ESCAPE ARTIST

ESCAPE ARTIST

MEMOIR OF A VISIONARY
ARTIST ON DEATH ROW

WILLIAM A. NOGUERA

SEVEN STORIES PRESS
New York ∗ Oakland ∗ London

Seven Stories Press
140 Watts Street
New York, NY 10013
sevenstories.com

FEATURED ART: courtesy of artist William A. Noguera/The William A. Noguera Trust/Artists Rights Society (ARS), New York.

GALLERY EXHIBITION IMAGES: courtesy of Alan Bamberger and artbusiness.com.

COVER AND CHAPTER ART IMAGE PHOTOS: courtesy of Melissa Ysais.

Library of Congress Cataloging-in-Publication Data

Names: Noguera, William, author.
Title: Escape artist : transformation through tragedy / William Noguera.
Description: First edition. | New York : Seven Stories Press, 2018.
Identifiers: LCCN 2017004932 (print) | LCCN 2017012083 (ebook) | ISBN
    9781609807986 (E-book) | ISBN 9781609807979 (hardcover)
Subjects: LCSH: Noguera, William. | Noguera, William--Childhood and youth. |
    Noguera, William--Philosophy. | Death row inmates--California--Biography.
    | Criminals--California--Biography. | Artists--California--Biography. |
    Colombian Americans--California--Biography. | Redemption--Philosophy. |
    Art--Psychology. | Self-actualization (Psychology)
Classification: LCC HV6248.N63 (ebook) | LCC HV6248.N63 A3 2018 (print) | DDC
    364.66092 [B] --dc23
LC record available at https://lccn.loc.gov/2017004932

Printed in the United States of America

9 8 7 6 5 4 3 2 1

DEDICATED TO
Guillermo Emilio Noguera.

I've loved you, sometimes hated you, worshipped your
strength, and feared it. But no matter what, you will always
be remembered and forever my dad . . .

Contents

ACKNOWLEDGMENTS

My gratitude to the following people for their help, confidence, and belief in me:

Margaret Bail, my agent, who saw the potential and took a chance on me where no one else would.

Walt Pavlo, Jr., who has walked a mile in my shoes, stumbled, and continued on.

Paul Reinhertz, my brother, my friend; words cannot reach the depth of my gratitude for what you've brought to my life—true friendship.

Melissa, none of this would be possible without your help. Thank you for not only believing in me, my work, and my words—but in the memory of that teenager you once knew, and recognizing he's still here. And finally, for helping me to understand there are second chances in life, love, and happiness.

FOREWORD

I spent time in a federal prison camp for a white-collar crime from 2001–2003. There is no pride in this proclamation, but it is through that experience that I have talked and written on white-collar crime for the past twelve years.

In September of 2011 I became a Contributor to Forbes.com and have interviewed insider traders, embezzlers, defense attorneys, prosecutors, and family members of inmates. In my work I attempt to create a mosaic of the people involved in our criminal justice system so that the general public understands how these crimes are perpetrated, who perpetrates them, how they are discovered, and the resulting punishment.

On reflection, my reasoning for digging deeper into white-collar criminal law has been as much about a search for self as it has been about an interest in the many cases that I cover. So I have been dedicated to understanding everything I can about the topic, the people, and the law. Then I met William A. Noguera, a man living a quarter of a century on San Quentin State Prison's death row.

On June 22, 2013, I walked through the gates of San Quentin State Prison just north of San Francisco. I was going to visit Noguera, a man sentenced to death in 1987 for a murder committed some years earlier. At the sentencing he was all of twenty-three years old and he had been in prison since he was nineteen. While I was interested in the case against him that resulted in the ultimate punishment, I was drawn to Noguera by his intellect, the disciplined life he leads in extreme conditions, and his beautiful art that he creates in the hell that surrounds him.

I was locked in a cage with Noguera for my visit, which is now the procedure for visitation at San Quentin's death row since a violent incident between two rival inmates broke out during visitation in 2000. I was allowed to visit for five straight hours and was not allowed to bring in any prepared notes, pen, or paper. I had wondered if I had five hours' worth of conversation in me with a man on death row, whom I had spoken with only a number of times via phone prior to that visit. It turned out that five hours was not enough time.

I left San Quentin that day wondering if I would ever see Noguera again or how I might further pursue telling his story. It was a long flight back to Boston, and in the following months I thought of William, his art, and our visit together. He left a lasting impression on me.

As I read a draft of this book, I recognize the man and the artist that I visited with in San Quentin. His transparency, acceptance of responsibility, and his passion for art come through with every word. He takes us along a journey of his life that is reflected in his own words and, more importantly, through his art.

After getting to know Noguera, reading this book, and viewing his art, his life continues to make me ponder deeper questions I have about my own life. First, can a person be seen for the good that they do now, no matter the wrong they have done in the past? This question is not one of forgiveness, it is about our ability to accept the good in the world without judgment. Was Picasso a saint? No, nor is Noguera. Yet we are able to look upon works by Picasso without analyzing the faults in his life. Art should transcend our ability to judge a person beyond what is on the canvas.

Second, how does a person live an ethical life in the face of daily challenges to conform with the unethical, the savage? Each semester I teach an Ethics class to MBA students at Endicott College, just north of Boston. Noguera calls in to the class and shares the surroundings he lives in and how he overcomes the temptations against falling into the demonic life of fellow inmates. For our students, it provides a view of a man in the midst of ethical temptations that go on in perpetuity.

However, Noguera offers hope to those students, insight and love from a place that is void of it. Our students have embraced the experience.

The third question that I have has to do with my own limitations in understanding art. Is Noguera a brilliant artist, or is he simply a good artist who is in prison? I have sat and looked at his paintings for hours and have been moved to tears. His ink-stippling pieces look like photographs and each tells a story. His abstracts are full of color, and I have enjoyed conversations with him as he described each piece in detail, though they had left his cell many years before. Is he an art master? I do not know, and Noguera himself wants to know. He wants to be judged by peers in the art world, critiqued, talked about, but he wants it to be based on his art, not the circumstances of his life.

"The limitations that I have on supplies and access to the outside world are the very things that make my work better, special," Noguera told me. Rather than look at his situation as one of limitations, he sees it as his unique signature on the world of art.

William Noguera is my friend. He is also, in my opinion, someone that the world needs to know. It is my hope that this book and Noguera's art will speak to you in a way that will leave a lasting impression on your life, just as he has left one on mine.

Walter A. Pavlo, Jr.
co-author of *Stolen Without a Gun,*
Forbes.com contributor

PREFACE

I live in a cage like the other 524 men in East Block, San Quentin's main death row housing unit. Built in 1927, East Block is a massive concrete and steel structure that looks like a large castle from the outside and a massive human warehouse from the inside. The cell I live in is four feet wide, nine feet deep, and seven and a half feet high. I've lived in this steel and concrete cage for nearly thirty-two years.

I am here for an event that happened at a time when my impulses were less restrained and my maturity still in development. My life should have been much different. This is how it actually turned out.

In an attempt to tell my story with honesty and integrity, including the dangers I face each day, I expose some of my deepest fears, pain, and desires. I share these candidly by detailing events and personal thoughts over the course of my life up to the present time. Some of these experiences are violent and criminal in nature. I use descriptive words such as warrior, gladiator, and rage, as well as racially charged slang. I don't include these words to glorify or sensationalize my actions. I feel great remorse for the pain I've caused. Rather, I include these words because they're a real part of my life and necessary to an understanding of how I developed into the man I am today.

I've faced conflict much of my life, and in prison survival depends on the decisions you make and whether you can defend your position each time. As you read, I invite you to ask yourself, *what would I have done?*

The most important question, though, is this: *Who holds the key that sets us free?* If you're honest with yourself, you'll understand, or at least take with you a sense of what some of us have gone through to find the answer.

THE SENTENCE

Orange County Superior Court Department 39
Friday, January 29, 1988. In open court:

"William Adolf Noguera, it is the judgment and sentence
of this court that for the offense of murder you shall suffer
the death penalty. Said penalty to be inflicted within the
walls of the State Prison at San Quentin, California in
the manner prescribed by law and at a time to be fixed by
this court in a warrant of execution; it is the order of this
court that you shall be put to death by the administration
of lethal gas. Said penalty to be inflicted within the walls
of the state prison at San Quentin, California. You are
remanded to the care, custody, and control of the sheriff
of Orange County to be by him delivered to the warden of
the state penitentiary at San Quentin, California within
ten days from this date. In witness whereof, I have here-
unto set my hand as judge of the said superior court and
have caused the seal of the said court to be affixed hereto.
Done in open court this 29th day of January 1988. Signed,
Robert R. Fitzgerald, Judge of the Superior Court of the
State of California, in and for the county of Orange. Good
luck to you, Mr. Noguera."

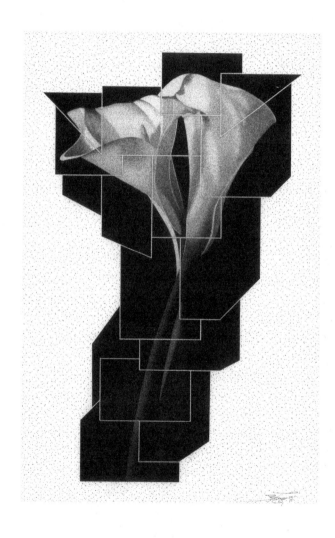

Chapter 1

Orange County Jail to San Quentin Death Row, 1988

I sat in silence as the judge read my sentence. None of it seemed real until that moment, when he said, "Good luck to you, Mr. Noguera." My raw emotions surfaced at that exact second and I cried from the deepest part of my being.

When we exited the courtroom, armed sheriff's deputies escorted me to a special holding cell separated from the prisoners I'd previously shared a cell with. Being sentenced to death changed everything. At some level I had known the death penalty was a real possibility, but I didn't believe it would happen. My world changed as I realized my name was on the list for San Quentin's execution chamber.

I sat in the holding cage for nearly two hours before I heard a deputy at the electronic door yell, "Open door." The sound of the door opening brought me back to reality. I'd sat there without moving or thinking—blank and too numb to feel or think rationally the whole time. Now I had no choice but to function. It was the beginning of a completely new life. I didn't know exactly what lay ahead, but I was committed to mastering and controlling my new circumstances. The alternative was to be killed, or something worse.

"Come on Noguera, time for a joy ride," the deputy prodded.

I stood and moved to the door as the deputy prepared to escort me from the cell and down the hall to the courtroom exit. Each step wearing the leg irons hurt the bones in my ankles, and I had to concentrate to keep from tripping or falling. My hands were in steel cuffs attached to a waist chain, with a long chain running down to the leg irons.

As they locked all the hardware I remember thinking how completely unnecessary it all was. *I'm not some dangerous animal—just a guy whose life should have turned out differently.*

My focus changed as we headed past the holding pens where other prisoners awaited their court dates. The prisoners yelled things like, "Alright now, big homie," "Take care of yourself," and "Stay strong, big dog."

We continued walking and came to another holding pen where a group of prisoners stood in silence. These men I knew. They were the elite—the convicts. Most were in for murder and wouldn't see the streets again. They were the men I'd spent the past four and a half years with—men who were no strangers to prison and the dangers that dwelled there. They were the proudest and most dangerous men I'd ever met. The prison system had honed them into fearless gladiators, and I was grateful for the respect they gave me in that moment.

I stopped as I came in line with the gate of their holding pen.

The deputy told his partner, "Give him a moment, he's earned it."

They backed away a few steps and left me alone facing these warriors. I nodded to the men I'd learned so much from about the thin line between sinking and swimming in the prison system. They were hardened convicts who lived by a code, not unlike a standard that promotes military cohesion and effectiveness among soldiers. Their code was all about the two most important elements in any prisoner's existence: fear and respect.

Those words represent an aspect of prison life that permeates every conversation and action of each prisoner for the total length of his incarceration. Who you fear, or who fears you, and whether you show appropriate respect and receive it in return are continually monitored by each prisoner in every situation. Being capable of intense physical violence is the obvious path to being shown respect and having no fear in prison. I would later learn other, more subtle ways that sometimes work, but an underlying capacity for violence is always the most reliable element for a peaceful existence.

I stepped close to the bars of the holding pen and, without a word, each and every convict shook my hand through the bars. Their eyes searched mine as if looking for a crack, any sign of weakness. I'd just been sentenced to death, and convicts always test you for weakness.

I needed the respect and loyalty they showed at that moment, but I'd learned not to be fooled. I knew they only respected who they feared or considered their equal. If I'd ever showed weakness or fear over the past four and a half years, they would have killed me.

As we all shook hands, Chente, a Mexican I'd known the longest, as tall as me and built like a seasoned warrior, said, "Órale, carnal, you take care of yourself. You know how we do it. When you get to Quentin remember who you are."

The rest of them said similar things.

"Okay, Noguera, let's get moving," the deputy said, prompting me to step away. I shuffled to the car and the next phase of my life.

The ride back to Orange County jail, the concrete castle where I'd lived for the past four and a half years, was short. I rode in a sheriff's car with two deputies and a chase car following close behind. Until then I'd been transported to court with all the other prisoners in a bus, accompanied by a couple of deputies watching the entire group. The only distinction between me and the others was my cuffs and leg irons attached to a waist chain, plus a red arm band marked "K-10," indicating the highest security level. Those additions let guards and prisoners know I was an escape risk or violent. After being sentenced to death, my travel arrangements were just one of many changes I'd face.

The gate closed behind us as the car passed into the jail courtyard. I took a deep breath and mentally prepared for the added scrutiny from other prisoners following the verdict. A death sentence changes the way people react to you. Guards who were once friendly before the sentence suddenly become more formal. Other prisoners show a new level of respect.

I didn't know the details of what living on San Quentin's death row would entail. Not knowing allows the imagination to invent new concerns and anticipate corrective responses. Strangely, it wasn't dying that concerned me, but the prospect of living while on death row until they were finally ready to kill me.

The deputy opened the door to take me out of the car.

"Step out and stand fast," he said. When I did, he pulled out his baton and stepped back. "Step to the side, Noguera. My partner will search you. Once he's done, I'll search the back seat."

I stood as he patted me down for weapons and contraband. Then the first deputy pulled out the back seat and searched behind it.

"Clear," he said. With deputies on either side of me, we entered the jail.

As the deputies escorted me past the normal holding pens and to the elevator, one deputy informed me, "The chains and irons stay on until we get you to your cell in solitary."

The other deputy remarked, "This is procedure, not personal. Hope you understand."

We kept walking and I didn't respond. I was tired and needed to be alone. I didn't know how long I could continue holding the mask in place—the one I wore when I was afraid or didn't want anyone to know what I was feeling. It was the mask I learned to wear as a little boy.

Again the escort deputy spoke. "Your property is stored. You're not allowed to have anything except your state-issued jumpsuit, blanket, sheets, towel, toothbrush, and toothpaste."

Standing to the side, two regular deputies I knew smiled and nodded to me.

"We'll take him from here," said Hunt, one of the deputies.

Hunt was older and had worked in the unit most of the time I'd been there. The other two deputies left. We rode the elevator to the fourth floor, where the solitary cells were. Hunt, who usually talked nonstop, didn't say anything. I was grateful for the silence. I wasn't in the mood for small talk. I needed time alone to think.

"Open five," he yelled.

The door slid open. I stood as the other cop removed the cuffs, chains, and leg irons, then I stepped into the cell.

"Close five." As the door closed, he said to me, "If you need anything, just ask. I know you'll want some time to yourself, but after that you know where I'll be."

I nodded, turned into the cell, and froze. As the emotions washed over me I slumped on the bunk where an old, thin mattress lay. The mask fell away and I allowed my emotions the freedom to run. I cried as I hadn't in years. Why do we regress at these moments and experience similar feelings from childhood? I cried for all the times I was hurt and beat up as a child. I cried for that child I once was who still lived deep inside me, but who I had locked away to keep safe. And finally, I cried out in rage to God.

Over the next few days I was in a constant state of anxiety about what lay ahead. Deputies would transport me to San Quentin within ten days. Each time a door opened, keys jingled, or I heard footsteps, I bolted to my feet, my stomach tight and fists wrapped around the cell bars. I don't know how many times I did that over the next eight days and nights. I could hardly sleep or eat. There was only the question: "When will they come for me?" As much as I dreaded the trip, waiting was worse.

When the mind is tortured, it searches for a way out, and for me, meditation served that purpose. It set me free. I could do anything, be anywhere, and most of the pain disappeared. But this time when I tried to meditate, instead of taking me away, I only had a heightened sense of the filth of the cell, and anger about what was happening to me. I focused on the unfairness I'd endured early in life, and wondered if my responses to situations later in life would have changed had I been treated differently. Normally I could steer my mind through hardship and doubt, adjusting and gaining strength that allowed me to feel empowered and in control. But I hadn't faced anything this serious before, and the methods I usually relied on weren't working. I had always quoted Nietzsche to help me mentally overcome adversity: "That which does not kill us makes us stronger." But that didn't work either.

I had fantasies about the moment they'd come for me. Dressed in black, an executioner with a battle axe and three guards would open the door, and I'd wait for my moment as I remained chained to the wall. Suddenly, I slipped my chains and the battle started. I fought in a frenzy, feasting on their fear. When injured, I fought harder, knowing it was for something bigger than myself. Those fantasies of battle eased my nervous anticipation about the future. Looking back now, I believe some part of my unconscious mind was showing me a path for surviving the coming months.

On the morning of the final day, well before dawn, I woke with a jolt. Something was different. A chill ran down my spine and I was on my feet instantly. I heard keys and a baton hitting the leg of a guard as he approached. I recognized the sound of the walk. There were no sounds from the kitchen, so it wasn't yet 4:30. The guard, Hunt, stepped in front of the cell.

"You awake, Noguera?" he asked.

"They're here for me, aren't they?"

"I just heard over the radio that they're on the way, and before they take you, I wanted to say a few things to you," he said, moving closer.

"Look," he continued, "I don't judge you. What happened is in the past. I've had the opportunity to watch you and I think you'll make it. What's important is what you do now. San Quentin is a terrible place, but like my father used to say, it is what you make it."

I nodded and told him I appreciated his words, and thanked him. Years later I would come to realize what he meant.

"Listen," he said, "Don't make me regret this. I know you'd like to say goodbye to your family. The phone's on in the dayroom. Make it quick."

He put his hand out and I shook it. For a moment he wasn't a cop and I wasn't a prisoner. We were just two men brought together by a moment of respect. He walked back up the stairs to the control panel and my door slid open. I hurried to the dayroom. I knew how much he risked by letting me make the call. Prisoners sentenced to death were kept isolated and weren't allowed to make calls. While the day and time for transport to San Quentin remained a secret, isolation ensured there was no risk of prisoners setting up an escape by notifying their friends of the details. Allowing me to make a call could place many people at risk, and guards are easy targets in that type of escape. He obviously trusted me.

I dialed my sister's number and the operator's voice answered, "How may I help you?"

"Collect call from Bill," I said. The phone rang as my stomach tightened like a fist.

On the third ring she answered, "Yes, who is this?"

"Collect call from Bill," the operator said. I could tell she'd been sleeping but my name brought her awake.

"I accept," she said. "Billy . . . oh God, they're taking you." She began to cry.

"Yes, they're here. I only have a few minutes but I wanted to call to say I'll be fine. Please don't worry and I'll call as soon as I can."

"Please be careful," she said.

We talked for a few minutes. I tried to make her laugh but I wasn't fooling her, or me. In the years to come, my sister's words and encouragement would provide the strength I'd need to overcome difficulties and make better decisions than I would have otherwise.

We said goodbye when I heard the unit door open, and the sounds of chains. I took a deep breath and let it out, empty but relieved to know the waiting was over. I was determined not to let this beat me, or die a broken man. I put the mask back on, and quickly returned to my cell.

I was transported from Orange County jail to the airport, then flown to Marin County Airfield. The plane ride was difficult. I wore a waist chain with cuffs and leg irons, but the hardest part was having to listen to the cop talk shit to me. I didn't say a word to him, but he wanted me to know from the start that he was in charge and that he was a tough guy not to be messed with. Even before takeoff he began his rant. He had bad breath and a bad attitude to match.

"If you move even an inch out of place I'll put a hole in you so big my fist will fit," he said as he pulled out his .357 revolver.

I looked at it and then at his eyes. I didn't show any emotion. I just read his face like I used to read the faces of fighters before a match. He was afraid, but like so many men he tried to hide it behind big talk and a big gun.

He looked away and the big talk continued. "I've read your file and you don't scare me. All that Karate shit only works on pussies."

I sat in the back seat of the small plane. He was in the front passenger seat about four feet in front of me, also facing the front. He was silent as the plane took off and I had time to take stock of the situation. He was out of shape, mid-forties, five foot ten and 250 pounds. He smoked and he was soft. He believed he was safe because I was chained and he had a gun. On the street, he wouldn't think of saying a cross word to me. However, the present circumstance gave him a sense of security and he took full advantage to verbally assault me. He was careless and confident.

The pilot was also from the sheriff's department, though he wasn't armed. He was just a pilot doing a job. He was six feet tall, 165 pounds, and married.

Once we were in the air, I watched out the window and wondered if all the drivers below knew how lucky they were. The cop began again with the big talk.

"I see you're a bad ass. What gang are you from?"

I didn't answer. I knew he wanted me to engage him so he could escalate the abuse.

He continued, "I don't think you're that special. I know your type. Without a gang, you ain't shit."

I don't know how he got the idea I was in a gang, but it couldn't have been further from the truth. Eventually the talk died down. With his superiority clearly established, he could relax.

I watched the landscape out the window, but kept an eye on the cop. He pulled out a thermos and poured some coffee, then tucked the thermos between his legs before sipping from the cup. He surprised me by placing his gun on the small console beside him, less than four feet from me. My mind immediately grasped the possibilities and focused on the options. I wondered if it was a trick to get me to reach for the gun and give him an excuse to kill me. I could see he hadn't emptied the bullets, so it wasn't a trick. My imagination took over: first, remove the cuffs from my wrists. I could do that in less time than it took a cop to do it with the key. Anytime I left my cell I carried a thin piece of plastic in the back of my mouth under my tongue. I made it a habit after seeing men severely wounded when they couldn't get out of their chains fast enough as another prisoner attacked them with a knife. Once out of the cuffs, I'd lean forward, grab the gun, and put it to the big-mouthed cop's head, cocking the hammer while ordering the pilot to fly to the coast. If he hesitated, I'd shoot the tough cop and level the gun at him. He'd comply. He'd do it because his mind would look for a way out, and he'd realize I was his only hope. Even if he believed he was going to die, his only chance was to follow directions and try to negotiate for his life later. Once within sight of the ocean I'd order him to fly low, place the plane on autopilot, shoot him, and jump out. I'd make it. The plane would continue until it ran out of fuel and sank in the ocean. By the time the plane was found, I'd be in Mexico.

Freedom was that close. I could easily do it. The judge, DA, and the twelve jurors had already labeled me a cold-blooded killer and I was on my way to death row, so what did I have to lose? Every fiber of my body was suddenly alive. The anticipation from thinking all of it through had placed me in a state of heightened awareness as everything seemed to move in slow motion. I weighed the pros and cons. I knew I could make it, gain freedom, probably never be caught, and make the idiot cop lose his arrogance before he died. On the other hand, I would have to kill the pilot, who probably had children and was just here to make an honest living. How could I live with myself knowing I'd murdered a man to gain my freedom? I just couldn't rationalize that. I'd fought and used lethal force to defend myself in the Orange County jail, but killing an innocent person in a purely selfish act was over the line. I took some deep breaths and remembered the earlier phone call. Sometimes the price was just too high.

As we landed and the small plane came to a stop in Marin County, I noticed the two California Department of Corrections cars parked just to our right. As the three bulls advanced, the cop started his big talk again.

"Now we'll see how bad you really are. Guys like you are turned out in San Quentin. Within a week you'll be somebody's bitch or they'll pass you around until you hang yourself or learn to love it. Welcome to Hell."

I looked directly at him, allowing the weight I knew my eyes carried to bore into him. He looked away.

Turning my focus to the bulls as they came close, I dismissed the cop from my thoughts.

"How we doing this morning?" one of them asked, then told me to step out.

"Watch your step," said a black officer. His name badge identified him as Hasman.

He was six foot six, 290 pounds and all muscle. He spoke with a roaring voice that commanded immediate attention, yet he didn't seem to be aggressive—just clearly someone not to be crossed. It was obvious he had spent years on an iron pile, and it was also obvious he understood the impression he left. I stepped out and stood there while the big-mouthed cop and pilot exchanged paperwork, my file, and small talk with the bulls from San Quentin. Moments later two of the bulls escorted me to the car while a third, a sergeant, got into the chase car. They all wore batons, and the sergeant and one officer had .38 revolvers.

The car picked up speed as Hasman merged onto the freeway and put on some R&B. Toni Braxton sang about lost love and passion.

"This your first time in prison? Your file's thin and I don't see any prior convictions or CDC record," the other bull asked.

I considered not saying anything but he wasn't pushing and he seemed like he was just curious.

"It's my first time."

"What the hell did you do, kill five or six people?"

Hasman answered him, "Nah, he's out of Orange County. Them folks hand out the death penalty like it's candy, especially if you ain't white. Ain't that right, dawg?"

I just nodded. The other bull, whose name I would later learn was Ovaldo, just shook his head and said, "Young or not, first time or career criminal, this ain't no joke."

He was right, it wasn't a joke, and after all these years this conversation is as fresh in my mind as if it occurred yesterday.

The car slowed as we got off the freeway, then made a right and passed through the exclusive San Quentin Village, right on the shore of the bay. Suddenly, there it was—the East Gate and, beyond that, the prison. Established in 1852, San Quentin looks like a medieval castle on 275 acres of some of the most expensive property in the wealthiest county in California. Across the pristine bay from San Quentin is a million-dollar view of San Francisco. No wonder the residents of Marin County continue to fight to close the prison and develop the property.

Hasman pulled up to the officer at the East Gate and reported, "One prisoner, one weapon, supervisor in chase car with one weapon."

The gate officer directed us to move the car to the side to wait for clearance to proceed. After a few moments, we got the all-clear and moved forward two hundred yards to the main entrance of the prison. This was where staff entered and left the prison each shift. It's also where guns are dropped off when returning to the prison with a prisoner. The armed bull and sergeant went to the armory to turn in their guns while I waited in the car with the one unarmed bull. Then the other bull and sergeant returned to the cars and we drove around the back of the prison to the main sally port where vehicles enter and leave the prison grounds.

Sally ports are common in prison as a means to prevent escapes. They consist of two gates, only one of which can be opened at a time. If the entrance had only one gate, a prisoner could wait for the gate to be opened, then rush the gate before it closed. The vehicle sally port allows a thorough inspection of vehicles entering and leaving the prison before passing through the second gate.

Inside the sally port Hasman handed the bull working there some papers and signed in. The sally port bull checked inside and under the vehicle, as well as inside the trunk and under the hood. When he was satisfied we were clear, the second large iron door opened slowly and we drove through.

Inside the thirty-foot-high walls of the prison, the road runs along the perimeter wall in a large oval. The main exercise area, the lower yard, is inside this loop on the right side of the road. The lower yard is roughly five acres. It's the largest exercise area at San Quentin and is used exclusively by mainline prisoners.

As a resident of death row, I wouldn't see that yard except from a vehicle. Prisoners could run on the large oval track, and tables were set up for card and chess games. It was interesting to see some of the men doing time here out on the yard. My attention went to the large amount of free weights on the iron pile where huge men lifted weights. The men could do commercials for any fitness center, but in prison their extreme physiques had a more practical purpose.

Once we arrived at R&R I was escorted to change into state clothes, have my pictures taken, and complete paperwork. They told me the basic rules, and gave me a rule book and my CDC number. From then on I was CDC prisoner William A. Noguera, D77200, assigned to death row.

From the R&R building we went to the building where I would be living, the AC. At San Quentin the Adjustment Center is the hole for condemned prisoners. It's where death row prisoners who don't conform to prison rules or refuse to renounce gang affiliation reside, and where all condemned prisoners are evaluated for classification when first arriving at San Quentin. Privileges are few in the AC, and guards are tough guys with bad attitudes.

As soon as I walked through the door of the AC, the stench hit me. Smoke from cigarettes and cigars and the stink of unwashed bodies assaulted my senses as I was led to the front of the first tier on the yard side of the building. The AC has two sides with rows of cells three levels high on each side. The sides are referred to by what's on the outside of the building, either yard side or chapel side.

The two bulls who drove me from the airport escorted me to my holding cell.

"You're gonna be placed in the quiet cell for ten days with just what you're wearing," Hasman said. "You get three showers every seven days and after the ten days are up you'll see the warden's committee. They decide if you'll stay here or go to East Block. 'Til then, enjoy the stay."

From there, two tier bulls took over. They made it seem like my presence had interrupted something terribly important. I would later learn this is a common attitude among AC bulls.

"What's your name?" said Ericson, a tall bull with a beard and bald head.

"Noguera," I said.

"I need you to step into this holding cage and take off your clothes, Noguera," Ericson barked.

I stepped into the cage, and as soon as the door closed I backed up to the food port so he could unlock the cuffs. He removed the cuffs and I began taking off my clothes, which included a pair of prison-issued shoes, blue denim pants, a blue shirt, and white boxers.

He ran me through the strip-out procedure: "Run your fingers through your hair, open your mouth, stick out your tongue, pull your ears forward, lift your arms over your head, lift your balls, now turn around, bend over, spread your ass, cough, lift your feet. Okay, he's clear," he said to his partner, an average-sized black bull with mirrored sunglasses, named Harland.

"Now put your clothes back on," he said, and continued. "Every time you leave your cell you will submit to this search. Do you understand?"

I nodded.

"Turn around and back up to the bars. I'm going to cuff and escort you to your cell. You will walk between my partner and me. Don't give us any trouble and we won't have a reason to split your skull."

The cuffs bit down on my wrists, and I clenched my jaw. They were testing me. They wanted to know if I'd complain or display some sort of disrespect. The cage door opened and the two bulls had their batons out. I wasn't afraid, but I also wouldn't give them a reason to beat me.

It was simply a test and, no matter what, I would pass. We walked down the tier. On the left were cells with screens in front of the bars. The screens were placed in front of the bars to prevent prisoners from stabbing other prisoners or staff through the bars as they walked by. Ahead of me four small mirrors slid out from the corner of the cell doors. I was being watched. I passed by without looking at the men who held the mirrors. I didn't care who they were, just faces in a crowd. My eyes burned as I walked. Just about every cell had a burning wick sticking out of it, made from tightly-rolled toilet paper. The bulls would light them with their lighters because, although prisoners could smoke, they couldn't have matches or lighters. Matches could be used to make a bomb.

We went to the end of the tier where the lighting was terrible. The four cells in the back were separate from the rest of the tier and could only be accessed by going through a locked door. Once through that door, each cell had a solid steel door with a small glass window in the center. They were the quiet cells, where new condemned prisoners and true J-Cats (crazies) were kept.

I was led to my cell and found the solid steel door was actually one of two doors. The second one, a regular door with bars and steel mesh covering it, closed behind me.

I backed up to the food port and placed my hands through. Warm blood trickled down my fingers from the cuts the cuffs had made. That wasn't normal. The cuffs had been altered to bite into a prisoner's wrists and cut him. Once the cuffs were removed I turned and faced the bull. I didn't look at my wrists. I just looked at him and then at the cell. I wouldn't give them the satisfaction of acknowledging they had hurt me. The bull closed the food port and stepped outside the cell's vestibule, looking at me through the outer door's small window, and at the blood that ran down my hands onto the floor. He knew what he had done. I said nothing as I stood in the dimly lit cell. Satisfied they had made their point, they turned and left. I stood there for a few moments, truly alone.

A hopeless void opened in the center of my chest. I'd lost so much and could lose even more if I allowed them to take it. This place was made to break men like me. I realized I couldn't let that happen. For all the things they were taking from me, they couldn't control my response to each insult to my humanity. I would keep my composure and not give them an excuse to make things worse. I would survive.

As my eyes adjusted to the light I realized the cell was filthy. The walls, bars, and steel mesh screen that covered the bars were caked with dirt and feces. I noticed writing on the walls, mostly names, dates, and poems. The words, *mom*, *love*, and *God* were the most common.

The cell was nine feet by nine feet with a steel bunk frame bolted to the right wall. A thin, dirty mattress lay on top. Next to that was a steel toilet and sink, covered in vomit. A dead rat floated in the toilet. I couldn't live like this. Both wrists continued to bleed, but when I looked around there was nothing to use to stop the bleeding. I didn't want to touch anything for fear of infecting myself. I took off my clothes except my boxers and shoes and went to the bunk. I moved the mattress to the side so I could place my clothes there. As I did this, a rat bolted from under the mattress and ran into a small hole under the toilet. I jumped back and nearly yelled. My heart pounded in my chest and I took deep breaths of the stale air, trying to calm down. I gagged and nearly threw up. After a few minutes I got control again and prepared to clean the cell.

First I tore strips from my state-issued shirt and tied off my wrists to stop the bleeding, then I searched the cell's hiding places. Searching the cage and finding all the items left by the last occupant is critical in prison. Many times, other prisoners hide things—contraband items—and either don't get a chance to remove them when they move, or purposely leave them there. Typical things left behind are shanks, razor blades, fishing poles, and string. Two things almost never found in a cell are money or drugs. Those are extremely valuable in prison and are kept in the prisoner's safe (their rectum, a practice called keistering). Sometimes bulls will purposely set up a prisoner by waiting two to three days after a prisoner has been assigned to a cell, then search it and find a shank they had planted. Possession of a weapon will land a prisoner in the hole for sixteen months. If the bulls don't find it, they know you flushed it, and they know you're on to their attempted frame job.

During my search I found six bars of state soap, a wash cloth, three pencils, a pen-filler, a razor blade, and an old newspaper that was hidden under the frame of the bunk. I flushed the razor blade along with the dead rat. The razor blade alone could extend my time in the AC an additional sixteen months. Anything that would extend my time had to go.

I heard men yelling from cell to cell, making football picks for the weekend and arguing about politics. I shut them out and continued with my task. I used my blue state-issued shirt and pants to clean, mop, and rinse the entire cell, bars, and screen. The light behind the metal bars at the back of the cell was much brighter after I cleaned it. I used a piece of my blue shirt as a mask to cover my face as I cleaned. The stench from the feces smeared all over the cell was overwhelming.

I continued to clean until I heard noise outside the steel door. Keys rattled and the outer door swung open. In the doorway stood two bulls. "Your name?" the first one asked.

"Noguera."

"Stand to the back of the cell. When the food port is opened, step forward and take your food tray."

I told him I was washing the cell and couldn't eat in the filth. He seemed to realize what I was doing as the smell hit him.

"Son of a bitch. Why wasn't this cell cleaned?" he asked his partner.

"You know Heckle and Jeckle, they're in their own little world," his partner said.

I assumed he was referring to the two bulls who put me in the cell.

"Stand fast, Noguera. I'll bring you some things to finish the job," he said.

The huge door closed and I continued cleaning. I didn't really expect to see him again that day, but after a few minutes I heard keys, and the outer door opened. He brought me three towels, more soap, a cup of disinfectant, a new set of state-issued blues, two sheets, a blanket, and two pairs of socks, as well as clean underwear.

"Because someone didn't do their fuckin' job, you had to clean this mess. I've brought you a few things you should have received. I don't do favors, so don't ask." He handed me the items through the food port.

"Thank you," I said.

He nodded and said, "After you're done I'll bring you a tray."

He turned and walked away.

I cleaned, scrubbed, and washed the cell six or seven times until the smell was gone. I plugged the hole under the toilet with the shirt I had used to wash and mop the floor, by soaking it in soapy water and squeezing it into place. I then stripped naked and took a bird bath in the newly cleaned sink. After drying off and putting on my new boxers, I sat on the mattress and relaxed.

Again, I heard keys and the outer door opened. The bull was back carrying a food tray and a milk carton.

"Maybe we'll move you to a new cell every day so you can clean it like this one," he said.

I didn't answer, but the look on my face told him I didn't know he was joking.

"That was a joke, son. Here's your tray. I'm the third watch CO. I'm here five days a week. If you have any questions, I'll answer them."

"Thank you, boss," I answered. "Do you have the time?"

"It's ten p.m. My name is Carlton."

I nodded and took the tray. I hadn't realized how hungry I was. I hadn't eaten since—I couldn't remember the last time. I ate everything, and then, concerned that the dirty paper plate would attract rats, I ripped it into small pieces and flushed them. Exhaustion was welcome after a dreadful day. Finally, I could rest. I fell into an uneasy sleep.

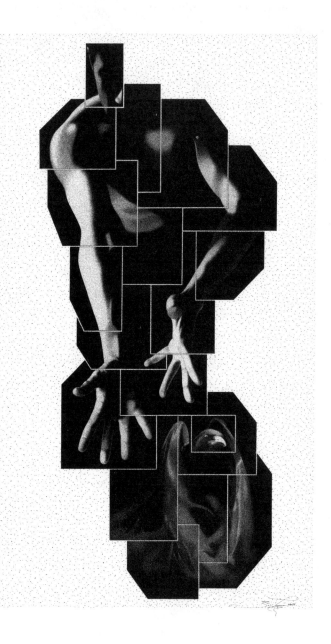

Chapter 2

San Quentin Death Row, 1988

I woke in the grip of a nightmare my first night in San Quentin, covered in sweat and gasping for air like a drowning man breaking the surface of the water. I'd been surfing my childhood spot at San Clemente, California, when I was pulled under by my leash. I tried to fight being pulled down, but the force was too strong. I was pulled farther and farther. It was dark and cold and I understood this was how I would die. I thought of my dog—a beautiful German shepherd named Bullet, who I loved deeply. In that moment I saw him watching me, only he wasn't alone. Next to him stood a little boy who also watched. I looked into his eyes and I knew him. I knew what he was thinking and what I had to do. I reached for my ankle and found the Velcro strap. I tore it open, freed my leg, and swam to the surface. In that moment, as I started to gain consciousness, I only thought of swimming to the beach and being free of the water's danger. I was a teen once again and my only concern was getting to the shore.

That split second of freedom ended with the realization of my surroundings. I stood up and stepped to the sink. The cement floor was cold on my feet and I checked the hole I had covered under the toilet. Would it hold? Was that rat, at that very second, moving toward my feet to bite me? But there was no rat. The hole was still securely plugged.

I pushed the cold water button in the metal sink and washed my face. I didn't know what time it was. Time stood still in a cell with no windows. I knew it was early because it was quiet. There was no yelling and I couldn't smell the smoke from the toilet paper wicks that prisoners kept alive so they could light their cigarettes.

I stripped naked and took another bird bath in the sink. I didn't know when the shower days were and I wouldn't rely on them. I had soap, towels, and water. After finishing, I wiped down the cell and made my bunk in a manner that would impress a drill sergeant.

I sat down to wait and began reading some of the foolishness written on the walls. There were silly drawings in no particular order, mostly of men and women engaged in sexual acts. It seemed like the same prisoner had done all of them over a period of several days. Only the wall across from my bunk was free of graffiti, except for a large dragon outlined in pencil. The wall had been painted fairly recently, so it held potential as a blank canvas if I could remove the dragon and clear the other stains first.

Once again, I thought about the little boy watching me during that moment in my nightmare. I knew him. I'd known him my entire life, but now, as I experienced the moment, he seemed more real—his eyes more haunting—than just a memory.

I fell into a sort of daydream sitting there staring at the wall, and I imagined using the pencils I had found yesterday when I searched the cell to cover the wall in a collage of my memories.

The sound of keys brought me back from my thoughts like a rubber band snapping back to its original shape. Closer they came until a face appeared in the small window in the solid steel door. He and his partner looked in, checking to see if I was alive. It was the two bulls who'd placed me in the cell and hurt my wrists. Heckle and Jeckle was what Carlton had called them. Instinctively I stood as the door opened.

"You eating? Stand back as I open the food port," Heckle yelled.

I stepped back and watched, like an animal in a cage, as the bull brought the food tray over and put it in the food port. Then he backed away and yelled, "Clear." Only then could I walk over and pick up the paper tray and small carton of milk.

"You want coffee?"

"I need a cup," I said.

Smiling, he said, "People in hell need ice water." He closed the door.

I stood there for a moment furious at the two of them for their dehumanizing words, but more at myself for playing into their hand and giving them the easy set up.

Heckle and Jeckle fed everyone on the tier, then picked up the trash. I didn't say anything to them, even when they spoke to me. I placed my paper tray in the food port for pick up but kept the empty milk carton to use as a cup for coffee the next morning. When they noticed I had kept the carton they pointed at it, then at me, and one of them said, "The monkey learns fast. Dance, monkey, dance."

I said nothing, but I was hot with rage.

Right after breakfast, I started pacing back and forth in my cell. I was lost in thought when I heard a lot of keys and what sounded like banging. I couldn't see what was happening, but it sounded like prisoners being removed from their cells.

I heard a bull yell, "Spike," which meant "Key," so prisoners were being taken out of their cells, but that didn't explain the banging.

A number of bulls passed in front of the steel door of my cell and then opened it.

"Bar check and search. Turn around and strip."

I did as I was told, going through the always disturbing and inhuman strip search that I've been subjected to for the past thirty years. No matter how much time goes by, a strip search is something I will never get used to. To be forced to stand naked in front of a number of bulls, lift up my nuts, then turn around, spread my ass, all while a high-intensity flashlight is used to look into these areas, is humiliating.

"Put your hands behind your back and back up to the bars," another bull yelled.

They put cuffs on my wrists. I anticipated the pain of the teeth biting into my wrists. While that pain never came, even having them properly placed on my wrists hurt because the cuts were still healing.

The cell door opened and they told me to walk backwards out of the cell. Once outside the cell, a bull grabbed the chain connecting the two cuffs and guided me to face the wall directly in front of the cell. Two other bulls entered my cell. All the bulls had their batons out, and as I stood there I noticed some of them had hammers in their hands which they used to hit the bars of the cell to check for tampering. Prisoners can cut through the thick steel bars in their cells, then launch a surprise attack on other prisoners, or guards when they walk by. By hitting each bar with a hammer the bulls can tell by the sound if the metal is solid. This was the banging I heard earlier. All the cells were being checked except one—the one next door to me remained closed.

How does a prisoner cut through steel bars? A man can do some amazing things when left in a cage with little else but time to think and plot, especially when he's angry. I saw a man use dental floss and nail clippers to cut a hole in the bars big enough to crawl through, then cut a bone-crusher, a large metal knife blade, out of his bunk that he sharpened by scraping the edge against the concrete floor. He did all this within thirty-six hours and attacked another prisoner. The attacker wasn't a smart man, but he was determined and completely focused on his objective.

The bulls went through my cell searching for contraband and testing the bars. When they failed to find anything of interest they put me back in the cell, removed the cuffs, and shut the steel door.

I have some difficulty describing what happened next because it's not a common experience, and many people doubt the reality of the perception. Nevertheless, I know it's real and will attempt to explain it with proper context. I get a feeling, which is like my personal psychic alarm system, when conflict is about to happen. My senses go into overdrive and I can actually smell the distinct odor of nervous sweat and testosterone as a man pumps himself up for an attack.

I'm sure men who have been to war will understand the experience, though I suspect the trait diminished gradually among humans after years of living in civilized society, not having to fight for survival. Many animals show clear evidence of having this sense of impending danger, and a few prisoners have it too.

I instinctively prepared myself for battle while taking off my shirt and shoes. I readily admit I was scared. I've come to learn that courage is not defined by being fearless, but by overcoming fear and acting as if the fear were not present.

Still, one thing was puzzling—they had already cuffed me and removed me from my cell, so if they were going to harm me they would have done it then. What was I picking up on? I could see through the small window in the outer door of the cell that the bulls had all gathered with shields and batons. Then I remembered the closed steel door next to mine. They weren't coming for me. I had allowed the unfamiliar surroundings to influence my judgment and I'd miscalculated what was really happening. I had to learn from the mistake and focus. Misreading situations and overreacting could cost me my life in prison. The tension in my muscles drained away slowly once I knew I wouldn't be hurt today.

The bulls opened the steel door right next to mine and I heard one yell, "Cuff up."

I had a sense that the bull and his partners didn't want the prisoner to submit. The way they were pumped up with adrenaline, they wanted one thing—a fight.

"Fuck you, faggot. I got something for you and your cock-sucking friends," yelled the prisoner.

He mumbled and screamed other things about the listening devices in his cell and that he wanted the camera taken out of his brain. He was a broken man with a shattered mind. Despite that, he was still ready for a fight because some part of his being told him to defend himself against the impending assault.

I sat on the bunk and listened as the door to his cell was opened and the bulls rushed in. There was yelling from both the prisoner and the bulls, but the most distinctive sound was their boots pounding against the floor as they entered. Soon there was only the sound of the prisoner screaming, "Help . . . Stop . . . Please."

They were beating him senseless and I wondered if they'd kill him.

They cuffed his hands and legs and took him away. The other bulls returned to search the cell and check the bars. I heard them talk about what they had done in excited tones.

"Man, did you see how he came off the ground when I kicked him in the nuts?"

"That crazy motherfucker will wake up with a bloody asshole from my baton," another laughed.

On and on, they boasted about the job they had done on him. I wished I could tell them they were punks for the way they'd treated a man who was clearly insane. Some other prisoners also realized what they had done and began yelling at them. But it wasn't my fight, and I couldn't afford the luxury of standing up for someone else. I had enough problems of my own.

Chapter 3

San Quentin Death Row, 1988

The next nine days were all the same. Breakfast, trash pickup, search, and bar check, lunch, and dinner. Showers were on Monday, Wednesday, and Saturday.

Each day I worked out, following an aggressive routine: five hundred pushups, five hundred sit ups, five hundred squats, a half hour of shadow boxing and another half hour of martial arts kicking techniques, fighting sequences, and meditation. Even this was a light workout compared to my daily routine when I was a competitive fighter.

The nights passed slowly and were filled with the same nightmare, only the nightmare had become something I looked forward to. At least in my nightmares I wasn't in a cell on death row. When I woke, it took a few seconds of conscious thought before I realized where I was—until that happened, I was free.

On the tenth day I woke and prepared to see the warden's committee. The hours passed without any word, until finally after shift change I saw Carlton walk past the small window in the steel door and I called to him.

"Carlton, a moment of your time, please." He opened the steel door that I'd come to think of as a door to a room in a mental ward.

"I'm sorry to bother you but I was supposed to see the warden's committee today. I've been here ten days."

"Let me check the log and I'll be right back."

Sometime later I heard the sound of his keys. The door opened and he stepped into the area right outside the cell.

"I checked the log. You're right, you've been here ten days, but it's Friday and the warden's committee and classification don't meet until Wednesday, so you might have to wait until then."

I nodded and he stepped out and closed the door. I was angry. I wanted to be classified and be allowed to call my family. As it turned out, I would be denied the privilege for many more months.

For the better part of the night I stared at the blank wall opposite my bunk, reliving love, hate, pain, anger, rage, passion, and thinking about how much I wanted my life back. I must have fallen asleep because the dreams came, only something was missing. There was calmness where usually a storm raged inside. This was the reason I'd surfed. It was the only thing that brought me real peace when I was a boy and through my teenage years. Maybe it was the rise and fall of the ocean, its peacefulness and sudden power. Harnessing that power by riding a wave was like being in total control.

Suddenly I woke. At the sink I washed my face in cold water. I sat on the bunk and stared at the blank wall. I knew what to do. I took a piece of rag, wet it, and began scrubbing the wall until the dragon was gone. Then I grabbed the three pencils I found during my search of the cell, and I began to draw. I drew with passion, as never before in my life. I allowed the emotions to pour out, and as they did I was no longer William A. Noguera, prisoner D77200. A mental door had opened and the little boy from my dreams was there with me.

Tears streamed down my face as I drew and poured out my deepest emotions. For the first time in years, I'd found a part of me, long ago hidden in order to protect it from all of the brutality.

My means of coping with the emotional stress caused by the continual turmoil early in my life was to subconsciously compartmentalize my inner self into two parts. One half dealt with the abuse I suffered—the conflicts of a fractured family, and the never-ending sorrow and affliction I've always had to fight against. As time went by, this half grew stronger, responding instinctively to threats with cunning and aggression. This was the face I allowed everyone behind the walls of San Quentin to see. He was my Sacrificed Child, the one who defeated my enemies. The other half was caring, sensitive, intelligent, and creative. I hid him deep in my soul to protect him and keep him from being contaminated by the venom that always surrounded me. He was my Radiant Child.

Sitting in a dark prison cell on death row overwhelmed me, and I realized my old methods of survival would no longer improve what really mattered—me. The Radiant Child had come to me in my dreams, slowly reconnecting as a guiding force, gradually transitioning into my conscious thoughts, making me whole like I'd never been before.

Days and nights went by. Wednesday came and went and still the warden's committee didn't call for me. Different bulls asked what I was still doing in the isolation cell and my reply was always the same, "I don't know, boss."

On the twenty-sixth day of my stay in isolation, Carlton opened the steel door to the cell and said, "Noguera, as I was coming in today I saw the associate warden and I mentioned your situation and how long you've been in this cell. He assured me he would look into it. Tomorrow's Wednesday. You'll probably be called for committee, so be prepared."

"Thank you, Carlton. I appreciate your efforts."

He noticed the wall and stepped into the area directly in front of the cell.

"Dear God," he breathed, and for the next several moments he just looked. Finally he turned to me and said, "That's amazing, I've never seen anything like it. You're gifted beyond words. You're an artist."

He stepped away and closed the door, leaving me alone again. But at peace.

That morning I'd finished the mural of the San Clemente shore where I'd surfed as a boy. I drew myself in various scenes: one struggling to the surface after freeing my ankle from my leash; one where I watched the little boy I'd dreamt of; and a third scene where I caught a wave and rode it. The entire wall was covered in photographic detail.

I found a missing piece of myself—long neglected but not forgotten. It was the beginning of my artistic journey, the start of what would fill my days over the next thirty years and allow my mind an escape from the inhumanity and filth I encountered along the way. I had found the key that would allow me to become the man I was meant to be.

The next morning I woke at 5:00 a.m. I paced the entire morning until Heckle and Jeckle came for me. Unlike their normal routine of fucking with any prisoner they encountered, they were unusually professional and simply said, "The warden and the committee want to see you. Put on your blue shirt, pants, and shoes. We'll be taking you."

I nodded. "I'm ready now."

I was strip-searched first, then one of them said, "Turn around and back up. I'll be double locking your cuffs so they don't tighten up on you and cut off the circulation to your hands."

This dirty motherfucker purposely hurt me the first day I arrived to show me his power, and thought it was funny. Now he was concerned about the circulation in my hands. I didn't say anything, but I knew the game and I hated their hypocrisy. I was about to see the warden, and if I complained about what they had done to me before, there would be an investigation. But they had nothing to worry about—I wouldn't say anything. My only interest was in being classified and getting placed in East Block where the majority of the condemned prisoners were housed. There, I would have access to a phone and visits, and start to put some sort of life together.

They escorted me to the second floor of the AC where the warden, Daniel Vasquez, and the committee waited. I entered the room and observed the impression my appearance had on them from their facial expressions and lack of eye contact. I wasn't a person to them. I was only prisoner number D77200. I was told to sit down and Heckle and Jeckle stood on either side of me, like I was an animal.

Sitting around the table were the warden, the associate warden, a captain, a lieutenant, a counselor, a shrink, and the AC senior sergeant.

The warden began by stating: "William A. Noguera, CDC prisoner D77200, you have been sentenced to death and until your appeals are completed you will be under my charge. This is my classification committee and we will review your file and determine if you meet the requirements to be given grade-A status and moved to East Block where you will enjoy the privileges of a grade-A prisoner. I'm sorry you spent so much time in isolation. I was not aware of your situation. Normally ten days is the maximum time a prisoner is allowed to stay in those cells. Nevertheless, here you are, so let's begin."

I foolishly allowed myself to think I'd be given grade-A status because of the mistake they made in keeping me in isolation so long, but soon my hopes were smashed.

The associate warden said, "I've reviewed your file, Mr. Noguera, and I'm particularly concerned with this attempted escape as well as your use of violence. Since your arrest you've had a number of incidents mentioned where you were involved in the assault of another prisoner. This is very troubling indeed."

Then the shrink cut in with an insulting tone, "You do understand that violence is not the answer to all conflicts?"

I cut him off, "I understand your concerns, but please allow me to explain." I thought no matter what I said, they wouldn't understand. They seemed to have already made up their minds.

I continued, "I've spent the past twenty-seven days in isolation when I should have been there for only ten. Your staff will verify I did not complain nor did I do anything that would indicate I will be a problem to you. I'm not a gang member nor do I have any affiliation to any gang. The incidents you refer to in my file were unavoidable under the circumstances. I was nineteen years old when I was arrested and thrown into a unit where the majority of prisoners were grown men with long histories in prison. I fought to stay alive and protect myself. Tell me, doctor, what would you do if a man—a convict—a killer, attempted to rape you and take away your manhood? Would you fight, or try to reason with him to end his pursuit of your ass? As for the attempted escape, I was placed in isolation for a year for something I was not involved in. An informant pointed me out, but he lied and I was never charged for it. It was all untrue."

"Thank you Mr. Noguera, this will all be considered. However, it is the opinion of this committee that you need an adjustment period. We will review this again in ninety days. Meanwhile you will remain in the AC during this period of observation."

The warden's words had the ring of a canned statement he'd used hundreds of times before. I'd wanted a fair hearing, but instead I was left feeling gut-punched.

He continued, "You are a grade-B prisoner. However, you will be placed on a group yard that goes outside three times a week and you will be moved into a normal cell by yourself where you will receive mail and go to the prison store for your necessities. You will not, however, be allowed phone use. That privilege is reserved for grade-A prisoners. Do you have any enemies?"

"I do not."

He assigned me to a group yard. I would be allowed outside Tuesday, Thursday, and Saturday. I was led away and back to the isolation cell.

"We'll be back for you in a while. We have to move a guy's stuff out of a cell for you. He got his grade-A," Heckle said.

After they left, I sat on my bunk, defeated. At least three more months in the hole. I stared at the mural I'd created on the wall. I was so far away from home.

I stayed in isolation for the rest of the day. Heckle and Jeckle were still recovering from their display of "professionalism" during the committee meeting and didn't have the strength left to move me. Bulls from the next shift moved me to another cell on the first tier after dinner. A part of me didn't want to go. Being in solitary confinement so long had affected me in ways I didn't yet realize.

I entered the new cell. It didn't have a solid steel door—just a door made of heavy steel bars covered with steel mesh. The cell was the same size as the quiet cell I moved from, but with cells on either side. In a cell with bars instead of a solid door, I could talk to my neighbors.

The cell had a steel toilet and sink, a bunk and a light with a switch that allowed me to turn it on or off when I wanted. Otherwise, the cell was bare, but clean. I took off my blues and folded them, then placed them on the bunk. I took a deep breath and set out to search the cell as I always did, looking for contraband and a possible set-up. The only thing I found was a copy of *The Count of Monte Cristo*. I had begun reading it when Carlton came to my door.

"Noguera, I have your property. It's not much, but I'm sure you want and need it."

It was depressing when he handed everything to me through the food port. The handful of things was all I owned in the entire world. I had fallen far and fast from where I had once been.

I noticed right away a new toothbrush, paste, and tumbler were in a bag with my property. I told Carlton there had been a mistake, those items didn't belong to me.

He smiled and said, "I'm by the book, convict. I never saw a thing," and he walked off.

He placed the items in my property. But why? He didn't know me. I decided to accept the gifts and inventory what I had: a pair of prison-issued blues (jacket, pants, and shirt), three pairs of socks, two towels, three T-shirts, three boxer shorts, two sheets, a wool blanket, a comb, a pair of state-issued shoes, a pair of Nike basketball shoes. Since mail was not allowed in isolation, a bag of unopened letters sat among my things. I put all my property on the mattress and rolled it up so I could clean the cell. I would be there for at least the next three months, so I was determined to make the best of it.

After finishing with the cell, I took a bird bath, made easier by having the tumbler. I dried the floor, then brushed my teeth. In isolation I couldn't brush my teeth because they wouldn't give me a toothbrush or paste. I unrolled the mattress containing my property and made my bed. After I finished everything else I opened the bag containing the letters. This would be difficult. For the previous twenty-seven days I'd basically shut out the world and lived in my inner world of childhood memories and dreams. Now I had to open myself up to what others were experiencing.

There were nine letters in all. I scanned them and read the ones from my mother and sister first. My mother's letter asked that I call her as soon as I could, and emphasized that I should pray and stay away from trouble because she loved me. My sister said similar things, and told me to always know she missed me and worried about my safety. There were no letters from my father. I hadn't expected any. My father and I had an understanding: words weren't needed. I knew he was on my side, and if I needed him I only had to ask.

The remaining letters were from Maxine. She was the person who taught me what friendship is. I met her years earlier through her brother. She was like a sister to me, and we had remained friends.

After reading her letters, I wished I could speak to her. What would she think? I disappeared after speaking with her briefly the day I was brought here, but that was nearly a month ago. Had she called the prison to ask about me? Did she know I was in isolation? Her letters gave no indication about this. They were all written in the first five days after my sentencing.

I had to put all of it aside. I didn't have the time, not when the next day would be my first day on the yard. I had to prepare myself mentally, emotionally, and physically. I didn't know the layout of the yard or who would be there. What I did know was that I was assigned to a yard where the worst and most dangerous men would be, at the worst prison in the nation. I knew I could be killed if things went badly.

I turned off my lights and plugged the air vent below my sink and toilet. I didn't want to wake up and find a rat gnawing on my toes. I kneeled and prayed as I had since childhood. I'm Roman Catholic and, although I have been taught all the laws of the church, and how to pray, my prayers have always been more personal.

"I kneel before no man, but at the end of each day, I bow to you, Father."

I have never prayed to saints or anyone aside from God. Why should I? My prayer was simple, and to the point.

"Thank you, Father, for my health, strength, and the food I eat. Please protect my family and those in need of your protection, especially the children who suffer and are in danger. I pray for strength to defeat my enemies and those who would see me harmed. Amen."

Sleep came quickly. Nightmares stayed away and I slept deeply and peacefully.

I woke in darkness. It was cold because all the tier windows were open.

Older prison cell blocks are built with an outer shell that resembles a huge warehouse on the outside, with another building inside of that, containing rows of cells. The cells in the AC are numbered through seventeen on the yard side, and eighteen through thirty-three on the chapel side. Each of the three levels, or tiers, is numbered the same way. Windows are on the outer shell and have steel bars on the outside of each one.

I could see my breath as I exhaled. I got up, turned on the light, and put on a pair of socks. I washed my face, brushed my teeth, and combed my hair. It wasn't dawn yet, but it was near. I made my bed and sat down on it. I was nervous. Uncertainty was something I didn't like. The moments came and went slowly, as if in quicksand. My mind was in overdrive. I imagined all sorts of things happening on the yard—from being attacked, fighting back and being shot because of it, to fighting someone who had a knife, using deadly force and killing him. No matter how the scenario went, it didn't go well for me. I had to stop this. If I got jumpy and misread a situation, or reacted to something that had nothing to do with me, I'd seal my own fate. Just then one of the bulls turned on a radio and CCR's "Born on the Bayou" began playing. Music has always done something to me. Emotionally it gave me resolve. My confidence grew and I knew that no matter what I faced, I'd survive.

Breakfast came and I refused everything. I wasn't interested in food and I didn't want anything in my stomach. Next, trash was picked up, followed by the bar check and search.

When that was done, Heckle and Jeckle walked the tier announcing, "Yard. All prisoners wanting yard, get ready. Yard release."

Cuffs were placed on my door and a flood of bulls entered the tier. Two bulls came to my door and said, "Name?"

"Noguera, D77200."

"Okay, strip."

I went through the routine.

"Clear," the bull yelled when he was done. I was handed back the two pair of boxers I was taking out, my shoes, socks, state-issued blue pants, shirt, and denim jacket.

"Just put on the boxers and shoes."

I did as I was told and backed up to the food port to be cuffed. Again I waited for the bite from the teeth of the steel cuffs, but there was no bite today.

"Spike here," the bull yelled again, and another bull came and opened my door. "Back out and stop."

As I did, both bulls, one holding my cuffs, the other following to my right with his baton out, escorted me down the tier into a holding cage where two more bulls took over.

"Strip," one barked.

I said, "I just went through this."

"You have to be strip-searched twice before you go outside," he said.

After going through the same routine again I was escorted outside by the two bulls. The morning sun warmed my face as I walked through the first gate of the sally port for my yard, and the gate closed and locked. I backed up to the door and placed my cuffed hands through the port. Once the cuffs were removed, the door into the yard slid open and I stepped through, into the concrete jungle of San Quentin's death row yard.

It's always an advantage to be the first prisoner to the yard, and that day I was first. It allowed me to begin my study of the new environment, and it gave me the chance to watch as each prisoner came through the gate. Questions ran through my mind as I mentally prepared for what was to come. Who runs the yard? Who are his followers? What are their gang affiliations? How strong are they individually and as a group?

There wasn't a single cloud in the sky, but it was bitterly cold. I quickly put on the few clothes I had and realized it wouldn't be enough. I blocked out the discomfort from the cold and focused on my surroundings. The yard was a large concrete pad, roughly fifty by thirty-five yards, enclosed by a large metal fence. A shower area with three nozzles, a toilet, and a sink were at the back, along with the pull-up and dip bars. A basketball court was on the other side. I looked up at the gunner who sat in the small shack up on the wall above me and he nodded at me. He carried an M1 rifle, a .38 revolver, and a whistle. That M1 was serious and I knew he would use it. San Quentin AC gunners were notorious for putting men in their graves. It was one more hazard to remember.

I went over to an area where the sun hit the yard, so I could warm up. A total of eleven men on Yard-C came out that day, and others were taken to the other yards. The AC had three large yards with gunner shacks above each one. Gang affiliation determined which prisoners were assigned to each yard. On the days I went outside, Yard-A was for the BGF (Black Guerrilla Family), a black prison gang, and the Bloods, a black street gang. Yard-B was for the NF (Nuestra Familia), a Northern California Mexican prison gang whose main adversaries were the Southern Mexicans and La Eme (Mexican Mafia). My yard, Yard-C, was the integrated yard where a mixture of prisoners with no affiliation went. On Monday, Wednesday, and Friday, Yard-A was for Southern Mexicans, La Eme, and the AB (Aryan Brotherhood), a white prison gang. Yard-B was for Crips, a mostly black street gang, and Yard-C was another integrated yard.

Prison gangs are distinguished from street gangs because the former originated in the prison system and normally don't maintain any kind of group organization or control outside of prison. La Eme is an exception. Although formed as a prison gang, they have a large street presence and control a vast criminal network outside prison as well as inside.

Once on the yards, most of the prisoners formed up for a very structured workout that closely resembles military basic training physical fitness. A single prisoner at the front directed the workout. They did pushups, squats, burpies (leg thrusts), and ran in place, all synchronized in time with the cadence called by the one in front.

I began to walk around the outside of the workout areas as I watched the activities and studied the players. No one had talked to me yet. I didn't sense any tension on the yard, but I didn't fully trust my ability to pick up on that yet. The best soldiers can disguise their intentions until the last possible moment, and only a man who has learned to read the slightest changes would know.

I continued to walk as the sun rose, and as I neared the pull-up bars I stopped to look at the men doing pull-ups. Four whites, with tattoos covering most of their torsos, were working out there. One of them broke from the group and came up to me.

"Morning," I said, as I looked at his eyes.

"My name's Benny. My brothers call me Pirate."

"I'm Bill."

"Where you from, Bill?"

I knew this was huge. Where you're from, who you know, and where your loyalties lie can mean life or death, depending on who you're talking to.

"Orange County," I responded.

"I know a lot of folks from them parts."

I noticed his workout partners had stopped and begun moving toward us. The men were all heavily muscled and in shape. I glanced at them and Pirate continued talking.

"Let me introduce you to my boys."

Pirate sized me up as he talked, playing the role of a friendly face in a large club while he evaluated my words and body language. He had noticed me watching his partners and my body tensing.

"This here is Bull."

I shook Bull's hand and he nodded.

"These two are Wicked and Tweak."

I shook both their hands.

"I'm Bill."

"All right, Pirate, stop stalling. We know you was tired and that's why you stopped to talk. Let's get back to the routine. Fuck all the bullshit."

Pirate smiled and then laughed.

"Fuck you, Wicked," Pirate retorted. "Bill, let me get back and teach these boys how to do a workout. Talk at you later."

"Okay, Pirate, good to meet you."

He turned and went to the pull-up bars where they continued their program. I stood for a few moments and then kept walking. The other men on the yard were doing their own programs and I discretely watched all of them. I wouldn't work out. That day was for observation.

At noon, yard recall was announced and I made my way to the gate. I had come out first and I'd be first to go in.

"Hey Bill, you coming out Saturday?" asked Pirate.

"If my door opens I'll be here."

"Noguera, first tier," yelled one of the AC yard bulls.

I walked into the sally port and the door closed behind me. I placed my hands behind my back and through the small port. Cuffs went on my wrists and the other door opened. Then they escorted me to the same holding cage I had been in earlier that morning. Again, I was strip searched then taken to my cell, cuffs removed, and finally released to my own little world.

Right away I saw the items on my bunk. Three books, a bag of coffee, a couple of instant soups, two candy bars, and a note that said:

> *Hey Bro,*
> *Just a few things to make your time easier.*
> *W/R*
> *Your neighbor, Blue*

I read the note twice, and went to the bars.

"Blue," I called out.

"Yeah."

"Was that you?"

"Yeah."

"Listen, I appreciate it, but I'm okay, you didn't have to do that."

Accepting gifts, especially from a stranger, can be a dangerous mistake in prison. Normally prisoners don't give away valuables just to be friendly. They usually want something in return and the repayment plan can be expensive, especially for those who don't have money on their books yet. There are only so many ways to repay someone in prison where we aren't allowed to have any cash.

"It's nothing. Besides, that little piece of work you did at county for that young Wood won't be forgotten."

The prison system is a small world, and word travels fast. I didn't say anything.

"Yeah, I know who you are, Sinbad, or do you prefer to be called Mad?"

"Listen, Blue, just call me Bill. The judge and jury called me killer and murderer, but I don't go by those names either."

He began to laugh. "I guess you're right, old son. Ha. But know, I respect what you did."

"I didn't do it because the kid was white. He was scared and asked for my help, so I did it out of principle."

"Well, enjoy the books and things. I feel what you're saying. Your reasons are your own. I respect that."

"All right now," I said and sat down to eat my lunch that had been placed in my cell while I was on the yard.

I live my life according to principles based on a personal code of honor. Few prisoners are able to do that. In here, men live or die based on principles—either their own or those of a larger group. This also determines whether other prisoners consider you to be an inmate or a convict.

An inmate thinks only about day-to-day survival in prison. He isn't governed by principle. He follows all the rules. If a bull tells him to jump he says, "How high?" He is a coward. If someone strikes him he will run. He is blind. If something happens around him, he doesn't understand it because he hasn't learned to evaluate situations. If asked what happened, he will tell. He is an informant. He has no self-discipline and no principles. He's a punk and a motherfucker.

A convict lives by a code. Often this code is twisted and dangerous, but by their own standards convicts are the elite because they believe in something. They have standards. Their class structure is established by the prisoners themselves, not by any official edict. Convicts build their own establishment. They function among themselves as contending forces. They instruct the young on acceptable behavior, train them to have honor and to live by a code. Often convicts test newcomers in order to make them strong, brave, and proud. Those who respond appropriately are on track to become part of their society. They're as hard as the steel which encloses them. They don't cooperate with the authorities, and they hate all cops. There are not many of these men left. The prison system has learned to separate the convicts from the population, and slowly the snake, without its head, has begun to die.

Not long after my arrest I realized there was no future in prison gangs and the only person I could rely on was myself. I began to discover the principles I would later forge into a code to live my life by, regardless of the circumstance or situation. That personal code has guided my life ever since.

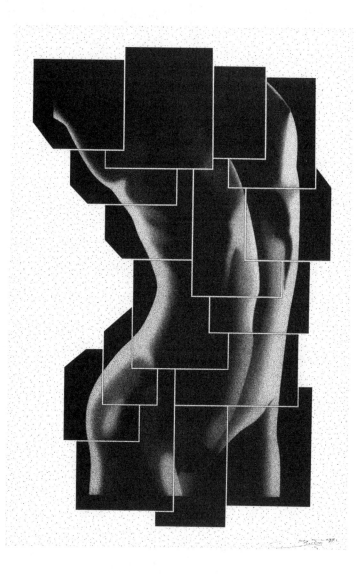

Chapter 4

Orange County Jail, 1984

I hate bullies, rapists, child molesters, or anyone who harms a weaker person just because they can. I identify with children who suffer at the hands of irresponsible adults, and I don't maintain my composure when one of those creeps is within range. I realize some view this way of thinking as Neanderthal, but I believe a real man can't stand by and allow the rape, molestation, or harm of a child to take place in his presence or with his knowledge. I also believe in using whatever force necessary to stop it.

That "little piece of work" Blue referred to happened at the Orange County jail and was not planned or expected. I was in the shower early on a Sunday morning when most of the men in the unit had gone outside to the yard. I stayed back to wash my clothes and just get away from the idiots. A young kid, maybe eighteen years old, who looked more like twelve, came into the shower area. I focused my attention on him because he seemed nervous. I wondered if he had orders to attack me. Even a twelve-year-old can inflict damage with a knife. He was scared, but I didn't think it had anything to do with me.

A few moments later I noticed a black man walk by, look inside, and signal to someone as he pointed into the shower area.

The kid said, "Help me please, they're going to rape me."

I turned off the shower and began putting on my shoes. Three black men came into the shower area. I stood and focused on them. I knew who they were. I had seen them taking items from other prisoners as they came back from canteen. Now they planned to rape the kid. At that moment I decided they wouldn't have their way. I wouldn't mind my own business and walk away while the motherfuckers raped that kid.

"What's up, Mad Bill? This don't concern you, homes. We ain't fuckin with no Chicans, just this sweet-ass cracker."

The one talking was Chili Red. He was a light-skinned African who had been to prison and rumored to be BGF. He was in good shape. I had seen him fight and, although he wasn't the best I'd seen, with two friends he wouldn't be easy. There was no turning back. Talking to them would do no good. I looked at the kid and he pleaded with his eyes. I'll never forget that look.

I turned to Chili Red and said, "Your business don't concern me."

For a split second he relaxed and at that moment I struck, hitting him in the throat. He grabbed his throat, and I advanced, kicking his feet out from under him. He fell to the floor and I smashed his face with my right fist. It all took less than a second and a half, and like most bullies or rapists he was a coward. I moved fast, kicking the second wannabe tough guy in the balls. As he doubled over, I kneed him in the face. Before I could turn, the third guy cut me with a razor blade attached to a handle. It cut a thin but deep line down the inside of my right elbow. I rushed him, deflecting his clumsy attempts to cut me again. I hit him in the mouth, and as he fell I hit him over and over again until he lay still. I looked at my arm and cursed out loud.

I grabbed my stuff and left the shower, followed by the kid. I had to stop the bleeding before the cops saw my arm and put two and two together. I walked into my cell and tied my arm off to slow the bleeding. My cellie, a Mexican named Spider, who had stayed back from yard as well, asked, "What the fuck happened, ese?"

"It's been handled."

He immediately pulled out a shank from its hiding place, and asked the kid what happened. I wiped off the blood and put tape around the wound.

Word soon spread about what happened. The rest of the unit returned from outside and the whites came to my cell to discuss the situation. I told them what I told Blue, that it wasn't racial. I got involved because no one was going to rape anyone—man, woman, or child—when I could stop it. Period, end of story.

It wasn't the first or last time I'd fight for that principle. It's what I believe in. Violence is the only answer when faced with those circumstances. In jail or prison, you're respected and feared for your capacity for violence.

A few days after the incident in the shower the cops transferred me to another unit. Someone talked to the authorities and they knew what I did. Instead of just writing me up, they placed me in the most notorious unit in the entire jail, A-1 and A-2. Known as Blood Alley because of the high number of assaults and stabbings there, it was also run by La Eme. The unit was for convicts—men who served many years in prison. The majority of them were "made men"—Carnales—soldiers, associates, or prospects of La Eme. There were also some AB members. I was the youngest prisoner in the unit. I was placed in A-1 cell-3, where my true education would begin on the finer points of prison life, like invoking fear in those who opposed me.

All cells in the unit were eight-man cells. There were five cells per tier. Each cell had a sleeping area with eight bunks. A day room off to the side had a shower, a large metal table, a phone (for collect calls), and a TV. It may sound like a college dorm, but believe me when I tell you that the men I met there are still the most dangerous I've ever met in the system. They were gladiators. The only way I could survive would be to compete and win at their deadly game.

Though fighting is important in prison, many good fighters haven't survived it. Equal in importance is the ability to understand and use prison politics to one's advantage. This is another subject I learned from one of the best.

As soon as I entered the cell, I knew I was entering a whole new arena. The men here were serious, well respected criminals—men who were looked up to by everyone in the system. I knew I would be watched and tested right away to see if I measured up.

I put my things down and approached a convict who sat in the day-room. I had seen him before and knew he was a Carnal of the Mexican Mafia. I also knew his reputation and that he ran the entire unit.

His name was Eddie Monster, and if you looked into his eyes, you'd understand the nickname had nothing to do with physical stature and everything to do with his intensity, as well as his reputation for viciousness as a gladiator.

I stopped in front of him and said, "Órale, mucho gusto, mi nombre es Bill. I just got transferred. Which bunk can I grab?"

"Órale, youngster, mucho gusto, I'm Monster. Four vatos caught the chain this morning. Go ahead and grab any bunk you want. But first, sit down and tell me qué paso with them niggers."

He, like many others, heard what I had done. I ran the entire deal to him and he liked what he heard.

"Watcha. I know Chili Red. He ain't no punk and he may try you again, but this time he'll come with a piece. Be ready."

The three other men in the cell came over and introduced themselves to me. There was Huero from La Habra, Midnight from La Jolla, and Richard also from La Jolla. They were Southern Mexican soldiers, and all would later earn the status of Carnales in the Mexican Mafia.

I put my things on a bottom bunk and made my bed. I didn't say much more. I was out of place with them and I wondered how I'd be tested.

At dinner we walked together to the chow hall.

"Sit with me," said Monster.

I noticed the respect he commanded. Everywhere he went, other prisoners nodded or wanted to get his attention so they could say, "Órale." The other three men in the cell got similar reactions from the others.

"You're a regular celebrity," I said to Monster.

"Yeah, as long as they pay I'm happy."

I won't lie—I was impressed. They projected poise and honor, especially to a nineteen-year-old kid. I saw the looks I got from many of the other prisoners. Many asked who I was. Others who knew, nodded or glared. I sat with an elite group. So what got me there? The answer was obvious: violence.

I've never been popular as a prisoner. Men like my new cellies, men who understood a certain discipline and code, usually didn't have a problem with me, but others find me arrogant and aloof. I don't like the majority of prisoners and I treat them with disdain. I have my reasons, and they're firmly based on the fact that most of these men are back stabbers and scumbags.

When we returned to the unit, more prisoners were in the cell and the open bunks were filled. All three of the men who had just arrived knew the rest of my cellies from previous time spent in prison. I was the only outsider. The other three were Shark from Bakersfield, Jack from Whittier, and Bugsy from Santa Ana. I was introduced, and right off Bugsy and I didn't get along. As he shook my hand, he asked Monster if he had claimed me. At first I didn't understand, but I soon realized he was asking if I was Monster's property. In other words, his bitch.

Monster's response was, "I don't fuck around, ese, and that youngster is firmé. He just took down Chili Red."

Bugsy didn't seem impressed, but let it go.

Later, Monster pulled me aside and said, "Listen, don't trip on Bugsy. He's an asshole, but no punk. He's dangerous. He just wanted to know if he could try you."

"I'm no punk. If that motherfucker tries me, I'll hurt him."

Monster stared at me. "Órale, I believe you."

Over the next couple of weeks I got into a routine of working out and practicing my martial arts with the same intensity I had before my arrest. All the men in my cell were workout fanatics.

I stayed to myself and watched everyone. It was natural for me to take note of their habits, their strengths and weaknesses, and find weak spots in their armor. I sized up all of them as if preparing for a fight. I knew one of them would try me and I had to be ready.

All of the men in the cell were from Orange County except me. I was from Los Angeles, which meant all of the men had other members of their gangs in the unit. If I fought one of them, I probably would have to fight more. The truth was, I was one of only three men that were not from Orange County in the entire unit. Not good odds at all.

The third week in the cell proved to be an eye opener. A shipment of drugs came in light and the two mules who brought it in were stabbed as the penalty for cheating. Drugs are usually smuggled in by men who know they are headed to jail on a certain date. They go to a drug dealer under the control of a gang, and offer to bring drugs into the jail for a "kick-down" (a small percentage). When they report to jail they turn the drugs over, minus their cut. Most of the time it goes wrong because the mule is usually a drug addict. He's strung out and needs a fix, and as soon as he can take the clavo out of his rectum, he uses all of his cut. After that, he begins to use from the other as well, which carries a severe price.

Monster received half of what came in. Later that night, all of my cellies were high. Monster asked me if I wanted to "get on the broom" (sweep the tiers), which wasn't about sweeping, but meant I would be trusted by everyone to handle drugs and deliver them from cell to cell, or in some circumstances deliver a shank to an individual. In my cell, there were three bone-crushers. Each one was at least seven inches long, made of stainless steel, and hidden so well the cops never found them, even during cell searches.

Because they were hidden so well to ensure guards didn't find them, they also couldn't be accessed very easily, and unless it was planned ahead of time any fight would be absent those weapons.

I reported to Monster at the end of each day on what was moved. I also gave him the kick-down I received in payment.

"Don't you use?" he asked.

"Only gesca (pot). I have to stay on my toes. I'll trade you for it."

I gave him all the coke, crystal, and heroin I received, and he gave me some gesca.

"Watcha, I don't have much gesca, not enough to cover everything you gave me, but I'll get back to you," he said.

"That's firmé. Gracias for the time on the tier."

"From now on, that's you. Every day you take care of business out there."

I nodded and went over to my bunk and rolled joints. I gave three to each of my cellies. It wasn't much, but the show of respect got their attention.

Bugsy came up to me to thank me for the joints and told me he hurt his back and asked if I would please allow him to use my bunk for a few nights until he could climb up to his bunk. I told him I understood and not to worry. I'd move my things to his top bunk until he'd recovered. Of course, he thanked me. He called me a "young stud," but I knew what he was doing. He wanted to see if he could talk me out of my lower bunk. If he could, he would progress and see what else he could take from me.

Over the next few days, I watched him improve until he began working out again. I waited yet another day, and while he made his bunk I said, "Looks like your back is fine. I need my bunk back."

He smiled and said, "Come on stud, you're young and can climb up like nothing. I'm getting old. Do me this favor."

"You said a couple of days 'til your back was okay. Time's up."

"Okay, okay, after chow."

I headed for the chow hall, and while walking I caught up to Huero and Monster.

"Watcha, this vato Bugsy is playing me. If we get into it, is he on his own?"

Monster responded, "He's a loud mouth. If you feel disrespected, handle your business. No one will interfere. But remember, he's not going to lie down. He'll fight and, if given a chance, he'll use a piece."

"Right on," I said, and continued to chow.

This would be it. I would once again ask him to move and I'd take it from there.

When we all returned and everyone was sitting around, I began to take my mattress off the top bunk.

"What are you doing, ese?"

"I'm taking my bunk back. Time's up."

"Come on, homie, let me keep it. Maybe we can share it, you bring your fine ass down here at night and I'll keep you warm."

They all stopped what they were doing to watch. I continued taking my mattress off the top bunk.

"Nah, ese, I'm taking what's mine," I said.

"Check this out motherfucker, the bunk's mine. I ain't giving you shit back. And starting now, when you go to the store you'll be paying me to live here and you'll give up that sweet ass if I want it."

There it was: his true feelings. He didn't like me and didn't believe I belonged there. He thought I was just a kid he could use and then throw away.

Bugsy was over six feet tall, and two hundred pounds. He was around thirty-two years old, a career criminal, and an associate of the Mexican Mafia. He was also used to getting his way. At the time, I was six foot one, 170 pounds, and angry.

He stepped up to me in a menacing manner and I didn't hesitate. Before he could extend his right arm to push me, I hit him in the face. As he fell I strapped my arms around his neck, and in less than ten seconds I choked him out. When he was out I let him go, took his mattress off the lower bunk, and put mine there. He began to come out of it and did what I knew he'd do. First, he allowed his emotions to override his mind. I'd embarrassed him and he wanted to satisfy his wounded ego. He stood up and walked past me to the shower area. I knew one of the three shanks lay hidden there—a big mistake. When he got it, he came out talking.

"Fuckin' punk motherfucker."

Prison-made shanks normally have a sharpened point, but the edges are not as sharp as a regular knife, so the user must stab or poke instead of cut. That's fine if the target isn't expecting an attack, but not so good in situations like this, where I knew he was coming for me. He needed to get close to me to use it. I hit him in the face, this time breaking his nose, and as he charged blindly, swinging like an idiot, everything slowed down. He scratched my shoulder and I felt the sting but it never went further. I moved in, smashed his ribs with my fists, and picked him up and slammed him to the floor. The shank fell out of his hands and I punished him—striking his face until it was a bloody mess and he didn't move.

I then dragged him over to the sleeping area and said, "This motherfucker tried to play me. I know you've known him longer than me, so if this is a problem, we can deal with it now."

"Fuck him," was all anyone said.

I would have fought them all if they backed his play.

Monster struck that idea by stating, "Get that piece of shit out of my sight. I told him if he tried you and lost, he'd be out of here. He lost."

I looked at him and narrowed my eyes.

"Before you got at me about him being on his own and handling your business, he asked for a green light to test you. He doesn't like you and thought you were here to rat us out," Monster said.

"I'm no rat."

"I had to see your reaction. If I protected you, it would have been a lot worse in the long run. Now they all know you won't hesitate to fuck someone up. All these vatos respect that."

The guards rolled up Bugsy soon after that. They asked what had happened and interviewed everyone in the unit. Funny, everyone said they hadn't seen anything because they were showering or asleep.

Bugsy was placed in another unit where he made the mistake of bad-mouthing Monster. For his mistake he was stabbed repeatedly and ended up in protective custody.

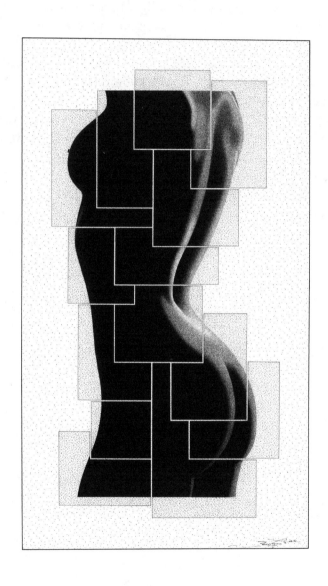

Chapter 5

San Quentin Death Row, 1988

I took advantage of each opportunity to go outside regardless of the weather. Each day, I worked out with intensity and purpose and also became familiar with yard politics and who the main players were. My yard was for non-affiliated prisoners, so in theory it was less prone to violence. The reality was that gangs often sent sleepers to other yards, including that one. Sleepers are active gang members who convince the warden's committee that they're threatened and can no longer function within their group. The committee will then change their yard assignment based on their word that they're no longer active. After that, the gang has a representative on a yard they previously couldn't reach. Sometimes gangs will even stage a fight with a chosen member so the bulls will take him off the yard and place him on another yard. Of course, it's all an act designed to get a member of their gang within striking distance of an enemy. Once sleepers are on the new yard, they may lay dormant for weeks, months, and sometimes years, until the designated target arrives.

Other prisoners who are sympathetic to a particular gang may also be ordered to "put in work" to get out from under some difficulty, such as a gambling debt owed to one of the gang members. The consequence of declining the order would likely be fatal.

My yard had three sleepers. All were extremely dangerous and two of them were activated just a few months later.

During that time I discovered the San Quentin library and its collection of books on art, poetry, and philosophy.

I devoured the books. Although I couldn't go to the library, I could order books and have them delivered to my cell. I read José Ortega y Gasset, the Spanish philosopher, as well as Søren Kierkegaard, and Alfred North Whitehead. I was delighted by the French poets, Baudelaire, Rimbaud, Mallarmé, Lautréamont, and Paul Valéry. But it was the artists and their work that moved me. That's where I found passion, love, hate, fury, and all of the human emotions that would later be the basis for my own work.

I studied Rubens, Caravaggio, David, and all the Masters of Realism, as well as the Impressionists, the Cubists, the Futurists, the Surrealists, and every art form available to me. But it was the Abstract Expressionists that captivated me most. When I looked at the works of the men of the New York school—Robert Motherwell, Jackson Pollock, Willem de Kooning, Franz Kline, Arshile Gorky, Clyfford Still, Mark Rothko, and others—a dialogue materialized between us. One look at their work and I was thunderstruck, and I knew immediately what was being conveyed. I discovered I was a "sensitive viewer," and the works came alive for me, breathing emotion and filling a void inside me.

Meanwhile, I lived two separate lives: one, as a prisoner inside the walls of the most dangerous prison in the nation, and the other as an artist. I think it's of great importance that I make a distinction here in my meaning of "artist."

There are many men in prison who can draw as well as an advanced student in art school, but that fact does not make them artists. If a man can cook, that alone does not make him a chef. The same applies to men who can draw. What makes an artist? There are many viewpoints, and everyone from the Realist to the Expressionist will give you theirs. For me, it is the ability to retreat from the world surrounding me where otherwise I cannot. It is the ability to escape by allowing my mind to actualize itself and render external what otherwise would be internal. It is also the process of accepting one's surroundings where we bear witness to the chaos within us and bring order to it by an abnormal sensitivity to a medium. I create because I must. Art to me is not a luxury, but a necessity.

San Quentin in 1988 was a violent place and I was not immune to it. For some reason as the heat of summer intensifies, violence explodes in prison. Men are moody and quick to strike as if cold blooded. The heat gives them mobility, as well as a thirst for blood.

Two of the sleepers on my yard were Tweak and Jose. Tweak was a white, extremely aggressive prospect of the Aryan Brotherhood.

The second sleeper was Jose, who had ties to La Nuestra Familia.

The tension on the yard was high that day. The whites were not working out and that was very rare, especially on a hot day. There were three new prisoners on the yard. One I recognized right away as Charles Manson. The other two were Africans I had never seen before. I decided to begin my workout and keep an eye on the various groups to see what developed. I began my three-mile run as I usually did, and watched.

The tension was still obvious after my run, so I headed over to Pirate and Bull.

"Morning," I said and shook hands with both of them. "Seems to be a little tense out here today."

"Yeah, that fuckin' nigger right there with the bald head stabbed and killed a Wood a few years back. It's time for him to pay the piper."

"You gotta do what you gotta do," I said. "I'm gonna finish up my routine, I'll talk to you later." I walked over to the pull-up bars.

I was hoping nothing would happen until the end of yard time. I wanted to finish my routine, shower, and not have to deal with the drama I sensed coming.

I noticed Charles Manson approaching, which interrupted my thoughts. He came right up to me, grabbed my hand, and said, "Brother, it's been years since I've seen you. It's good you're back. What do you need?"

I pulled my hand away. I had never met this piece of shit before, and fixing my eyes on him, I said, "If you ever touch me, talk to me, or even look my way, I'll rip your fucking face off. Do you understand me, you fucking baby killer?"

He backed away and stumbled, then turned and got away from me. I don't play well with child killers or molesters. What his friends did to Sharon Tate makes them child killers in my book, and I won't tolerate any of those motherfuckers touching me or talking to me.

Normally, convicts do not respect predators who were famous

on the street. They are not dangerous in prison. Men like Charles Manson, Richard Ramirez, Richard Allen Davis, and William Bonin are the lowest form of life in prison, and many convicts would take them out in a second if they were on the yard together. The public considers them scary monsters, but convicts consider them vermin and resent the fact that they are still alive. That's why they always end up on a protective custody yard, with the other child killers and molesters, or don't go to yard at all.

Tweak struck just as I finished showering. It was about a half hour until yard recall. The African came to the back of the yard area, where he began to undress to take a shower. He must have thought he was safe. Everyone had been friendly to him and no one had said anything to make him suspicious. He made a fatal error by not being aware and alert. Tweak approached him from behind and, as the African turned to look at him, Tweak stabbed him four times on the right side of his torso between the ribs. They were kill shots. The African realized the threat too late and didn't have enough time to defend himself. He took two steps and fell. The gunner sounded his whistle and ordered everyone to lay flat on the ground.

"Everyone down. No one move," he yelled. Then he addressed the African, "Can you walk? Try and make it to the gate."

The other bulls came to the sound of the whistle and waited at the gate with a gurney. The African got up and fell, but got up again and stumbled to the gate. Blood flowed freely from his wounds. Then I looked closely at the bone-crusher Tweak used. It was a six-inch steel blade. There was no possible way he got that outside without the help of a bull looking the other way. Tweak smiled.

"See you in about ten," he said.

I nodded.

"All right now. If you need anything while you're in isolation, let me know."

He was placed in isolation for ten days and then he'd return to the yard. Later I learned the African survived. He had a collapsed lung and other damage. He was lucky. However, he never returned to the yard and neither did Charles Manson.

Chapter 6

Childhood, 1970–1975

I began studying the martial arts at age six, after my father grew frustrated that his only son was constantly being picked on and beat up at school. I was the only Colombian boy, which meant I was different. Different, for the only and eldest boy in the family, meant a target was on my chest from the beginning.

I once took a horny toad to school for show and tell. I caught it on one of the many hunting trips my father and I had been taking since I was five. One of the bullies wanted to hold it as I waited my turn to show it to the class. I refused, knowing the boy would not give it back.

He got angry and said, "Give me the lizard, punk, or I'll take him."

He was used to getting his way. His brothers were all in the Blackwood Street Gang and at age six he was already on his way to becoming a member. He wasn't the only one. Most of the boys in the school had older brothers in gangs who would back up their little brothers in any conflict. I had no one.

I was not going to let him take my lizard and kill it, even if that meant I would be hit. I once saw him take a bird from its nest and smash it. So I said, "No."

What happened next would stay with me for the rest of my life. The boy tackled me, hoping to get me on the ground. As he did my head hit the corner of a desk and I lost consciousness. When I came out of the haze, kids were screaming and the teacher was calling for help. My head was split open and blood covered my face and shirt. I was scared, but mostly it hurt my feelings because I understood I wasn't liked there. I wanted to fit in but no one wanted me. This would continue for years. My father enrolled me in martial arts classes, but still the beatings continued. How could I fight and win against members of a gang? I retreated further into my imagination and daydreamed of being someone else and living someplace nice.

My refuges from all of the bad things in my life were the martial arts and my family. It's where I was safe and accepted. My parents loved each other and cared deeply for their children. My little sister, Sarita, who is sixteen months younger, was always close to me, and although things were bad at school and in the neighborhood at least I could come home and feel safe and loved.

All of this ended in 1973, when we returned to Colombia for a vacation. That's when my father learned from his sister, Elvira, that my mother had betrayed him by sending money home to her family without his knowledge, for living expenses and to build a house. That's when everything changed in my family. My father and mother never again showed each other affection, and they became very distant. My father began drinking heavily, and although he and I still hunted, fished, and went to tournaments together, my mother and sister were excluded.

My sister chose to remain close to our mother and was never again close with our father. I couldn't choose between them. I loved both my parents and it killed me inside to see what was happening to my family.

Not choosing my father's side made him angry and I often received physical beatings and emotional abuse as he vented his frustration. My mother added to the turmoil by withholding affection unless we told her we loved her and not my father. Other times she would bully my sister and me, especially when she became upset at my father for refusing to give her the amount of money she wanted.

The drama didn't end there. My mother would lock herself in her room and announce to us she was going to kill herself. Other times she would take off in the car and tell us she would never return because we were bad and it would be our fault if she killed herself. I remember sitting at the door of her bedroom for hours begging her not to kill herself. I believed she'd do it. When she came out or returned in her car, my sister and I would agree to anything, including loving her more, if only she wouldn't kill herself.

My parents each competed for their children's affection and placed the responsibility for family peace squarely on our young shoulders. We both blamed ourselves for any family disturbance since each parent made it clear we had the power to keep things peaceful. If only we acted right and said the right things no turmoil would erupt. This was a terrible burden to place on a child.

My relationship with my father was complex. I loved him, worshipped him, feared and hated him. He was a good father when he was sober and not angry, and during those times I liked being with him and would do anything to please him.

Tragically, he was obsessed with controlling everything following the betrayal he believed my mother had committed, and that fueled his darker side. He still provided for us, but his drinking increased and he became mean. Worst of all, he began to beat my mother.

I developed my ability to read body language and nonverbal cues as a survival mechanism while living with my father. He was usually normal until Friday, and then as the week drew to a close I'd grow more and more nervous anticipating how the week would end. I spent a lot of time waiting and watching. I'd sit on the curb in front of the house on Fridays, waiting for my father to come home. If he arrived by 5:30 p.m. we were safe—he had left work and driven straight home. He'd hug and kiss me, then announce we were going hunting, fishing, or to a tournament. I could relax. If he didn't arrive by 5:40 p.m. I'd start to get nervous and begin to cry. I'd run in the house, get my finished homework, think of jokes to tell him—anything so he'd be happy and not in a dark mood. I'd sit on the curb and wait until he arrived. If it was past 5:45 p.m. I knew he'd stopped at the store, cashed his check, and bought alcohol.

When my father arrived home and I'd see the bag from the store, my effort to divert his attention went into overdrive. I'd try to please him, but normally to no avail. He'd walk through the house, put down his things, open a beer, and comment on all the things wrong with the house. He'd demand to see my newest martial arts forms and my homework. He'd listen to my piano songs. He was only getting started, pumping himself up.

He'd check my sister's chores, then go into the backyard and inspect all of my animal cages. Were the pheasants fed and clean? Had I let the pigeons out? Had I washed my dog's area? Had I fed the snakes? Cut the grass? On and on it went, until he eventually found some shortcoming that I was guilty of. I was only nine years old then, with more responsibilities than anyone that age should have had. When he found a mistake or something that didn't meet his standards, we'd get hit hard. Then he'd confront my mother about her lack of control over the house, and he'd start inspecting everything. All the while he drank, and his mood darkened.

After that he'd sit in the backyard drinking and I'd watch him from behind a window shade. I saw him thinking, and I knew that soon his anger would reach a boiling point. I sensed it, and tasted it in the air. Suddenly he'd rise and storm into the house. His temper terrified me. I knew where he was headed and soon I could hear the yelling, followed by the sound of him hitting my mother. At that moment I hated my father. I'd push into the room and try to defend her only to be thrown into a wall or punched. The physical pain wasn't nearly as hurtful as the understanding my family was in trouble and my mother in danger.

I learned early on that I had two fathers. One was kind, loving, and most of all he made me feel like the most important person in the world. I loved him. From the age of five, he began teaching me how to track and hunt animals. He taught me everything I knew, and I experienced a world most could only dream of. To me my father was a god—a man who other men respected and feared.

My second father was a drinker, and mean. On his dark days, he would hit me as easily as speak to me. My sister and I were terrified of him, and although I loved him, a resentment was growing. My anxieties got worse as this side of my father took over. Even the sight of him coming towards me was often enough to make me wet my pants. A monster seemed to be living in my father's body.

As the abuse and stress grew in my life, other parts of my life suffered as well. I found myself staring at a fly, and from there my mind would jump to some other distraction, and then to something else. It seemed like it never stopped. My attention span was extremely limited, which made school difficult. I never failed a grade, but learning was always a struggle because I couldn't fully concentrate on the subject at hand.

Prior to 1975, Attention Deficit Hyperactivity Disorder (ADHD) wasn't recognized as a treatable medical condition. It was simply called hyperactivity and the response was typically punishment intended to reform the difficult child for not concentrating enough. No one, including my parents or me, really understood what the problem was, yet educators believed it merely required more effort from me. They grew more and more frustrated when their pressure tactics did not improve the situation. Teachers thought students with "hyperactivity" were just stubborn, and focused more attention on the students who were trying to learn.

By age eleven, I was withdrawing more and more to minimize the pain caused by others. It seemed like the whole world was against me and I didn't understand how to change that. I was punished at school and beaten at home.

Things at home got steadily worse. My father continued his downward spiral and seemed to find new and worse things to do to my mother when he drank. I remember thinking he must plan while he was sober and act them out when he was drunk.

My mother also changed. She began to fight back with verbal insults, seeming not to mind that it only escalated the problem. I couldn't understand why she would do that when she knew his response would be violence. Maybe it was her way of maintaining some element of control. Whatever the reason, it only added fuel to his rage. He responded with his fists, and by kicking down doors and tearing apart whatever she was working on. Many of my mother's paintings were smashed as a result.

Their fights always seemed to be about money. My father maintained control by withholding money from her, and she constantly tried to wrest control from him by getting more of it. He'd give her the exact amount to pay the bills, and only enough to buy the food we needed. No name brands or anything fancy for my father or his family. This enraged my mother. She was used to the best of every-thing, and didn't want to settle for what he'd give her. Even with what she made, it didn't cover the expenses for what she wanted to buy, so she began to steal. My mother was too proud to shoplift. That was beneath her. Instead, she switched price tags of lower priced items with the things she wanted to purchase and paid the lower amount. This happened every time we went shopping, and my sister and I thought it was normal. It allowed my mother to buy us name-brand items for school and everyday needs.

Anyone looking at our family from the outside would think I was lucky. We had a nice home, nice clothes, toys, bicycles, and I even had a motorcycle. My father and I often went hunting, fishing, bike racing, to martial arts competitions, and surfing. To the casual observer, it looked like I lived a very privileged childhood.

My parents, and especially my mother, were experts at false appear-ances. If my mother was asked about her marriage, she would say how loving and good my father was and that our family was very happy. I still don't understand this, but to my mother it was vitally important that others believed we lived a charmed life. Of course, the neighbors and anyone close to us knew the truth, so when she told them how great things were they'd smile and nod, but the looks on their faces said it all.

During one of my father's more violent episodes, my mother man-aged to call the police after she was beaten. My father announced they'd have to kill him if they wanted to take him, and before that happened, he'd kill as many of them as he could. He started loading his guns and preparing for battle. I knew my father was wrong. He had beaten my mother and he should have stopped and given up. But there I was, knocking on the door of the room he was in. I could hear him inside and I said, "Dad, it's me. Open the door." Everything grew quiet.

"Billy, what do you want? Get out of here."

"Papa, let me in. I'll help you."

The door opened and there stood my father. I could see the rage in his eyes and the heat rolling off his body. I also noticed something else—pride. He was proud of me for standing with him against the outside forces. He hugged me and I felt at peace in my father's embrace, even in the middle of the storm. I stood there hugging my father wishing the moment would never end. But it did.

"Check the rifles and load all of them," he told me.

I looked on the bed at the arsenal he'd laid out. I did what he said without question. I told him how no one could stand up to him and that they didn't understand who they were messing with. Gradually I changed the subject and talked about his job, how he'd soon be manager and run the entire company. I then switched to the competition I had coming up the following week and reminded him he still had to teach me some new strikes because I was ready to fight at the next level. Slowly my father calmed down and his anger drained away.

His rage faded and I pressed on. "Dad, remember how you taught me that spinning back fist I used on that guy in the Four Seasons Open? I need you to show me that combination where you go low and high, like you did a couple of weeks ago at the studio. That was awesome. You knocked that guy out."

My dad was finally calm and almost back to normal.

There was a knock on the door. "Mr. Noguera, this is officer Deacon of the Industry Sheriff's Department. We need you to open the door and talk to us."

At that moment my father's next move would decide everything. He looked at the guns and then at me. He took a deep breath.

"Give me a moment, I need a moment to think."

"Mr. Noguera, we just need to talk. Everything will be all right. Is your son in there with you? Is he all right?"

"He's fine, just give me a moment."

"Can he say something so we know he's okay?"

My father nodded.

"I'm fine, we're finishing up the laundry," I lied.

My dad smiled and relaxed. "Okay, I'm opening the door. I'm not armed. I'll talk."

As he opened the door they crashed in and rushed him. They were aggressive and angry and they beat him with their batons. I heard him cry out, "No. No." Blood hit my face as they split his head, even though he wasn't resisting. They weren't paying attention to me. I decided my father needed my help and I moved in quickly. I kicked the cop closest to me in the leg and tried to pull him off my father as he turned to me. I didn't see the blow, but his punch drove me against the wall and I lay still. My father looked at me before being knocked unconscious and dragged away. In that moment I understood my father. He felt like I did. It was him against the world. That day it had been us against the world.

This was not the only time my father and I fought side by side. Later that same year, two brothers, Robert and Ernie Hernandez, jumped me while we were at school. Both of them were bigger than me, and members of the Cadbrook Street Gang. They wanted the necklace my parents had given me at my first communion. It was a cross on a gold chain and it was hidden under my shirt. They saw it during P.E., and as I left Sparks Elementary School on my way home they demanded I give it to them.

Why couldn't they just accept me and leave me alone? I knew they didn't like me and didn't want me in their neighborhood, but how could I make it end? Every day it was something else.

I took the chain off and I'm sure they believed I would give it to them. Instead, I put it in my pocket and said, "I'm not giving you shit. Fuck you and your brother."

Two against one was not fair, but my life had never been fair, so I was well acquainted with odds being against me as a young boy fighting the world.

As I realized a fight was coming, I heard a reassuring internal voice telling me, "I'll do this. Nothing in my life matters except this. No moment in my life exists except this moment. I am born in this moment, and if I fail I will die in this moment."

I punched, kicked, and did everything possible to defeat them, but as I fought Robert, his brother picked up a rock and hit me in the head. One moment I was fighting, the next I woke up in the street. I touched my throbbing head and found a large bump on one side and blood all over my face and shirt. I tried to stand, but couldn't. The world spun and I managed to get to my knees, where I noticed my pockets were turned inside out. The chain and cross were gone and so was my lunch money for the week. I walked home bloodied and bruised, crying hot bitter tears.

I didn't want my mother to see me, so when I got home I went to the backyard to feed and water my animals. I didn't want to see anyone but my father. My sister came out and saw me. I told her what happened. She sympathized with me. We had a special bond and she was always protective. But what could she do?

When my father arrived home, my sister told him, "Papa, Billy's hurt and needs to see you. He's in the doghouse."

The doghouse was my father's workshop.

My father put his things down and went outside. When he entered the doghouse and saw me, I recognized the fire in his eyes. He was mad at those who had hurt me.

"What happened?"

"Robert and Ernie Hernandez wanted my first communion chain and cross. I wouldn't give it to them, so they jumped me. I fought, but Ernie picked up a rock and hit me. That's all I remember. When I woke up my chain and money were gone."

"Are you okay?"

"My head hurts, but I'm okay."

"Do you know where these fuckin' Mexicans live?"

"Yeah."

"Okay, let's go. Get in the van."

We drove to their badly neglected house which had old cars parked everywhere. My father knocked on the door, and when the door opened I smelled the odor of food cooking inside.

"Are you Robert and Ernie's father?" my father asked.

"Yeah, what's up?" asked the man who stepped outside. He was as tall as my father, had a gut, and was a lot heavier.

"Your two sons jumped my son and took his money and chain. I'm here to get it back."

The man turned into the house and yelled, "Roberto, come out here."

When Robert appeared, the man asked him, "Did you and your brother take his chain and money?"

"No, we've been home and Ernie's at baseball practice," Robert replied.

"He's lying. He has my chain on right there," I said and I pointed at the chain and cross.

The man smiled and said, "Do you have a receipt or something that proves it's yours? Because right now, it's your kid's word against Roberto's."

My father, sensing this wasn't going anywhere, said, "Yeah, I have the receipt right here," and punched the guy's teeth in. It was so fast and such a powerful hit, the guy had no chance at all. But then, not many men had a chance against my father. The guy tried to fight back but my father beat him and only stopped when the man was out cold. Robert was there without his brother and I went to work. I floored him with a single punch and kicked him when he tried to fight back, then I collected my chain and cross.

As we drove away, my father smiled at me. "Never allow anyone to take shit from you. If they do, remind them what the price is, okay?"

"I will, Dad."

The school year was coming to an end and it would be a couple of years until my path crossed Robert and Ernie's again.

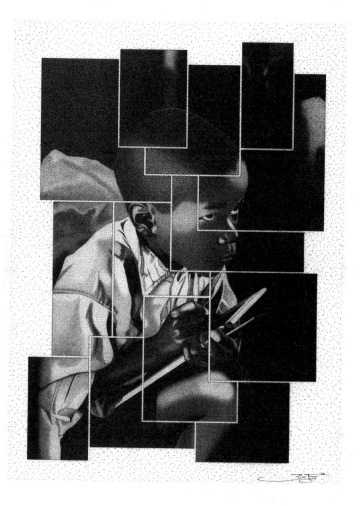

Chapter 7

San Quentin Death Row, 1988

After three months in the AC, the warden's committee scheduled me to appear before them once again on Wednesday. Would they allow me to go to East Block? I had received no write-ups or 115's, which are reports of rule violations. I kept to myself and was building a rapport with some of the AC bulls.

Some of the bulls were so impressed with the mural I did in the isolation cell they asked me to draw something for them. They seemed moved by the detail and imagery of that work. Drawing was starting to become a compulsion for me as I continued to put together compositions on paper. It seemed like something inside me needed release through my work.

I would sit on the concrete block of my bed for hours at a time and allow the world that surrounded me to melt away. In that place, there were no bars or threats. In that state of mind, I created images that were parallel to my mind's wanderings during dreams.

The storm within became quiet and a door opened inside me. There, at the open door, was the Radiant Child. The part of me I hid from harm for so many years surfaced to give me what I needed most—an escape.

At first it was difficult to find the door where that part of me lived. I eventually realized music provided the emotional trigger I needed to access that part of myself. Going to that inner place gave me inspiration and consolation. At times, it even brought me to a state of ecstasy.

I bought a small stereo and headphones through a prison vender and listened to music while I drew. At times, I was so far away I forgot to eat. In those moments, nothing else mattered. I was free.

The warden's committee was a joke. Once again they escorted me in, and after a few moments of lectures on my use of violence and their concerns about how I justified my actions, I was again denied grade-A status and told to return in ninety days. I thanked them for their time and efforts in the process and assured them I understood their concerns and would do everything asked of me to earn their trust. I was learning their game.

I knew I could alter their perception of me by how I carried myself, and how I acted every day. It was simple in theory but more complex in practice. On one hand, I needed to convince the bulls and the administration I was a well-adjusted prisoner who understood their authority and respected them, while earning their respect for me. On the other hand, I needed the other prisoners to know my potential for violence was extremely high. In fact, they should expect it. Finally, when by myself, I removed both masks and worked toward my salvation within the realm of expression and imagination.

After four months of going to the yard, I had my first confrontation. It didn't surprise me. Being prepared is part of my normal state of mind, which I based on an awareness of the kind of people surrounding me. Anyone who goes out to a yard without this frame of mind is a fool attempting to bury his head in the sand. Every time I leave my cell to go out to the yard I tell myself, *Today they'll try to kill me.*

You could live next door to a prison and still be light years away in terms of understanding the rules that govern prison society.

After years in prison, men's hearts blacken and many become creatures of violence. Paradoxically, while they're dangerous, they're also weak. They commit violent acts because they want acceptance. In fact, they will do anything they're told by the gangs to earn that acceptance.

I don't need acceptance from anyone. I alone define my boundaries. At the end of each day, I look in the mirror and know I've been true to myself.

Make no mistake, I am capable of extreme acts of violence, and I've had my share. For me, it's a matter of survival. I get no pleasure from violence, other than to defend myself and demand respect. The fact is, respect is necessary in prison. Without it you become someone's punk and property, or risk being killed. In here, the most respected and honored men are those who have killed other prisoners. The more potential a man has for that ultimate outcome, the more respect he receives.

When I speak of prison and its societies or culture, I mean places like Folsom, Trenton, Angola, and, of course, San Quentin. In those places, men are broken or made. You learn never to trust anyone. You learn how men deceive and plot in order to hurt you. For some, their sole objective is to murder you.

I wear the scars of many battles like badges of honor. They are a testament to the fact that I stand alone with dignity and that I demand respect. I will not allow anyone to hurt me or take anything from me. I am neither good nor bad, neither right nor wrong. Touch me in an attempt to harm me and I'll make you regret it.

It was a hot day in June 1988. Fourteen men came outside to the yard that day. After all the men were out, I began my workout as I had for the previous four months. Aside from the casual "Good morning" to Pirate, Tweak, Wicked, and Bull, I said nothing else to anyone.

As the sun rose above the southeast wall of the yard, I finished my bar work and got ready to shower when suddenly I felt it. It wasn't much, but it had touched a part of my awareness I've developed since childhood—the part of my mind that sensed tension, smelled fear, and knew the intentions of men as they prepared to act. I slowly and carefully scanned the yard. Tweak's eyes met mine. He had sensed it, too. None of his crew seemed aware, so I knew the threat was not from him. I continued to prepare for the shower, but as I did I looked at Jose, the Northern Mexican, who was a sleeper for the NF.

He had finished working out, but was shielding as hard as possible, trying to act normal, hoping no one would "see" him. I kept him at the edge of my vision and started to shower. I wasn't sure yet if I was his target, so I didn't rush or give away the fact that I knew he was shielding. The gunner was sitting, looking at the yard, though he didn't have a clear view of the entire shower area. That was where the NF soldier would make his move. I got out of the shower, dried off, and put on my boxers and shoes. I spotted him walking to the showers. He carried his roll and jacket. As he walked, he began to pump himself up, and his shields came down.

The heat from his adrenaline and fear hit me like walking out of an air-conditioned store in the hot summertime. His intentions were clear and his eyes locked on mine. Everything slowed down. I dropped my shields and allowed that place within me to come alive. Rage and hate filled my every fiber. My storm rushed forward. I saw him flinch as it reached him, but he had committed himself. In a split second, in the moment when two warriors meet on the battlefield equipped with their true nature, I knew him and his biggest fear. He feared defeat at my hands. He pulled his shank from its hiding place in his jacket and rushed forward, dropping his shower roll and striking in a short thrust aimed at my torso.

Most men carrying a piece expect little resistance from their intended victim. It's no surprise that if they get hit, their plan dissolves. As his blade kissed my flesh, my fist connected with his eye socket, and I followed through with strikes to the throat and face. He dropped the piece and I kicked him in the groin and finished him with a crushing blow to his jaw. All of this lasted maybe three to four seconds. The gunner saw nothing. I picked up his piece and flushed it.

I looked around daring anyone else to challenge me. My message was clear. Don't fuck with me.

Understand that I live in a world where one must speak the language spoken. Here, that language is violence. I would prefer to live in a world where men respected kindness and understood the deeper qualities of the soul. The road I walk is one of dignity and honor. I am not like the rest of these men, but I speak their language.

The Northern Mexican never came out to the yard again. When the bulls saw his busted up face he explained he had fallen while playing basketball. He didn't come back out because he knew what would happen. In prison if another prisoner attacks you, there is no longer a chance to be friends. There is no possibility of restoring trust. He'd have to try and kill me again. But I would not allow him to position me with smiles and disarm me with friendliness. No, one of us would have to die, and it wouldn't be me.

Later, I found out he had orders to kill me. I still don't know the reason.

Perhaps they thought I was a sleeper for La Eme, or maybe it was my arrogant manner and ability to stand alone. Many gangs take issue with someone strong enough to become a dominant Alpha alone. It sets a precedent which conflicts with their premise that everyone needs a gang to survive.

This does not mean I openly defy anyone. I stay to myself and respect other Alphas as well as gangs and their codes. However, I will not engage in any activities that conflict with my moral code. My code is part of me and doesn't change regardless of circumstance or situation.

Chapter 8

Orange County Jail, 1984

I'm far from perfect. I've made grave mistakes in my life and I readily admit to my faults. We all make mistakes, but it's what we learn from the mistakes that defines us. Not long after I arrived in A-1 cell-3, I started using drugs again. For a while I stayed away from the heavier stuff and just smoked pot, but as the guy "on the broom" each day, the amount of drugs that passed through my hands was incredible. Every day I handled heroin, coke, pot, LSD, crystal, and everything in between. I was trusted, and although I was not a gang member, everyone knew who I associated with and what I was capable of.

At first I took LSD and snorted coke, then heroin. I trusted my cellies enough to let my guard down around them, so I got high and partied.

Most of the men in the unit got high, but I didn't do it because everyone did. I did it because I wanted to, because I found pleasure in my senses going into overdrive, and because it allowed me to escape. I became more aggressive, difficult, restless, and irritable because of the drug use. It muddled my thinking and drowned out my pain, making my situation seem less real and not as serious. It was a dangerous mindset to have in a place where life and death decisions were made by men who constantly preyed on any weakness they could find.

For the next few months, I continued my job as "sweeper." I passed drugs, money, shanks, and kites, which are notes with instructions about the most sensitive matters that occur behind prison walls.

On a number of occasions, I dealt out serious beatings to those who challenged me or attempted to disrespect me. The truth is, I became as unstable as I had been on the outside. Drugs, power, and my temper controlled me. I wasn't thinking. I acted without thought.

Looking back, I'm ashamed I allowed myself to sink to that level. I was young and I didn't understand the consequences of my actions. How could I, when the men who made the rules respected me based upon my ability to take care of business?

Another encounter with Chili Red enhanced and elevated my status even more.

The unit went to dinner as it normally did. We entered the chow hall, walked in a straight line to a small port in the wall, and one by one received a tray passed to us through the port.

I was halfway to the port when I looked at the far wall of the chow hall and saw him. He sat among a score of his warriors and stared at me openly. I glared back and continued on my way to pick up my tray.

Huero touched my arm and said, "You see Chili?"

"Simón, ese, I got him," I said.

"He won't be coming alone. That puto has his guerrillas with him. I know some of them," he said.

At that moment Richard, who was about six feet tall and 210 pounds of muscle, cut in line along with Monster and said, "Watcha, get your tray and sit down and let's see what this bitch wants to do."

Chili could summon more than thirty Africans to his side. It was the first time I had seen him since our dance in the shower. He was in F-unit on the fourth floor and I was in A-unit on the third floor. Normally, we would never cross paths. They ate in one chow hall on the fourth floor, and we ate in the one on the third floor.

Later, I learned repairs to their chow hall was the reason our paths crossed and they had advance notice of the possibility, which gave them time to prepare.

I picked up my tray, walked over to a table, and sat down along with Monster, Richard, and Huero. No one ate. We waited. The tables surrounding us were full of seasoned gladiators including Roy-Boy from San Diego, Shark, Midnight, and Jack from Whittier, Sporty, and Chente. There were at least forty Southern Mexican soldiers and Mexican Mafia associates with us. But none of that mattered to me. My eyes focused on Chili. There was no pretense here, no shield to drop at the last possible moment. I freely allowed my intent, my desires, and my hatred to show. This piece of shit was a rapist and I would gladly finish what I started. There was unfinished business between us, and as far as I was concerned, it was just him and me.

"Watcha, Monster, let me handle this. This punk motherfucker is scared. I'll walk through him," I said.

"He ain't coming alone, ese," Monster responded.

I continued to watch him as word spread among us that the shit might hit the fan, but everyone was to wait to see how things went.

Chili got up with six Guerrillas following close behind. They all left their trays on the table. The cops told him and his crew to sit down, but they ignored the cops.

I stood up and tipped my tray over to empty the food. The trays were made of metal, and even if he had a shank he no longer had an advantage. Huero, Monster, Shark, Chente, Richard, and Roy-Boy stood with me and advanced on Chili. I knew from the sound that some of them followed suit and carried their trays.

As we approached them, he and some of his crew pulled out shanks. Until that moment, I hadn't fully understood their intentions. They didn't want to simply fight and beat me up. Their intent all along was to kill me.

They kept coming, and at the last possible second I flipped my tray sideways and threw it like a boomerang, hitting Chili across the face. The edge of the tray opened up a gash on his cheekbone and staggered him. In his wildest nightmare, he never expected that. He made a mistake of epic proportions in underestimating me. He believed, since he had a piece and position, he had the advantage, and normally he would. However, battle is a moving, breathing element that changes. Unorthodox fighters will always surprise those who can't adapt to change.

As he began to recover, I kicked him, and my right foot connected with his stomach, which knocked the wind out of him. He looked at me, and just as he reached out to steady himself on a table, I grabbed the hand that held the shank and twisted it to the side and toward me, breaking the wrist. He screamed, the shank fell to the ground, and I pounded him. The entire chow hall erupted into a fighting frenzy. All around me, men fought, and the cops ran out of the chow hall in fear for their lives.

After leaving Chili broken and bloodied on the floor, I turned and engaged another African, but, realizing their advantage was gone, he turned and ran. Huero pounded another into the ground, and as I looked around, most of the fighting had stopped, except Monster, who was in a frenzy.

One African lay at his feet and he had another one by the throat and was stabbing him repeatedly. He had taken the piece from one of them and was making them pay for their mistake of following a flawed leader into battle. The viciousness of his movements was incredible to watch. He reminded me of a dancer, and my admiration for him grew. He was a gladiator, a warrior, a man who backed up his words with action.

When it was all over, which took less than a minute, more than thirteen of their ranks were taken to the hospital with serious wounds. Only three of us had fallen, and of those, only one was serious. Chango, from Los Angeles, soon recovered from the many stab wounds he received during the fight.

The bulls took a number of us to the hole, but somehow Huero, Monster, Richard, and I escaped that fate. We returned to the unit and then to our cell. We were quiet until Monster and Huero smiled and nodded at me.

"Carnal, that's what I'm talking about. The way you took care of your business is the way it's supposed to be done," Monster told me.

"Órale, what's up with the boomerang? That fuckin' tray hit that fuckin' nigger and opened him up. That puto never expected that," Huero said, and laughed.

They continued to talk about what had happened and I mostly listened. When everyone was getting ready for bed, I went to Monster, who was sitting in the dayroom drinking a cup of coffee, and sat down.

"You did good, ese," Monster said to me.

I nodded. "Where did you learn to fight like that?" I asked Monster.

"You noticed, huh? Yeah, you're not the only one who's trained in the arts. I never competed like you, but I took lessons for about two years, and what I learned I practiced every day until I mastered it. I had to quit the lessons because we couldn't afford it, but I had plenty of crash dummies to practice on," Monster responded.

"Yeah, but what I saw in that chow hall was poetry and destruction rolled into one," I said.

He studied me for a moment.

Only you noticed that. In all my years of war, only you have seen it for more than just me being a good fighter," Monster responded.

"I recognize in you something that lives inside of me as well—rage."

Monster again looked at me for a long moment. "I can't help it. I hate niggers. When I was coming up in the system, one of them fuckin' Africans always tried to take what was mine. So my hatred has grown and I love it. I love the fear in their eyes when they see this Mexican coming to get them. I want to be their boogey man."

He was solid. He knew who he was and, more importantly, he accepted himself.

"Gracias for having my back," I said.

"I would follow you into any battle, ese," Monster replied and shook my hand. He looked at me with those eyes, his gaze met mine, and he said, "I knew I was right about you. Ever wonder who would win between us?"

I stared at him and then we both started laughing.

He was right. I asked myself that same question after seeing him destroy those two men.

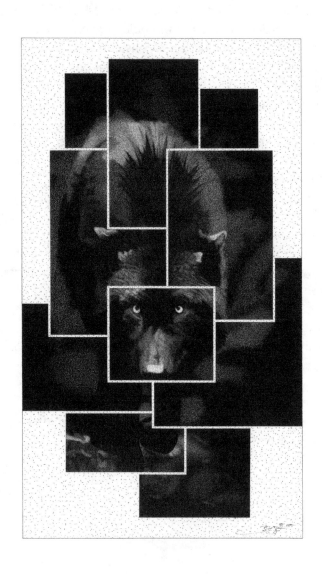

Chapter 9

Childhood, 1975–1976

The summer before my seventh grade year, my mother convinced my father that both my sister and I would not be attending Sparks Junior High School. Instead, she would find a better school, one that didn't have gangs, so I could concentrate on studying. That seemed like a good idea on the surface, but as usual my mother ignored the obvious. The gangs and bullies were not my biggest problem. I had a huge disadvantage because I couldn't concentrate. My mind seemed to be in constant motion. I had ADHD, made worse by my emotional state and by my home life.

My parents continued to fight. My father drank and continued abusing my mother, and in turn she abused both me and my sister emotionally. She also began to dominate and control us physically. When she became upset or frustrated, she yelled, threw things, and worked herself into a frenzy, hitting us with whatever she could pick up. She sometimes broke down and cried uncontrollably, then just as quickly seemed fine again. All of it confused both my sister and me. We couldn't make sense of our mother's behavior.

By the end of summer, my mother announced she had found the school we would attend. It was a private school in West Covina, California, named Immanuel First Lutheran. No gang members went there, so my mother expected I would become a straight-A student. Most importantly, her children would attend private school, which was a huge boost to her ego.

My home life became a living hell. My anxiety, isolation, and resentment grew each day. Neighbors and family friends began to notice.

The private school was my mother's desperate attempt to keep up the appearance that everything was fine and that we had money. To my mother, the appearance of success would keep the outside world from becoming aware of what really happened inside our home. My father also ignored the obvious and agreed to pay for our school. Somehow, both my sister and I were excited about getting away from those who knew us and starting with a clean slate. We thought none of our baggage would follow us since the school was far from our home.

I anticipated how great it would be at the new school. There would be friends who would like me, who would include me in their games, and call my house. I even imagined I would be popular.

That summer, I got away from the house as much as possible. I didn't want to deal with all the problems there. Early each morning, by 4:45 a.m., I woke, fed, and watered my animals, then my father gave me a ride to the bus stop. From there I'd catch two buses to Huntington Beach. I'd surf until around 9:45 a.m., then catch the bus back and arrive home around 12:30 p.m. I'd eat, and then pull out my skateboard or BMX bike, and I was gone again. I'd return at 4:00 p.m., in time to get ready to leave for my martial arts training. My sister and I both rode our bikes to the sessions at the studio, where I'd train until 7:00 p.m.

When I arrived home, I'd eat and go to bed. This was my schedule the entire summer. I was never home during the week except to sleep. It angered my mother because all the time spent in the sun darkened my skin more than usual. She believed darker skin equaled lower social status. To change this, she put lemon juice on my skin and peroxide in my shampoo to lighten my skin and hair. Pictures from that time show our hair was a shade of red/brown. Of course, my mother told anyone who would listen that our hair was naturally that color because of our German and Spanish bloodline. In her world, it made us superior. My mother was fixated on ensuring everyone believed her version of reality.

Friday nights were either heaven or hell for me. The good times were when my father had something planned for us, and we'd be off. As long as my parents were apart, my father was fine. My mother, on the other hand, got worse as time went by, whether my father was around or not.

I showed an interest in working with my hands at age twelve. My father was an artist—a sculptor—and I'd watched him work with stone, titanium, glass, wood, and marble. Even when he worked through the entire night, I didn't want to leave his side, and sometimes I'd fall asleep there at his feet.

The passion my father demonstrated through his work allowed me to see a side of him no one else knew. He loved his work—not just the finished piece, but also the process of exercising his skill and vision.

I absorbed everything he did with his art, how he touched the materials, and his familiarity with the shape as he created it. A few times he even took me to his job and showed me how to run a mill and lathe. We'd spend hours talking about shapes, and how numbers correlated with different geometric forms. The forms spoke to me in a language of their own. I didn't know it at the time, but I was seeing the world differently than most people, just as my father had. By placing shapes in a certain order, I could set a series of numbers to work toward a solution.

The first day of seventh grade started out great. I was excited to be going to a new school. Every year since I could remember, I feared going to school. Would someone try to take something I had? Would last year's bullies still be there? Would I have to fight to make it through the day?

All those concerns were absent as my mother drove my sister and me to our new school. As soon as we arrived, I noticed there were no gang members anywhere.

All of the kids were white. Relieved, I got out of the car, kissed my mother goodbye, and my sister and I ran to the playground. As soon as we got there, the bell rang and a teacher named Mr. Shultz instructed us where to go. Since my sister was in the sixth grade and I was in seventh, we were in different classes and homerooms. My first class was history. I followed the other kids who I heard talking about being in the seventh grade. I hadn't spoken to anyone yet. I waited to see where everyone sat, and then I picked a desk with a couple of empty ones close to it. I didn't want to make waves. I just wanted to fit in.

I sat down and looked around. The classroom appeared like any other. The second bell rang, a signal that all students must be in class, and the room began to fill up. All the desks filled and kids began to talk about their summers.

Listening to how they spent the summer, I realized many of the kids knew each other and had spent part of the summer hanging around together. I listened and smiled as the boy who sat in the desk right behind mine told the other boys sitting nearby about his summer at the Colorado River, and all the hot older girls he kissed. He bragged about the girls letting him feel them up and described how a four-teen-year-old girl had pulled out his dick and said she couldn't believe how big it was. When he noticed me listening, he stopped talking to look at me.

He said, "Turn around, wetback. I wasn't talking to you. If I want my grass cut, I'll call your dad."

The words stung. Everyone heard what he said. How could I respond? The boys in his group all laughed and repeated the word—wetback.

I turned around and faced the front, embarrassed and hurt. I wanted to cry, but I didn't. Everything I imagined a new school would offer, and the possibility of fitting in, dissolved in that moment. Nothing had changed. I was still different, still singled out, and still picked on. I didn't hear a single thing the teacher said during the class.

I was brought back to reality when, just as the class ended, the boy who had called me wetback flicked my ear with his finger. It stung and I jolted to my feet and faced him.

Everyone looked at me, including the teacher, and the boy yelled, "Mr. Shultz, the Mexican gang member wants to beat me up. Please tell him to stop."

I'd reacted to the idiot, which made me the bad guy.

"Sit down, William. Here now, you kids cut the foolishness. It's the first day of a long school year. I expect you to behave or you'll soon meet my paddle," Mr. Shultz said.

I sat down, but I was shaking with hurt and anger. The bell rang and everyone rushed out of the class.

"Donald, William, please come to my desk," said Mr. Shultz.

When we did, he asked, "What's the problem?"

I didn't say anything. I learned early to keep my mouth shut and deal with it later.

"Mr. Shultz, I was just sitting there listening to you when I turned the page of my book and he jumped up ready to fight. I don't know what his problem is. Maybe he doesn't like us," Donald responded.

"Well William, do you have anything to say?"

I said nothing.

"Donald, I suppose both William and I are crazy, because I'm sure the reason his ear is red has nothing to do with you hitting it, does it? It's the first day of school and you will keep your hands to yourself or I'll be introducing you to my best friend," Mr. Shultz told him.

He pulled out a two-foot-long paddle. The handle was round with tape around it and the business end had holes drilled in it to reduce wind resistance.

"How do you like it? I just made it and I'm dying to use it on someone's behind. Are you interested in breaking it in, Mr. Hamilton?"

"No, Mr. Shultz. I understand," said Donald.

I still hadn't said a word.

"Get to your next class before you're late," ordered Mr. Shultz.

I followed Donald to the next class, and unfortunately I had to sit next to him.

The whole time I re-played what happened over and over in my head, not paying attention to the teacher, the class, or anyone.

The bell rang and the next class was recess. I went to the bench next to the pull-up bars. Many of the kids were in line to buy food or something to drink. I hadn't brought money, so I sat and watched. The whole time I felt left out and hurt. When my sister saw me sitting there, she ran up to me and sat down.

"Hi, Billy. This school is so cool, I love it," she said.

My eyes began to water.

"What's wrong?"

I told her what happened.

"Oh no, not again. Are you alright?"

"Yeah, I just don't know why he called me that. I hate it here," I said. My sister hugged me and then went to play and talk to her new friends. She always fit in and always had friends. She was lucky and I was grateful she didn't have to deal with what I had to. Better me than her. She was my little sister, and with all the problems we had at home she deserved to have a little happiness.

I noticed Donald and his friends standing in line to buy something. He laughed and played around, and enjoyed all the benefits of being accepted for who he was. I noticed there were no Hispanics anywhere except my sister and me, and she was a lot lighter-skinned than I was.

Then I saw a tall black kid walking up to the food line. He was taller and more muscular than everyone else. Donald and his friends immediately started talking to him and I could tell, although they all seemed friendly, they feared him. They were friends only because it was in Donald's best interest.

I took note of that, and I've never forgotten it. It doesn't matter if you're black, white, brown, yellow, or red, beautiful or ugly, if you're feared you will be respected, and being respected ultimately leads to acceptance.

The Hapkido studio was the only place I found acceptance and safety. Master Yim believed in me and my skill as a fighter and made me the youngest member of the Hapkido Fighting Team. However, other parts of my life were affecting my study and practice of the martial arts, and it hadn't gone unnoticed. Master Yim believed that through meditation and visualization one can attain all that one truly needs. He knew about the abuse I received because I showed up with black eyes and bruises. He never asked me about it, but he knew.

One day he saw me alone in the back of the studio practicing my kicks. He asked me in to his office, and after sitting there for a few moments without saying a word he finally spoke. "Boy, did you know that through meditation you can change the future?"

I didn't say anything.

"I can see the rage that lives inside of you. I can see it in your moves, in your eyes. I'd like to teach you how to control it and use it to make you better, faster, and stronger. If you fail to control it, some day it will control and destroy you."

My rage was a constant companion since early childhood. I was so comfortable with it I considered it to be almost like a friend. It was never far away and always available to fill the emptiness inside me after pushing away the hurt inflicted by others. It is the only constant I've ever known.

"I don't want my rage to go away. It gives me power to fight against the people who want to hurt me," I said.

"Meditation will not make it go away. It will allow you to control and use it better. You will learn to be its master. If you decide to learn, come here every day an hour early. I will leave a key to the studio next door for you. From now on, this will be your hallowed ground."

The following day, I went to the Korean store beside the studio to pick up the key. Despite many years of training at the studio, I had never gone inside the store. I stood just inside the door and noticed all the wonderful things they had on display. The Korean girl behind the counter had large almond-shaped eyes and long straight hair. She came out from behind the small counter and said in a heavily accented voice, "You Bill? Master Yim say you come for key."

I nodded and she placed a key in my hand.

"You want look around?"

"Thank you," I said.

I explored the store. It wasn't very big but had everything from herbal tea to clothes, including martial arts uniforms which looked much better than the one I wore.

The girl saw me looking at the uniform and said, "You like? That fighter uniform. Master Yim say you fighter."

"It's better than the one I have. I like it."

Just then she brushed past me to take the uniform off the hanger so I could look, and when her skin touched mine I looked at her more closely and noticed how young she was—not over fourteen. What really got my attention was how beautiful she was. She smiled at me and her teeth were perfect. Her scent was unique and attractive. I was intoxicated in her presence.

"My name Michiko. I see you every day when come for key."

"I'm William. I'll see you tomorrow."

I didn't want to leave. Michiko was beautiful and I wanted to continue talking to her. She also seemed nice and didn't make fun of my appearance or laugh at me.

The studio was different early in the day. There was no smell of sweat, no yelling, and no training.

Leaving the lights off, I began to stretch and then went through my fighting forms. While doing them, I closed off the world. The only thing that existed was war. I battled my enemies, and sometimes the enemy wore my face. It's still this way for me, all these years later.

During one of those forms I noticed Master Yim standing a few feet from me. I stopped. I hadn't heard him come in.

"Boy, come. Sit."

I sat down in a meditation position for martial artists. Knees bent under me, I sat on my heels. Master Yim began.

"I know you can fight, boy. That is not the reason I asked you to come early. I'm going to teach you how to control your beasts so you stop fighting yourself. You have two parts inside of you. To become one, you must master yourself, then your beasts."

"I don't understand," I said.

"You are angry. It fills you. I see it in your eyes. I want you to close your eyes and relax. Breathe, boy. In through your nose, out through your mouth. When you are calm, go to a place only you know. In this place, you are safe and master. When you find your place, picture your surroundings and know them. When you know every inch of it, you will become one with your place. Then and only then will you be able to bring your beasts there and control them."

For the next few months, I went to the studio early each day and meditated. A part of me felt Master Yim watching me, so I did what he said. What I really looked forward to was seeing Michiko.

Somewhere along the way, something began to happen. During the meditation sessions I found myself in a small cave that I knew. During a deer hunting trip with my father, I had found the cave behind a waterfall. A reflection caught my eye as I walked by, and when I investigated I found that, just behind the falling water, I could squeeze between the face of the rock and the water. Suddenly the rock opened up to a cave.

It was approximately eight feet high, twenty feet wide, and forty feet deep.

I meditated, and found myself kneeling in the cave. I heard water falling and felt the coolness in the air. Opening my mind's eye, I stood and searched my cave, touching everything and getting to know my surroundings. A presence brought my eyes to the mouth of the cave where the water fell, but nothing appeared.

For many months after that, the same always happened. A presence, nothing more. Then one day I arrived at the studio one summer afternoon after being jumped by three black members of the Greenberry Street Crip Gang. They had knocked me off my bike and hit me over and over again with a water hose and sticks. I fought back but they were much bigger than me. There was nothing I could do except take another beating.

When they finally stopped, I walked my broken bike to the studio. With each step I took, rage and hatred filled me. Michiko saw how beat up I was but said nothing. She didn't want to embarrass me more, but I saw the look on her face and I hated that she pitied me.

I entered the studio, prepared to meditate, and knelt. My mind opened up. I was in my cave. The presence again arrived, and at the mouth of the cave a large black wolf leapt through the water and landed in front of me, shaking the water from his pelt. He looked at me and bowed his head. Reaching out, I ran my fingers through his fur and immediately knew he was my rage. Again, a presence caught my attention, and as we both looked to the mouth of the cave another large black wolf leapt through the water, landing before us. Identical to the first, he bowed and I knew him also. He was my pain. Rage and Pain were with me, and for the first time I began to understand I could only rely on myself to even the playing field.

Chapter 10

San Quentin Death Row, 1988

My sixth month of confinement in the AC was difficult. Reflecting on the choices I made that brought me to this point only magnified my sense of loss. Time dragged by as I anticipated the upcoming warden's committee scheduled for the end of the month. Would they deny me yet again? I dreaded the possibility of spending another three months in the AC before another committee review.

I spent almost every waking moment creating compositions on paper, and as my desperation grew so did my intensity and feverish pace. I became a madman with a driven sincerity. Sheets of paper with compositions and drawings in all stages of completion covered my cell walls. Even more drawings were under my mattress. My work began to reflect a distinct undertone—darkness. My photo-realistic nightmares and dreams lay before me as if my mind's wanderings and demons were taking on a life of their own.

My subconscious spilled over into my waking hours, and when I wasn't drawing and recreating my mind's pictures, I entered into a visual dialogue with the paintings of the artists I read about.

My dreams are a series of stark black-and-white images, like an old silent movie. Each image is like a picture cut out and placed in my view, followed by another, and then another. I've never heard of anyone else who sees dreams like this, but I always have, and always in black and white.

Even though condemned prisoners are not allowed inside the San Quentin Library, I have requested and read every book there regarding art. My art education is extensive, largely from studying those books, alongside my endless passion for expression. My art education is extensive, largely from studying those books, alongside my endless passion for expression.

A bull keyed the AC speaker and announced, "10-12 in the unit." This is the code for a high-ranking official, and announcing it alerts all the bulls in the unit to be awake and put any contraband items in their lockers so they are not caught. I was so engrossed in my study I didn't notice the warden and one of his captains had entered the tier where I lived.

I had my headphones on when they came by my cell. Engrossed in Robert Motherwell's writings, I only noticed the group after a flashlight beam crossed my eyes to get my attention. I took off my headphones and stood up. Warden Vasquez, along with the captain, Heckle, and Jeckle, were standing outside my door looking at me.

"Morning, gentlemen, how can I help you?"

"I had the opportunity to take a look at your work on the wall of my quiet cell. I am very impressed by your talent. I've never seen anything like it. The detail and overall feel of the mural is enormously powerful."

I didn't say anything, and the warden continued.

"I see you're condemned, so you'll soon meet my committee for review. When you are given your grade-A status, I expect you will continue what you are doing. Do you do portraits?"

"I can draw anything I can see in here." I pointed at my head.

He looked closely at all the drawings and compositions on my walls.

"Impressive. As a grade-A prisoner you will have the chance to participate in the handicraft program and you can get art materials. I'm sure you will sell most, if not all, of your work, since you're the best I've seen."

"I look forward to that. However, your committee has turned me down twice, and I fear the same will happen again," I said.

"I believe things will be different this time. My staff tells me you are no trouble and always address them with respect."

"I try to treat everyone with respect, like I want to be treated."

"Words to live by. I'll let you get back to your work. I look forward to seeing you soon, Mr. Noguera."

"Good day, Warden Vasquez."

"Ah, good day, Mr. Noguera."

They all turned and left. I stood there for a moment replaying the conversation in my mind. Had he just told me I'd get my grade-A status? My concentration was broken when my neighbor, Blue, called me to the bars.

"I heard what them bottle stoppers said. Looks like you'll be getting that grade-A real soon, old son."

"I don't know, bro, I'd hate to get my hopes up only to get them smashed."

"Nah, I know Vasquez. That old bull is pretty straight up, and he likes your work. I've checked out that mural you did in that cell back there, and so have a lot of these bottle stoppers, and every one of them leaves saying you're the best they've ever seen, and I agree. That thing you do with an image is far beyond skill and talent. It's magic."

"Yeah, now you're blowing smoke up my ass. What, you need a drawing for that fine twist and twirl you're writing?"

He burst out laughing.

"Yeah, I'd love another drawing, but the truth is what it is."

"Man, I'd really like to get over there to East Block and call my family."

"Them cats over there get on the moan and groan, yard, and leaning tower every day. Plus, you'll be able to get in that art program."

"The warden mentioned I'd be able to sell my work. How does that work?"

"They got a gift shop just outside the main gate where you can put your art, and bulls and the general public can buy it. There's also a specialized contract the warden's office puts out, so if a bull wants something special you and him can enter into a contract. You do the work and he pays. I have a feeling you'll have a line in front of your cell waiting to buy your work."

"Yeah, that would be something. I'd like to be able to support myself and send a bit home to my family."

"Man, I'm going to miss having you as a neighbor when you're gone."

"I'm not gone yet. For all you know, I'll be here another year."

"I doubt that, old son. I'll get at you later."

"All right, take it easy," I said.

Those few but powerful words from the warden brought a light to the darkness. I imagined what I'd encounter in East Block and what I could accomplish there. I didn't completely understand what lay ahead, but I started to form an idea that could utilize my mind's potential and the potency of my work. It could possibly restore the inner freedom lost during a lifetime of pain and mistreatment.

As my date with the warden's committee approached, I tried to occupy my mind with work, exercise, music, and yard every chance I got. The committee was constantly on my mind. I was nervous, excited, and anxious to get an answer.

I paced back and forth the night before my hearing. I tried to sleep, but it was impossible. Sleep would not visit me that night. Instead, thoughts raced until an old enemy awakened.

I've been haunted by migraines since I was a small child. At times, they were so bad I'd throw up and have to close my eyes. Any light caused immediate pain so intense that nausea overwhelmed me.

I remember holding my head with my hands, and rocking back and forth when one of the headaches assaulted me, the whole time wishing I could break open my head to relieve the pressure and pain that throbbed like a heartbeat.

The headaches continued into my adult life. Anxiety was normally the precursor that set them in motion, subsiding only after hours or days of torture. I tried to relax as the headache came on. I washed my face in cold water and laid down on the concrete floor of my cell to meditate, using thoughts of the ocean and the joy it brought me.

The memory helped me relax and sleep came. There were no dreams, just sleep.

I woke suddenly. The headache had receded like an ocean tide. My cell was completely dark, but I could see the sky from where I lay on the floor. From that angle, I could see out the tier windows about fifteen feet from my cell. The sky took on a purplish glow. It was Wednesday morning. I had only slept about forty-five minutes, but I was ready.

After a bird bath I wrote out the points I wanted to make to the committee. As I waited to be called I wondered if my notes would do any good. Was I fooling myself? Had the committee already made up their minds? Was it all just a formality?

John Wooden's famous words came to mind: *Failing to prepare is preparing to fail.*

At 9:45 a.m., Heckle and Jeckle came to my cell.

"You ready for committee, Noguera?"

"Been ready."

"You know the drill."

After the standard strip procedure they escorted me to the hearing, where the warden sat with the same captain who had come by my cell earlier in the month.

The change in mood was obvious from the moment I entered the room. Both the warden and the captain nodded to me in recognition.

"Mr. Noguera, please sit down."

I sat and the warden began.

"Good morning. As you know, we are here to review your possible entry into the condemned grade-A program. Since your arrival at San Quentin you have been housed here in the AC for observation because of your possible attempted escape from the Orange County jail, as well as your violence on a number of occasions while you awaited trial. My staff and I have interviewed a number of prisoners and the officers who work your tier."

As soon as he mentioned other prisoners, I feared someone told him about the incident on the yard with the Northern Mexican sleeper. That would be a reason to deny me grade-A once again.

The warden continued. "Everyone we interviewed told us you are not a gang member and have no ties or affiliation to any gang. Further, you have received no write-ups in the seven months you have been with us. In essence, you have done everything asked of you. Before I conclude this hearing, I'd like for you to consider the following. I have seen many men come to my prison with artistic talent. Granted, not many with the talent you possess, but I've checked up on them years later, and they used their talent to tattoo other prisoners or to create just enough art to support their drug habit. The question is, will you be different? When I check up on you, what will I discover? Will I find what I always find, or will you be that one I'll never forget? Any thoughts, Mr. Noguera?"

"I've thought carefully about this moment and what I'd say to you, and I realize many men have come before you with words full of promise only to fail. I won't make promises to you. My actions will speak for themselves. I'll leave it at that and I'll thank you for your consideration."

"Nicely put, Mr. Noguera. Associate Warden, anything else?"

The associate warden turned to me. "I've been working at San Quentin since I left the Marines when I was twenty-three years old. That was over thirty years ago. When the warden said I should come to the AC to look at something a prisoner had drawn, and that I should bring my son who is also an officer here at the prison and who recently graduated from art school, I didn't know what to think. I'll tell you something, both my son and I were deeply moved with what we saw in the quiet cell. We also went to your cell while you were outside and examined your drawings and compositions. What you possess is a gift. What you do with it is entirely up to you, but mark my words, in thirty years in CDC I've never seen anyone like you."

The warden then spoke. "It is the decision of this committee that you, William A. Noguera, CDC D77200, will receive grade-A status and will immediately transfer to East Block. You are assigned to Yard-1. I hope you appreciate this chance and take full advantage of it. If you come before this committee again, I promise you I will make it a point to keep you in the AC until I retire. Don't forget that."

"I won't, Warden. Thank you for this opportunity."

Finally. I'd get my chance in East Block. They took me back to my cell and Blue was waiting at the bars. He waited for the cuffs to come off and the two bulls to leave. Then he called.

"Bill, what happened?"

"Vasquez gave me a shot. I got my grade-A status. They said I'm going to East Block immediately."

"Man, old son, that's all right. Listen, they're not going to come for you for a couple of hours, so pack up your stuff and then holler at me. I have a few things I want to run down to you before you leave."

"Right on. Give me a few and I'll be with you."

I turned and looked at the cell I'd lived in for the last six months. There wasn't much to it. Most of the things were state-issued, except my shoes, small radio, headphones, drawings, and hygiene items. I quickly gathered my personal things and placed them all inside a pillowcase. I felt like I'd just won the lottery.

As I think of that day now, I realize just how sad and pathetic it all was. Nothing had really changed. I was still on death row, surrounded by killers, rapists, and child molesters. They're the worst men in our society, all corralled together waiting for their execution date. Still, I found a silver lining in all of it. I would not waste the opportunity.

I placed my pillowcase with my property next to the cell door, rolled up the mattress on the bunk, and placed a few items on top of it for the next prisoner who would occupy the cell: soap, towel, bowl, cup, quarter tube of tooth paste, and three pencils. It wasn't much, but that's what I started with. I'd give the next man the same chance I had. When I finished packing, I stepped to the bars and said, "Blue, what's up? I'm done packing. I didn't have much. Do you need anything?"

"I appreciate it, brother, but I'm fine. I do want to give you a heads up about East Block and what you'll find there."

"I'm all ears."

"Don't be fooled about grade-A and what it's supposed to mean. The men there are just as dangerous as the ones here, maybe more so, because they're smarter and haven't got caught. Keep your eyes open and don't fall asleep. When you get there, a lot of people will know who you are because word travels fast and people talk. What happened on the yard with Jose is no secret. Some will like it, others won't."

He continued, "In East Block, every yard has over a hundred men and each one is integrated. You'll have Crips, Bloods, Southern Mexicans, et cetera, mixed together, so stay on your toes. You feel what I'm saying? Trust no one but yourself."

"Hey, right on. I understand and I appreciate you taking the time to tell me these things. Believe me when I tell you I've enjoyed having you as a neighbor and getting to know you. Is there anything I can do for you once I'm in East Block? Maybe make a call for you?"

"I'm good. I'm used to writing, so I really wouldn't know what to do or say on a phone. Can't remember the last time I used one. Hell, come to think of it, I've been in the hole so long I think I'd be uncomfortable using a phone. Can you believe that? Damn, this place has truly fucked up my mind."

At that moment, I heard keys and footsteps coming.

"Noguera, you ready? East Block is here to get you," said Heckle.

"Blue, that's my ticket. My best to you. I hope our paths cross again under better circumstances. Until then, I have a little something for you," I said.

"All right, Bill."

I gathered my things as Heckle and Jeckle stepped in front of my cell. "Just get your things. We don't need to strip you. You're grade-A and no longer our responsibility," said Jeckle.

"May I give Blue this small drawing?" I handed the drawing to Jeckle, who looked at it and then handed it to Heckle. He opened the tray slot and cuffed me behind my back.

When the door opened I stepped out on the tier just as Heckle handed Blue the drawing in between the opening in the cell door and screen.

"Old son, this here is a fine gift. Thank you. Best of luck to you and keep your head on your shoulders. It's been a pleasure knowing you," he said.

"Same here, Blue. You take care."

With that, I turned and walked off down the tier where an East Block bull waited for me.

Heckle and Jeckle followed behind but were not their usual selves. They didn't shout "Clear" or "Escort." Getting grade-A status somehow made me less dangerous. It's funny how that works in prison. The word of the committee can suddenly transform an animal into a human. That's a trick even David Copperfield would envy.

The East Block bull took me out of the AC at 11:15 a.m. It was late

September 1988, and as we walked I took in everything. Mainline prisoners wandered around freely, and as we walked by they stopped to watch me. They knew I had a death sentence and came out of the AC. Some nodded. Others just glared. This was San Quentin State Penitentiary, the most notorious prison in the United States, and I was headed for the main death row housing unit. The walk took a few minutes, but I didn't mind. The buildings were old and showed serious neglect. I could smell the decay. This place was so different from the world I'd once lived in.

As we rounded the corner to East Block we passed a brass fire hydrant with a prisoner kneeling next to it in the process of shining it. It was the only thing that seemed cared for in the entire prison. The prisoner seemed in a frenzy as he polished it. The bulls laughed and said, "That's Corky, he's a nut. He doesn't shower and no one will go near him because of the smell, but he spends all day polishing that damn fire hydrant. Looks nice, huh?"

Nodding, my thoughts returned to Blue. I don't know why he came to mind. Something had changed in him over the previous couple of months, but at that moment I didn't know what it was. Blue was one of the highest-ranking members of the Aryan Brotherhood. Some even said he was one of its original founders. I never asked him about it. It didn't matter. To me, he was a good neighbor who often talked to me about his views of the world and San Quentin. At fifty-five years of age and after thirty years of a life term for murder, I saw something different begin to form inside him. He seemed tired of the dog-eat-dog world we lived in and longed for a normal life. He often spoke of washing and cleaning his soul and being reborn. As I neared East Block I wondered if he was looking at the drawing I left for him.

In it, I created the world he longed for. An island, where he was free and reborn, where the shackles of the burden he carried fell from his wrists and ankles, where childhood resilience and memory gives hope and a future.

We finally came to the huge iron doors of East Block. A sign at the top read, "Death Row." The bull hit it with his baton. A small window at the center of the door opened and another bull looked out, then the doors swung inward.

"New arrival for the row," my escort said.

"Name and number, convict," said the doorman.

"William A. Noguera, D77200."

The doorman wrote it in the unit log book and the other bull escorted me to the front desk.

"We have Noguera from the AC, where do you want him? He got his grade-A."

"Place him in the holding cage while I figure out what cell is open and get him his bed roll and state-issue," said the desk officer.

Once in the holding cage on the first floor, I studied my surroundings. The place was filthy. I gagged from the strong urine smell. Looking down on the floor, I saw water ran freely from an unknown source, and roaches seemed to materialize out of nowhere. I placed my pillowcase over my shoulder. I didn't want to put it on the floor. I looked up into the East Block housing unit and couldn't believe how big it was. There are six floors to it. Five are tiers with rows of fifty-four cells per tier on both the bay side and the yard side. The first tier on the bay side uses eight cells for the sergeant, lieutenant, and other officers. That leaves just forty-six cells on that tier. The sixth tier is for the property officers and storage.

It reminded me of a massive birdcage. It seemed to fit since there were hundreds of birds everywhere, even a few seagulls. The combination of the birds and the yelling prisoners made the noise truly deafening.

Water ran off the tiers like a cascade where men washed out their cells. It was a lot to comprehend. I had never seen anything like it in my life. It was a madhouse.

The desk officer announced over the loud speaker, "Third tier officer, bayside, you have a new arrival in the holding cage. Come get him."

I looked up and noticed a bull coming down the tier. He was blond with a handlebar mustache, about six feet tall, two hundred pounds, and wore sunglasses. He came down the stairs, briefly checked with the bull at the desk, then came over to me.

"You Noguera?"

"Yeah, boss."

"Is this all your property?"

"Yes, I didn't get my state-issue yet."

"We'll get it on the way up. My name's Stevenson and I'm the third tier bayside officer. You'll be living in cell-83. Let's get you settled in."

I turned around so he could cuff my hands behind my back. Stevenson opened the cage door and we went to the laundry exchange next to the front desk. He grabbed three sheets, three towels, three boxers, three shirts, two wool blankets, and two pillowcases.

"Everything came in new yesterday, so let's load you up," he said.

After getting everything I needed, we climbed the stairs to the third tier, and into cell-83.

"The cell's clean, but I put a few extra towels in here, plus soap and scrub pads in case you want to wash the cell. Shower days are Monday, Wednesday, and Saturday, but if you go out to yard, you can shower out there every day. What yard were you assigned?"

"Yard-1," I said.

"You'll be allowed out every day to that yard. It's a normal yard, unlike Yard-4, which is P/C (Protective Custody). They don't go out on Wednesdays."

"Boss, what are the rules on using the phone? I'd like to make a call to my family. I haven't spoken to them in over six months."

"The tier phone man schedules all phone calls. Phones run from seven a.m. until ten p.m. The phone man is your neighbor. When he comes in from yard, ask him to schedule you."

"Thank you," I said.

Stevenson left and I looked at my cell. The first thing I noticed was how small it was. Approximately four by nine feet. I could stand in the center of it and place my hands on opposite walls. I could reach up and touch the ceiling. It was a box. A very small box.

Chapter 11

Orange County Jail, 1985

More than a year had passed since I first went to mod-A, cell-3 in the Orange County jail. I spent most of my time there with Monster. We worked out together, and usually the workouts led to sessions where he'd give me his perspective and opinions on racial issues, political problems, and views on the world I lived in. I took everything in and listened carefully. I was getting the best "clecha" one could ask for about prison from one of its leading professors. At the core of everything he taught me were a few simple rules: never rat out anyone, never half step—if you commit yourself, believe in it and follow through—and never break your word or back down.

Monster saw my potential and made it no secret that I was his road dog and had his backing.

His power carried the weight of the most powerful organization in the prison world, La Eme. That was important beyond words. Because of who he was, I had his political power, and by invoking his name I could essentially open doors or close them on someone.

On more than one occasion, I made it clear to Monster I was not interested in ever becoming "made." I respected him and what he stood for, but that life was not for me. Following orders from another prisoner was not my style, especially when it meant killing someone over prison politics.

He explained that in prison or on the street, being part of a brotherhood had its advantages and those advantages should not be taken lightly. Of course, this dialogue between us went on all the time. At first, he was convinced that at some future time I would see his point of view and agree with him.

That never happened. I understood all too well what he said was true. However, from everything he taught me I also saw the danger in his words. Prison gangs are all about politics. If you make the mistake of aligning yourself with a member who goes out of favor, you too will fall because of fear that you'll retaliate. It's no different from what happens in the Italian Mob. There are different "crews" in a family. If the captain of a crew falls because of in-house politics, usually all his crew members also fall.

Monster respected the fact that my position never wavered. Over time he realized my mind wouldn't change, and he trusted me. He didn't have to fear I would one day stab him in the back in a grab for power.

One can look at my stance and interpret it as having my cake and eating it too. I knew the power he had and the benefits I received by being his road dog. Our friendship was based on respect and a mutual interest. We were both machines and we both benefited from it. Around me, Monster was free to be himself. He could express his views and innermost thoughts without political backlash. In prison, peace of mind is priceless.

In unit-A, known as Blood Alley, the assaults and stabbings continued and the captain of the jail was tired of it. He set up a meeting in the chow hall after breakfast one Saturday, with two men from each of the cells in unit-A, twenty men in all. After a ten-minute wait the captain entered the chow hall with twelve of his deputies and addressed us.

"Gentlemen, I'm going to come right to the point and tell you that if one more beating or stabbing takes place in unit-A, I'm going to break up the unit and send you all to different units. Believe me, you won't like the change."

With that he turned and left. His deputies followed.

They kept us in the chow hall another hour and then we returned to the unit. Monster told the rest of our cellies what the captain had said. No one seemed concerned.

"Man, fuck that red-nosed puto. He can break up this unit and shove it up his ass. I wouldn't give a fuck," said Monster.

Most of my cellies were waiting to catch the chain to prison, so they'd be gone in the next week or so, including Monster. What happened here didn't concern them.

Exactly two days after the meeting with the captain, a prisoner named Dan Viola returned from court and later that day created a problem. He was upset because the judge in his case refused to drop the special circumstances on a case that was over ten years old. That made him a candidate for the death penalty.

He and his cellies were watching TV when he suddenly bolted up, picked up the TV from its shelf, and slammed it against the floor. Of course, the loud crash brought the cops to investigate. When they arrived at his cell, the prisoners all said the TV fell while they were cleaning it.

I don't know if the cops believed the story, but they returned to their booth and opened the door to the cell so the broken TV could be removed. It would take a few weeks to get a replacement.

I'm sure most thought it was over, but I knew better and so did my cellies. Dan was a convict and a stone cold killer. He had a reputation for having a hair-trigger temper. He would stab anyone who crossed him. At six feet two inches, and over 240 pounds of muscle from years of driving iron, he was a serious force. However, it wouldn't matter. He disrespected his cellies by breaking the TV, and brought heat to his cell. He would pay a price for that.

The next morning was unusually quiet. I sensed the tension in the air as soon as my eyes opened. It was 5 a.m. I slept from 12:00 a.m. to 5:00 a.m., just as I had my entire life. Five hours is all the sleep I require. Any more and my old enemy, the migraine, awakens and tortures me as punishment for sleeping too much.

I showered, and when I stepped out Richard and Monster were both up and having a cup of coffee.

"Buenos días," I said.

"Órale, buenos días, carnal," said Monster.

"Richard, you jumping in the shower?"

"Simón, I want to grab a quick one before the fireworks start."

He smiled at me and inhaled. "Damn, you gotta love the smell of violence in the air. Violence is the only answer."

I laughed and sat down next to Monster to put my shoes on.

"I was hoping for a peaceful day of intellectual stimulation over a cup of tea," I said.

"Yeah, you're a fuckin' humanitarian. Remind me to nominate you for a Nobel Peace Prize," Monster quipped.

He laughed and his eyes came to life as they usually did when something was about to happen.

"Who do you think will do the deed?"

"My money is on Casper," I said.

"Not mine. Prince will take care of it. He loved that TV."

Prince was a huge mountain of a man who looked like he was created in a Russian lab. At six feet four inches, close to 270 pounds and with tattoos covering his entire torso and arms, he could be the poster child for what a killer should look like. Nevertheless, looks aren't everything. I knew for a fact he was weak. If cornered, he'd fight and hurt you, but I knew he was also an informant, and that he was cutting a deal with the DA's office where he'd be let out in exchange for his testimony against his co-defendants in a murder trial. About a month before, I saw him in the attorney visiting room speaking to the DA's office investigator. On another occasion while we were in court, I caught sight of him en route to a hallway where the deputy DA waited for him. I don't believe in coincidences.

I never told anyone what I knew about Prince. If I had, they would have killed him and I didn't want responsibility for that.

Richard came out of the shower and began to get ready for breakfast, as did the rest of our cellies.

"Check it out: if Prince does it, I'll make your bed and give you my dinner for a month," I said.

"Fuck that, I won't be here for a month. Let's make it an even hundred grandes."

"Deal. Locked in. If Prince does it, you win. If Casper does, I win."

Richard jumped in and said, "But if you two vatos are wrong and someone else does it, I win."

"Put up or shut up. If you're in, then the winner takes two hundred," I said.

"Órale, I'm in, and thank you for your donation," said Richard.

A few moments later the unit cop came into the booth, racked all the doors in the unit, and announced, "Chow time. All inmates wishing to have breakfast, prepare yourself. Chow time."

For the next ten minutes, all the doors remained open while everyone prepared for breakfast. The cop left his booth as he normally did and went into his office on the other side of the unit, where he couldn't see our cells. We exited our cell and waited by the wall directly in front of all the cells. We all knew it was when Dan would be hit. The cops would have a hard time finding the perpetrator since all the doors were open.

Dan came out of his cell acting proud and defiant, as usual. That wouldn't last. Just then, Casper appeared without any shoes or socks on.

It was easy to miss him. He wasn't a face you'd remember because he looked ordinary. He was just another face in a crowd at five eleven, 170, short blond hair, clean shaven, and no tattoos. Hell, he was the guy next door. Never judge a book by its cover, though. Casper was a killer. He would spend the rest of his life in prison serving three life terms. This was his opportunity to earn his bones and get the attention of the right people by killing Dan.

Just as Dan came in line with our cell, Casper called and walked up to him. "Dan, Shady is taking your stuff and rolling it up. You better go see what the fuck he's doing."

"That motherfucker." Dan turned to walk to his cell. Knowing Dan's mind was on Shady, Casper pulled out a steel bone-crusher nearly eight inches long and stabbed him repeatedly in the chest. Dan staggered in shock but fought back. He tried to grab Casper and wrestle him to the ground. Because he was bigger and stronger, it seemed like the only rational move. But Casper was relentless. He stabbed repeatedly, covering Dan's torso in gaping wounds. With blood pouring from his wounds, Dan pushed Casper off in a desperate final move and ran to the door at the front of the unit.

"Deputy, help me, I'm bleeding," he yelled from the door. The cop, who was in his office, saw Dan covered in blood. He rushed over and opened the door.

Casper removed the handle from the piece, then gave the blade to Cowboy, who wiped it down and hid it behind the sink in the mop room.

Casper stripped off his jumpsuit, threw it in the mop room sink where the water was already running, and Cowboy poured bleach and soap on it. Next, Casper jumped in the shower and washed off Dan's blood. He was out within two minutes. Cowboy checked him for blood or any signs of the incident. Finding none, Casper put on new boxers and a new jumpsuit. It all took less than three minutes. Finally, he put on his socks and shoes. He hadn't worn shoes because he didn't have an extra pair he could throw away if they got bloody like his jumpsuit.

I looked at Richard and Monster. "When do I get paid?" They mumbled they'd get their people to put it in my account by the weekend, and I smiled.

"Thank you for your support."

We finally made it to the chow hall about two hours later. We were interviewed separately after eating. I told them what I usually did, "I was in the shower. I saw nothing."

The next day, true to his word, the captain broke up the entire unit. They sent Richard and me to unit-F31, cell-3. It was an eight-man cell like our previous one. As soon as we were settled in, word came from Monster, who was in unit-C15 cell-2. Richard would be running the unit. All of our new cellies accepted that as if God himself had spoken. They knew who Richard was and they immediately offered him a bottom bunk, which he took. I, on the other hand, grabbed a top one. I'd wait until someone left and then I'd take a lower one.

Our new cellies gladly accepted it all. Being cellies with the shot caller in the unit gave them the benefit of the respect he received.

That night I took over as the man on the broom and went to see who was in the unit. I was familiar with the prisoners who lived on the tier because at dinnertime, while we waited to go to the chow hall, a lot of the men had come by to introduce themselves. I already knew many of them from unit-A. The captain had miscalculated. By breaking up unit-A, he only temporarily inconvenienced the normal play in the game within those walls. Nothing really changed. The men who made mistakes would still be dealt with, the drugs would continue to come in, and the politics would never end. As I was about to climb the stairs to unit-32, I saw Cowboy and Casper standing in the area directly outside the unit.

"What's up, Sinbad? I see ain't nothing changed," said Cowboy.

"Nah, just taking a look at the neighbors to see what's up. You headed in here?" I asked.

"Yeah, a lot of us from A will probably end up here or in unit-C. They don't want to throw a bunch of wolves in with the sheep," said Casper.

Just then, Casper came close to the gate where I stood. "Dan didn't talk and these bottle stoppers are too stupid to figure it out. They found the gang and plank but they won't find anything. Cowboy wiped it clean." He smiled from ear to ear and said, "Man, that cocksucker didn't die, but he'll be shitting into a bag for a long time and won't be smashing anymore TVs."

The cop came out of his office with a pair of cell cards in his hand. "You'll both be in 32 cell-2."

Casper and Cowboy picked up their bedrolls and came through the door when it was keyed open. They went up the stairs and into cell-2. I followed them up the stairs.

"I'll let you get settled in. Time to see what the word is up here."

Walking down the tier, I came to the last cell, where all the prisoners were black. Unit-A had no black inmates. They wouldn't have lasted more than a night there.

One of the Africans came to the bars when he saw me. "How you doing, Sinbad? I saw you earlier but I wanted to wait until we had some privacy to talk."

"What's on your mind, Snake?"

Snake was a Crip and a convict who had spent most of his life in prison. The blacks respected him, as did Mexicans and whites. Snake was small, maybe five foot seven, wire thin, and black as night.

"Look, homes. That deal with Chili awhile back got out of hand. I just want you to know we're not a part of that and don't want no trouble with any of you eses. I speak for all of us, and you know my word is good as gold."

"I feel what you're saying. That beef was between Chili and me. He brought his people into it and I finished it as I always do. As far as I'm concerned, it's done and doesn't involve you or your people."

"Right on, homes. Chili's gone. No need to bring the past back. Besides, from what I hear, the beating you put down on him should leave little doubt who came out on top. Listen, I got a little something here for you and Richard. Send him my regards." He handed me a balloon with both heroin and coke inside. "There's a gram of heroin and two grams of coke there. I got something going we can talk about later, but for now just enjoy yourself."

"Good looking out. I'll get at Richard right now. Take it easy, and gracias. Don't worry about that other pedo. I know where you're coming from."

I walked down the stairs to my cell and called Richard. "Hey, Snake sent this carga and soda for us. He says he's not with that pedo with Chili and wants no trouble."

"Yeah, he's scared, but he ain't going to do shit. He knows the position he's in," said Richard. "Let me tell the placa I'm done sweeping and I'll come in. I just wanted to see what the word was and look around. Casper and Cowboy are in 32-2. Dan kept his mouth shut, as did everyone else. Now it's party time."

Chapter 12

Childhood, 1975–1976

I had a terrible first month at Immanuel First Lutheran. Hardly anyone talked to me and I felt isolated. My mother insisted it was a good school with no gangs, and told me I should be grateful to attend a school so many kids wished they could afford. The message was clear. I would attend this school no matter what.

I thought a fresh start in a new school would mean the past could be forgotten. What I failed to understand was that, even though we changed our environment, we still carried the emotional garbage from our past. I didn't have to fight at school but the challenges were, in some ways, even worse. I knew how to deal with gangs and those who tried to physically harm me. At the new school, the bullies were weak physically but used emotional and intellectual manipulations to achieve similar results. I had no skill in fighting those battles, and I lacked any ability to get beyond their bias and make friends.

At first, no one picked me for their team during P.E. That changed when Mr. Tonjes forced a member of Donald's inner circle, Stephen, to take me on his team. We won that game because I hit three home runs. I also excelled in basketball, football, and track.

I suddenly had value to those people when they needed to win a sporting event. That year I even won the merit award for excellence in sports. The following year I earned a presidential award signed by Jimmy Carter for my athletic achievements, as did my sister.

Only Degan Jackson, the black kid, was faster and better than me in any school sport. They recognized my value as an athlete, but they still didn't include me in their social events. The kids would come back excited after weekend parties and trips to the beach, but never invited me. They only knew me when they needed my help to win. I still didn't have friends.

I reached a breaking point in my life in terms of my willingness to accept my fate as an outsider. My resentment fueled a desire for revenge against the people who needlessly made my life more difficult as I struggled to fit in. I was developing a new coping strategy that would progress over time and result in severe consequences for me later.

I have a unique ability to remember numbers. Locker combinations became imprinted in my memory after seeing the locks opened once, and I could recall them any time. One day I noticed one of Donald's friends, Jimmy, go to his locker during a break, open the combination lock, and remove a snack. After that, I knew Jimmy's locker combination, and it gave me an idea.

As I returned from the bathroom, I stopped next to Jimmy to open my locker and get a notebook.

"What's up, Jimmy?"

He continued eating his apple pie and didn't answer.

"Did you see Kiss on TV last night? They were at Magic Mountain." He finished the pie.

"Can't you see I'm eating, spick? Damn, get away from me."

His words struck like blows. I turned and went to class. It was the turning point for me.

The next day, I asked to use the bathroom during second period and I went straight to Jimmy's locker and dialed the combination. It opened. My heart pounded as I reached for his lunch bag. I glanced around to make sure no one saw.

I took it out and briefly looked inside. It was huge. I placed it under some trash in the garbage can and went back to class, smiling to myself. I had finally scored points for my team and I enjoyed it.

During recess I watched Jimmy go to his locker as he spoke to Kenny. Kenny always pretended he was playing the drums and constantly talked about the band he was forming.

Jimmy dialed the combination at his locker, but when it opened he frowned as he looked inside, moving his books and gym clothes around.

"Fuck, where's my lunch?"

"Maybe you didn't bring one?" offered Kenny.

"Bullshit, I always bring one."

I smiled to myself. I had a lingering unease someone had seen me, but mostly I was satisfied. I just walked away. They usually ignored me anyway and this time was no different.

We all went to our homeroom at lunchtime. Jimmy sat alone, looking dejected. *How does it feel to be me?* I thought.

A week later during one of my classes, Mr. Shultz asked if we knew what products our neighboring countries exported. A kid named Oliver raised his hand and when Mr. Shultz called on him, he answered, "Well, I know that Mexico exports wetbacks because Bill, or Guillermo as he's known in Mexico, is sitting right here."

Everyone in the class laughed.

"I'm not Mexican, I'm Colombian, you idiot."

"Here now, you kids. That's enough. Bill and Oliver, you will see me after class."

As soon as the bell rang and the class emptied, Mr. Shultz closed the door, walked over to his desk, and pulled out his paddle—two feet long with holes drilled through. He called both of us over.

"Oliver, what makes you think it's okay to call people names?" No answer.

"Your comments will earn you two swats." He bent Oliver over his desk and hit him twice.

"Now Bill, just because Oliver here cracked a joke about your culture doesn't mean you can attack him with your own verbal insults."

"That wasn't a joke he cracked. He called me a wetback, just like many of these idiots have since I've been here, and you think it's funny. I've seen you laugh when they do it," I said.

"Listen here, this isn't up for debate. Three swats."

"For what?"

"For talking back and calling Oliver an idiot."

Oliver smiled and I couldn't help feeling defeated. There was no winning in this place. They were both white and I wasn't. It was as simple as that.

Mr. Shultz was mad. It was obvious as soon as he grabbed me and I resisted. Oliver had just bent over to be hit because he knew he was at fault. I believed it was just another mistreatment by someone who didn't like me.

"Stop resisting, Bill, or it will be worse."

"I didn't do anything wrong. Why am I being punished?" I asked.

With that, he shoved me into the desk with force and my mouth hit the corner of the desk, splitting my lip. Mr. Shultz roughly took hold of me and began hitting me as hard as he could manage. He hit me five times. I stood up and looked at him. I could see the anger in his face. When he saw my bleeding lip, he said, "You brought this on yourself. You made me lose my temper."

He was no different than the bullies who had beat me up my entire life. I hated him and everyone at the school. As I went to my next class my ears rang and my vision clouded red with bitterness and hurt.

Sitting in my next class, I calmed down and the anger drained away. My vision returned to normal, but then the physical pain set in. Right after class I went into the bathroom and looked in the mirror. My lips were swollen and cut, but my legs hurt the most. Quickly lowering my pants, I saw the reason for the pain. My legs were badly bruised from the middle of my upper legs to my butt. I allowed myself to imagine I was somewhere else. A place of my own.

Through the rest of the day I kept to myself and began thinking about what I could take from Oliver, as I had from Jimmy, so he'd experience a piece of what I did every day. I imagined stealing his girlfriend and taking her to the school dance. As we danced, we'd laugh at him. They were silly fantasies, but they eased the pain of my damaged ego.

I left my last class and nearly bumped into Oliver. As soon as our eyes met he taunted me.

"Now Billy, temper, temper. What have we learned today? Ah, yes, foreigners are not welcome here."

He laughed and walked away with Donald and Jimmy. Watching him go, it suddenly hit me. I knew what I'd take.

Chapter 13

San Quentin Death Row, 1988

Speaking to my family the first night in East Block seemed more like a stage performance than reality. There were the usual tears from my mother and sister as I assured them I was fine. To me they seemed worlds away, and to bring them into my world would only upset them more. I kept their minds at ease by downplaying my situation and how dangerous things truly were.

The last call was to my father. I dialed his number and the operator answered.

"How may I help you?"

"Collect call from Bill."

The phone began to ring.

"Hello."

"Collect call from Bill."

"Yes, Billy?"

"Hey dad, it's me."

"Are you okay, son?"

"Yes sir. I was finally given grade-A status this morning and I'm now in East Block."

"How are things there?"

"Well, I'm not sure. I'll probably go outside tomorrow and get a feel for this place."

"Son, I need you to be careful. Keep your eyes and ears open. I know you'll survive this. Trust no one."

"I won't, Dad. I know where I'm at and who surrounds me."

"You know if you need anything, don't hesitate to ask. I'm here for you."

"I know, but I'm okay, thanks."

We spoke for about fifteen minutes and my dad told me of his marriage to Maria, a Colombian woman twenty-three years younger than him. He also mentioned I should expect to be a big brother soon because they planned to have a child.

"You have to do things differently this time. I don't want another child going through what I had to."

"Things are different now. This is a whole new ball game."

"Raising a child is never a game."

"No, it's not. You'll see. I give you my word."

"I better get going. I have to prepare myself for tomorrow."

"Listen. I'm very sorry about everything I put you through. I never intended to hurt you or to have things turn out like this. Knowing what I know today, I would have done things differently. I'm sorry, son."

"Don't worry about it, Dad. I don't blame you."

"I love you, son."

"Me too, Dad. Goodnight."

"Goodnight."

I hung up the phone and sat on my bunk for a few moments. My father is the only one who has ever apologized to me regarding my childhood. Not that I blame him, or anyone else, for what's happened to me. But I could hear it in his voice. He blamed himself and the burden weighed heavily on him. It takes a certain type of man to own up to his mistakes and take responsibility for his actions. I admire my father despite all of his faults. He is a man who takes responsibility, and I love him for it.

My thoughts were interrupted by the tier bull.

"Are you done with the phone?"

"Yes, thank you."

The bull closed my food port and pushed the phone away to the next person on the list. The phone was on a wooden cart with wheels, which the bulls rolled from cell to cell according to the phone schedule the tier phone man made each day.

My neighbor, hearing I was off the phone, called out, "Hey, Bill, did you get through to your people?"

"Yes, thank you."

"Listen, I can put you on everyday if you'd like. Ju . . . ju . . . just, you know, look out for a guy when you ca . . . ca . . . ca . . . can," he stuttered.

"I appreciate the offer, but I'm good for now. Goodnight."

"Ah, yeah. G . . . g . . . g . . . goodnight."

I already didn't like my neighbor. As soon as he came in from the yard and noticed someone new was next door to him, he called over, introduced himself, and asked if I wanted to use the phone. His name was Silent, but I couldn't figure out how the hell he got his name since he hadn't shut up since coming in from the yard. But that wasn't the reason I immediately didn't like him. It was the fact that he attempted to sell me phone time. He hadn't done it in a direct way, but it was clear it had to be dealt with right away.

In a penitentiary like San Quentin, only those who are weak or on a P/C yard pay another prisoner for something that's state-issued. If I let it go unchecked, he and then others would take it as a sign of weakness and attempt to prey on me. Even if I didn't need to ever use the phone again, the fact that he'd played it like that meant I had to pull him up and make my position clear.

I finished cleaning my cell and put the few items I had in a box Stevenson had given me. The cell was fairly clean, but I followed my normal routine to search and then completely clean any cell I am assigned. I took a bird bath and made my bunk, then laid down with my lights turned off and thought of what I might encounter the next day on the yard. So many things crossed my mind. I recalled what the warden told me, what Blue said, and finally, as sleep came for me, I thought of how much I missed being on hallowed ground.

Upon waking that first day in East Block the smell of the ocean filled my senses, and for a moment I lay on my bunk wondering what I'd do today. Surf, then go hang out with my friends. The speaker just to the right of my cell clicked twice and brought me back to reality. I had forgotten where I was, and just for those few seconds I was free. I sighed, and got up. It was 4:45 a.m. I stripped naked, took a bird bath, brushed my teeth, and combed my hair. As I finished, the birds in the unit began to sing.

After making my bunk I placed a five-gallon bucket next to the bars of the cell door and sat down. A large window was directly across from the front of my cell. Four feet wide and twenty feet long, most of the glass was broken out, but the bars on the outside remained intact. The sky was still dark, but I could see light reflecting on the bay water. Looking across the bay, I could see the lights of Richmond, an urban war zone where drugs, gangs, and violence held residents hostage. But from inside the walls of San Quentin at that time of morning, the city looked as beautiful as Oz.

The prisoner on the floor above me flooded his cell and the area outside of my cell door became a waterfall. The sound triggered a memory and I knelt down and closed my eyes. The bars melted away and I was once again inside my cave, only it was empty and abandoned. So much time had passed. The drugs, the grief, and the pain had kept me from that place for so long, but no more. I was back. I would never again allow anything to come between me and my hallowed ground.

Reaching deep inside, I called to them and they came. Leaping through the mouth of the cave and landing before me, my Rage and Pain. How long had it been? Far too long. I touched them both and suddenly there was another presence at the mouth of the cave. No wolf leapt forward. Instead a small child came forth and knelt in front of me. Looking into his eyes, I knew him. The Radiant Child. Never before had all of my parts come together, and it made me strong, complete, and ready to fulfill my potential.

I opened my eyes and saw the sun had lit the sky. I had meditated for about fifteen minutes, and now it was time to prepare for yard.

The bull came by at 6:00 a.m. and asked if I wanted to eat breakfast. I said, "No thank you."

Upon hearing this, my neighbor, Silent, said, "Hey Bill, can I have your tray?"

"Good morning, Silent. Go ahead, I won't be eating this morning." I said it in a manner that made him wonder what was on my mind.

"Ah . . . ah . . . g . . . g . . . good m . . . m . . . morning, Bill," he stuttered. I noticed he stuttered when he was unsure of himself.

"Wh . . . what yard are you on?"

"Yard-1."

"M . . . m . . . me too. Wh . . . wh . . . where you from?"

I knew he sensed a shift in me. I also knew others would be listening.

"Orange County."

"Man. We . . . we . . . we're homeboys. I'm out of O.C. too."

"Listen, Silent, I'm preparing to go outside, so I'll get at you on the yard."

"All right, bro."

"Yard release. All inmates prepare for yard release. Officers report to your yard assignments," the desk officer said over the loudspeaker.

Taking a deep breath, I focused and reminded myself, *Today, they'll try to kill me.*

Bulls began to file down the third tier to strip and escort prisoners to yard. The tier bull came for me.

"First day out to yard, huh, Noguera?"

"Yeah, time for some sun and exercise," I said.

"Let's get you stripped and on your way. Hand me everything you're taking out and then go through the dance."

"Okay, clear. Get dressed, Noguera."

When I was ready, I turned around and backed up to the food port. Stevenson put the cuffs on my wrists. The door opened and I stepped out backwards, then turned to walk down the tier.

Stevenson took me to the first tier, where another bull used a metal detector wand to check for any metal I might have hidden in my mouth, under my arms, taped to my spine, in my ass, or under my nuts. Then another bull gave me a final pat down.

From there, I walked out the door to Yard-1 and got my first look at where I'd be spending my time when outside the cell. It was very similar to the AC yards—basically just a square concrete box surrounded by a fifteen-foot-high corrugated wire fence on two sides, and concrete walls the same height on the other two sides. One of those blocked the view between our yard and the bay. The main difference between Yard-1 and the AC yard was the larger number of prisoners.

I stepped past the first gate of the sally port for Yard-1 and 2. The gate closed and I backed up to the door so the bull could remove the cuffs. Next, the main door to Yard-1 opened and I stepped through. There were already over sixty men on the yard. It seemed crowded, which meant it would be extremely hard to detect moods and intentions among so many people.

I went to an empty table and placed my things there, then just watched the entire yard for a few minutes. It wasn't that big—maybe half the size of the AC yards. The front of the yard had a shower area, sink, and toilet, all surrounded by a four-foot-high concrete wall. A row of steel tables lined the fence between yards 1 and 2. A basketball court was in the center; the iron pile, dip bars and assorted bench presses, and equipment were all in the back.

After a few moments a prisoner I recognized said, "Órale, carnal, qué pasa? How you been."

We shook hands.

"I'm okay, Mouse, it's been a few years. How're things with you?"

"Man, you know, just doing the tiempo. I never thought I'd see you here. Watcha, let me introduce you to some of the vatos here so you know how things are."

"Not just yet. Give me a minute. I got some business I have to handle before anything."

"What's up, man? Need help?"

"It's nothing, but gracias for the offer."

Silent was standing by one of the tables, talking to another Peckerwood, and I decided to take care of business right away. I glanced up to check the gunner. He was looking out over the fifteen-foot wall at the bay.

I wanted to make sure the gunner wouldn't see anything if Silent did something foolish. As I walked over to him I could sense I was being watched. I stopped to his right and he turned to look at me.

"Silent, right? I'm Bill. You got a moment?" I could tell he knew I was not happy.

"Hey homie, wha . . . wha . . . what's up? Y . . . y . . . you n . . . need the phone?"

"Nah, I just need to get at you for a moment." I looked at the cat he was talking to.

"Give us a minute," I said, leveling him with the weight I knew my eyes carried.

He walked away and I faced Silent.

"Check this out. If you charge some of these lames for phone time, that's your business. But I don't pay no one for state-issue, you feel me? If this is a problem, say so right now and we can deal with it."

"Hey, n . . . n . . . nah B . . . Bill. L . . . l . . . listen brother, it's not like that. I w . . . was, you know..."

I cut him off.

"I know what you were doing, and I'm telling you it's a dead issue with me."

"Yeah bro, I don't want no trouble. My bad. I'm s . . . s . . . sorry."

"Are we straight?" I said.

He nodded.

I turned and went back to the table where my things were. A moment later Mouse came over with a heavily muscled Mexican. "Mad, this is Sporty."

"Órale pues, mucho gusto, carnal," said Sporty.

"Mucho gusto. Just call me Bill. I don't go by any nickname."

"Órale, that's firmé. What happened with that Gavacho?"

"I just set him straight about the phone, that's all."

A number of other Southern Mexicans on the yard came over to us and began introducing themselves. Flaco, Chino, Diablo, Danny-Boy, Dino, Capone. One by one they shook my hand and went off to get ready to start exercises. Mouse and Sporty stayed behind to run down the yard rules.

"Watcha, Bill. The Blacks use the iron pile first, from seven a.m. to ten a.m. We can't go back there and lift until ten a.m. when it's our turn, and we have it until one p.m. The Woods lift at the same time we do. See that line in the cement there? That's the start of the iron pile area. We respect their time and they respect ours. The pull-up bars, dip bars, heavy bag, and speed bag are also part of the iron pile and off limits until our time. We usually do our line exercises for an hour or so, run, then play basketball or bullshit until ten a.m."

He was including me as part of "we" and he assumed I would go along.

"Órale, gracias, Sporty. I'm going to kick back today and just get a feel for the yard. I'll get at you later."

"That's firmé. I'm going to start my line routine," said Sporty. He walked off to be with the rest of La Raza.

It was obvious that Sporty was the shot-caller for the Southern Mexicans. I still wasn't sure of his rank. Was he simply a Sureño (Southern Mexican gang member) who had the authority to speak and make decisions for the Sureños? Was he an associate of La Eme? A soldier working his way up, making his bones? Or was he a full-fledged carnal, a made member of La Eme?

"Hey, Mouse, you're not going to work out?"

"Nah, not today. I'll kick back with you until we can go to the iron pile."

I had hoped to be alone and study the yard. With that many men, there would be a pecking order, and the faster I understood it the better it would be for me.

Since Mouse would be tagging along, I decided to get as much information from him as possible. I'm sure Sporty was thinking the same. He hadn't called Mouse over to work out because he was hoping Mouse would later tell him about me. What Sporty didn't know was that Mouse and I were cellies in Orange County, and Monster and Mouse were from the same neighborhood. Not that it mattered. When the time was right and I knew who all the players represented, I'd make my position crystal clear to everyone.

Mouse knew me fairly well so it didn't surprise him when I asked, "So what's the deal with Sporty? Who is he?"

"He's from Varrio Nuevo Estrada (VNE). He's a good dude, a solid Sureño. He just wants to know what you're about."

On yards like this, everyone was interested in a new player because the balance in power is usually based on strength in numbers.

"Are you wondering what I'm about?" I asked.

"Fuck no. I know exactly what you're about. If Monster couldn't recruit you and you two were perros, no one can. I know you're a free agent."

Sporty and the rest of the Southern Mexicans were already doing their line routine, and I continued toward the back of the yard with Mouse.

There were a number of different teams, or workout crews, at work on the iron pile and I considered all of them carefully. Only two crews caught my attention. A large African who I'd met in the AC on the Crip yard ran the first one. As I neared, he noticed me and put down a pair of hundred-pound dumbbells. Stan "Tookie" Williams was approximately five eleven and weighed over 270 pounds, with massive arms and a huge chest from years of lifting iron.

"How you doing, Bill? I see they finally let you out of the sandbox."

"Yeah, they figured it was either that or I'd continue to run up the cost of repainting the walls I was drawing on."

He laughed. "It's good to see you. If you need anything, look me up."

"I appreciate the offer. Thank you."

We shook hands and he went back to his workout.

"Hey, Mouse, who's that vato with the blue muscle shirt lifting in the corner?"

"That's Marcel. He's a Crip from L.A. Him and that vato Tookie don't get along. Something about their neighborhoods on the streets not being firmé."

Marcel was impressive, and to me he seemed more dangerous than the rest. He stood about five eleven and weighed around 220. He was young—maybe twenty-three years old. The way he moved caught my eye. He knew how to use the muscle that surrounded his frame. I made a mental note of it and looked over to where the Peckerwoods sat.

Mouse said, "I know what you're thinking and the answer is..."

I answered for him. "Wicked. He runs the show for the Woods. I was on the yard with him in the AC and we're cool."

We walked across the yard, and when Wicked saw me he grinned and called out, "What's up, Bill? Shit, it looks like we meet again. How's it going?"

"I'm good. Just getting a feel for the cats here and hanging out."

Mouse shook hands with him and I met his crew.

"Hey Bill, let's take a walk," said Wicked. I fell in step with him. After a short walk, he began.

"Listen, I heard what happened with Silent and he didn't mean anything by it. He's shook up because you checked him, and he's worried you might fuck his ass up."

"Man, it's over. I checked him to make sure he understood where I'm coming from. End of story. Tell him not to trip. I mean him no harm."

"It's what I figured, but I had to ask."

Prison protocol demanded that Wicked, as the shot-caller for the Whites, investigate where I stood. If there was a problem it would have to be solved either by the Whites dealing with Silent on their own and satisfying the offense, or by coming together against me. If that happened, and if I were a member of the Southern Mexicans, a war would erupt.

This is the protocol for any offense that crosses racial boundaries. But I dealt with things on my own. If a prisoner happens to be of another race and brings his people into it, that would be his choice. Bottom line, it wouldn't make a difference. He and I would eventually dance and he would lose.

We went back to where the rest of his crew stood and I excused myself.

There were four major forces on the yard—the Southern Mexicans, two Crips factions, and the Whites. Everyone else on the yard had some connection with one of those groups. There were no Northern Mexicans, Bloods, or BGF members on the yard, which made things easier. The absence of those groups meant fewer problems and fewer people to watch. Of course, the groups present were certainly dangerous. It's just that by nature Crips and Bloods don't get along, and neither do Northern and Southern Mexicans.

At 10 a.m. sharp, the Blacks cleared the iron pile area. As soon as they crossed the line, all the Mexicans, Whites, and Indians crossed over and began to set up shop. The new groups set hundreds of pounds of iron in the order to be used, and all began to lift. Crews of three and four prisoners formed a team that worked out on each of the many bench presses in the iron pile.

Turning to walk away, Sporty called. "Hey ese, give me a minute."

I waited as he grabbed his shirt.

"What's up?" I said.

"Nothing. I just wanted to kick it with you. I'll take the day off."

We began to walk up and down the side of the yard by the tables.

I started, "I know you have questions about me, so let's get to the point. I'm a no-nonsense type of cat. I'm straight up. I don't beat around the bush."

"I know you just got here, so if there's anything you need, I can help you out."

"I appreciate it. Gracias, but I'm okay. My main concern is tomorrow, and where I can lift."

"Ah, homes, these vatos can't keep up with me, so maybe you can team up with me on my bench. All the other benches are already taken."

"Yeah, that'll work, but there's something you should know about me."

"What's that?"

"I do my own thing. I'll lift with you, but you have to know, I don't make moves for anyone. I don't take orders and I'm not anyone's puppet. If someone asks me to do something, I'll lay them the fuck out right then and there. If I have a problem, I'll deal with it. If you see me fighting against three or four cats, don't get involved. Sit back and watch the show. It's only going to last a few seconds before they're laid out. As you get to know me, you'll understand. I'm an extremely serious motherfucker. I hate drama and bullshit. If you can live with that, then you get a workout partner. Otherwise, I appreciate the offer but I'll find another bench."

"Nah homes, I can live with that. I don't like bullshit either and the less drama the better. Besides, I wouldn't have asked you to lift with me if I didn't already know a little about you. I heard about what you did to Jose in the AC, and I like your style. I know you're Colombian and have no ties to anyone but yourself. I like that."

We continued to walk and he explained his weight lifting routine and his theory on muscle development and response. Sporty knew what he was doing and I liked his discipline. It was obvious he lived what he preached.

"I saw the line routine you did with everyone and I won't be doing that," I said.

"Why, you don't like Mexicans?" He laughed.

"Nah, I just have a routine I've been doing since I was five that I stick to."

"That's fair, do what you do, ese."

"What's the deal on the showers? Is there a set time I can use it?"

"You can shower whenever you like, but we normally go in there after we lift. As you can see, the shower is full of changos now, and they set up bodyguards that stand there and watch their backs while they shower. They don't want one of these big bad Mexicans to sneak up on them."

I looked and, sure enough, while the Blacks showered, four bodyguards stood watch.

I showered as everyone was going in at the end of the yard day. I waited until the end because I wanted to talk to Wicked.

When yard time was over and the bulls called my name, I walked through the first gate into the sally port. I turned around and the cuffs went on my wrists. Taking a deep breath, I thought, one day down.

Chapter 14

Orange County Jail, 1985

Richard transferred to Folsom Prison soon after we moved to unit-F. Monster and most of the other men I knew also transferred to prison. The players were different, but the game remained the same. I remained too. I was fighting a capital case and would be there for a couple more years.

My new cellies were Chente from Santa Ana, his homeboys Lucky and Crow, the darkest Mexican I had ever met, Handsome from Stanton, who looked like the Hunchback of Notre-Dame, Psycho from Fullerton, Apache from Orange, and his homeboy, Slick Rick. They were all extremely violent convicts fighting cases that carried many years in prison. All were ages twenty-four to twenty-eight, and each one had something to prove. Facing long prison terms, they wanted no doubt in anyone's mind that they were serious soldiers.

Those men were all respected gang members and they treated me as one of them. I had a reputation for taking care of business and I had Monster's backing, and his influence continued to affect behavior there. Chente and I hit it off right away and worked out together.

Every day with those men was a day with potential for death, and any sign of weakness was an invitation to be killed. I often demonstrated why I was called Mad. It was important they saw it for themselves. I wanted those men to know that any attempt to harm me would become a nightmare for the one who tried it.

My life was a mess. Although I acted like I didn't have a care in the world, I lived in a constant state of despair.

I think if a few things in my early life had turned out differently I would have been a great actor. My performance there surely deserved an Academy Award. I was playing a role, and any slip of the theater mask could bring deadly consequences.

I drew late at night while the others slept. Early each morning, before they woke, I threw away my latest creation and put the mask back on. No one knew. At least not for a while.

A new prisoner arrived in the unit named Chango, who always joked around and had a grin fixed on his face. Chango always talked about his family. He had a wife, and a little boy and girl he loved and who came to see him on visiting days. His little boy sometimes smiled at me and played peek-a-boo behind his hands when I'd see them in the visiting room.

Chango was in jail for receiving and selling stolen property. Unfortunately, his assignment to our housing unit was a mistake. Thinking no one would recognize him or remember his past, he didn't provide the classification committee information they needed for placement in a P/C-unit. That would cost him dearly. Nothing is forgotten in prison and word travels fast.

A gang member from Chango's old neighborhood recognized him and sent word to Primo, a San Quentin convict who Chango had testified against. Within days, another gang member about to start trial for murder had his attorney subpoena Primo to testify. Two weeks later, Primo was on a bus headed for Orange County. Primo's testimony was just a cover for a more sinister plan.

Ten years earlier while both Primo and Chango were teenagers, they killed a rival gang member, and Chango's testimony led to Primo's conviction and assignment to San Quentin.

A prisoner can have his attorney subpoena convicts from any of the California prisons to testify at his trial, and because the meetings to prepare for trial are legally protected from monitoring, it's a secure way for gang members to meet and conduct business. One item of business is to confirm "hit lists." Most of the time the attorney has no idea he's being used for gang business. He subpoenas the men his client says he needs to prove his innocence.

A hit list is active once confirmed, or green-lighted, by a made member of the gang. Once active, everyone on that list is marked for death and any member or associate can do the deed. Primo carried an active list and Chango's name was on it. Primo also carried the paperwork that proved Chango was a rat.

Primo expected to be housed in a different unit than Chango at the Orange County jail. Once there, he'd have to show paperwork and order someone in Chango's unit to carry out the hit. Imagine his surprise when he found out Chango was in the cell next to his.

Primo had taken to prison life like a fish to water. He trained, lifted weights, and became a Mexican Mafia soldier. Many wars later, he was a made member of the Mexican Mafia with a deadly reputation and temper.

When Primo arrived he was the only carnal in the unit, so he was immediately in charge. At lunchtime when all the doors opened, he came to our cell and shook hands with Crow, Lucky, and Chente. They introduced me.

"This is my perro, Mad," said Chente.

"Mucho gusto, Primo. Es un placer," I responded.

"Órale, carnalito, mucho gusto." Primo said.

We shook hands.

Primo was a seasoned warrior, built like Conan the Barbarian.

"Hey Crow, gracias for pulling me down from the pen."

"It was nothing. I just did what was supposed to be done. If it weren't for Lucky, I never would have recognized Chango."

"Simón, that's firmé." Turning to Lucky, he laughed and said, "Maybe I should start calling you Hawk Eye instead of Lucky."

All of it happened right under my nose, but I didn't yet know what it all meant. No one did except Crow and Lucky.

"So what's the plan, Prime Time?" asked Crow.

"I want to handle this alone and right away. If Chango sees me, he'll run and tell."

"Órale, what do you need from me?"

"A piece. A bone-crusher. I want this puto six feet under."

Crow went over to the wall phone, next to the shower and above the toilet. He got a small Allen wrench, hidden in a bar of soap, and unscrewed the bolts that held the phone in place. Then he pulled the phone off the wall. Behind it, a steel bone-crusher nine inches long, one and a half inches wide, and one-eighth inch thick, was taped to the wall.

Crow grabbed it and reattached the phone to the wall. He walked over and presented it to Primo.

"Here, use my personal work on that rat. This should fix him."

"This is what I'm talking about. This is a wicked piece."

Primo was right. The piece was indeed wicked. It was cut from a steel towel rack and sharpened to a razor's edge on both sides with two bloodlines on each side. It was made to kill. The bloodlines are grooves worked into the blade so when the body tissue contracts around the blade, the user can easily pull the blade out and continue to stab over and over again. Without the grooves, the blade is harder to pull out and slows the attack.

As soon as I saw it, I knew Chango didn't have a chance. My thoughts went straight to his little boy and how he'd be devastated when he learned his daddy was hurt. I'd seen plenty of men stabbed, but I felt bad about this one. I was so moved by the thought, I didn't hear Primo talking to me.

"Hey ese, where you at?"

I focused on him. "I was just thinking of some work I'd like to put in with a piece like that."

"Yeah, Primo. This vato knows that secret shit. Last year he took Chili Red down twice. The last time in the chow hall with a bunch of his guerrillas with him. Man, this motherfucker puts in serious ass-whippings," said Chente.

"Watcha, Mad, can you put a handle on this for me?"

"Yeah, but it's Crow's piece and no one knows a piece like its maker."

"Primo, I made it. Let me put the finishing touches on it."

"Alright, ese. Get to it. I don't have a lot of tiempo."

Crow set off to work on the handle, which wouldn't take long. Using a razorblade, he cut two pieces from a chessboard approximately one and a half inches wide and four inches long, and placed them on the blade. Then he cut strips off a sheet and wrapped the pieces of the chess board tightly. After the handle was secure, he wrapped it in thin plastic and lit it on fire, allowing the plastic and strips of sheet to become one with the pieces of chessboard.

Crow ran cold water over the handle to cool it, then dried it and gave it to Primo. I always tense and mentally prepare myself anytime someone near me has a piece in their hands. I just don't trust anyone.

"Muchas gracias, Crow. I won't forget it."

A few moments later, the unit returned from lunch and the doors were opened.

Primo shook all our hands and said, "I'm going to go kick back at the pad and wait for this puto. I'll hopefully catch his ass at dinner." And just like that, he was gone.

Chango wouldn't see it coming. At least not until it was too late.

The rest of the afternoon, I busied myself writing and washing my sheets and other whites, but nothing helped me forget what was about to happen. I secretly hoped Chango had learned of Primo's arrival and was moved to a P/C-unit. At 4:10 p.m., Chango and a couple of other men walked by en route to their cells after returning from court.

"That rat gonna finally have its day," Crow said, smiling.

I knew Primo was preparing himself in his cell. He would not take anything for granted. He'd approach his foe as if he believed Chango was armed for battle.

At 4:30 p.m., the unit officer stepped into his control area and announced, "Chow time. All inmates prepare for chow." Then he opened all our doors. As usual, after opening the doors the cop went back to his office on the other side of the unit.

Chente and I stepped out of our cell into a busy tier where men met before chow and talked. Men from every cell began walking by, but I didn't see Chango. A few seconds later Primo came out of his cell in his boxers and tennis shoes. My eyes focused on his right hand where he held Crow's bone-crusher.

He walked by briskly and entered Chango's cell.

I felt a tightness in my stomach and emptiness in my heart. Mostly, I felt bad for his little boy and the pain he'd suffer. Chango had fucked up, but his children would pay a price for the actions of their father.

Rage filled me, and a part of me considered taking action, but that would be suicide. Even if I managed to stop it, my name would go on the death list. Sometimes doing nothing comes with a heavy price too.

I couldn't see into the cell, but the sounds told the entire story.

Chango must have seen Primo enter the cell because he screamed, "Primo, por favor, no."

The sound of scuffling shoes on cement, then the distinct sound of a steel blade entering flesh reached our ears, followed by the bone-chilling screams from a scared man who knew death had come for him. Before this, he probably thought his only threat was hundreds of miles away in a cell at San Quentin. Every action has a consequence and price, and Primo was collecting his fee.

The unit officer finally heard the screams and ran toward the commotion. He stopped when he came in line with the cell where Primo was slaughtering Chango, and he could see the whole thing. With his flashlight, the cop hit the Plexiglas divider that separated us from the cops.

"Garcia, stop."

The cop yelled to no avail. Suddenly the screaming stopped and Primo emerged from the cell covered in blood. The sight of him startled the cop. To be honest, it left an impression on me as well.

Primo still carried the bone-crusher, and his eyes were filled with primal, animal-like intensity. But it was his smile, now that his hatred was satisfied, that had the most impact.

"Time to go home," he said, and went to the door where the scared cops waited for him.

He was sent to the hole first, and from there back to San Quentin. The DA's office rarely prosecuted prisoner-on-prisoner violence, even if someone died.

They rushed Chango to an outside hospital. I didn't know if he'd live or die. At the core of everything for me was what I knew his little boy would experience when he found out what happened to his father, and a part of me cried with him.

Late that night I sat down to draw and experienced a rare moment of clarity as my emotions and vision became one with my imagination. As I allowed that to happen, a frenzy overtook me. I poured my fear, hatred, and finally love into what I created.

While in this state, I hadn't noticed Chente wake up and walk over to me. He stood behind me and watched as I worked. I don't know how long he was there, but suddenly a part of me sensed his presence and I bolted upright to face the possible danger.

Not expecting my response, Chente stumbled backward and fell in surprise.

"Hey, what's the deal, ese?" he said.

I got a hold of myself and saw him through rational eyes, and recognized him.

"You surprised me. Never do that again. You understand?"

I shook the emotions away from me, but it was too late. Chente had seen it, and the evidence was still present on my face in the form of tears and on the table in the drawing. Chente stood up and looked at me.

"What are you doing? I woke up and saw you here. I talked to you, but you didn't answer, so I came to see what was up. But man, you were somewhere else."

I looked at him and anger swept through me. He had interrupted me, intruded on my most intimate moments, and a part of me hated him for it.

I grabbed the sheet of paper I was working on and went to throw it away.

"Carnal, wait. I saw you were drawing. Let me see it."

I hesitated, then turned to face him.

"Watcha, I'm sorry, dispensa, for disturbing you. I didn't know what you were doing and I came over to talk to you."

"Don't worry about it. You surprised me, that's all," I said.

He repeated his request. "Can I see what you were working on?"

I handed him my work.

"Fuck, ese. I didn't know you could draw like this."

"No one does."

"Damn, this is some deep shit. Look, I saw what you were going through when you were drawing. I can still see it on your face. You shouldn't hide this. This is you."

Maybe he was right. After he went back to bed, I sat and looked at my work. I wasn't ready to let anyone truly see me. How could I when I couldn't truly see myself?

No, I'm not ready, I thought. I stood up and threw the sheet of paper in the toilet and flushed it. I watched it go down. As it disappeared, so did the part of me that felt. I slid the mask back in place and got ready for another day in hell.

Chapter 15

Childhood, 1976

The bruises from Mr. Shultz's beating were still on my legs and butt a week after Oliver instigated the situation that led to my punishment. They had turned an ugly purple and black, and I wanted to cry every time I looked in the mirror. More and more I anticipated how I'd pay Oliver back.

Book reports were due the following week. Everyone had picked a book to read and write a report about. The grade we received from that report would count as a quarter of our grade for the entire class.

I read *Of Mice and Men* and had already finished my book report. Many of the kids in class were still reading their books and Mr. Holtz, the Lit class teacher, continued to remind everyone that only a few days remained to turn in the book reports.

My anticipation grew as the due date approached. I constantly thought of the different things that could go wrong with my plan. Success depended on perfect timing, good weather, and Oliver sticking to his habits.

I woke up the morning the reports were due and immediately looked to the window and thought I may never get my chance because it was raining.

I was proud of the job I had done on my report. Since I finished it early I had the opportunity to think about how best to present it, and I decided on a nice blue cover that gave it the look of a professional folder.

It continued to rain as my mother drove me and my sister to school, but just as she pulled into the parking lot the rain stopped and the sun peeked through the clouds.

My sister and I got out of the car and kissed our mother, and waited as she made the sign of the cross and blessed us. My sister met up with some friends and ran to the playground. I watched her go then headed for the classrooms. It was a few minutes before class started, but I wanted to know if Oliver was here. For it to work, he'd have to go outside at recess and remain on the field until the last possible moment, then rush to class, arriving late. This was his normal pattern and would make it unlikely he'd stop at his locker to collect his report until just before Lit class.

Opening my locker, I pulled out books for my classes and went to a bench in front of my homeroom. Oliver arrived a few moments later. He opened his locker and put a folder inside, then pulled out his baseball glove and ran out to the field to play.

I watched him go and wished I was popular and had friends. If I did, I would be happy. I had never had a real friend, but I thought I could be good at it. I even began to wonder: if I were white, maybe Oliver and I could be friends. I would forget all the hurt and pain he caused me. I would forget it all, if only he'd be nice to me and truly be my friend.

The bell rang and I continued to daydream.

Mr. Tonjes passed me and said, "Bill, the bell rang. You'd better get to class."

"I'm on my way, Mr. Tonjes."

"I expect you to go out for track and field. We need you."

Nodding, I went to class thinking, *Yeah, you need me to help you win. Then once I've done my part, I'll just be the stupid wetback again.*

I arrived in class as the second bell rang and sat down. Mr. Shultz was at his desk going through the newspaper.

"Everyone take your seats. I'll be a few moments."

I pulled out my book report when Donald, Jimmy, Oliver, and Kenny came in late.

"You four are late. Didn't you hear the bell? Maybe you'd like a date with my paddle. She just loves to kiss bottoms."

"Ah, sorry, Mr. Shultz. We were practicing our baseball signals. We want to win against Hope Lutheran," said Donald.

Mr. Shultz went back to his paper, and as Oliver and Donald passed my desk, Oliver flipped the folder with my book report off my desk. When it hit the ground, Mr. Shultz looked up and then went back to reading. I got up to pick up my book report.

"Bill, what are you doing? Sit down," said Mr. Shultz.

"I'm picking up my book report."

"I don't care. Sit down."

He knew what Oliver had done, but it didn't matter.

"You saw what happened, but you only pick on me."

"What did you say?" he asked.

"You only pick on me. When others do something you ignore it, but when it's me, you always yell at me or punish me."

"Come here."

I stood up and went to his desk.

"You will learn to keep quiet and not talk back."

"I wasn't talking back, but you won't listen. Why is it okay for anyone to do anything to me, but if I complain you punish me?"

Mr. Shultz stood up and said, "Shut up."

It was hopeless. He didn't care what anyone did to me. He didn't like me, and no matter what I did he'd find fault in it.

"Your mouth will cost you a swat."

He pulled out his paddle, grabbed me by the arm and pushed me forward. The sting of the paddle hurt the already bruised flesh. Once again he had become angry and hit me to satisfy that anger.

Walking back to my seat, Oliver smiled at me.

I sat down and anger crept into every part of my body. I didn't pay attention to the class or anything being said. The only thing I thought about was Oliver. It's strange, but usually no matter what I'm doing, focusing is always difficult because of the ADHD. But when angered or hurt, my focus is laser sharp.

The sun continued to shine, and at recess Oliver did exactly what I expected him to do. He was so proud of himself for the swat I received, he didn't even notice me watching him. And why should he? In his mind, I was nobody and couldn't hurt him.

He ran to the baseball field, along with Donald, Jimmy, Kenny, and a number of others, and I stayed there, even after the first bell rang. I watched, and before the second bell I slipped into class and waited. Sure enough, after hearing the second bell, they ran in straight from the field without their books.

The next class would be English Lit with Mr. Holtz, the class where all book reports were due. Halfway through the class I got permission to go to the bathroom. The hallways were empty. Everyone was in class and it seemed peaceful as I walked to the locker area. I checked behind me to make sure I was alone. Despite all the scenarios I had planned for, getting caught had not crossed my mind until now. That thought quickly vanished when I neared Oliver's locker.

My heart pounded in my chest. Power and adrenaline flowed through me as I took control. I touched his lock and my fingers went to work, 37-12-16. The locker opened. I grabbed the report and locked the locker.

Just as I had with Jimmy's lunch, I put it under a bunch of stuff in a large trash can. No one would find it.

Walking back to class, I felt vindicated. I was getting even for the times I was hurt, laughed at, and singled out. Although I was far from being even, I took comfort in the fact I was fighting back.

The final twenty minutes of class seemed to take hours, but the bell finally rang and I practically ran to Mr. Holtz's class. I didn't want to miss a thing. Everyone was seated when the second bell rang— everyone except Oliver.

Mr. Holtz began the class and passed out the list of books we could choose from for our next book reports. I looked at the list, but my mind was on Oliver. Where was he? It was ten minutes past the start of class and he hadn't appeared. After another five minutes, Oliver walked into class.

"So glad you could join us, Mr. Young," Mr. Holtz remarked. "Did you get lost on the way here?"

"No, Mr. Holtz. I can't find my book report. I brought it to school and put it in my locker, but it's gone."

"Should we call the stolen book report police? Or maybe we should ask your dog if he's seen it."

"I'm not lying. I did my report and brought it to school."

"Sit down, Mr. Young. If you can't produce it by the end of class, you will receive an F."

At the end of class, Mr. Holtz said, "Please pass your book reports forward. Is there anyone else whose report has vanished?"

No one said a word. Mr. Holtz went through all the reports briefly, then came to mine.

"Nice touch, Mr. Noguera. It seems you actually gave this some thought."

I didn't say anything.

"Mr. Young, have you found your book report?"

"Mr. Holtz, I don't know where it's at. I did it."

"Since you have not turned in your assignment, you will receive an incomplete, which translates to an F for a quarter of your grade. Maybe next time you will be more careful."

Oliver looked defeated, and a part of me sympathized because I knew what he was going through, but when he caught me looking at him he said, "What are you staring at, greaseball?"

I turned away, and when the bell rang he walked past me. He didn't say anything to anyone. He was alone and I thought, *How does imported medicine taste?*

Chapter 16

San Quentin Death Row, 1988

Blue was right. The men in East Block were no different from the ones in the AC. Their answer to most problems was violence.

On my second day in the yard, after coming through the yard sally port, I went to a corner near the front of the yard and set my things on the floor.

I scanned the yard for any sign of tension. The Blacks were at the back of the yard setting up to drive iron, and most of the Mexicans and Whites were drinking coffee or standing around talking before starting their line routines.

Nothing seemed out of place, so I began to stretch and warm up. Mouse came up to me and said, "Good morning."

We exchanged small talk as I warmed up, but he soon left. He knew I hated being disturbed while I concentrated on martial arts. To me, it was one of the most intimate forms of expression I practiced. To reach the state of concentration required to abandon myself to the purity of my senses, I needed to be alone.

He must have told Sporty and the others, since no one interrupted me.

Wicked had seen my routine during his stay in the AC, so when our eyes met he simply nodded.

During this state of concentration, my mind does not close itself off from the surrounding sounds, smells, or influences. In fact, my mind grasps everything within the scope of my senses and enters a state of hypersensitivity. In this state I become so in tune with my senses and body that when I start to move and practice the martial arts I'm like a machine—I can accomplish anything.

I was aware of eyes on me when I took off my shoes and meditated before going through my fighting forms and techniques, and for the next hour and a half I practiced. At the end of my routine I knelt and meditated for five minutes, bringing my breathing to a controlled rhythm and disengaging my mind. During martial arts practice, I am at war. There is no other description that comes close to the mental state I enter to reach the goals I have for myself.

Standing from my meditation position, I put on my shoes and started to run. I had time to run approximately two miles before it was our turn to cross the line and enter the weight area.

As I ran, I thought of the area I ran as a boy and teenager: Hacienda Heights, La Habra Heights, and Turnbull Canyon. I knew those roads, all the turns and smells, from so many years of running them. Now as I ran, my mind knew by the subconscious count of footsteps just how far I had gone and where I would be if I were running the hills. Mental pictures came to mind, and at moments the vivid memories overwhelmed my senses and I'd catch the fragrance of a tree or flower I once ran by.

When I finished running, I went to the sink at the front of the yard next to the shower. Some African prisoners were showering and their bodyguards watched me as I approached.

"I need some water," I said. I didn't wait for an answer and stepped into the area directly next to the shower with my tumbler in hand and filled it. I drank deeply and refilled it, then walked away.

Sporty asked, "What's up, ese? How's it going?"

"I'm good. Just getting ready for that iron."

"You ever lift iron before?"

"Not much. My routine is about endurance, bar work, and overall balance in the martial arts. But I look forward to getting started."

"I saw what you were doing earlier. What was that?"

"A combination of Hapkido, Karate, Taekwondo, and Jeet Kune Do I've molded into a more focused form of mixed martial arts."

"Man, it was impressive. All these motherfuckers, especially the Changos, were checking you out."

I didn't say anything.

"You got enough left in the gas tank? Because my workout is going to push you to failure," Sporty said.

"I'll be all right. I won't be lifting the weight you can, but give me a minute and I'll catch up."

"Yeah, I've had a lot of vatos say that, and they end up quitting. So I hope you're different."

"You'll soon find out that when I say something, I do exactly that. No ifs, ands, or buts about it."

"Órale, ese. Relax a few because we start at ten a.m."

"I'll be there," I said, and left to get my things. It got hotter as the sun rose above the fifteen-foot wall at the back of the yard. Many of the Africans had finished working out on the iron pile and were either showering or near the tables. It wasn't 10 a.m. yet, so I just sat and looked at the yard and took note of who was doing what. Learning the habits of those men was a good way to understand and identify when something changed and a good indicator when something was about to happen.

Over the years, I've become a student of human behavior. In prison the ability to read a person, group, or entire yard can be the difference between living and dying.

At 10 a.m. Sporty stepped over the line along with the rest of the Mexicans, Whites, and Indians. I helped Sporty stack the iron in the order we would use it. I wondered what Sporty had in mind as we stacked thousands of pounds.

"Watcha. On Monday, Wednesday, and Friday I work torso: chest, back, shoulders, and abs. On Tuesday, Thursday, and Saturday it's arms, abs, and legs. One day light, the next heavy. I work fast and it's about trust. Trust that when I'm doing a set, no one's going to sneak up on me because you're spotting me. If we work out together, trust is the first and last thing. I give you my word that no one will ever harm you while we work out together. If someone attempts it, I'll smash him."

"You got my palabra, ese."

We shook hands.

"Órale, let's put the lick down. We'll be super-setting everything. Today's Friday, so it's torso. Let's warm up," he said.

We placed a two-hundred-pound bar on the rack and Sporty pressed it eight times as if it were paper. He then stood and stepped to the pull-up bars and did eight pull-ups.

"That's one set, ese. We'll be doing over seventy-five sets today."

I got down on the bench and un-racked the two hundred pounds and pressed it eight times. Shit. It felt like three hundred pounds.

"Feels heavy, huh?"

"Yeah. What's up with that?" I said.

"This is pig iron. It's not balanced. The ends are welded on so we can't use the plates as weapons, and as you've noticed, the bar doesn't rotate like weights should."

"Damn, that's rough man," I said.

"You'll get used to it and soon you'll crave this shit," said Sporty.

I laughed and we continued to work. After two sets on the two-hundred-pound bar, we took it down and placed the two-hundred-fifty-pound bar up and did sets again. Sporty did eight reps. I managed only three each set and eight pull-ups.

"Okay, I'm going to keep raising the weight until we reach the four-hundred-forty-pound bar. When you can't go up anymore, we'll exchange the weight so you can do your set."

At that moment he smiled. "Yeah, you didn't realize when you signed on that I was crazier than a bed bug, huh?"

"Man, that's some serious iron. I admire your workout," I said.

"Our workout. You'll soon be doing it as well. You'll see. Any fat idiot can hit four hundred pounds once. But it only counts if you can hit it after you've finished your workout. Endurance and strength, speed and explosiveness, is what our routine is about. You'll need all of it during a war if you find yourself in the middle of one, and from what I hear and saw this morning, you would be unstoppable. You feel me, ese?"

Sporty was right. If I could combine the strength, explosiveness, and endurance he had with what I already possessed, I might very well be unstoppable.

Nearing the end of the workout, I noticed a shift on the yard. It wasn't much, just a slight change, but enough to raise the hairs on the back of my neck. I continued to work out, but I began looking at each group carefully. Nothing really seemed out of place. Either I was overly tired and the fatigue had me jumping at shadows, or someone was extremely good at shielding his intent. That wouldn't surprise me, but it would bother me. On that yard, with so many men in such a small area, it would be easy to shield and strike without warning.

"Hey Sporty, ponte verga." I looked at him in a manner that left little doubt he should stop and pay attention.

"What's up, ese?"

"I'm not sure, but something's going down. I can feel it."

He looked at me, then at the yard. "It's all good. No one's trippin'."

I let it go, but I knew better and I also knew Sporty was nothing more than a thug. He survived out of dumb luck. He assumed because of his physical size and strength he was superior, but he was incapable of reading a yard or a person. He was not sensitive to shifts or reading the intent of men. At some point that might cost him his life or mine, since I had to trust his ability to watch my back while I lifted hundreds of pounds of iron.

Continuing to lift, I went through the motions, but my eyes and senses were on alert. Something was about to happen, but I hadn't figured out who the players were.

From groups to individuals I scanned until I focused on a Peckerwood who, as he got a drink of water and began to stand, dropped his shields. It was that fast, but the heat rolled off his body as he reached in his jacket and pulled out a piece of plastic with a pair of razorblades melted into it so the blades formed a makeshift straight razor. It's a deadly weapon, but one reserved only for men not worthy of the time and effort it takes to make a bone-crusher.

Rapists, rats, or child killers are typically the ones attacked using razorblades. A warrior would be insulted if someone used that weapon on him. I know I would.

I grabbed the bar just as Sporty was about to lift it off of the bench rack and said, "Check it out," and shifted my gaze to the yard tables. Sporty got up from the bench and looked. The Peckerwood walked straight to the tables where four whites played cards.

One of the whites was my neighbor, Silent, who had his back to the yard. The Peckerwood, Domino, grabbed Silent by the forehead with his left hand and pulled his head back. At the same time he brought the razors across his throat, leaving a cut from ear to ear.

Silent grabbed his throat and stumbled backwards as the blood ran down his shirt. The commotion caught the gunner's attention, and he blew his whistle and ordered everyone on the ground.

Bulls from every part of the unit came running at the sound of whistles from the yard. Silent lay on the concrete holding his throat. Domino sat a few feet from him, laughing.

"Yeah, how's that feel, punk motherfucker? Just die," he said, and continued to laugh.

"You, on the ground. Can you walk?" the gunner yelled. "I need you to get to the gate where staff can assist you," he directed and aimed his M1 at Domino.

"I'll help him, CO," said Domino as he laughed.

"You, don't move," yelled the gunner and chambered a round.

"Okay, I was just trying to help this piece of shit," he laughed.

I watched as Silent dragged himself to the gate, where staff cuffed him and placed him on a gurney, then carried him to the hospital.

The gunner yelled, "You, come to the gate," while pointing at Domino.

"I'll see you in about two," he said to Wicked.

"All right, bro, give my regards to the fellas," said Wicked.

The Peckerwood knew the routine. He would go to the AC, and if he kept his nose clean they'd let him back to East Block in two years.

Sporty turned to me. "You were right, ese."

I nodded.

After the entire yard was cleared, the investigation squad took pictures and gathered evidence that would eventually go to the DA's office, where the file would sit unopened. What can you do to a man already sentenced to death? Not a fucking thing.

After returning to my cell, the tier bull came to my door.

"Noguera, how do you feel about the shower and phone job? They're yours if you want them."

"What would I have to do?"

"It's simple. The shower job is cleaning the shower after everyone's done. You'll be able to shower every day, and you'll receive an extra tray each meal, plus all the extras. The phone job doesn't really pay, but it gives you a chance to use the phone whenever you want and all you have to do is make a schedule every day and give it to the tier officer. It would be a favor to me if you'd take the jobs. I want someone who can handle it."

"How do you know I can handle it?" I asked.

"Carlton and I have known each other for years, and he told me about you. He said you're a talented artist and carry yourself well."

"Carlton's a good man, boss. I appreciate the offer and I'll take the jobs. Thank you."

Silent's loss was my gain and I would take advantage of it.

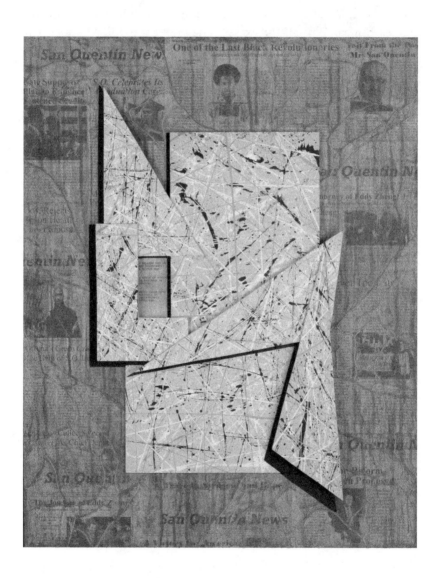

Chapter 17

Orange County Jail, 1985–1986

The men who lived with me in the eight-man cell never seemed to mind being in jail. For them, it was a time to meet with crew members and wait for transport to prison, where, as they put it, "all the action is." Family members or women who came to see them were just a form of entertainment, like going to a movie on the weekend.

They would write a woman and eventually she'd come to visit. It was as normal to them as if they had asked her out and they agreed to a date together. They were so used to that life, they didn't see anything twisted about any of it. They were "institutionalized," and their whole world existed behind bars. The world outside was just a place they sometimes visited. With this state of mind, it was natural they spent most of their lives in prison. In prison they were respected and honored. The prison culture was what they loved and where they thrived. It called to them and they answered readily. Outside prison culture they became uncomfortable and uncertain. Those men truly had no place in society other than as pawns to support the prison industry. Despite all that, men resent being locked up and think about getting out and living free, ignoring the fact they're more suited for life inside.

At the end of 1984, two of the men I lived with, Lucky and Crow, took deals of fifteen years to life. Those deals spared them a possible death sentence and meant they didn't require a trial. They were transported to Folsom State Prison within two weeks. The two men who replaced them, Shotgun and Trigger, were from the City of Orange in Orange County. Both men were Mexican and facing more than seventy years in prison for a string of robberies and a possible murder charge that was still pending. The district attorney did not have enough evidence to charge them with murder, but they were nervous about him getting it. It was only a matter of time, and they could both possibly face a death sentence.

Shotgun and Trigger were always together and always seemed to be planning something. They were known gang members with tattoos covering most of their arms, chests, and backs. Both men were short, heavily muscled, and bald, and across their stomachs the word "Orange" was tattooed in Old English font.

They soon got into a routine and got along with everyone in the cell, but they stayed to themselves. Both Chente and I believed they were up to something, but it was nothing more than a feeling. I wasn't surprised about a month later when Trigger approached me while I swept and said he and Shotgun wanted to talk to everyone in the cell.

"Órale, Sinbad, me and the Camarada want to get at you and everyone else about something, so if you can, stay in tonight and let someone else get on the broom."

"All right," I said, and went to cell-5, where Chente was playing poker. As soon as he saw me outside the cell, he folded his hand and came over to me.

"What's up, carnal?"

"Trigger just got at me about staying in tonight because he and Shotgun want to rap to all of us about something."

Chente thought for a moment.

"What do you want to do?"

"I'll do what he asked and stay in. I just wanted you to know what was going on in case you had some pedo with these two."

"If I did, you'd know about it."

"All right, I'm gone," I said, and left.

I had gone to Chente to note his reaction and see if he was hiding something from me. Trigger had come to me, and wanted me to stay in. Everyone else would already be in the cell, so if someone else was a target, I wouldn't be needed in the cell.

So the target was me, and Chente had no idea what was going on. I had learned to read him and I knew he wasn't hiding anything.

At dinner time, Chente caught up to me.

"Hey Mad, you thought about what Trigger told you earlier?"

"Not much. A bit."

"He asked you to stay in. All of us except you would already be in the cell. So it's you they need. You feel what I'm saying?"

I looked him in the eye. "I figured the same thing. I'll be ready."

We walked to the chow hall and I ate everything they served. It was a good day. Hamburgers and fries, salad, milk, chocolate cake. Normally I couldn't eat when I felt threatened. But I was numb. The drugs, despair, and the overwhelming grief caused by the murder of a piece of me had taken their toll and I'd lost the ability to feel anything. If I was the target, they would regret trying me.

After dinner, I asked Smiley, a tall Mexican who lived in cell-1, if he wanted to stay out and handle the broom because I was tired. Of course he jumped at the chance. He knew that, besides being able to walk around until 11 p.m., he would get a cut of all the drugs being moved and sold. He thanked me and went off to gather the broom.

Once we were all in the cell and settled in, Trigger turned on the TV and turned up the volume. Then he asked all of us to come into the sleeping area so we could all talk.

It didn't feel like I was being targeted, or that anyone was, for that matter. Chente and I looked at each other and stayed ready, but when Shotgun sat down and took off his shoes, it became obvious. Whatever was going on, it had nothing to do with violence and, more importantly, nothing to do with me. I relaxed a little, but not completely, because with them anything was possible.

Trigger knelt down on the floor in the center of us and began to talk.

"Watcha, we wanted to talk to you vatos out of respect and we hadn't said anything before because we needed some tiempo to see if we could trust you. Me and the Camarada are looking at some serious fuckin time. I know all of you got muertes, so maybe you want in on this. The bottom line is we're out of here. Here's the deal. I got business I need to handle out there, so we're pressed for time. The problem is, to get out of here it has to be done off the roof at night, and we need help getting the rope up there and cutting the steel cage."

I relaxed and sat down on my bunk. Not much surprises me anymore, but that clearly blindsided me. Never in a million years would I have guessed what they had in mind was escaping. I continued listening to Trigger.

"We got a vato turning himself in tomorrow night, and he'll be packing hacksaw blades so we can cut through the cage. Next Friday night we're scheduled to go outside at night, so that day we need to get the rope ready. We'll cut strips of sheet and braid it together until we have two hundred fifty feet; that's about how high the building is."

"How the hell do you expect to get all that rope on the roof? They search us before they allow us up there," said Chente.

"We'll need seventeen more people we can trust to carry five feet of rope in each shoe. They search us for weapons, and that's usually just a pat-down. So unless something changes, we'll be all right. Once we're up there, Shotgun and me will begin to cut the cage. We'll need everyone carrying rope to stand around behind the ping-pong table as if the game is the most interesting thing in the world. That way, you block the cop's view of the fence where we'll be working. Then one by one you'll go to the bathroom, where someone will be tying the rope together. Once you give that vato your rope, walk back to the ping-pong game and wait until we're done. It'll take approximately forty minutes to cut the fence. That'll give us twenty more minutes to climb down and split."

Everyone in the cell seemed excited about it, but I wasn't sure it would work. Involving seventeen more cats in it besides the eight in our cell was necessary for it to work. But all it would take was for one of those idiots to brag to a friend or girl outside and the house of cards would fall.

I decided to shower and get in while everyone talked and watched TV. When the hot water hit my face, I took a deep breath and allowed the water to relax me. Fifteen minutes before, I had been ready to fight for my life. As I showered I was overcome with a moment of relief and exhaustion. I didn't want to be there. I was tired of pretending. I wished so badly I could somehow wake up and find myself home in bed where all I had to worry about was a beating. I knew I'd survive that. But in that cell with all of those gangsters and killers, I wasn't so sure.

Chapter 18

Adolescence, 1977–1978

Taking something from someone who hurt me seemed fair. Although it started off like that, the truth was I liked stealing. Through my seventh and eighth grade years, I routinely took things that didn't belong to me. I believed I was justified since those people hurt me first, and I used that as an excuse to steal.

It was normal for boys my age to have rapid growth spurts, but for some reason it hadn't happened to me. My parents were concerned and took every opportunity to remind me about it.

My father seemed the most upset since he was six feet tall, and white. I was short and very dark.

During one of his rage-filled nights of drinking, he grabbed me by the neck and said, "I know your mother is a whore and that she fucks others, maybe she fucked a nigger and that's where you came from."

He smiled and left. He was drunk, but I've never forgotten those words. They stung and hurt me deeper than any beating I'd ever received. I loved, worshipped, and sometimes hated my father, and after that I knew deep down he thought I wasn't his son.

The next day we went to a martial arts competition, where I fought in a class for black belt fourteen- to sixteen-year-olds, and won. My father was very happy, and as I lifted the trophy over my head and he hugged me I remembered his words and they stung again.

It may have started with my father's words, or it may have been the special "vitamins" he began buying in Tijuana, Mexico for me, but a new resentment started growing inside me. I thought everyone was against me, and that deep down inside everyone hated me and wished I'd die and go away.

I trained harder and with a renewed dedication, fueled by rage and pain. I learned to control my beasts, but they seemed to take on a life of their own. Normally, when I wasn't upset I was fine. But as soon as I got angry, my vision clouded over in a red haze and, depending on the degree of the rage, I'd lose all control.

It happened overnight. I don't remember how or when, but I began to grow, fast. My knees hurt terribly from the rapid growth, and so did my head. The headaches were the worst.

With the growth I also gained confidence, though that was short-lived. We were coming to the end of my eighth grade year and that meant the school dance was coming up. After winning competition after competition in the martial arts, I thought that would translate to popularity.

A girl at school had caught my attention. Wendy was very beautiful and popular. She was blond, with big blue eyes and a beautiful smile. I imagined asking her out, and her accepting, but I never had the courage to do it. She wasn't seeing anyone, but I just didn't believe she'd ever go anywhere with someone like me. But I felt confident. Unstoppable.

At recess I saw her talking to her friends, and I walked up to her.

"Hi Wendy. How's it going?"

"Oh, hi. I'm fine."

"Are you going to the dance next week?"

"Probably, how about you?"

"Maybe. Has anyone asked you?"

"No, but I'll probably go anyway."

"Umm, do you think maybe, I mean, do you want to go with me?"

"Oh my God, that's so cute."

For a moment I thought she'd say yes.

"Have you looked in the mirror?"

I was confused. Did I have something in my nose or teeth? She saw that I didn't understand. She pulled out her make-up mirror.

"Look at yourself. Now look at me. Do you think I'd ever go to the dance with a wetback?"

She laughed at me and her friends all joined in.

What had I ever done to cause her to make fun of how I looked? Honestly, I wanted to cry. No matter what I did, it was never good enough. I went and sat down next to the basketball court. I wished I could have crawled into a hole and died. Not that she had said no, but that she and her friends had laughed at me and called me a wetback.

A week before the end of my eighth grade year, I was walking to class when the school principal and English Lit teacher, Mr. Holtz, stopped and asked me to come to his office. As I followed him, I wondered why he needed to see me in his office. Why couldn't he tell me whatever was on his mind there? We entered his office and he sat down behind his desk. He didn't ask me to sit, so I stood there while he went through some papers.

"Do you know what these are?"

The papers he held weren't familiar.

"I'll tell you. They're reports. Over the past two years, students have lost things with no explanation. Food, homework, sports gear. The list goes on. All of the missing items have come from boys, and you are one of the few who has never had something turn up missing. Can you explain that?"

I knew he suspected me of stealing the items, but I also knew he was fishing, hoping I'd admit it was me.

"I keep track of my things."

"No," he yelled and stood up. "I know the rest of the students here and I know they would not take anything. But you," he pointed his finger at me, "you are a thief."

I said, "Why, because I'm not white? Because you don't come to my house for dinner? Because you think everyone that looks like me is a wetback?" I was getting angry. "I've seen you laugh when people call me that. All of you think it's funny, but it's not."

"I know you took those things. You are a thief. It's written there, all over your face," he said as he pointed at me.

I thought, *Yeah, you're right. I am a thief, thank you for making that so clear.* But I said nothing. I just stared at him.

"You know what, this is a closed issue. It's the end of the year, and if

I could prove you took those things I'd expel you. Get out of my sight. You're nothing but a common wet . . . ah . . . thief."

During the next class, which was Lit, Mr. Holtz asked everyone to please not leave their personal items unattended because there was a thief among us. He looked directly at me as he said this.

At graduation, Mr. Holtz smiled broadly as he shook my parents' hands and told them how proud they should be and that I was part of the school's proud history.

I thought, *Fuckin' hypocrite.*

That was 1978, the summer before my freshman year in high school. My father and mother were sleeping in separate beds and the tension at home had never been higher.

The only difference was me. I had changed. I was tired of being the butt of everyone's jokes and their punching bag. I didn't really know what I'd do to make things different, or change how people saw me, but the first change had to come from inside of me, and it had. I was stronger and felt like I could do anything. I didn't know it then, but those vitamins my father began giving me months before were more than just vitamins. They were anabolic steroids.

During a fighting competition, he learned from a fighter in the men's division that steroids would provide fast results. As a matter of proof the fighter offered himself and his record, as well as the Russian and German Olympic teams and their success. It was all the proof my father needed, and shortly after that conversation he took a trip to Mexico, where he bought several cycles of Dianabol.

I'm sure my father had no idea about the possible side effects of the drug. How could he, when no one did in 1978? He only knew the results and that outweighed everything else.

That summer my routine was the same as the year before. Every morning I'd wake up early and my father would give me a ride to the bus stop where I'd catch the bus to Huntington Beach, surf the morning break, come home, put in three to five miles of road work, train at the studio until 7 or 8 p.m., then sleep.

My beach routine was about to change for the better. I always surfed off to the side so I wouldn't drop in on any of the locals. They were all older and guarded their territory like they owned the beach. I simply wanted to surf and not attract attention.

I was off to the side looking out over the beach as I waxed my board when a couple of the locals came up to me. "What's up, brah?"

"What's going on," I replied.

"We've seen you come out here for the longest, but never see you around. What's up with that? Where you from?"

"Look, I get it. I'll leave, you don't want me here because I'm not from Huntington."

"Nah, pup, it ain't like that. You're cool. We just wanted to see what's up with you. Maybe you want to line up with us."

"No doubt, that would be cool," I said.

I thought they wanted to chase me off but they'd just asked me to join their line and surf with them, and the guys impressed me. They were surfers. Long-haired, all of them were at least seventeen and older, and they were cool. They were also feared. I knew from watching them that no one surfed their break unless they allowed it.

There were a total of eight of them, all wearing black and blue O'Neill wetsuits. As I made it to the line-up, they nodded to me. After catching a few sets with them, Brody, who had asked me to join them, introduced me to his brothers. There was Sandman, Turtle, Jeff, Go-Go, Robert, Matt, and Silver, who was the only blond in the group.

"These are my brothers, my tribe, The Pack. We hold down Huntington because it's ours. From now on, whenever you come out, this will be your spot. If we're not out that day and any motherfuckers tell you to move, tell them you're with us and to go fuck themselves."

"Thanks, Brody. Man, when I saw you and Matt coming over earlier I thought you were going to make me leave. I've been watching you guys for a while and I've seen you kick dudes out of here. I always thought it was only a matter of time until it was my turn."

"Listen, last year we noticed you. Go-Go had seen you out here to the side and thought you had some skills, so we just let you do what you were doing. You didn't try to line up with us or get friendly, you just did your thing. We basically ignored you. Then I noticed you taking the bus inland and figured you traveled a ways to surf. Where are you from?"

"La Puente," I said.

"Damn, that's a fuckin' long bus ride."

"Yeah, but I like to surf and I need to get away from my house. It sucks there."

"I hear you, man. I know what that feels like. But from now on, when you need a place, this is it. All right, brah?"

I nodded.

This guy, who was cool and The Pack's leader, had offered me a place many wished was theirs, but he'd picked me. He didn't care how I looked or if my skin was dark. When they looked at me, they saw a surfer.

"Let's head in, brah, I'm fuckin' hungry. You?" Go-Go asked.

"Yeah, I could eat, but I only have enough money for the bus fare."

"Don't stress, brah, I got you," said Go-Go.

Go-Go was the youngest of The Pack. He was seventeen with long black hair, green eyes, a wiry build, and always seemed to be going a hundred miles a minute. We made our way in and the rest followed. When we reached the shore and I stood next to them, I realized I was only an inch or two shorter than the tallest. I smiled. Walking to the parking lot, we came to a four-wheel-drive Chevy truck that belonged to Silver and most of the guys put their boards in the back and began to take off their wetsuits. Brody walked past us to a beat-up older VW bus and placed his board in it.

"Let's shower and get some food. Put your board in my ride," said Brody.

As I did, I noticed a girl was asleep in the back of the bus.

"That's my girl, Brenda. Let me wake her. Babe, you want to eat?"

"Brody, noooo . . . just bring me something," she pouted.

"What can I say, brah? She needs her sleep."

We showered to get all the salt water off of us and then crossed Pacific Coast Highway to a bagel shop where Matt ordered us all bagels and coffee.

When we got our stuff and returned to the parking lot, Brenda was up and three other girls had joined her. I couldn't help but notice how beautiful they all were. I mean, they were every teenager's dream. As we approached, Go-Go picked up one of them and she turned and kissed him deeply. The rest of The Pack opened the bags of bagels and ate. Silver, Go-Go, Brody, and Turtle paired up with the girls who were obviously their girlfriends.

"So who's the stray," asked Brenda.

"That's Bill," said Brody.

"Oh noooo, Mr. Bill," laughed Brenda, making reference to the popular *Saturday Night Live* character. But the look on my face must have shown I didn't like being made fun of, because Sandman cut in.

"Yeah, Bill doesn't fit you. We gotta come up with a name for you."

"How old are you?" asked Silver's girl, a dark-skinned Asian with green eyes and blond hair.

"I'm fourteen."

She laughed. "I should set you up with my little sister. She's fifteen. You'd like her. She's cute."

"Yeah, brah," said Go-Go, "she's the kind, if I weren't tied down, I'd scam on her."

Just then his girlfriend elbowed him in the ribs and he laughed. "What? It's true, she's hot."

Everyone laughed and I joined in. Everyone but Sandman. He was thinking.

"I've seen that look on Sandman's face before," said Silver.

"Yeah, just before he came up with my nickname," said Turtle.

"How did you get the name Turtle?" I asked.

"It's because I'm smart and take my time to make decisions."

"Bullshit. It's because this motherfucker is slow as fuck," laughed Go-Go.

Sandman said, "You like to swim. I've seen you swim around the pier, reach the shore, turn around and swim around it again. That's a long swim in the ocean."

"I'm used to it, and I love the water."

Sandman kept looking at me and then smiled. "Oh shit, he's got it. The prophet is about to speak," laughed Silver.

"Wait. Before you say anything, how did you get the name Sandman?"
I asked.

"Brody gave it to me. When we were kids."

I looked at Brody. "It's simple. No matter how many times he showered, you could always find beach sand on him, in his pockets, hair, ears, everywhere. So I began calling him Sandman."

I smiled and then laughed. "Makes sense." Then Sandman got up and began eating a bagel. When he finished, he turned to me and said, "You swim, you're fearless, the ocean is your home, and you got serious skills in carving up a wave. When I look at you, I see a serious waterman. I see Sinbad. That's what we'll call you."

"Sinbad, that's hot," said Mika, Turtle's girl.

"Why Sinbad?" I asked.

"Ever see the cartoon—or how about the movies? In the cartoon, Sinbad pulls his belt and becomes bigger and stronger. He's a sailor who smashes his enemies. He always finds himself in the water swimming or fighting. And in the movies, he's this dude who is on a long journey where he fights mystical monsters," said Sandman.

"Yeah, I know the cartoons and movies. I like the name, but I don't know if I look the part."

"Brah, believe me, you do. You don't see yourself like I do, but it's there," he said as he pointed at me.

I couldn't wrap my head around it. When I woke that morning I couldn't wait to get to the beach and surf, but I never imagined what waited for me. I looked at my watch and realized I'd miss my bus if I didn't get going. I picked up my board and suit and Go-Go said, "What's up, brah? Where you off to?"

"I gotta go. If I don't hurry, I'll miss my bus, and if I don't get home on time my old man will kick my ass."

"Don't sweat it. I got you covered. I have shit to handle in Whittier, and La Puente isn't far from there. I'll give you a ride. That cool?" asked Brody.

"Yeah, that would be really cool. Thanks."

Later, as he drove me home, we talked and I liked him. I just didn't understand why he asked me into his circle. There were an endless number of people who would have jumped at the chance to hang out with them.

"Brody, why me? Why did you ask me into your line up? Why are you driving me home?"

"Brah, you've been surfing that spot for the longest. You were just a little pup when we first saw you. And although you're from La Puente, you're like us. You held down your spot and surfed it."

"Yeah, but so do a lot of people. Why did you ask me to join your line up? You guys don't allow anyone in. I've watched you as long as I've been surfing and the first thing I heard was don't fuck with The Pack. Don't surf their break unless you want to get pounded."

He was quiet for a time and then he turned down his stereo.

"I asked you because you remind me of someone."

"Who?"

"My little brother, Justin. We called him Bomber. He died in a car crash a few years ago and you look like him."

"I'm sorry, Brody. That's fucked up."

"He was my best friend and he, Sandman, and me formed The Pack. That's why we wear the black and blue wetsuits. It's in memory of Bomber. He's the one who began calling us The Pack. The Wolf Pack," he said, "because killer whales, Orcas, are the wolves of the sea. When I saw you for the first time, I thought of Bomber and it stuck in my head. This morning while you knelt down with your board across your knees and waxed it, I remembered Bomber used to do exactly the same thing. He'd kneel like that, stroke his stick while looking at the break. I looked at you closely and it hit me hard. So I told Matt I was going to ask you to hang with us. Everyone said go for it. He belongs here."

I didn't know what to say, so I said nothing. He turned up his stereo. Led Zeppelin's "Black Dog" played and I just sat back and listened.

When we arrived at my house, I grabbed my board and suit and Brody said, "Hey, brah, I come this way every day for work. I can drop you off if you like. It's no sweat."

"That would be cool, thanks. I'll see you tomorrow, brah."

The next day, and for the rest of the summer, I surfed with The

Pack almost every day, and pretty soon everyone knew me. Even other surfers recognized me and knew not to mess with me. My confidence was sky high, and I noticed girls had even begun to look at me.

Near the end of summer, I arrived at the beach early. Sandman and Brody were already there kicking back in the parking lot when I showed up. They both said, "What's up, Sinbad?" No matter how many times they called me that, I wasn't used to it and it always caught me by surprise.

"What's up?" I said.

"Man, dead calm. It's flat. There's no swell, no nothing. It's going to stay like this all fuckin' day. As soon as the rest of us get here, we'll load up and head down to find the kind waves," said Sandman.

"Hey, I know a spot. It's in San Clemente—Trestles Beach. I've surfed it a few times and it breaks good. The only problem is there are a few locals who think they own it and run off anyone they don't like," I said.

"What? You mean they run around like they own the beach, chase people off, and surf it like it's their backyard? The nerve. Hell, they sound exactly like us," laughed Sandman.

I looked at Brody and Sandman just as Jeff, Robert, Go-Go, Silver, and Turtle arrived.

"I'm serious. These cats are trouble and if all of us go they'll probably fuck with us," I said.

"What are you talking about?" asked Go-Go.

"Going to Trestles," said Sandman.

"Fuck it. Let's have at it. There ain't shit going on here," Go-Go said.

After Matt arrived, we piled into Silver's truck and Brody's VW van and headed to San Clemente. The ride there was as crazy as rides got. I was in Brody's van with Turtle and Jeff, while Go-Go, Sandman, and the rest of The Pack were piled into Silver's truck. They wheeled in and out of traffic, and at one point Go-Go jumped out on the hood of the truck while going about sixty miles per hour, pretending he was paddling into a wave, and then jumped up on the hood like he was surfing. The guy was crazy, but everyone was laughing and pointing at him.

When we got to Trestles there were some nice swells and we all got our boards and suits and ran down to the shore. We stopped for a moment to suit up, and I was the first to paddle out. Everyone else followed. We caught wave after wave and were out there killing it, when I noticed a guy on the shore taking pictures of us.

"Hey Sandman, check out the ho-dad with the camera. He's taking our picture."

I took the next wave in and walked up to the camera guy. "What's up with you taking our pictures? Who are you?"

"I'm Spencer Wells. I'm a photographer and I represent Aquatic Pulse. I was checking you out. You have some very aggressive and clean moves. Ever thought about entering a surfing contest?"

"Nah, I just surf because I like it."

By then, the rest of The Pack had come out of the water and were standing listening to him.

"Well, you should. I think you'll do well in local contests and maybe at a higher level."

"You think, brah?" said Go-Go.

"Here's my card. If you decide to give it a shot, I'll fund you. I'll pay your gate fee, travel expenses, and you'll wear our logo. We'll also give you a new board and suit."

"No doubt? I surf in a contest for you and you give me all that stuff?" I asked.

"Yes, we're forming a team and all team members get the same treatment."

"Brah, go for it. It sounds like a sweet-ass deal," said Go-Go.

I took the card and said I'd give it some thought. Spencer then went to his car and came back with a couple of shirts for me with Aquatic Pulse written across the front and back.

"There's a small contest in three weeks in San Diego. I'd like you to enter. Give me a call within two days if you decide to do it. I'll get you in."

"Not even. Two days . . . he'll tell you now. He's in. Go for it, brah. Are you scared? Man, I know you'll shred," said Go-Go.

"Okay, I'm in," I said.

"Fantastic. What's your name?"

"It's Sinbad. He's from Huntington."

After he left, I turned to Go-Go. "What, you're my manager?"

"Yeah, brah, as your manager, I get everything you get." Everyone started laughing.

"Looks like we're going to San Diego in a few," said Brody.

We all stood around, talking and looking at the shirts. The sun was rising quickly and more people showed up on the beach. Then a group of ten guys approached us, saw the shirts, and told us this was their spot and that those shirts and sponsor were meant for one of them, not us. All of them were between seventeen and twenty years old. They were the guys I had told Sandman about.

They were known as The Boyz and they held down Trestles, much like The Pack held down Huntington.

"What are you talking about, lame? You snooze, you lose. My boy got the sponsor, so you and your boyfriends go suck yourselves off," said Go-Go.

Leave it to Go-Go to jump-start a situation. One minute we were all standing there, the next, one of their older guys punched Matt in the face. That quickly, all of us were in a fight right there on the beach.

A guy about eighteen with long wavy blond hair pushed me backwards and I fell on the sand, but as quickly as I fell I rolled and came up kicking him in the stomach, and then head. He tried to side step my kicks, but when he did he walked right into my left knee and he crumpled to the ground. Two of The Boyz were on Sandman, beating him pretty badly, and I went to him. I pulled one of them off, and as soon as I did he swung at me, missed, and I caught him twice in the face with my fists and he went down.

Sandman was hurt and couldn't defend himself, and as the guy beat him, rage exploded inside me and a red haze clouded my vision. I grabbed the guy who was beating Sandman and threw him to the ground with force. Before he could recover, I leapt on top of him. Everything from that moment was blank. The next thing I knew I was in Brody's VW van and pulling up at his apartment in Huntington. I was awake the whole time, but I have no memory of what I did or anything from the moment I saw red and threw that guy off of Sandman. One moment I was blank, the next, it was like a switch was thrown in my head and I was conscious again of what was going on around me. I must have acted no different than I usually did because, as I became aware of my surroundings, Brody continued talking.

"We'll kick back at my pad for a little while. Clean up and then I'll drive you home. I have to be at work by twelve thirty. Is that cool?"

I nodded.

"You haven't said a whole lot. Everything cool?"

"Yeah, I was just thinking." It was then I noticed my hands hurt. My knuckles were sore and swollen. I looked closely at them and checked for any breaks. Sandman's voice surprised me. He was in the back of the van with Turtle and Jeff.

"Are your hands all right, dude?"

"I'm okay, just a little sore, and hungry."

We must have stopped at Carl's Jr. because, as I became more aware of my surroundings, I smelled the food and my stomach growled. All of us got out of the van and climbed the stairs to Brody's apartment. Silver's truck was already parked in front, and when we walked into his place everyone got up to see how Sandman was. It was then that I noticed his face. He had a black eye that was nearly closed, a cut on his eyebrow, and his mouth was pretty badly swollen. All of us had small bruises and minor cuts, but Sandman looked like he'd been beaten badly.

"Oh my God, what happened?" cried Brenda. "Are you okay, Sandman?"

"I'm fine, Brenda. Nothing the echoes of time can't make into a distant memory," replied Sandman.

"I know you," she said. "You always talk like that when you're going through a tough time."

"Ah, she walks in beauty, like the night of cloudless climes and starry skies; and all that's best of dark and bright. Meet in her aspect and her eyes."

"Man, you gotta give me some of them lines. Cause if I could talk like that, indeedest all the legs would spreadest for my dickith," laughed Go-Go.

I laughed and I couldn't stop myself. For unknown reasons, what Go-Go said just seemed like the funniest thing in the world. I laughed until tears blurred my vision, maybe to hide the real tears I was crying. I sat down and closed my eyes and Sandman went with Brenda to the bathroom to clean up. Everyone sat down on the couches and ate. Between bites, they recalled the fight with The Boyz. I just listened and kept eating.

"So what's the deal? Where did you learn to thump like that?" Matt asked.

"Yeah dude, that was some hairball shit you did to them fuckers," said Go-Go. He stood and kicked and punched as if he were in a Kung Fu movie.

"I was wondering the same thing," said Sandman as he entered the room. After cleaning up, he somehow looked worse.

"Damn, brah, who hit you with an ugly stick?" laughed Go-Go.

Sandman shook my hand. "Man, you saved my skin back there. I need you to know that the blood you sacrificed for me will be the blood that bonds you and me forever. I will forever be in your debt."

At that moment, two souls shared the intimacy of brotherhood.

Go-Go cut in. "You see, that's what I'm talking about. Man, you make taking a shit sound romantic. You gotta teach me the Shakespeare shit. Cause then I'll get all the pussy."

"Brush your fuckin' grill and you might get some, mumble-mouth motherfucker," laughed Brody.

Everyone was laughing by then and I turned to Sandman. "It was nothing. You needed help and I gave it. You would have done the same for me."

"Yes I would have, but I never thought that much help would come from you or in that form. I knew you would help, but believe me when I say you dish out a serious ass kicking. What was that? Do you study the martial arts?"

"Yeah, since I was little. My whole life has been about training. That's where I go when I'm not here surfing."

By then, everyone was listening to me.

"What did I do that was so special? I mean, I know I can fight.

I've gotten my ass kicked my whole life, but why are you guys so surprised?"

I didn't want them to know I didn't remember anything after my vision turned to red. It was the first time I had no memory of what I'd done. Usually rage, or fear, would taint my vision, but I had never completely gone blank. I needed to know what had happened.

"Man, anyone would be surprised if they saw what you did. I was getting my ass beat by two of them dudes, and out of nowhere you appeared, pulled the first guy off, and a second later you picked up the second dude and threw him down. You just beat the shit out of him. The first guy was still out cold when we pulled you off of the second dude," offered Sandman.

"Yeah, I saw you run over after thrashing the guy you were fighting first, then pull the dude off of Sandman. He took a swing at you but you punched him in the face and he went down," said Turtle.

"I saw Sandman being hurt and he needed me, so I acted. I'd do it for any of you."

My hands hurt and were swollen, but I continued trying to remember what had happened earlier. A steel wall had gone up in front of those memories and I've never been able to break through.

Summer came to a close, and on the last weekend before I started my freshman year of high school, I was sad. I'd spent just about every day at the beach with The Pack and it was about to end. They'd continue to surf every day, but since I lived so far away I wouldn't be able to make it there and be back in time for school.

As soon as I arrived at the corner where the bus dropped me off, I hurried to the beach and breathed deeply as if I were taking as much of it in as possible, to use later when I needed the memory.

I put on my wetsuit and, although it was still dark, I swam out, needing to experience the ocean alone. Before The Pack asked me to surf with them I had found a certain bond between the ocean and a part deep inside of me, and it gave me peace. Nearing the halfway mark to the end of the pier, I filled my lungs with air and opened up my stroke. I felt strong and alive and somehow free. Each stroke, each breath I took, brought me closer to the end of the pier, and a thought occurred to me. Why turn around? I usually reached the end of the pier, swam around it, and headed back. I'd done it twice each morning, but as I neared the end of the pier I didn't want to turn around. Turning around would have been following the rules, and those rules kept me from freedom. I swam on, passing the end of the pier and breaking free to a place where I controlled my life. Life or death were literally mine to control, so I swam on.

Suddenly I became aware my ears were cold and I stopped. The sky was becoming light, so I turned around, and at first I was taken by surprise. I was at least a mile out. I'd never swam that far and for a second I was scared I wouldn't make it back. But I dismissed the thought. After all, I was Sinbad, a waterman, and the ocean was my home.

I swam like a machine and my thoughts only came back to the present when I neared the pier and heard Go-Go's voice above me. He was on the pier yelling and pointing at me, but I couldn't make out what he said. My ears were numb. Halfway past the end of the pier, Sandman and Turtle were at my side on their boards and I picked up my pace. All I could hear was the pounding of my heart in my chest. Nearing the shore, I body surfed a wave in and emerged from the water. Brody, Silver, and Matt met me there.

"What were you doing, brah? When we got here we saw you go in and do your swim, but as we set up our shit and watched you keep going, we didn't know what to think," said Brody.

By then the rest of them were listening.

"I was just feeling it, so I pushed on," I said.

"Brah, I went to the end of the pier to watch you, and when I lost sight of you I freaked. I thought you were dust," Go-Go said.

"You scared all of us. We lost one of ours when Bomber went down. We don't want to feel that again."

Sandman said, "It's the last week of summer. We know you won't be here every day because of school, but know this: in our hearts you'll be here. We'll surf and your spot among us will remain, because you're one of us. The Pack never leaves or forgets one of our own."

Then I noticed Turtle held a new black and blue wetsuit. He handed it to me. "We all pitched in to buy it. Try it on."

I took mine off. It was old, cracked, and much too small. I put on the new one. It fit perfectly. "Damn, you almost look as good as I do," laughed Go-Go.

"You're one of us. You're Pack," said Brody.

One by one we picked up our boards and paddled out. Brody and Sandman were on each side of me, and as we neared our spot, Sandman said, "I was right about you. You are Sinbad."

Chapter 19

San Quentin Death Row, 1988

I settled down to read a new book—my third in the seven days after Domino slit Silent's throat. Everyone on Yard-1 would remain on lock-down for ten days with no yard program. After that we'd go back to normal schedule. In the meantime, I busied myself reading, and drawing all manner of compositions. In East Block I could order books from a larger part of the library than I could when I was in the AC. It seemed like no one had any interest in the books I ordered since they were often dusty and moldy. Most of the men in prison are not interested in art or its history and movements. Instead, they concentrate on racial, cultural, and religious study, then they use their knowledge as proof of their intelligence, and ultimately as a weapon to argue their superiority over other races, cultures, or religions. This is a complete waste of time—like a dog chasing its tail.

The new books I discovered on the writings of Motherwell, Kline, de Kooning, and Rothko were a wonder to me and I couldn't stop reading them. In them I found a language I understood and could relate to. Ideas such as, "A consummated experience between picture and viewer," and, "The point is to end this stillness and loneliness and to be able to breathe and stretch one's arms again," were a revelation and excited me beyond all else.

Reading the words of Rothko, a man I had never met but felt I knew intimately through his words and work, was a very moving experience for me. I also found Friedrich Nietzsche's writings extremely meaningful, and his belief that music is the true language of emotions was like water to the lips of a thirsty man.

"Mr. Noguera? Excuse me, Mr. Noguera?"

I looked up. "I'm sorry. I was reading. How may I help you?" I said.

I had not heard the woman approach my cell. I'm temporarily in my own world while I read and I rarely notice my surroundings.

"I'm the handicraft manager and Warden Vasquez asked me to stop by and offer you a place in the program. I brought the latest catalog so you can order materials if you need anything."

She handed me the catalog and a membership application through the crack at the top of the cell door.

"Fill the application out and pick a medium you'd like to work in. I'll collect it tomorrow, along with your order sheet so your materials can be processed. Usually approval for orders takes a few weeks, then they arrive a few months after that. It's best to order in bulk so you don't run out."

"Thank you. I appreciate you coming by. I'd like to get started as soon as possible. I'll have the application and order ready for you tomorrow."

"The warden tells me you're extremely talented. Do you have anything I can look at?"

Normally I don't like anyone seeing my work until I've had time to digest the feelings associated with what I consider a very personal experience, but it wasn't the time to be difficult. I turned and picked up a small folder I had made from cardboard, where I kept my drawings and compositions. I handed it to her. She opened the folder and examined the contents for a couple of minutes.

"These are very good—and at the same time very disturbing. There's a rawness to your work. If you're interested in selling your work in the gift shop, you may consider landscapes or flowers. They seem to sell the best."

Her suggestion annoyed me. Landscapes? Flowers? Was she kidding?

Apparently not. She handed my folder back and then reached for a large portfolio she had brought.

"The warden asked if I had any art materials available so you could get started, so I brought you a few things. A prisoner who paroled last week left these materials."

"I appreciate it. I'll use whatever I can."

"There's a list of items you can order inside the portfolio, and the rules for the program. I only come into the unit once a month to pass out orders, pick up art for mail-outs, or to place pieces in the gift shop. I put three contracts inside the portfolio in case a staff member orders something from you. He signs the contract and then it's approved by the warden. That's about it. Any questions?"

"Not that I can think of, but thank you for coming in today and bringing me these materials."

"Oh, you're welcome. I'm Katharine, and I can be reached by institutional mail if you need anything."

She left and I looked out the large window directly in front of my cell. Wind surfers passed by in the bay, and a part of me was sad. Having a window in front of my cell is a huge bonus, but it's also hard to deal with. The other men in here only see the wind surfers and bay as beauty and a form of entertainment. For me, however, it's a form of torture because I know what it's like to ride a wave and feel the spray of the ocean on my face—to feel its power and harness it. To have had it then lost it is much worse than never having had it at all. A man who has never experienced something can't long for it. This is why I believe prison was made for men like me. I am tortured and punished by being here. Most men here have never had anything, so prison serves no purpose except to warehouse them.

The sound of keys brought my attention back from the wind surfers. I had already learned to distinguish each bull by the sound the keys on his belt made as he walked. It sounded like Stevenson. He had finished releasing the remaining inmates for showers and was coming for me so I could clean the showers.

"Ready to go, Noguera?"

"Give me a moment to get my things. Could you put that portfolio in my cell when I go clean the showers? The art manager left it for me."

"Not a problem. I see you're getting settled in. I look forward to seeing what you can do with the right materials."

So am I, I thought, *so am I.*

"I'm ready to go."

I turned around and he placed cuffs on my wrists through the food port then opened my door. I backed out and went to the showers. This was the best and worst part of my day. Worst because no matter how good a job I did cleaning them, the next day they were back to a state of filth. The men who used the showers each day seemed to forget they were human for the time they spent in there. Some spit, others urinated, and some even masturbated. The stench was overwhelming and the first twenty minutes or so were terrible while I poured bleach and scrubbed the walls and floor. After they were clean I showered as long as I wanted. I usually brought all of my dirty clothes to wash each day instead of sending them to the prison laundry service. I'd seen men who sent their laundry out end up with rashes that they always seemed to be scratching. I avoided all that whenever possible.

After I finished cleaning and washing, I turned the hot water on, showered, and allowed it to relax me. Much of that time I spent daydreaming I was somewhere else.

I turned off the water and put on my shorts. I wondered what was in the portfolio. I still wasn't sure what I'd need to order and how much it would cost. After five years of incarceration, my savings were nearly gone and I had no means to support myself. They didn't allow death row prisoners to work jobs for money. I wasn't like the rest of the men here who asked their families for money, or convinced some woman to support them. I would find a way to support myself.

"Hey Noguera, you done?"

"Yeah, boss, but I need some more bleach to clean these showers."

"I'm way ahead of you. I put a gallon in your cell, and a bag of extra fruit I got from the kitchen."

"I appreciate that. Thank you."

After I returned to my cell, I put away the bleach and hung up my clothes to dry. I looked in the bag Stevenson had brought me. There were four grapefruits, six oranges, five bananas, and ten apples. I put them in a plastic bag, then filled up a five-gallon bucket of cool water and placed them there. Getting the shower job had been a huge plus for me since I didn't eat any prison food that was cooked or opened. The kitchen workers often did things to the food going to death row because they knew a lot of the men there are rapists, child molesters, and child killers who deserved what they got.

As shower cleaner, I received enough extra food so I could pick only the things that were still sealed and avoid problems. It also allowed me to save the remaining funds for things I really needed until I figured out a way to support myself.

Of course, in prison there are always ways for a convict to make money and I had the required tools for all that. Dealing drugs was lucrative, and so was gambling and extortion. But I was done with that life. I would rather starve.

Finally, I looked at the portfolio. It was twenty-six by thirty-six inches, made of black plastic. As I picked it up to set it on my bunk I noticed it was a lot heavier than I expected. It had a large zipper along three sides that, when opened, folded out like a book. Inside, I found ten sheets of illustration board, each twenty by thirty inches and twenty-ply. They were professional grade materials, far superior to the low grade materials I'd grown used to. There was an eighteen-inch ruler, erasers, graphite, pencils, pens, brushes, ink bottles, and a specialized set of pens for drafting. It was exactly what I needed to get started.

I sat back and thought about what I'd do first. I didn't want to waste any of the boards because everything had to count.

The next day the handicraft manager came and picked up my application. She approved it on the spot and took my order sheet. By that time I knew what I had to do. It was obvious to me there was a market here for art. A lot of prisoners did cards and small drawings, and some even painted. But from what I could see, most of their work seemed more like a hobby than art. I guess that's what the prison had in mind when the program opened. For almost all the prisoners, art was nothing more than a cell hobby. They did landscapes, seascapes, Southwestern cowboy or Indian scenes. Others did prison art that included unique combinations of gun towers, cell bars, and Chicano and gang motifs.

I started to work on a strategy to sell my art to the staff members at the prison and to the public. To do this, I needed to create art unique to me—art so powerful they wouldn't be able to look away.

I sat down on the other five-gallon bucket and rolled back my mattress. I placed a sheet of illustration board on the steel bunk frame and just stared at it for the next few hours. I only stopped to get my dinner, which I didn't eat.

I allowed my mind to wander, using my imagination, and I opened it to the possibilities that lay there.

Sometime during the night I must have gone to bed, but as soon as I woke up I was back on that bucket, staring at the board. I did this for the next two days until the hand that held the graphite pencil began to move across the board. Once set in motion, my mind, vision, and hand became one. I worked in a frenzy for the next three weeks. I developed a routine designed to satisfy all my needs. I woke at 5 a.m., ate breakfast, read, went to yard at 6:30 a.m., returned at 1 p.m., cleaned the showers, worked from 2 p.m. until 11 p.m., read until 11:45 p.m., and slept from 12 a.m. to 5 a.m.

After nearly three weeks I finished my first piece showcasing my talent and skill as a realist. It was a scene of everyday life—a father and two boys playing in the front yard of their home. They had smiles on their faces as they played. I paid close attention to the detail of the house, their faces, landscapes, and the reaction generated by the interaction between the father and his sons.

I was satisfied I had accomplished what I set out to do. It was a piece anyone could relate to. It was appealing, yet contained every ounce of my talent and my skill to convey powerful emotion. I placed it at the back of my cell, facing the front for all to see.

During the next yard release, when dozens of bulls passed my cell, I made sure all of my lights were turned on so anyone who walked by and happened to look in would see it. I arranged my cell in a way to emphasize how clean I was and the discipline I lived by. The added PR element would help me sell pieces. I wanted to leave an impression on any bull who looked in my cell and spoke to me. I also wanted them to see my work for what it was—real art, not a cell hobby project.

"You going to yard today?" asked a bull I had never seen before named Tucker. He was an African American with white hair and a jumpsuit uniform instead of the regular pants and shirt.

"Yes, boss."

I began to strip, but he stopped me.

"Just hand me your shoes. You got any knives or swords I should know about?"

I laughed. "No, not today."

"Get dressed. I'm sure if you had anything I wouldn't find it. In my twenty-seven years here I've learned an important lesson. No matter how hard I look, I'll never find anything on a convict, even if he has something. An inmate is a different story. They're stupid and easy to catch. You don't strike me as an inmate so let's get you outside."

He seemed very easy-going with a confident manner, as if he knew what he was doing. He wasn't lazy. He was studying me and through our exchange had learned much more than if he had gone through all of my things and had me strip.

I decided to try something. I had been rehearsing in my mind to engage a potential buyer for my work. I knew just being an artist wouldn't be enough. I had to be my own dealer, PR person, and a likable individual to generate interest. Most of all, people had to remember me. I had to set myself apart from everyone else and earn their respect.

"That's interesting that you can read someone so quickly and distinguish between a convict and an inmate. That says a lot about your skills as an observer," I said.

"After so many years of this, believe me, I know."

"I believe you. Do you mind if I step back and put my work to the side? I don't want someone to see it and decide to take it."

"You did that?"

"Yes. It's a form of Hyperrealism in graphite." I picked up my work and brought it over for him to see close up.

"That's excellent work. I've never seen anything that detailed outside of a gallery. You go to art school?"

"I learned from my parents and on my own."

"Do you sell your work through the gift shop?"

"No. If I create a piece for a client it's through a contract approved by the warden's office."

"How does that work?"

"The warden has given me contracts to enter into with staff. It's like any business contract where we agree on a service and a price for that service."

"Do you have these contracts?"

"Sure."

"How much would you charge me for one of your pieces?"

"The price depends on the difficulty and size of the work." This was it. I had the conversation going and he seemed interested. But many deals are never completed because the seller doesn't know how to finish. I needed to finish. I pressed on.

"Do you do portraits?" he asked.

"I can take any idea you have and create it for you, including portraits. The materials I use are all professional grade and the piece will last for many generations. My work is guaranteed. If you take it to any established gallery and they don't appraise it for double what I charge you, I'll return your money and you keep my work. You will learn that my word is good, and that no one can do what I do."

I was taking a huge risk. If he didn't like my work, he could easily demand his money back and I would be out my time, work, and money with the guarantee I had given him.

"Depending on how much you charge, I'd like two pieces. One would be similar to the one you have there, except with African American people. For the second one, I'd like a portrait of Martin Luther King, Jr."

"Two pieces of that type and detail will take five and six weeks to finish, approximately one hundred twenty-five to one hundred fifty hours apiece. And my price is one hundred seventy-five dollars per piece, three hundred fifty dollars total, plus tax. I will need a signed contract before I start because another officer will be coming this afternoon, so the first one to sign a contract will be the one I start first."

I didn't want to press him too much and scare him away, but I also didn't want him to think he could come back later and sign. If he did, he might have to wait many weeks or months for me to make room for him on my busy schedule. I also knew that once he left he might forget to come back or decide not to buy my work.

"Let me see one of them contracts," he said.

By that time, everyone had gone by and yard had been released on the third tier, and they were releasing the fourth tier. I had to get the contract done quickly.

"I'll write both pieces up on one contract. When they're both finished, and you've seen them, I'll seal them and you can pick them up from the art manager to complete the sale. I do it this way to prevent someone from seeing your pieces and buying them on the spot."

"Go ahead and write it up and I'll sign. I don't want anyone touching what's mine."

I quickly wrote a description of the work I would do for him. We both signed.

"Thank you for the order. I look forward to starting your pieces."

"Thank you. I can't wait to see them when you're finished. I'll check in next month to see how you're doing."

"That sounds good. I should be close to finishing by then."

"Let's get you outside before someone starts wondering why we're up here shooting the breeze."

I laughed. "By the way, my name's Noguera. It's been a pleasure meeting you, Tucker."

"Call me Tuck," he laughed. "And the pleasure's all mine."

He escorted me downstairs, where I went through the pat down and wand before going outside. I was satisfied with myself that I had two pieces to do for pay. I had taken a step in the right direction. It was the first step in a very long journey.

Chapter 20

Orange County Jail, 1986

The guy with the hacksaw blades Trigger and Shotgun were waiting for came in and was placed in unit-A. During church the following Tuesday night, Trigger got the blades.

Prisoners from any part of the jail, regardless of housing assignment, could meet at church. Drugs, shanks, information, and in this case hacksaw blades, were passed along there.

As Friday drew near, I believed the escape would actually happen. The seventeen other men needed to carry the rope upstairs to the roof had been recruited, and in cell-4 a number of them were braiding long strips of sheets five feet long. They would be placed in each shoe of the twenty-five men involved. Of those men, only six planned to escape. I was sure, once others saw what was happening, they would run too, but I would not be one of them. For whatever reason, I had a bad feeling about the plan. It seemed solid, but I didn't like the number of people involved, and being on the run with no real goal just didn't appeal to me. Deep down, I still had something to lose.

On Friday at lunch time, Trigger asked me if he could get on the broom because he wanted to check all the braided rope and give everyone involved their ten feet.

I went into the cell and sat down at the dayroom table to watch the news when Chente approached me.

"What's up, man?"

"Nada, just kicking back while Trigger takes care of his business," I said.

"You haven't said much about this. Are you going with us? I got a place we can go to, get a ride, some cash, and be gone."

And then what? I thought. No one had a real plan after getting out. Being gone was not a plan, and if I decided to go it wouldn't be with any of them. They were killers and warriors, but fighting and killing was different than making it on the run. All of them would get caught within a week if they got out because they'd stay close to what they knew.

To be successful after an escape, you have to cut all ties, get far away, secure identification, and stay under the radar by living a normal and attention-free life. None of those guys could do that. Their plan was escape, have fun, continue to rob, steal, and kill. In other words, do exactly what they'd done their entire lives.

I respected them because of how dangerous they were, but they were not the type of men I would associate with outside of jail. I admired some of their qualities, but outside of these unique circumstances we would not be on friendly terms. I wore a mask that fooled them all and I would continue to wear it, but my act never fooled the one person that counted—me.

"I'll check it out and decide when I see how things turn out, but you should know this: if I decide to fly, I won't be going with you or anyone else. If I go, it'll be alone. My chances of making it are better that way," I said.

"I hear you, but my offer stands," he said.

"Gracias, I appreciate it."

He watched the news for a few more minutes, then got up and went to his bunk to lay down. He wasn't happy. He wanted me to come with him, but when I refused it was as if I'd let him down. Maybe I should have kept my thoughts to myself, but the last thing I needed was for him or any of the men to think I'd be going with them, then once out, change up on them. That could cost me. Maybe even my life.

I had to play my cards right. Although I had no intention of escaping, once I saw the open cage and others leaving, my mind might change. If it did, I wanted no misunderstandings.

Trigger gave everyone their pieces of the braided rope and placed handles on each of the four hacksaw blades to make sawing easier.

We went to dinner and got back by 5:30 p.m. Roof-yard would begin at 7 p.m. In the meantime I got on the broom and took note that everything seemed normal. The men involved were doing what they usually did. If I didn't know what was about to happen, I wouldn't have been tipped off by their behavior.

Maybe I was the one acting different. I had ten feet of rope coiled at the bottom of my shoes and I was nervous. Since I wasn't planning to escape, it all seemed like a bother to me and a completely unnecessary risk. The consequences behind the attempt, successful or not, would be huge. That's what I feared the most.

At ten minutes to 7 p.m. the unit officer stepped into his control booth and I hoped he would announce roof-yard was canceled. I've always had a sixth sense, and when it tells me something isn't right I listen. But what could I do in those circumstances? Could I say, "I'm sorry I don't want to be involved?" If I did and something went wrong, I'd be the scapegoat. I'd be blamed, or it would be rumored that I didn't want to help and maybe I told. My reputation would probably save me if that happened, and those who knew me would speak up for me, but what about those who didn't think highly of me? There were those who hid among the smiling faces who would love to see me brought down. They'd float the rumor again and again until someone smelled blood and they'd kill me like sharks.

As much as I didn't like the idea, I couldn't think of a good reason for not believing it would work. I still had a bad feeling about it, but voicing the concern would only bring unwanted attention.

The unit cop picked up the microphone. "Roof-yard. All inmates wishing to go to the roof, get ready. Five minutes to release."

All the doors opened and everyone stepped out. Normally about half the unit went to the roof, but that night everyone was going, which meant a lot more people knew what was going on and didn't want to stay behind. Maybe they wanted a chance to escape. Some likely didn't want to be the subject of scrutiny if something went wrong. Staying behind might suggest they told the cops what was happening. They could be stabbed and killed based on someone's speculation and frustration over the failed attempt.

I put the broom away and went over where Trigger, Shotgun, Chente, and another Mexican named Goofy were talking.

"This is good. With this many vatos going to roof, that lazy-ass placa won't search us. As soon as we get upstairs, Goofy will start tying the rope together in the bathroom. When he's done, he'll fold it up and carry it down to us. While he does that, Chente, go over and talk to the placa in his booth. Ask him the time and then bullshit with him about whatever to keep him from seeing Goofy with all that rope," said Trigger.

"Órale. I got it covered. Just do some fast cutting," said Chente.

"All right, gentlemen. Roof-yard release time. Everyone going, file out," yelled the cop.

We made our way to the hallway outside the unit where we were normally searched, and, as Trigger had said, the cop asked us to empty our pockets without even looking, then told us to go ahead to the roof.

As soon as I stepped out into the night, I was hit by sadness and a sense of longing. I'd been in jail for nearly two years and I was alone. I had never been in jail or done time before, and seeing the night sky always affected me in a way I didn't care to dwell on. But I couldn't help it. I thought of all the things I missed out on. I wondered where I would be if I hadn't lost control that night, and finally I bowed my head and thought of William and all of the things we could have done together. If only he hadn't been taken from me, he'd be two and a half years old.

This was how the thoughts always ended. I wiped my eyes to hide my tears, and replaced them with anger to fill the void where my future used to be.

I walked over to the rail in front of the ping-pong table and stood there as a game started. The roof was a huge area with a top level where I stood and a bottom level where there was a basketball court, handball court, volleyball court, and track.

An officer sat in his office in front of me and read a book. He was the only cop there, and he wouldn't step outside his office with as many prisoners as there were on the roof. If he saw something he'd simply call for backup and wait for the cavalry to arrive.

Whatever he was reading, it must have been great because he never looked up. In the meantime, Shotgun was directly behind me on the bottom level cutting away at the cage. I cast a glance his way and it occurred to me he wouldn't make it. There was just too much to cut in the time he had left. I turned back around to see the clock above the cop's office. It read 7:30 p.m. By that time, one by one, men were filing into the bathroom where Goofy was tying the pieces of braided rope together.

I waited another five minutes then made my way to the bathroom. When I stepped through the door, Goofy looked up and smiled at me.

"Órale, Sinbad. I'm almost done. Three more vatos' shoes and I'll take this to the fence. Think this shit will hold?"

"Man, if it doesn't, it's a long way down. Maybe only one should go at a time so there's not so much weight on it."

I took off my shoes and handed him the two pieces of braided rope I carried. As he took them and started tying them to the rest of the rope, I noticed how much rope there was and how difficult it could be to walk it all outside unnoticed.

"All right, ese. I'm gone," I said. I made my way back outside. Instead of watching the ping-pong game, which had too many people watching anyway, I went to the bottom level and walked around the outside of the basketball and volleyball courts. When I reached the handball court at the far side of the roof-yard, I allowed myself to look in the direction of where Trigger and Shotgun worked on the fence. Trigger cut and Shotgun kept watch. When Trigger got tired they'd switch places. They had cut about four feet straight down and needed another cut four feet across the bottom so they could fold the fence back and slip through, but they weren't going fast enough. They should have been working together while someone else watched their backs.

Goofy came out of the bathroom with all of the braided rope inside his jumpsuit. It was a dead give-away, but other prisoners surrounded him as he made his way to the bottom level of the yard and the cop was busy talking to Chente so he didn't notice anything.

Once he made it to the level where I was, Goofy took the braided rope out of his jumpsuit and laid it on the roof. He rolled it up in a bundle, similar to the ones rock climbers carry. Once the fence was open, he would have to slip out and tie the rope to the ventilation system and throw it over the side, hoping it didn't get tangled.

I glanced at the clock. It was 7:36 p.m. There wasn't enough time to finish at the pace they were working. When I neared them, Chente came over to see how far they needed to go and he must have also sensed they wouldn't make it. He grabbed one of the hacksaw blades and began to work on the fence with Trigger.

I continued to walk, stealing glances at their progress, and it seemed with Chente helping they had a chance. If they'd had the right tools from the start, it would have taken less than half an hour. But with plastic and cardboard handles attached to the blades themselves, it was far from easy, and luck would have to be on their side.

At 7:45 p.m. the bottom of the fence was close to being done. They attempted to fold and bend it back, but the cut wasn't big enough for them to fit through. Realizing this, they started to cut the remaining two links as fast as they could.

At 7:56 p.m. the cop in the office got on the loud speaker and announced the end of roof-yard time.

I looked at where Chente and Trigger were—they had failed. They'd tried to fold the fence back in place so it wouldn't be noticed right away, but that would depend on who came out to the roof next. If it was unit-C, they wouldn't say anything. The fence and braided rope would be ignored. But if it was a unit for soft inmates or P/Cs, they'd run and tell the cops as fast as they could.

Chente and Trigger managed to bend the fence back to where it wasn't easily noticed, but the braided rope was an entirely different story. If Goofy had five more minutes he could have taken it back into the bathroom and, with help, flushed most of it down the toilet. What was left could go back to the unit and be flushed there. But he hadn't thought ahead. By 7:50 he should have known the fence would not be cut on time, but it was too late. He hid the rope behind the equipment locker on the lower level. If no one noticed it, there stood a good chance no one would know which unit had been involved, especially with the segregation units using the roof in the mornings.

I climbed the ramp to the top level where the main door stood open and everyone filed out. I could tell a lot of the men were upset. Others understood that when the cops found out about the attempted escape they would tear our unit apart and a number of people would go to the hole for a very long time.

Once we were back in the unit, a quiet lingered. Everyone waited for the second shoe to drop. I got on the broom as I usually did because changing routines was a clear indication something was different, and the last thing I wanted was to draw attention to myself.

It was close to 10:15 p.m. when the unit cop walked into his control booth and told me to lock up.

"It's not eleven yet. I still haven't mopped the tier," I said.

"Don't worry about the tier. Just lock up."

I nodded and put the broom in the storage room, then went to my cell. The microphone clicked.

"All inmates . . . all inmates . . . emergency count. All inmates stand at the bars in full jail issue. Emergency count," the cop barked.

As soon as I entered my cell, a number of cops entered the unit holding books with our pictures in them and counted us. I could hear the same in other units.

They knew we went to the roof, but two other groups had gone after us and said nothing. It was the 10 p.m. roof group that told, which meant any of the Friday roof groups could have done it, and if no one had inspected the roof in the morning, as far as the cops were concerned, the attempt could have happened yesterday.

As soon as the cops left, Chente pulled me up.

"What are you thinking?"

"That they don't know who cut the fence. They'll find out no one's gone and relax. Then they'll begin interviews, but they'll wait to see if someone begins to brag about it or what rumors pop up. Hopefully these idiots will keep their mouths shut, but the entire unit knows about it and someone will open his mouth."

"Damn, we almost had it. A few more minutes and that would have been it."

"Yeah, that and twenty-five cents will buy you a fuckin' cup of coffee. Forget what could have been and worry about what's going to happen."

"Man, fuck these placas. They don't know shit. They're stupid."

"Maybe you're right," I said, but I knew different. The cops weren't stupid. If they didn't find out what happened, they'd wait, shake the tree, and see what fell out.

The weeks passed and nothing came of the attempted escape. Once everything went back to normal, everyone relaxed. We were allowed back to the roof and the evidence of the attempt was obvious. The entire bottom four feet of the fence had been double reinforced, so cutting it would be impossible. Mirrors had been installed in all the corners, so the cop in the roof office could see every part of the roof. All blind spots were eliminated, along with the possibility of escape.

I sat watching the news nearly six weeks after the attempt when the unit cop got on the microphone. Before he spoke, I knew something was wrong. I don't know how, but I knew it and I also knew it involved me. Over the previous couple of weeks I'd overheard conversations about the attempted escape, and the prisoners speaking were not in the unit when the attempt was made. Prisoners from another unit talking about it in such a casual manner meant the cops would soon know all about it.

"The following inmates, roll it up for housing change."

My stomach tightened.

"Gomez, 830-122; Martinez, 830-124; Silva, 818-145; Noguera, 730-256."

I looked at Chente. "Damn it. This is all I need," I said.

The names and numbers they had called belonged to Trigger, Shotgun, Chente, and me.

The announcement didn't include where we were headed, but as soon as I was in the unit vestibule and saw the red jumpsuits and chains waiting for us, I knew we were going to the hole.

They took and stored our property. We stripped naked and handed over our normal mustard yellow jumpsuits and put on the red ones worn only by prisoners in the hole. Our orange wrist bands were replaced with red ones that read K-10.

K-10 is the highest security level in the jail system.

I said nothing as we went through the process, but I knew it was about the attempted escape. If it were for drugs, fights, extortion, or any of the many things that routinely landed prisoners in the hole, we would simply be thrown in the hole for ten days. Changing the wrist bands meant our assignment had changed to segregation.

Even after completing our time in the hole, we wouldn't return to a normal unit. We would go to a four-by-eight-foot single-man cell in an isolation unit. There would be no TV, shower, or phone in the cell. If we wanted to shower, it was every other day, and we would have to walk down the tier and be locked in a dark and dank shower stall.

Finally, they put chains on us—leg irons, wrist cuffs, and chains to connect them all.

We walked to the hallway just outside the hole and were told to wait while the cops prepared our paperwork. I stood there, getting very angry. Another cop came up and explained the hole program. Breakfast and dinner were like normal for inmates, but for lunch we would only get onion soup. We would not be allowed phone calls, mail, or any communication. Showers were twice a week. There would be no talking. We would receive a mattress and sheet at 8 p.m., and at 3 a.m. we would turn it in. We would get it back the following night at 8 p.m.

I knew the routine, but it didn't ease my anger. I said nothing.

Trigger started joking around with Shotgun and laughing. I didn't know what was so funny, but it set off a firestorm of rage inside me and I began to boil. I watched Trigger as he continued his clown act.

"Hey, ese. Shut your fuckin' mouth," I said.

Maybe I shouldn't have talked to him that way, but I didn't care. I was angry and I wanted any excuse to focus my rage on someone so it wouldn't consume me.

"Fuck you, Mad. You ain't nobody. When we get out of here, we'll see if you have anything to say."

That's all I needed. I didn't say anything else. I had a goal when I got out of the hole and Trigger was it.

We were escorted down the stairs and into the hole where I was placed in a single-man cell with a heavy outer steel door. Inside was a toilet, sink, and bunk—nothing else in the cell. It was extremely hot and dark.

As the heavy door closed, a thought entered my mind. What would my father think if he had known as he held me at the age of six months that his son would one day be held in a dark cell, surrounded by killers. Alone.

Chapter 21

Adolescence, 1978–1979

I argued about what high school I wanted to attend, but it accomplished nothing. My mother had her own agenda and she was determined to put me in a private school.

She took the position that, since I had not been in a single fight at Immanuel First Lutheran, I should continue on at a private high school. She told my father that La Puente and Los Altos High Schools were full of gangs, and that instead of beating me up they would shoot me. She told him if he truly cared about me he could sacrifice a few dollars.

My mother ignored the obvious if it didn't fit her interpretation of reality. My main source of stress and abuse was centered at home from the two people who said they loved me—my parents.

If only I didn't care so much about my parents, then their problems wouldn't have affected me so deeply. But every time my father drank and my parents fought, I was consumed by distress, fear, depression, and despair. The turmoil I experienced meant one thing—I loved my parents, and while destroying themselves, they were also destroying me.

Throughout the summer, my mother scheduled appointments at private high schools for entry examinations, including Don Bosco, Bishop Amat, St. Francis, and others. The memories of Immanuel First Lutheran were fresh in my mind, and I didn't want to be singled out any more in a private school. I just wanted to be normal—another face in the crowd. I didn't believe going unnoticed would be possible at a private school. It was so overwhelming, I wet my bed almost every night, and that shame led to even more emotional scars. I was determined to somehow avoid the fate my mother had planned for me.

I sat outside under a tree waiting for my turn to take an entrance exam at Don Bosco. Another kid came over and asked if I had a light. I didn't know what he was talking about until he pulled out a cigarette.

"I don't smoke," I said.

"Oh well, no biggie. You here for the entry exams?"

"Yeah, but I don't wanna go to this school or any other one. I want to go to a public high school."

"Just fail the test. It's what I'm gonna do. They never give your parents the score, and you're scheduled to do the meet-and-greet today, right? Well, your parents will never know why they didn't accept you. As far as they're concerned, it could have been because they didn't like you. It's no big deal. These schools turn down just about everyone who applies, so don't sweat it. The main thing is you won't have to go to this school."

"Man, are you sure my parents won't see the score?"

"I'm sure. My brother did it last year and all my parents got was a nice letter saying that the enrollment had been filled."

I wasn't sure if I believed him. The last thing I wanted was for my parents to find out. If that happened, I'd be in serious trouble.

"Hey, I'm Kent. Sit next to me and just watch me. I'm going to fill out the little squares without even looking at the test. Then I'll sit for a while and leave. It's that simple."

"I'm Bill. All right, I'll check it out."

We walked in together and, true to his word, he did exactly what he said he'd do when he received his test. I took a deep breath and did the same. Halfway through, I looked over at him and he was almost done. But what if things had changed since last year? What if they sent my parents the test score? Even worse, what if my mother came to the school and demanded to know why I hadn't been accepted?

I decided attending another private school was worse than any beating my father could give me, and I continued filling in the blank squares without looking at the questions.

On the way home, my mother was excited about me attending Don Bosco, and talked about how it was a great school, and that from there I would attend a major university.

On and on she talked, until she suddenly stopped and began crying. I was used to my mother's changes of mood, but it still confused me and made me uncomfortable.

Nevertheless, I purposely failed every test I took that summer, and as the school year neared it seemed I would end up at Puente or Los Altos High. At least that's what I thought. My mother was more resourceful than I gave her credit for, though. Since I had not been accepted at any of the private schools that required an entrance test and interview, she simply found one that only required tuition payment.

What my parents didn't take into consideration was the simple fact that, since no entrance test or interview was required at Heights Lutheran, a lot of the kids there were trouble and had been kicked out of other schools. All of the kids weren't bad, but plenty of them were there only because their parents could pay the high tuition. Heights Lutheran was in Turnbull Canyon, in the midst of some of the most expensive homes in the area.

As the school year started a lot of things were different in my life. Most notable was the physical difference. By the midway mark of my freshman year, I was no longer the little five foot two inch, one-hundred-pound boy with short hair and painfully awkward looks. In his place stood a six foot one inch, 170-pound young man with lean muscle and long black hair that reached past my shoulders. Still, the biggest change was internal. I no longer feared anything or anyone.

The steroids my father continued to give me changed everything. I was a walking time-bomb with a hair-trigger temper.

I was still me, but my mood swings were sudden and violent. One moment I was fine and the next, for no apparent reason, I'd become angry and the storm inside me would explode, led by my beasts.

I was sensitive to anyone's criticism, and more than that to any attempt to push me around. Of course in high school that sort of thing always happened, but I made it obvious that if anyone messed with me they'd be sorry.

I was only a freshman, but thanks to my height and athletic ability, I went out for the cross-country and basketball teams, making varsity in both.

All of those accomplishments only added to my confidence. Unlike other freshmen, I was accepted by the older kids. Although I felt good about all of those things, resentment grew inside me and led me to hide who I truly was. I still believed if anyone saw the real me they'd laugh, as so many had in the past. I was so afraid that I buried my true self deep down and wore a mask to compensate. I wore one at school, one at home, another at the beach, and at fighting competitions, yet another.

It came to a point that I didn't know who I was anymore. It was all a performance and the lines of truth blurred. I simply changed my personality according to environment and those who surrounded me.

The one true thing I knew—the thing that never changed no matter what mask I wore—was my rage and pain. To me, those elements were as real as the clothes I wore. They protected me and gave me the will to take on anything, simply by touching that part of me. With my beasts, I could overcome any odds.

Sometimes, when my emotions were raw, I didn't have to reach for the beasts. They simply took on a mind of their own and controlled me.

It became apparent after the fight at the beach with The Boyz. When it happened again and the results were the same, it didn't scare or worry me because it gave me the reputation I wanted—to be the guy nobody should mess with.

In high school, being feared made me popular and it led to acceptance. I knew I didn't want only to be feared. I wanted to be liked too. But a part of me felt that if I couldn't be loved, then being feared wasn't a bad alternative.

To say I was extremely sensitive to other's opinions of me would be an understatement. I still didn't see how I appeared to others. To me,

I was still an ugly kid no one liked, and the only real reason anyone spoke to me was because of my reputation and the mask I hid behind.

Most days, I went to class alone. A lot of people said hello to me and I'd always acknowledge them with a simple smile or "what's up." No one knew a lot about me aside from what they saw at school, and heard. I was aloof without trying to be. I was just unsure of myself, so I kept everyone at arm's distance.

As I walked to class just after the Christmas holidays in 1978, I came around a corner and saw three juniors had a little kid up against the wall, messing with him. I was late for class, but I slowed to see what was up. One of the juniors, a guy named Benny, had the small kid up by the neck and had slapped his glasses off his face and kept calling him "Frogman." His friends, who I knew as well, were Mark and Greg. They were all bullies and they thought they were being funny.

As I neared them I saw a scared kid who was powerless and hated that he couldn't do anything to help himself. I knew exactly how he felt because, not long before, I'd been him.

"Hey, give it a rest, man," I said.

Benny and his friends turned around, saw me, and ignored me.

I walked up to them and noticed the little kid was crying.

"What, you didn't hear me? I said leave him the fuck alone."

"Fuck you, Bill. You ain't gonna do shit," said Benny.

I passed Mark and Greg and shoved Benny back.

"Fuck you, punk, I said leave him alone."

Benny, used to bullying anyone he wanted, didn't hesitate and attempted to push me back. I didn't have time for a shoving match. Before his hands touched me, I sidestepped his advance and punched him twice in the face. He fell and turned to look up at me.

"How does it feel? Get up. I'm dying to trash you," I said.

He got up, but the look in his eyes said it all. He was afraid. But I didn't want it to end there. I knew his ego was hurt and he was scared, but it wouldn't take much to get him to react.

"You just going to stand there, punk motherfucker? I knew you were a bitch and all talk."

I hadn't finished the sentence and he was already moving toward me, which was exactly what I expected him to do.

"Fuck you, I'll kick your ass," he screamed as he rushed at me headfirst as if he meant to tackle me.

Benny didn't know how to fight. He pushed people around and bullied them because they were smaller and weaker. But when faced with someone who hit back, he was lost.

As soon as he lowered his head and attacked, I jumped up and kicked him in the face with a jump front kick, and he pitched forward and fell again. This time he didn't get up.

I turned to his two partners. "If you fuck with him again, if you even call him some fucked up name, I promise, I'll fuck up both of you punks," I said as I went to Greg and shoved him hard.

"You hear me, punk?" I asked.

"Dude, we were only playing with him."

I slapped him hard across the face.

"Shut the fuck up. You heard me. Fuck with him and I'll fuck you up."

I turned around and walked up to the kid, who I didn't know.

"If anyone fucks with you, come tell me and I'll make them sorry."

He just nodded. God, I felt bad for him. I was once that little scared boy. We were the same age, but I had changed. No one would ever make me feel that way again, and if I saw someone doing it to someone else, they'd have to answer to me. I hated bullies and I was just looking for an excuse, any excuse, to make them feel what they made others feel.

Benny and his buddies had recovered enough to give me a dirty look, but they knew better than to say anything to me.

"Are you all right?" I asked the kid.

"Yeah." He was still crying. "Thanks. They always do this to me and I don't know why." He began to cry harder, and my anger simmered.

"They won't anymore, okay?"

He nodded.

"Come on, let's go to class. What class do you have? I'll walk you."

"Algebra with Ms. Shelton," he said.

My mom and dad in
Colombia, South America,
before their marriage and
arrival in California. (1962)

My first baby portrait at
six months old. (1964)

Mom and Dad celebrating my first birthday and waiting for the birth of my little sister in Los Angeles, California. (1965)

Me at age three at my desk, practicing drawing fundamentals. (1967)

My first boxing lesson,
at age four. (1968)

My little sister and me
in happier times. (1969)

My third-grade school portrait at Sparks Elementary. (1970)

Duck hunting with my dad in Bakersfield, California. (1971)

In competition at the Four Seasons Open Tournament, where I won my first junior title. (1972)

Our last family portrait, taken soon after our return from vacation in Colombia. Shortly afterward our family was destroyed. (1973)

My father wheeling his katana swords at a martial arts demonstration in Long Beach, California. (1973)

Portrait of me at eleven years old, upon earning my sixth-degree blue belt and becoming a member of the Hapkido Championship Team. (1975)

Hiking at Monrovia Peak, California, with a friend and my dog, Bullet. This is where I would soon discover my secret cave and hallowed ground. (1977)

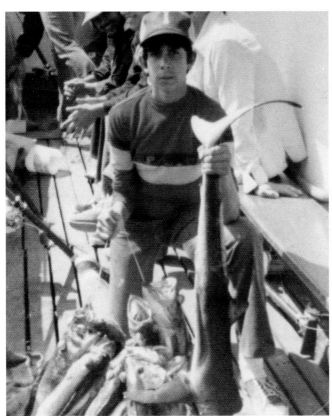

Deep-sea fishing for Rock Cod and Blue Shark in Seal Beach, California. (1977)

In my backyard with my first buck after hunting at Monrovia Peak, California. (1978)

The Hapkido Championship Team members (left to right): Jeff, Carlos, me, and Jim. (1979)

My teacher Master Yim and me at the Hapkido Championship Tournament, where at sixteen years old I won my first men's title. (1979)

Hunting for deer with my father near Monrovia Peak, California. (1980)

Sitting on my dad's Honda GL 1000 Gold Wing motorcycle on our way to the ski-lifts at Mount Baldy, California. (1980)

With my 12-second 1963 California Bug, shortly after meeting Vanessa. (1981)

Meditating before my match at the Long Beach Open Tournament. (1981)

At the Long Beach Open Tournament, connecting with my first kick on the way to my second championship. (1981)

With my grandfather at my high
school graduation. Later that same
evening I'm nearly stabbed to
death. (1982)

With my dog, Sebu, next to my '62 VW convertible only a few months after
I was attacked at knife-point. (1982)

My daily routine of
practicing martial arts at
San Quentin State Prison. (1991)

On the yard at
San Quentin Death Row,
age twenty-eight. (1998)

Visitors to my self-titled art exhibition at the San Francisco Design Center Galleria
artSFest Arts Expo Gala. (2005) PHOTO: ALAN BAMBERGER AND ARTBUSINESS.COM

A replica of my cell on display at my "Shadowed Views" art exhibition at the Space Gallery. (2006)

"Shadowed Views" art exhibition at the Space Gallery. (2006)

My solo art and film exhibition at Yerba Buena Center for the Arts. My work is placed leading to the entrance of the film-screening based on the work titled *Ghost in the Material.* (2007)

My solo art exhibition titled "Drawings" at Braunstein Quay Gallery. (2008)

With my dad during a visit at
San Quentin State Prison. (2009)

A visit with Melissa, my lifelong friend
and executive director of the William A.
Noguera Trust. (2012)

My first visit meeting with friend and mentor Walt Pavlo Jr. of *Forbes*, with Melissa. (2013)

I took him to Ms. Shelton's room, and when she saw us she came out.

"What happened, Bobby? Are you okay?"

I answered for him. "Some guys were picking on him and I stopped it. He's okay."

She looked at me, and for a moment, I could tell she wondered if it had been me who had bullied him.

"Ms. Shelton, Bill helped me and beat up Benny because he was hitting me." Bobby was crying again.

"It was nothing. They won't hit him anymore. I'll make sure of that."

"Bobby, go sit down," she told him. He went inside and, as he did, he said, "I'll see you later, Bill."

"Right on, Bob," I said.

Ms. Shelton turned to me. "Thank you for helping Bobby. He's small and everyone picks on him and he just doesn't know how to deal with it. But please don't get yourself into trouble."

"No worries, I'll be fine," I said.

She nodded and I went to class.

By lunch time, just about everyone knew about what I had done to Benny and his friends, but most importantly they knew why I had done it. I sat alone next to the stairs at the front of the school drinking an Orange Crush, just watching the cars pass by, when Bobby came up to me.

"What's up, Bill?"

I turned to him, but the look on my face must not have been pleasant because Bobby started to walk away.

"Hey Bobby, what's up? Come and kick back with me."

"Are you sure? I don't want to bother you and you don't look happy that I'm here."

"It's not that. You just surprised me. You're cool, and any time you feel like talking, don't trip. We're friends."

Bobby had seen my face when I wasn't hiding behind a mask. What he saw was hurt and pain—raw and in plain sight. When I realized what he had seen, I shoved the mask in place so the anger would show through my eyes.

"So, what's on your mind? Are you okay? Benny and his girlfriends haven't messed with you, have they?"

He laughed. "That's funny. No one's ever called them that. But they're afraid of you, so you can say anything."

"Yeah, but if they pick on you, tell me. I want them to know that picking on you is like picking on me. We're friends and friends look after each other, right?"

"Yeah, but what can I do for you? I don't know how to fight."

"That's the great part about being friends, you don't have to be or do anything. Just be you, all right?"

He nodded, but I could see he was uncertain. No one like me, or at least who looked like me, had ever offered him friendship, and he didn't understand. The truth was I wasn't entirely sure myself.

I wanted to protect him from the pain and humiliation he suffered at the hands of bullies. I also didn't want him to go through what I had, and that's what moved me to action.

Maybe it wasn't friendship I offered him, but he didn't have to know that. What was important was he wouldn't be messed with as long as I was around. That thought alone made me smile. It gave me the excuse I needed to make bullies pay.

High school is a strange place. Appearances and opinions are everything. Something so simple, such as hanging around the right person or group, can give you a certain authority or right to act a certain way. I was a varsity athlete, but I never hung around with the team. It just seemed cheesy to put on a letterman jacket and hang out together.

Most of the time, I was just off listening to music, drawing, and doing my own thing. I did that in part because I had spent so many years alone and felt uncomfortable in groups. I still wasn't sure how well I wore my mask, or whether there were holes in it where people could see the real me.

Another reason was, none of those guys measured up to The Pack. To me, the guys in high school, at least the ones I knew, were lames and wannabees. They dressed and talked like surfers, and some even surfed a few times, but that didn't make them surfers.

Bobby didn't want to impress me and he didn't try to be someone he wasn't. For that reason, I talked to him and sometimes we ate lunch together. In the process, I began to like him. His father was a doctor and his mom was a lawyer, and often they'd wave at me when they picked Bobby up.

Nearly a month after my confrontation with Benny and his two partners in crime I came out of my world religion class and was heading for my locker when I saw Mark by the far corner of the gym standing watch. Normally I would have ignored it, but something told me I shouldn't. It was lunch time, and since I wouldn't be late to any class I decided to see what was up. Taking the long way around the gym, I came to the opposite corner from where Mark stood and looked. There, about halfway down, near the stairs that led to the parking lot, stood a bunch of people looking at something. I knew Benny was involved since Mark was keeping watch.

I went down to where everyone stood and that's when I saw Greg push Bobby to the ground. Bobby got up and tried to walk past Greg, but was pushed back again. Benny sat just a few feet away, lighting Bobby's model planes on fire. He placed them on the small wall where he sat and, one by one, he burned them.

I guess after a month, a bully's brain resets itself and forgets everything, because otherwise he had to know I'd find out. Or maybe they talked themselves into believing they'd be able to deal with me. Either way, I was done playing. This time I'd make sure they remembered me and why I punished them. I jumped down to where Greg held Bobby. I took three quick steps and, as Greg saw me, I hit him in the face. He doubled over to cover himself and I kicked him in the face, staggering him before he turned to run.

Benny saw it and stood up, leaving Bobby's planes in ruin. I didn't say anything. He knew what to expect and acted on it. As soon as we were close enough, he threw two looping punches, hoping to connect with my face, but he missed. In return, he got a vicious upper cut to the jaw that turned his legs to rubber. I picked my shot and connected a crushing right cross to his eye, dropping him to the ground. When he tried to stand, I grabbed him by the throat and got in his face.

"I told you. Fuck with him and I'd fuck you up. Do it again and I'll break your fuckin' arm."

I punched him in the face again. I looked at Bobby, who had tears in his eyes, but I could see his anger, too. He hated Benny and Greg, but he hated himself even more for not being able to do anything about how they treated him.

"You okay, Bobby? I'm sorry I wasn't here fast enough."

"My models are ruined. I worked all summer on them and now they're ruined."

Only then did I have the opportunity to look closely at his models, and I understood. They were not simple models. They were small-scale replicas of the real thing. Bobby had put the fighter planes together perfectly and painted them to match.

Benny and his buddies would pay for them. It was as simple as that, and I would be the collector.

The next morning I arrived at school early. For the past few months, I'd ridden my bike to school on the days it didn't rain. Since I ran the hills surrounding the school each morning before school, riding my bike saved my mom the trouble of taking me. At least that's what I told her.

The truth was, I liked being alone and the four-mile bike ride gave me that.

That day, after locking my bike at the school, I ran four miles and showered quickly. I normally ran five miles, but I wanted to be in the school parking lot before anyone arrived. I had a job to do and I didn't want to be late for my first day at work.

I stood by a large tree just to the side of the parking lot and waited. Benny pulled up in his mini truck. It was all fixed up, lowered with chrome wheels and a nice paint job. Greg and Mark were with him. As soon as he parked and they got out, I peeled away from the tree and walked up to them. As I neared, I could see the effects of my beating on their faces. Benny had a black eye and his mouth was swollen. Greg had a large bruise on his cheek. But other than that he looked fine. As soon as they saw me, they stopped and watched me. I went right up to them.

"I told you not to fuck with Bobby. You ruined his models, so you'll be paying him back."

Mark said, "I'm not paying for—"

Before he could finish, I slapped him hard across the face.

"What? I didn't hear you. You're not paying?" When he didn't respond I said, "Yeah, that's what I thought."

Mark just looked at me while he touched his face. I knew it stung.

"The way I see it, you owe Bobby a hundred bucks for his models, his time, and because I told you if you fucked with him again I'd trash you."

"Man, those planes aren't worth a hundred bucks," Benny said.

"Maybe not. But your truck is, right? Every day goes by that you don't pay me, I'll take something from your truck. Piss me off and see what happens. I promise you, paying Bobby back will be a lot cheaper than fixing the damage I'll put on your ride."

I looked at Greg. "I've always wanted a killer skateboard like this." I grabbed the board he was holding. "Man, this is clean. Thanks." I turned and walked away.

"What about my board?" Greg said, and without turning back I replied, "You'll get it back when you and your girlfriends pay up. Piss me off and I'll light it on fire."

As I climbed the stairs to the gym, I saw Bobby running toward me. "What's up, Bill?"

"Nada. Just thought we could try out my new board."

"That's a really nice board. When did you get it?"

"A few minutes ago. Greg donated it to the Bobby fund."

At first he just looked at me. Then he realized what I was saying. "Oh. You took it from Greg. That's funny."

"Yeah, try it out. It's ours 'til they pay you back for messing up your models. I told them they had to pay you a hundred bucks and every day they don't pay I'd take something from them." Bobby seemed unsure, but I said, "Don't worry. I'll handle it, and this time they'll learn to leave you alone."

Bobby smiled. "All right, can I try out our board?"

I laughed. "Yeah, go for it."

While Bobby played, Benny, Mark, and Greg came up from the

parking lot. They looked at me, then at Bobby riding the board. I smiled at them and thought, *Payback's a bitch.*

I carried the skateboard around the rest of the day. I liked that Bobby told everyone what I had done. The news about the fight yesterday also spread through the school. When I passed people I saw their looks and heard what they said. To me it was the easiest lesson I'd ever learned. They respected me because they feared me.

At lunch time, I sat talking to Bobby when a girl came up. I knew her name was Michelle, but I never really talked to her. She was a junior, so we didn't have classes together.

"Hi Bill, can I talk to you?"

"Hi Michelle. Yeah, what's up?"

Bobby smiled and made his eyebrows go up and down real fast. I laughed.

"You're an evil little guy, Bobby."

I stood up and took a few steps to where she stood.

"I was wondering what you were doing this Saturday night. I'm having a party at my house and my parents will be gone. Do you want to come?"

"Yeah. That would be cool. I don't know how long I can stay, but I'm there."

She smiled at me. "Here's my number. Call me and I'll tell you how to get there."

"No doubt. I'll call you. Thanks for inviting me."

She walked away and I couldn't help staring at her. She was something else. About five foot five, with long, straight black hair that fell past her shoulders, blue eyes, and a nice body she showed off as often as possible in short, revealing outfits. And she wanted me to come to her house. I looked at the number she'd written.

"So, are you going?"

I had forgotten Bobby.

"Yeah, I think so. I'll call her and see what's up. I have a lot of stuff to do, but I'll probably go."

"She lives in the Heights, about a block from me." I suddenly realized she hadn't invited him.

"Hey bro, I'm sorry you weren't invited," I said.

"Don't worry about it. I'm only a freshman."

"Yeah, but so am I and she invited me."

"You don't look like any freshman I know. Don't sweat it. Even if she invited me, my parents would never let me go."

I looked at the number again. I'd go, but I wouldn't stay long. I just had too much to do. It seemed like no matter what, I always had something, some responsibility, to attend to. During the week my day started at 5 a.m. with a light breakfast and twenty sets of pushups, jump squats, and pull-ups. I'd then ride my bike to school and run five miles, shower, then go to class. After school, depending on the sports season, I'd go to basketball practice, or track. Then I'd go home, eat, feed my animals, and do the rest of my chores. On Monday, Tuesday, and Wednesday I'd ride to the Hapkido studio and train for three hours, return home, and do my homework. Then if I had time, and if I could sit still, I'd pull out my sketchbooks and draw and arrange mathematically-based forms.

On Thursday and Friday my schedule was the same except, instead of going to the Hapkido studio, I went to Jeff Runge's small training school where I learned wrestling, grappling, and ground-fighting techniques. On the weekends I surfed early and met up with The Pack, went hunting or fishing, and on certain weekends entered surf competitions or participated in fighting competitions. Since being sponsored by Aquatic Pulse, I had entered three surf contests and, although I didn't win, I did well, loved surfing, and enjoyed being part of a team. Fighting was a different story. I rarely lost, and when I did, it was because I was disqualified for being too aggressive and hurting my opponent. The competitions I entered were based on a points system, or controlled fighting. As I got older and more aggressive, the rules made me angry. I didn't see the point in pulling punches and kicks, so when I fought it was for one objective—to knock my opponent out. Anything else seemed silly to me and a waste of time. The steroids made me more and more aggressive, impatient, and short-tempered. I couldn't sit still before because of the ADHD, and I'd become even worse on steroids. My mind was in constant motion, and I often felt as if I'd lose control.

I had a fighting competition in two weeks, and although I was in the middle of training, I'd go to Michelle's party. I liked her, and for the first time someone had asked me to a party.

I wondered why she'd asked me to her party. I realized it was out of respect and because of my reputation and how I looked. From that moment on, I saw myself differently. I understood how I appeared to others and how well the mask I wore fit.

That afternoon before school ended, I asked to use the bathroom, but instead went to the parking lot. I went directly to Benny's truck and popped off his Tornado mirrors, then threw them in the trash as I went back to class. I smiled to myself. Now that I had power, I could make up for all the years I'd suffered at the hands of bullies.

The next morning before school started, Benny, Mark, and Greg came up to me while I spoke to Michelle, and gave me a hundred dollars.

"Can I have my board back?" asked Greg.

"Yeah, go for it." I pushed the board to him.

"How about my mirrors?" Benny asked.

"What mirrors?"

"The ones you took off my truck."

"Dude, I don't know what you're talking about. But I'll tell you this, fuck with Bobby again and we'll do this all over again, but it will double. Now get the fuck away from me."

I watched them walk away.

"Oh my God, that's so cool. You made them pay you for messing with Bobby," Michelle said.

"No, I made them repay him for ruining his models. This money's for him."

"I've known Benny since elementary school. He's always picked on people and gotten away with it."

"Things are about to change for him."

On the way to first period, I saw Bobby and gave him his money. He just stared at it.

"Thanks, Bill," he said.

"Listen, I know it doesn't make up for your time, but maybe you can buy some new ones and rebuild them. The bottom line is that everyone knows not to fuck with you. If they do, I'll pound them."

"Yeah, but what do you get out of all this?"

I laughed even though there was nothing funny about it.

"I get to beat up bullies."

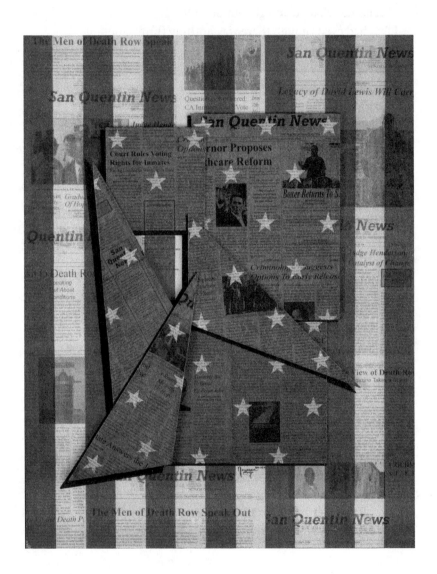

Chapter 22

San Quentin Death Row, 1989

Drawing always came naturally to me. I was determined to use it as my anchor to ground and protect me from the world inside San Quentin.

During my senior year in high school, I took an art class and learned a unique way to draw solely using dots. I don't remember much about the class except this technique, and after so many years an idea formed. Using the set of technical pens the handicraft manager gave me, I experimented until I fully grasped the potential of the technique.

After only a month, I replaced working in graphite pencil with ink stippling, and when a potential buyer came to me for one of my pieces, I would show him and explain my unique way of drawing with only dots. It seemed to fascinate everyone who saw the drawings, and after only creating two of them for staff members of San Quentin, word spread about my work. I'll admit, I didn't believe my technique or my delivery was as clear as when I drew with graphite and regular pen. Nevertheless, the orders continued to come, to the point I was turning them down until I could catch up. That only seemed to put me in more demand. I raised my prices and was still a year behind. I had a real sense of accomplishment because my work was so sought after. No one at San Quentin sold their work solely through contracts as I did. The handicraft manager even suggested I reduce my prices, as she put it, "so everyone can afford to buy one."

I wasn't interested in her suggestions. If anything, I thought my prices were too low. But I wasn't complaining. I had work. I was practicing and perfecting my voice and technique and being paid for it. I was also sending money home every month to help my family.

Most men here would be satisfied with that, but I wasn't. That ambition, that sense of wanting to be heard, drove me forward. I didn't want to merely "work for" someone. True, I needed to continue to get commissions to support myself, but what I truly wanted—what I thought of constantly—was the freedom to work for myself. As an artist, I wanted to create what I felt and needed to express, without limitation. I couldn't do that while I spent most of my time working on commissions.

My solution to the problem, at least temporarily, was to make a personal expression book, where I drew and expressed myself fully, crossing into dark territory where my subconscious and vision became one.

Each night, I'd completely abandon myself to expression and the power I seemed to be able to invoke but not fully control. My time was limited, so for one hour each night I crossed over and worked. This, at least, was the plan. But often I didn't stop until morning. Time ceased to exist. The only thing that mattered was bringing my emotions to life.

Those drawings I showed to no one. They were a look into the deepest part of my soul where my emotions and dreams, mixed with the influences around me, took flight and demanded attention. There, also, in those drawings and images, I worked with mathematically-arranged geometric forms and broke up the layout of the drawings and images. Each form was based on a coordinating number system that brought order and ended the chaos inside me when arranged together to complete a number combination. The images weren't simply for the eyes. Beauty wasn't the goal. Truth, an accurate representation of my interior sensation and experience, was what pushed me to those depths. And although I wasn't ready to show anyone my work, an idea was born. It burned inside me and drove me forward. I wanted the world to see me, and wanted my voice to be heard. I constantly thought of exhibiting my work. The pieces I did on commission were simply pretty pictures and, to me, as insignificant as wallpaper. I believe true art is about rendering the barest of human emotion for the world to see through images that trigger the mind's wanderings and fill the viewer with the very emotions that possess me when I create them.

I wanted to be known as an artist and respected in the art world by my contemporaries. But I wasn't ready. I needed to be comfortable with my true work and I needed to complete a body of work I could show.

I also feared that galleries wouldn't take me or my work seriously. I didn't want them to use me as if I were a circus act. I decided to wait and bide my time. I'd labor to complete a significant body of work, and only then present it to a gallery for serious consideration.

Meanwhile I continued taking on commissions and perfecting my technique and style. Late at night, when everyone slept, I crossed over into dark territory and truly worked out my problems, calming the chaos that seemed quieted only by the complete embrace of my imagination and vision.

Sales of my work had not gone unnoticed by the man who gave me a chance to do something with my talent. Nearly a year to the day after he gave me my grade-A status and sent me to East Block, Warden Vasquez and one of his captains appeared in front of my cell. Just like the first time he came to my cell in the AC, I didn't notice they were there. I had my headphones on while I worked and I was oblivious to their presence until they flashed their light in my eyes.

I took off my headphones and was surprised by the warden standing at my door.

"Mr. Noguera, how are you? I've come by to see how you're doing."

"I'm doing well, Warden Vasquez. I'm finishing up a piece for one of your officers. I'm sorry I didn't respond right away. I listen to music while I work and it's hard to hear anyone at my door."

"It's quite all right. I've been following your progress and noticed you're taking on a lot of contract work. Honestly, you've surprised me. I normally give a convict a chance like I gave you, only to find myself regretting it. But with you, I must say, you've exceeded all my expectations. May I see what you're finishing?"

"Of course. I have only about ten hours more and I'll finish it, but I believe you'll get a good idea of what I'm doing."

The warden and the captain both looked at the portrait of Joe Montana I was finishing.

"Captain Hales, was I wrong in telling you Mr. Noguera would help you win your bet?" the warden asked.

The Captain laughed, "There's no doubt in my mind. No doubt."

"Mr. Noguera, the Captain is interested in commissioning you to do two pieces, both portraits. One of JFK and the other of Ronald Reagan."

"Gentlemen, I'm presently booked solid until next year. I've even turned down orders because of the long list of clients already waiting for my work."

"That's unfortunate. I was really hoping you could help me."

I did a quick mental evaluation and decided to make an exception. I needed high ranking officials to appreciate and allow me to order the materials I needed to reach the level I envisioned I'd someday reach.

"Captain Hales, I'll finish this piece by tomorrow and I'll make room for you. What do you have in mind?"

"Well, as the warden mentioned, I'd like two portraits. I've brought you two small pictures I'd like you to use. I'd also like them done in dots like the portrait there of Montana. The portraits are for me, but an associate warden at Folsom Prison is convinced he has the best artist in the system there. I want to prove him wrong and win the bet we made."

"I'll be happy to prove you right, but please understand, art is not about who makes a picture look life-like. There are different types of styles and mediums, so it's difficult to judge whose is better. But I understand what you want. You want the work to be hyper-realistic as if it were a photograph."

"Yes, that's exactly what I want. How much will you charge me?"

"Two portraits, approximately twenty by twenty-six inches, will take one hundred fifty to one hundred ninety-five hours per piece to complete, and will run three hundred seventy-five dollars per piece. A total of seven hundred fifty dollars."

I was taking a risk in raising my prices. But I believed the work spoke for itself, and everyone who bought one of my pieces always came back to order more, telling me how the galleries that framed the work spoke highly of the unique style and technique I used.

"That's fair. When will they be done?"

"Give me five weeks and I'll have them ready for you. Let me fill out a contract and we'll both sign it, making this agreement official."

I prepared the contract and we both signed, then, to my surprise, the Captain opened my food port and put his hand through to shake my hand.

"Thank you for taking time from your other work to help me. I appreciate it," he said.

"The pleasure's mine, Captain. Thank you for the order and for believing in my work."

I then turned to Warden Vasquez. "Warden, I never had the opportunity to thank you for asking the handicraft manager to stop by when I first came to East Block so I could enter the program. She brought me art materials at your behest. Thank you." I put my hand through the food port and the warden shook it.

"I gave you a chance, much like I've given many other men. You made something of it. You did that, not me. This job rarely gives me the chance to see someone actually grow into something positive. Seeing what you're doing gives me that chance."

"I appreciate that."

Once they left, I sat and stared at the contract we signed and then at the pictures he gave me to work from. I knew what I'd do and how I'd do it. I also became very aware of how badly I wanted the Captain to win his bet. Not for him, but for me. It was me, my work, that would be judged and I wanted no doubt in anyone's mind who was the best. I wanted my work to be known in and out of prison. I wanted my name to be recognized and respected. I decided nothing would stop me from accomplishing that goal. Prison walls would not be enough to stop my escape.

Two weeks after finishing the captain's portraits, he stopped by my cell while I got ready to clean the showers.

"How are you, Captain? I see you picked up your portraits. Were you pleased with my work?"

"I am more than pleased. The portraits are absolutely stunning. I've framed and compared them to the work my friend in Folsom was so pleased with. Although his work was very nice, what you did, and how photo-realistic it is, blew him away. I came by to tell you that and, again, thank you."

"You're welcome. I was happy to help."

The Captain nodded. "Enjoy your day, Mr. Noguera."

After cleaning the shower, I turned on the hot water and, as the water cascaded over me, I thought, *I've taken yet another step with many more to go, but I'm on my way. Art will be my vehicle of escape.*

Chapter 23

Orange County Jail, 1986

In a moment of anger I allowed myself the freedom to say exactly what was on my mind. Usually once the anger fades following a heated exchange, we regret the harsh words that seemed so appropriate in the passion of the moment. During my nine days in the hole, I repeatedly played back my last conversation with Trigger. But each time the result was the same. I didn't regret it.

Trigger would be coming for me. In fact, at that very moment he was probably developing a plan to deal with me. Chente, Shotgun, Trigger, and I would move to a segregation unit on our tenth day. I had to be ready to deal with Trigger.

I thought of ways I could avoid the confrontation. Since I started it, I could apologize and say I was just angry. I quickly dismissed that option. Gang members like Trigger are consumed with protecting their reputation, and the way I talked to him demanded action. He would accept my apology, then wait until I relaxed and thought everything was fine—then he'd try to kill me. It was as simple as that. Trigger was a soldier, a convict, and a killer who couldn't allow anyone to disrespect him as I had.

I wondered if he still had a hacksaw blade. If he did, he would cut a piece with my name on it. We both knew there could be no turning back. But when the time came, knife or no knife, Trigger would fall.

I briefly considered another option. I could apologize to him, then wait for my chance to strike when he let his guard down. But using deception to gain a tactical advantage was cowardly and had never been my style.

The afternoon of the tenth day, we were escorted to the segregation unit in chains. From that point on, I would be in chains with an escort anytime I left the unit. The chains consisted of handcuffs and leg irons, both attached to a chain around my waist.

We stood in the vestibule of the unit as the officer in charge decided which cells to put us in. Trigger and Shotgun said nothing to me the entire time.

Finally, Chente stood next to me and said, "Ponte trucha. Watch out." I nodded.

"Silva, Noguera, 29-9 and 29-10," the unit cop said.

My escort removed my chains. When he uncuffed my ankles, I glanced at Trigger and Shotgun. They were both tense and expected me to act, which meant, if they had been unchained first, they would have attacked. The unit door opened and I went down the stairs to the bottom tier toward the open single-man cell. I knew a majority of the men who occupied the other cells.

"What's up, Sinbad?"

"Hey, Mountain Man. So this is where they keep you, huh?"

"Yeah, these fuckin' bottle stoppers fear little old me. But that's okay, because I'd be afraid of me too if I was them," he laughed. "Ain't nothing changed here but the place and time, old son."

"I suppose not." I neared the bars and shook hands with him. "It's good to see you, Olaf."

"Same here. Get settled in, and when I get out on the broom we'll talk."

I nodded and stepped into the cell. Olaf, a.k.a. Mountain Man, looked every bit the name. He was six foot four and 275 pounds of muscle, with long black hair and a beard that came down to his chest. He looked exactly like a lumberjack cliché. He was also a fierce fighter who loved nothing more than scaring the hell out of cops.

His eyes were his most distinctive feature. They were ice blue, so bright you sometimes thought they were white. I first met Olaf over two years earlier in the hospital. At the time, I'd been seeing the doctor to treat my headaches. I was also depressed, had intense rage, and persistent feelings of doom. I didn't know it at the time, but I was suffering withdrawal symptoms from the steroids I'd taken for so long.

When we met, Olaf was being treated for gunshot wounds. His ex-girlfriend and her boyfriend had emptied a .38 revolver into him. When that didn't put him down, they started shooting him with a .44 magnum. Unfortunately for them, Olaf picked up a hammer and ended the argument for good.

The cell door next to me opened, and a few moments later Chente walked by and into the cell.

"Hey, Mad. They put them vatos upstairs in cells 3 and 4. You know the business."

"Yeah, fuck them clowns and the car they rode in on. I'll deal with them later."

"I have no doubts about that, ese, but you know I got your back no matter what. I'm there."

"Right on, Chente. I hear you."

Sometimes it's a comfort to know those around you are interested in helping. The only problem with that is, one minute you're showing your hand to someone you believe wants to help, and the next thing you know there's a knife sticking out of your back. Trigger had been right when he said I was nobody—meaning I wasn't connected to a gang or crew.

Therefore, politically I had no muscle and anyone who sided with me would be taking a big risk. That was another reason not to trust any Southern Mexican, including Chente.

He may want to help me, but I would not take the chance. Trusting him could prove to be fatal. I was alone in my fight, and I would deal with it alone.

As soon as all of us were locked in our cells, Mountain Man stepped in front of my cell.

"I'll bring you some cleaning supplies so you can clean your cell."

"Right on, Olaf."

When he went to the mop room, I searched the cell. The cells were extremely small and there weren't many places to hide things. I searched every inch of it and found nothing.

Olaf returned with the mop bucket, scrub pads, towels, and bleach. By then I had folded my mattress back and taken off my jumpsuit.

"Here you go. I put some smell-good in the mop water, and here are some things to maintain your pad."

"Right on, man. Good looking out."

"Not a problem. I'll get with you in a bit. I got some things I want to look into."

I nodded and began cleaning the cell. I would be in the cell twenty-three hours a day. No more walks to the chow hall—all my meals would be served to me in my cell. I'd be out to shower for ten minutes, and to use the dayroom—a large cell with a table, toilet, sink, and phone—for an hour each day with my group. In the dayroom I could make calls, play poker, or work out.

About an hour later Olaf came by to pick up the mop bucket and we had a chance to talk.

"So what's the deal? Why did they slam you in here?"

"They haven't said shit to me. No write-up, no nothing. All they said was that it's an ongoing security concern, but it's probably because of the attempted escape off the roof."

I ran the entire deal to Olaf and he listened. When I finished, he laughed and said, "Well, fuck 'em if they can't take a joke. It's their job to try and keep us in and it's ours to try and fly."

He suddenly stopped and smiled. "So did you find it?"

I knew Olaf, and he loved to have his secrets.

"Find what?"

"Come on, old son. Did you search the cell?"

"Of course I did. There's nothing here."

His smile widened.

"Okay, where is it? Because I can't find it."

He looked up and I followed his eyes to the top of the door.

"Here, use these."

In his hand he held two bent combs with all the teeth missing except the ends. I took them but I still didn't understand what they were for. Seeing my confusion, he said, "Take the combs and slide them into the slot above your head where the door runs. Inside, there's a lip right above the track where the door runs, and on that lip I put one of my babies."

I took the combs and slid them along the lip above the door track until I heard the distinct sound of metal rubbing against metal.

"Careful now, you don't want it to fall, because everyone will hear it. Just slide it to the edge of the slot where you can see it, then grab the end and slide it out."

I did as he said and pulled the piece from its hiding place.

"Nice piece of work."

"Wicked, isn't she? It took me a few days in the shower to sharpen it to a razor's edge, but it can cut paper."

Olaf was right. It was one of the best pieces I had ever seen. Eight inches of steel that was sharpened on both sides, with bloodlines running down both centers. It had one purpose: to kill.

"She's yours if you need her."

I looked at Olaf.

"That guy who came in with you is upstairs cutting a piece from the towel rack," he said. "He sent a kite to Boxer, who's also from Orange, asking to get on the broom tonight so he can get at him. I also heard him talking to his neighbor who came in with him about you, and it wasn't good. What's the deal?"

"I basically told him to shut the fuck up because he was acting like a clown and I wasn't in the mood for it."

"So how you going to handle it?"

"Don't know yet, but I'm sure it'll happen. He can't do all this talking and not do anything, especially in front of his homeboys and crew."

"You got that right. Just keep your eyes open. It'll take him a few days to get used to the program here. When you want to know how to get to him, let me know."

"Right on, Olaf. I'll keep that in mind."

I looked at Olaf's piece. I'd never used a piece on anyone, and wouldn't start now. I needed to find a way to catch Trigger alone and without the shank he was making. I decided to play it by ear and get to know my new surroundings. I'd see things much more clearly after that.

The next morning I woke at 5 a.m. After washing up, I stood by the bars and listened.

I could hear the sound of breathing, and men snoring. Other than that, it was quiet. I stood there and thought how much I wished none of this was happening. It was hard to understand just how things had gone so wrong—not just the pending situation with Trigger, but everything.

I knelt down and bowed my head and asked for the strength to overcome my enemies, and for victory. I've never been religious, but I've always had a personal connection with my God. I hold my beliefs close and won't share them in detail, not even here in these pages. In general, I believe I won't be given any burden so great I can't bear it. I am so confident in this, I rarely ask for more than strength and victory over my enemies.

That afternoon, I went to the dayroom at four and stayed until six because the next group didn't want to use their time.

I took the extra time to observe how the program was run and who was in charge. For the Mexicans, it was Boxer. For the Whites, it was an Aryan Brotherhood member named Little Steve. I didn't know the men aside from their reputations.

My dayroom group consisted of Chente, Indio from San Pedro, and Diablo from Azusa. Indio and Diablo were crime partners and, I later learned, both made members of the Mexican Mafia. That didn't surprise me since they were in administrative segregation (high-power). But they were laid back and their biggest concern seemed to be finding a newspaper to see which NFL teams had won on Sunday.

When we got to the dayroom, Chente asked what I would do about Trigger. I played it off by saying I wasn't worried about it because we would never be close enough to do anything to each other. We were on two different tiers and I doubted a chance would ever present itself. I don't know if he believed me, but he didn't say anything else about it.

Being in high-power meant I couldn't walk around and I was in a solitary cell. I'd adapt. I always did. But part of me was bothered that I had simply adapted to so many changes over the past two years.

Maybe compared to what I'd already lost and had been through, this was something I knew I could survive.

After two weeks in high-power, I looked up from the book I read to find Trigger at my door. I was surprised, and it must have shown on my face because he smiled.

"Órale, Mad. Watcha, I wanted to come down here and get at you so we can squash this pedo between us. We had a misunderstanding and it's over. If that's firmé with you, we can go back to how it was before."

"Yeah, don't trip. I lost my temper and you know how that is."

"Órale," he said, and put his hand through the bars. We shook hands. I didn't believe a word he said. I knew he wanted me to relax and then he'd try to kill me, and for some reason it didn't bother me. I went back to reading my book and didn't think about it until the next morning when I woke up.

The question on my mind was, "How?"

He must have a plan already. I just had to figure out how he'd attempt to murder me. He swept the tier at night, a job his homeboy Boxer had given him. That meant Boxer knew his plan. Trigger had to tell Boxer what he wanted to do and get a green light to do it. Obviously he'd received the green light.

After breakfast, Olaf came out of his cell to sweep and pass some things from cell to cell.

He came to my door. "Old son, let's smoke this joint. This is some prime shit."

He handed me the joint and I pulled out a book of matches and sparked it. I inhaled and passed it to Olaf who took a lung full. We passed it back and forth and then allowed it to take effect.

"I see that cat Trigger is now the sweeper at night. I heard what he said to you last night." Olaf smiled, which meant he had something in mind. I decided at that moment Olaf didn't mean any harm and that he didn't much care for the Mexicans.

"Do you buy it?" he asked.

"Not a lick of it. He got that sweeper gig because he has something in mind, and Boxer gave him a green light. Otherwise, he wouldn't be on the broom."

"Good, you see the picture. Now, have you figured out how he'll do it?"

"Not a clue, but he has a plan. I'll just stay on my toes, because he'll try soon enough."

Olaf smiled again.

"Listen, they lock us up every time someone else is let out of their cell. We're either locked in our cell or we step out into the vestibule. Either way, he can't get to you. What he has planned has to be done while he's out, which is at night when the lights are off and you're in your cell. There's only two possibilities. One, he throws hot oil on you and lights it, or he'll make a spear and try to stab you. He's too stupid to rig the oil, so he'll try and spear you."

I thought about the oil and being burned alive and it scared me more than any stabbing.

"What are the chances he'll try and burn me?"

"Not a nice thought, huh? Don't worry about it. It's too hard to make, and Mexicans like to stab. It's more personal."

He placed a small domino on the bars of my cell door.

"Think about that for a while."

He walked off. Olaf loved his games. He loved making you think and guess, so at the end he could show you just how much he knew and how that knowledge could help you.

About half an hour later he came back.

"Figure out how that little domino will give you what you need?"

"There's no way I'm going to figure it out."

"Man, you're no fun." And he seemed sad for a moment, then smiled.

"Okay, what I know that no one else does is that, if you place that domino at the upper corner of your door with a piece of tape when your door closes, it won't really lock. The control panel will show it's closed so the cop will leave, but you, by grabbing your bars and pulling hard, can open it. Look at the domino. See how it's been sanded down on one side? It's thinner than a normal domino and works perfectly."

If he was right, I could easily open my door, get out, and finish my business with Trigger.

"I see the wheels in your head turning," he said. "But here's the best part. You'll get away with it because, when the cop comes back and turns on the control panel, your door will automatically close and the cop won't know how anything could have happened when all the doors are closed."

"You're an evil genius, Olaf."

He smiled, bowed, and walked away.

The next morning at 5:45 the tier cop got on the speaker and announced roof-yard. No one said anything, so he began to call out each dayroom group. When he got to my group, I put my towel through the bars to get his attention. My door opened and I went to the front of the unit and into the vestibule.

"I'd like to go to the roof."

"You know, it's cold as fuck up there and you'll be up there until your hour is up."

"I understand."

"A judge has mandated we offer you roof-yard three times a week, starting today, so I'm to inform you that each morning at five for-ty-five an announcement for roof-yard will be made. Your schedule, because you're in dayroom group three, will be Monday, Wednesday, and Friday. However, if no one wants their time up there, I'll go down the list and release whichever group wants to go."

"Sounds good," I said.

The cop put chains on me and escorted me out of the unit to the elevator and up to the roof.

As soon as I stepped outside the door the cold and wind hit me. The cop wasn't lying. It was cold as fuck. To my surprise, my escort began removing my cuffs and chains. When I looked at him, he simply said, "Judge's orders. You have to be given exercise time up here and you can't exercise with chains on. You have an hour."

I turned and walked down the ramp to the lower level of the roof, and as I walked I let my lungs fill with air and I began to run. Sud-denly I was no longer on the roof of the Orange County jail, and I wasn't prisoner 730-256. I was sixteen and running the hills near my home. I didn't think of any upcoming trial or all the grief I'd experienced. I didn't think of how Trigger was planning to kill me. I simply ran.

The next morning no one wanted roof time, so I took advantage of the opportunity. I went out every time it was my roof day, plus whenever no one wanted their time, no matter how cold or wet it was. I had to be in complete battle mode. And that meant being in perfect physical shape. I was in danger and I couldn't leave anything to chance.

Each night at six the large lights were turned off on the tier and Trigger came out to sweep. I kept my eyes on him, but I didn't make it obvious. I knew he'd try soon. If he didn't, he'd be considered scared. With all the talking he'd done to get on the broom and get the green light on me, if he didn't handle it, his own people would take care of him.

Every day after I came back from the dayroom I'd place the domino on the upper corner of my door, and I remained ready. I'd allow him to make the first move, then I'd finish it.

I didn't have to wait long. One night, after being let out, Trigger came by sweeping.

"All right now, what's up, Mad?"

"Nada, just kicking it. You?"

"Tú sabes. It's all good. Hey, I got some bomb-ass gesca. You want to smoke it with me?"

"Órale, gracias. That would be firmé."

He gave me the joint and then pulled out some matches and sparked it up for me. I took a hit and passed it to him. The whole time, I watched him. He took a few hits and gave it back to me and said, "Go ahead and kill it. I got more and I promised the carnal I'd smoke one with him."

"All right, Trigger. I appreciate it. Gracias."

He left and I put out the joint. Every muscle in my body was tense. I knew it was coming, but I stayed at my bars with my right arm hanging so he'd be sure to see it. I was tired of playing cat and mouse with him. I wanted it over and done with.

He came back with the mop bucket and mop, and placed it in front of Chente's cell, then went and got the disinfectant and poured it into the bucket. He returned the disinfectant, and when he came back, he did so quietly. As soon as he came in line with my cell and where I stood, he rammed the broomstick, which had a shank attached to the end, through the bars and into my right shoulder. It was a fast strike, but he tried to ram it through me. I saw it coming and rolled to my left, avoiding the spear, but he caught my shoulder. As the tip entered my shoulder and struck bone, my arm went dead. He pulled out and tried to spear me again, but I moved out of his range.

"Yeah, puto, how you like that? You ain't shit and never have been."

I pulled off my shirt and wiped off the blood so I could look at the wound. It was a puncture, nothing more. It bled, but it didn't really hurt aside from the sting, and it was no longer numb, so I could move my arm.

I was embarrassed that I'd allowed him to do even that much damage. But rage and hatred soon followed. I put on my shoes and went back to the sink to wipe the blood from my shoulder, where it still bled freely. I pressed my shirt to the wound with pressure that made me wince, but I held it there until the bleeding slowed.

By then, Trigger was pretty proud of himself. He went upstairs to tell Shotgun, then went to Boxer to report.

"Hey Bill, you all right?" Chente asked.

"Yeah, it's nothing. I got this."

I didn't want to talk to him, or anyone. I focused on Trigger and when I would make my move. I waited for the unit cop to return to his control panel, do his check, and leave again. Once he was gone, he wouldn't return for at least an hour. That would give me the chance I needed to take care of Trigger and not get caught.

A few minutes later, I heard keys and my stomach tightened. The cop walked by to his control panel, checked his doors, and left. Moments later Trigger came by pretending to sweep, but he was curious. He wanted to see how much damage he'd done. I stared at him, allowing my hatred to show, and he took it as a challenge.

"You can look all you want, ese, but remember who's running this motherfucker."

By then, everyone knew what had happened and was at their bars, listening.

"You think so, huh? You're good when a door's between us, but you're a bitch and always have been. You'd run if this door weren't here, and scream for the placa to save you."

"Sounds good, Sinbad. You'll get your chance and we'll see what you're about."

"Why wait? Now's a good time."

I grabbed the cell door and pulled hard on it and, just as Olaf said, it opened and I rushed out.

The look on his face was worth the pain in my shoulder. He was frozen by surprise, fear, and the realization of his mistake. I didn't hesitate to take full advantage of it. He tried to bring the broom up to swing it, but I was already too close for that when my right fist connected with his jaw, followed by my left. He dropped the broom and tried to hang on to me. I continued to pound his face. In a desperate attempt to stop me, he grabbed me around the waist and tried to wrestle me to the ground. At that close range it was hard to punch him, so I elbowed him instead, which opened up his face. He let go as he fell and I followed him to the ground, where I climbed on top of him and pounded his face with my fists, stopping only when he was out cold.

I dragged him over to where the cells were. Just in case someone came by and looked down the tier. I was angry. Rage filled my vision until I was shaking with it. But I wasn't done. I wanted him to remember me beyond the ass beating I gave him. My shoulder bled freely again and it only added to my anger. I wanted all of the men to know, if they didn't know it already, I was not to be fucked with. It didn't matter if they were a carnal, or an associate, or anyone else. When it came down to it, it would be me against them, and I would win.

Trigger sat up, looking dazed—like he had been hit by a car. I squatted down in front of him.

"Got anything to say now, puto?"

He just looked at me.

"That's what I thought."

I got up, and he tried to do the same, slowly at first, to get his balance. When he came in line with Boxer's cell, he stopped and Boxer handed him a towel to wipe the blood off his face. He said something to him, and Boxer's reply was, "That's on you, ese."

Trigger then turned to me and spit a mouthful of blood and saliva, hitting me on the arm, and said, "Fuck you, punk."

That was his ego and pride talking, but I didn't care. I moved in, kicking him in the head, and punched him in the mouth. He crumbled to the ground.

I grabbed him by the front of his jumpsuit and was ready to destroy him when Boxer spoke up.

"Ya estuvo. He's had enough."

"You green-lighted it, now I'll finish it."

"Simón, but he's done. It's over. He ain't going to be on the broom any more. Palabra, this is done."

He didn't scare me. I knew he was trying to save his homeboy's ass, and it was far from over. But short of killing him, there was nothing else I was willing to do. Slowly I let him go.

"Keep your kids in line. This'll happen to anyone who steps up to the plate."

"Órale, Mad."

I knew he wasn't used to anyone, especially someone so young, talking to him like that, but I wanted him and anyone listening to know I wasn't afraid and that I would be respected.

I went back to my cell and stood just inside the door, listening and watching.

A few moments later, through the reflection in the Plexiglas that separated us from the cops, I watched Trigger climb over the tier rail on the upper tier and into his cell. Half expecting him to come out with a piece, I stayed ready until I heard the unit cop approach and Trigger telling him he was done for the night and to lock his cell.

I took in a deep breath, then went to my sink to wash up and apply pressure to my shoulder, again. I looked at my face in the polished piece of steel that served as a mirror, and saw for the first time the effect this had on me. A piece of me was dying. I could see the agony in my eyes. If something didn't change, I'd be lost. I shoved the thoughts away, hardening my will as I washed my face. I would survive. No matter what, I'd never be a victim again.

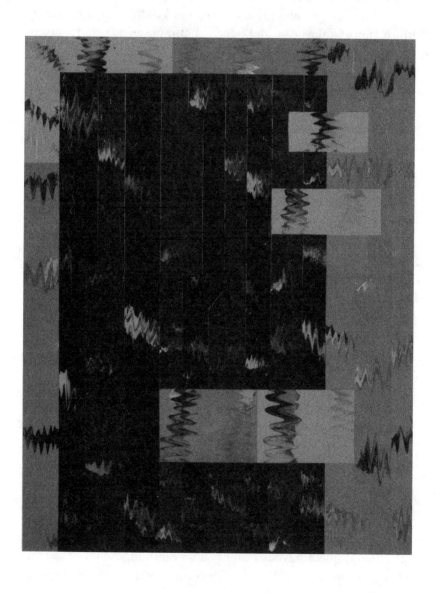

Chapter 24

Adolescence, 1979–1980

In December of 1979 my parents had their final face-to-face fight. I was fifteen years old. I came home from the studio, where I was preparing for the Hapkido Middleweight Championship. As soon as I opened the door and stepped into the house I sensed the tension. I was familiar with it, but it always hurt me deeply because there was nothing I could do to stop it, and I knew it would destroy our family.

My little sister was crying, and as soon as she saw me she ran and hugged me. She kept repeating over and over, "Dad hit mom. Dad hit mom. Dad hit mom."

She shook violently, or maybe it was me who was shaking. I noticed a metallic taste in my mouth as fear, anger, despair, and hatred filled the pit of my stomach.

I was no longer thinking, only reacting. The door to my parent's bedroom was closed and I don't remember how I got there, but I was at the door and I knocked.

"Mom, open the door."

When the door opened my mother stood there crying silently. Her face was bruised and her blouse torn. I took one look at her and walked away. My vision clouded, and rage flowed through my veins. I didn't know what I'd do, but I searched for my father.

I found him in the backyard sitting at a marble table and bench, watching our birds as he drank. As soon as he saw me, he looked away, but I'd seen the scratch marks on his face.

"You promised never to hit her again." I stood in front of him, clenching my fists.

"She started it. And who the fuck do you think you are to ask me anything? I'm your father. Now get out of my face." He shoved me back and I stepped right back in front of him. I was taller than my father and, although he outweighed me by thirty pounds, I realized at that moment I no longer feared him. I loved him and it hurt me beyond words what that confrontation would mean, but I didn't back down.

"You're a liar. You blame everyone but the person whose fault it is. You've destroyed our family. You're drunk."

I slapped the beer off the table and sent it flying.

His response to it was immediate. He grabbed me by the throat and slapped me across the face. I allowed it to happen. I wanted him to hit me. A part of me needed to be consumed by the moment. My face stung, but I got right back in front of him and he hit me again. This time his closed fist struck me hard on the side of my ear. I saw stars when he connected, but he was off balance and drunk and his momentum carried him and he stumbled and fell. I stood over him, crying.

I don't know what I felt. I don't know if I cried because my father had died in my eyes and was just a man, or because I knew my family was finally dead.

I walked past my father and left the house. I don't remember how I ended up near the school, but I ran and I didn't stop until I was totally exhausted. It was very late, and the next thing I remember was waking up on the side of a hill in Turnbull Canyon. I was mentally, emotionally, and physically drained. Then I remembered what happened and went home. It was the first time I stayed out all night without anyone knowing where I was.

When I arrived home the house was empty. It was Saturday. My father was probably at work and had already forgotten what he had done, or he would simply play it down and apologize as he'd done a thousand times. But this time felt different, more serious. I took off my clothes and showered, letting the hot water wash over me.

When I got out, I heard my mother and sister come into the house and they were in a hurry.

"Mom, qué pasa?" I asked.

"Get your suitcase and put all of your clothes in it and some things you'll need for a few weeks."

"Why, what's happening?"

"We're leaving, and until we get a judge to sign a court order to make your father leave, we'll be staying at a friend's house."

"I don't want to leave our house."

"Fine, stay then. I know you've always loved your father more than me. Even after he's done all the things you've witnessed. But remember this. If you stay, when we come back and your father is ordered to leave, you will not be welcome here with us."

It was always like this with my mother. It was always about choosing a side, which I didn't want to do. Why did I have to choose? They were still my parents and, just because they would no longer live together and were obviously getting divorced, that didn't mean I had to pick a side as if I were going to war. Yes, my father was wrong. Yes, he should never have done those things to my mother. But why couldn't I salvage as much as I could from my family? No matter what, I still loved my father. And although I allowed my mother to manipulate me again, I was determined not to choose sides.

My sister was different. She saw a lot of the things my father did over the years and she felt justified in cutting my father out of her life.

I packed my things and my mother drove us to Carlos and Irene's house, which was a block from ours. I didn't want to stay there. Carlos was a nice guy and I didn't understand why he'd get involved. He was one of my father's best friends, but his wife was distant. I felt like we were a burden to her, as if she had been pressured to allow us to stay.

That night my father came to Carlos's house and knocked on the door. When Carlos answered, he asked to speak with me. He was very calm, which concerned me. My father was not known for his passive manner or etiquette.

"Mijo, I came home and your things were gone. I see your mother has moved out."

"Dad, she's getting the divorce and she's getting a judge to order you out of the house."

I could see his jaw clench, but he kept calm.

"Are you all right?" he asked.

"I'm okay, but I don't want to stay here."

"Then don't. Come home with me."

"I can't. Mom said if I did, I wouldn't be welcome in her house when you're ordered out."

"Well, no matter what, you are always welcome in mine."

"I know, Dad."

"I just wanted to see if you were okay. How's your sister?"

"She doesn't want to talk to you."

"Okay, I understand. Tell Carlos I'd like to talk to him for a moment."

Carlos came to the door and my father very calmly said, "You betrayed me. I thought you and I were friends. After all these years, this is how you repay my friendship? Fine, you don't want me as a friend. Let's see how you like me as an enemy."

He never raised his voice and it seemed to unsettle Carlos. My father was normally an in-your-face kind of guy. But that change made his words somehow more serious and a prelude to something much scarier.

My father left, but his words hung in the air. Carlos went inside and sat down. The fear on his face made it obvious he regretted letting us stay at his house.

It didn't take long for my mother to get the order, and I'll never forget the look on my father's face when he left our home. It was painful for me to see him like that. My father looked defeated, somehow smaller. The burden seemed to weigh on him, slumping his shoulders as he walked away.

I went back into my room and put all my things back where they belonged. My sister and mom were happy. My mother turned on the stereo as if she were celebrating, while I mourned the death of my family. My mother and sister were a team, but I didn't belong. What had made our house a home was that our family lived there, but after my family split up it was just a place where I slept.

It would be easy to view that moment as the start of my downward spiral, but it's much more complicated than that. I was angry and I resented my parents for not finding a way to work things out. My mother was cold to me every time I asked when I could see my father. My father had guided and supported me my entire life. His presence gave me a sense of security. After he left I had none of that, and my mother made it difficult for my father and me to see each other. She made up stories to make visits difficult or stressful. If he came by for a scheduled visit and I was in the shower, she'd tell him I had gone to the beach. She seemed to enjoy the frustration she caused my father, but didn't notice what it did to me and how withdrawn I became.

Soon after that, I got a job at Skate Junction. I was the youngest member of the skating rink staff, but because of how I looked the manager put me in the adult rotation, so I worked all the adult sessions.

Adult nights were no different than working at a popular night club. Within a month I became floor guard, which was basically a bouncer on skates. I was there to keep order and make sure everyone followed the rules. I spent more and more time at work, choosing to make money a higher priority than school, training, or anything else. I continued to attend Heights Lutheran, but at that point I was just going through the motions. I didn't try, and my grades suffered because of it. My only goal was buying a car. I thought of it constantly. After working a couple of months, I did exactly that.

A guy at school had a '71 Chevy Nova I really liked, and when he put it up for sale I bought it. The car was exactly what I wanted—a machine to boost my already bad reputation. It was lowered in the front and had chrome wheels, a 427 big-block engine—chromed out, with duel Holley 750 carburetors. It had a turbo 400 transmission with shift kit and stall converter. The interior was all tuck-and-roll mohair. The car was an extension of me and projected the badass image I was going for.

I also had a girlfriend. A pretty, petite blonde with hazel green eyes, who was two years older than me.

I had everything a teenaged boy could wish for. The ugly duckling had turned into a swan. But it wasn't enough.

After a couple of months away from the studio and my training, I returned. My trainer made a deal with me that seemed fair. He would train me in exchange for me teaching the men's advanced fighting class and fighting for his team. I accepted and went back to my training routine. I no longer relied on my parents. At the age of fifteen I was basically on my own and answered to no one.

My mother left to spend a few months in Colombia with my sister. I stayed behind, unsupervised and without support of any kind, except for my father coming to my fighting competitions. He didn't know my mother and sister were gone, and I didn't mention it. My father's main concern was that I continued to train and take my vitamins, which was how he referred to the steroid cycles. Every forty to forty-five days my father would give me a cycle to take, and many times the cycles were stacked without a rest in between.

My headaches were worse than ever, and the steroids were a major factor in their intensity as well as my overall attitude and behavior.

I had a particularly bad headache one day while my mother and sister were gone. Light only made it worse, and I thought my head would explode. Go-Go, a member of The Pack who was staying at my house for a few days while my mother was in Colombia, offered me some pot. I'd never smoked pot. I'd heard all the warnings about it, and had never really wanted to try it, but there was Go-Go, a good friend of mine, offering it, and I knew the rest of The Pack smoked it too. They all looked fine. They weren't dope heads and didn't act like their brains were fried.

Go-Go had a good pitch about smoking pot and how it would help me.

"Brah, this shit will stop your headaches. Seriously, take a few hits and it will mellow you out and the pain will go away. I take a few hits before I go to sleep and I'm out like a light."

I don't know if I believed him, but what did I have to lose? My head hurt so bad I just wanted it to stop. I took the small pipe he offered and did a small hit.

"Man, hit that shit," he said.

I inhaled deeply and coughed. My throat burned and I gave it back to him. He took a deep hit.

"Man, this shit is the kind—see how it expands in your lungs? That means it's working. This is Buddha Thai."

I took another hit, and pretty soon my headache was gone.

"Man, my head stopped throbbing. The headache's gone."

"I told you this shit works."

I felt a little funny and later learned that was the high from the pot which, as Go-Go said, would mellow me out. For the first time in years, I slept without waking up in pain.

Chapter 25

San Quentin Death Row, 1992–1993

Robert Alton Harris was executed at San Quentin in April 1992. Before that, I understood my death sentence only on an intellectual level, but with the Harris execution it became all too real. Prior to that, California had not executed anyone since Aaron Mitchell, who was the 194th person to die in the gas chamber, in 1967.

The thought of execution hardly crossed the minds of men here, even though we were all sentenced to death. The threat of being killed was far greater on the exercise yard than from any state-sanctioned procedure during those twenty-five years between the Mitchell and Harris executions. On any given day, an attempt on my life could be made. Extreme violence was common and expected. That threat seemed normal. Put four hundred convicted killers on an exercise yard and, of course, there will be violence.

I'm not afraid to face a man coming at me with a knife and trying to kill me because I'm trained to deal with that. That's a situation I've experienced and have total confidence I can win. In a fight, I determine the outcome, and, although I may be killed, I'm not afraid. Being strapped into a chair and executed by inhaling poisonous gas is a different story because I have no control. I can't use my ability to survive based on my training. It's being helpless that I hate. I have a deep-seated aversion to dying in a hopeless manner where I am nothing but a spectacle in a macabre theater. The most intimate moment, coming at the climax of one's life, becomes a stage performance with a gawking audience and news reporters seated in rows on the other side of clear Plexiglas.

That was what gripped me so tightly, not the fact that Robert Alton Harris was being executed. I never spoke to him. He was one of many men in prison for killing children, and I have nothing to say to his kind. Still, I imagined how it would be for me at the moment of execution.

It was so real to me on April 21, 1992 that fear overwhelmed me. I shook violently. The walls seemed to close in on me until the act of breathing became difficult. Since the moment they came for him, a week prior to his execution date, my emotional state was totally out of control.

He lived directly above me, on the fourth tier in cell-77. I heard them tell him in hushed tones they were there to take him to North Segregation where he would remain in a cell just above the gas chamber while they waited for any last minute appeals or stays. They cuffed him and opened his door, and he compliantly walked with them on the last walk he would ever take.

I went outside every day during the week prior to his execution. I worked out as if my life depended on it. The emotional turmoil I experienced happened internally and no one saw the changes going on inside me. Each day when I went back to my cell from the yard I imagined it was my death walk, heading for my own execution.

Because Harris was the first execution in California since 1967, the media made it even more of a circus act. Every channel ran coverage of it, with the reporter speaking in front of the gates of San Quentin, and showing historical footage of his arrest. They called him the smiling killer. All of it drove me closer and closer to a breaking point, where my mind plunged into a state of hyper-reality. I relived the best and worst parts of my childhood, similar to the certainty with which a person who is drowning reviews in the span of a second all the insurmountable moments of his life. As midnight neared and his execution approached, I put on my headphones, hoping to block it out.

Suddenly, at 12:15 a.m., East Block erupted in the sound of men cheering. I took off my headphones and tried to understand what they were reacting to. I turned my radio to KPFA, a station that covered social and political commentary, and learned Robert Alton Harris had received a temporary stay of execution.

I didn't share the relief the other men did. The pending execution triggered a thought process that made me realize my own mortality. The stay of execution didn't change my state of mind.

Fear had been part of my life for as long as I could remember, but the conscious realization of my mortality was an element I never considered.

Sleep came to me late that night. But for the first time in my life, images saturated in color filled my subconscious. The colors were so intense I thought I would drown in them.

I woke suddenly very early in the morning. I washed my face in cold water and went to the bars of my cell, stopping to listen. It was absolute silence. Dead calm. Even the birds seemed to know that silence was appropriate.

I turned on my radio and heard that, during the night, Robert Alton Harris became the first person since 1967 to be executed in San Quentin's gas chamber.

He received a stay of execution at the last moment while sitting in the chamber, and was escorted back to his cell. A short time later a higher court revoked the stay, and he was escorted back to the chamber, strapped in, and executed.

I didn't know exactly how I felt about it, aside from tired and drained of emotion. I sat on my bucket and looked out the window in front of my cell. I wasn't really thinking, just looking at the water of the bay and allowing its movement and color to touch me. I don't know how long I sat there, but the breakfast trays being passed around brought me back to my surroundings. It was still very quiet, but I could hear men talking and the sound of toilets flushing.

When the bull working my tier came by with the trays, I refused and sat back on my bucket. We were all on lockdown that day with no movements, no showers, and no yard.

Around 10 a.m., a couple of shrinks came by asking questions to anyone who would speak with them.

"How are you this morning?"

"Do you feel like hurting yourself, or others? Are you hearing voices?"

I refused to acknowledge them and they didn't press me.

I sat on my bucket the rest of the day, the execution fresh in my thoughts. I came to the conclusion that, more than ever, time was something I couldn't waste. I didn't have the luxury of an entire lifetime to ponder—not when someone would eventually decide my time had come. More than ever, I wanted to be heard, to be relevant, to make an impact. I didn't want to be just another number on a long list of men who died in prison. I wanted my life to mean something.

Men with the strongest wills rebel when oppressed. I'm no different from the many men throughout history who've suffered the chains of oppression and struggled against them in order to change their circumstances and better themselves. However, rebellion without true cause, goal, or structure, is nothing more than chaos. True rebellion begins within. It may begin in the form of anger, but until it is purified in the fires of intellect, it is short-sighted.

Rebellion starts with rehabilitation. I don't mean rehabilitation in the sense that prison administrators have in mind. Rehabilitation, in its purest and truest form, is to return to our true former self— before the influences surrounding us affected our behavior. To do this, we must become conscious that each of us holds the key to our own freedom. Not through religion, or by following prison rules, or through fear of torture. My rebellion is to survive these brutal circumstances and prove my worth. In doing so, I understand who I am, but more importantly, why. I know what I must do to grow and mature, channeling the explosive forces inside me where I alone control them, and I alone hold the key to my freedom.

Tamed? Nothing could be further from the truth, and those who say it see me, the world, and themselves through eyes permanently impaired by prejudice and intellectual impotence. My weapon of choice is my mind. And its product is to actualize itself in the form of expression—art, where I retreat from the world that surrounds me and escape its suffocating embrace.

Chapter 26

Orange County Jail, 1986

I went out to the roof every day it was offered, where I ran and practiced martial arts. After that I did an intense workout of pushups, pull-ups, dips, and squats.

I lived in a constant state of vigilance, always checking my surroundings to ensure I left no openings for someone to harm me. Being constantly on-guard exhausted me, but I knew that one mistake on my part could land me at the wrong end of a bone-crusher. Though I'm confident in my skill as a first-rate fighter, I'm also aware that on any given day even the best can fall.

Friendship is a difficult thing to find and maintain in jail. I lived in the high-power unit with men who gave up on friendship—if they ever even knew its power. The only times I experienced a sense of kindness in jail were the moments I spent reading letters I received from Maxine, then pouring my heart out in pages I sent back. With her, I could express my frustrations, fears, and doubts. I told her how I felt and exposed the fact that behind the mask I was afraid, that I'd been afraid since I was a little boy, and all I truly wanted was to turn back the clock and undo what was done. She gave me what no one ever had—friendship. She listened to me when I had no one to turn to.

In the four years I spent in the jail before my trial, I saw my lead attorney, Martín Gonzalez, only once. I called him over five hundred times pleading for him to come see me, but he never did. He always sent someone I didn't know or trust. When I saw him during a hearing, he always said everything looked good to shut me up. He was not my lawyer—he was my mother's lawyer and he was there to protect her interests and her version of reality.

I'd attempt to tell him what happened that night, how I simply lost my temper during an argument and I didn't remember anything after my vision turned red. I told him I needed to be examined by a psychologist and we should talk to the DA and tell him what really happened, and more importantly, why. He told me I was in Orange County and they wouldn't listen, and we would only be giving them evidence to use against me. The only defense he would present was complete innocence. All or nothing. It was what my mother wanted.

He knew all of the things I had experienced as a child. He was my mother's divorce lawyer and knew about the things that went on in my home—the abuse, the violence, everything. But he refused to show any of it. Instead, he hid it all to protect my mother and her secrets while sacrificing me.

What could I do? I knew nothing about the law. I'd known Martín Gonzalez since I was a small child and it was hard for me to stand up to him. Sure, I was great at dealing with things in a physical manner, but in matters of law I was out of my element. Around him I felt like a child among adults. Gonzalez and my mother made all the decisions about my defense. I had no power.

It frustrated me, and all I could do was watch as my life was thrown to the wolves. I'd pour out all of those things to Maxine and she'd listen. But what could she do? She was younger than me, and when she decided to take action and contact Gonzalez to change his approach, she was simply patronized or ignored.

So while it was the State of California that imprisoned me, it was my own lawyer and mother who had placed a gag in my mouth to make things easier for them. I had no voice. I was treated like a child, and when I did finally testify, I did so under the worst type of distress and coercion.

My anchor through all of this was Maxine's friendship, letters, visits, and phone calls. I think a part of me clung on from absolute desperation, like a drowning man clings to a life jacket. She was the only friend in my life. I was surrounded by the worst of the worst, yet her friendship provided hope if only for a moment.

I spent over a year in high-power, and each day I lived in that four-by-eight-foot cell a piece of me died. The darkness closed in on me every time I saw the brutality that surrounded me.

After the confrontation with Trigger, I was left alone. Although I was aware Boxer resented me and he made a number of comments to others about wanting to kill me, it never materialized. Trigger, Shotgun, and Boxer soon took deals that sent them to prison for years, and once they left I was relieved. Their presence always worried me. I don't know if I can describe how it feels to know that every time they saw me, heard me, or thought of me, they wanted one thing: to murder me. If asked, I would say that I didn't care what they thought, but in truth it bothered and worried me to my core. Those were men not to be taken lightly.

About a month after Trigger left, four men arrived who I'd never seen before. I returned from the roof one day and walked into the vestibule to see them there in chains. I could tell they'd just come down from prison. All four were Mexican and had tattoos covering their arms and torsos. They projected authority by the way they moved and I suspected they were all high-ranking members of La Eme.

The cop removed their chains, one person at a time, then sent them through the door leading to the cells on the lower tier where I lived. The last one to go was the youngest of the four and I guessed his age about thirty-two. He was tall with a large mustache and a light complexion. Although he wore a baggy oversized jail-issued jumpsuit, his overall muscle development and size from years on an iron pile was obvious. He was a serious physical threat.

As the last of his chains were removed, the two cops stepped back with their batons ready. He smiled at them in a way that acknowledged their fear.

I could tell he liked the effect he had on them. Then, to their horror, instead of opening the door and stepping through it, he turned and came to me. I was calm as I watched him. I was in chains, so if he chose to attack me there was nothing I could do to prevent it, but we didn't know one another and he didn't seem crazy. He walked up to me because he wanted to. He was a man who did as he pleased.

"Órale, carnalito. Mucho gusto. Soy Chapo," he said.

I shook his hand as best I could. The chains and cuffs made it difficult.

"Órale, carnal. Mucho gusto. Me dicen Sinbad."

"Are you here with us?" he asked.

I nodded, "Simón."

"Órale, I'll see you in a few."

He turned, smiled at the cops, then walked to the door and went through it. I looked at the cops and their faces said it all. They knew, even with their batons, they would be in serious trouble if he attacked them.

He hadn't threatened them in any way, but his size, attitude, and presence was enough to let them know he was the real deal and was to be respected.

They removed my chains and seemed to need to come off as tough guys to re-establish their authority with me.

"Noguera, you go out almost every day when no one else does. We're going to check into this because it's a pain to take you up there. Maybe we can limit you to only the days you're assigned."

I opened the door and walked to my cell. I didn't engage them to satisfy their hurt egos. They wanted a confrontation, but they wouldn't find one with me.

After the door closed behind me I took off my jumpsuit and washed it, then took a bird bath. By the time I finished, a lot of the men in the unit were up and I could hear my dayroom partners, Indio and Diablo, talking to the four men who just arrived.

I learned they were in my dayroom group. When the time came, my door slid open and I went to the dayroom. A lot of the men go to the dayroom in their shower flip flops and see it as a time to relax and socialize. Not me. I wouldn't make that mistake. I always wore my shoes and kept my eyes open, just in case.

Chente entered the dayroom next, then Indio, followed by Diablo, who was talking to three of the four new men. Chapo came last. He had stopped at a couple of cells to talk to other men he knew.

When the dayroom door closed, I met the other three men who came from Folsom with Chapo. Topo and Nemo were brothers from La Puente, which was where I grew up. The other guy, named Apache, looked like an Indian except for his mustache. He was from 18th Street in L.A., and Chapo was from Maravilla.

When Topo and Nemo heard from Indio I was from La Puente, they became much more open with me. As soon as Chapo heard this, he turned and said, "Sinbad, you also go by Mad?"

"Yeah, that's me. What's up?"

"Your road dog, Monster, sends his regards. He was my cellie at Folsom and he says you're firmé and that he trusts you."

"Simón, Monster's a good man."

"Watcha, I gotta get with some of this business, but when we're done I'll cut it up with you."

He turned and the six of them sat at the table to discuss business. The four had been called down by Indio's attorney to testify in his trial, but they wouldn't be testifying. That was just an excuse to get them to Orange County to have a meeting.

Chente and I sat as far away from them as possible to give them their space. About an hour later they each made phone calls to confirm the decision. The phones there weren't monitored because of court orders mandating a pre-trial defendant's right to privacy and attorney-client confidentiality. It meant the men could conduct business of a sensitive nature without fear of the cops listening. That's something they could never do in prison, where all their phone calls, mail, and visits were screened.

After their calls, they sat down again and talked briefly. They seemed much more relaxed. The business must have gone well, because they were soon laughing and talking about women and about people they all knew.

Chapo, Nemo, and Apache took off their shirts and I noticed their tattoos. Chapo had a black hand on his chest with the word "Emero" in the center. Nemo had the word "EME" across his entire chest in block letters, and Apache had a black hand with a large "M" at its center on his right shoulder. I had been right. They were all high-ranking members of the Mexican Mafia. I also discovered both Indio and Diablo were made members and part of Chapo's inner crew.

Somehow it didn't bother me or impress me. More and more,

I thought of it all as just "it is what it is." At one point I had been extremely impressed by men who everyone feared and respected, but at that point I saw them as just men. They were dangerous men, but still just men. They bled just like me and could be hurt just like me.

Chapo came over to me and shook my hand again.

"I heard that you put a beating down on Boxer's homeboy Trigger, and that you came out of your cell on his ass after he speared you."

"I just took care of my business. I don't let anyone, especially a clown like Trigger or even Boxer, step on me."

Chapo laughed. "Yeah, Monster told me how you and some of the camaradas took care of them Changos and some of the other pedo you did. He speaks highly of you. But he says you're a shadow and won't hook up with us."

"With all respect, I like being on my own. I'll take care of business, but I'm not into taking orders from anyone."

"Yeah, ese, pero tú sabes, once you get to the joint it won't be easy to be on your own. If the Norteños, Guerrillas, or someone else targets you, without us you're a sitting duck. Watcha, you know all of this. What I'm saying is, whenever you decide to come over, the door is open."

"Gracias, Chapo. That's firmé."

Nemo and Topo came over and we talked a bit about where I grew up and parts of La Puente. I learned they lived only a few blocks from where I grew up and we knew some of the same people.

When the dayroom time was up and I returned to my cell, it didn't surprise me Chapo stayed out on the broom. He was a take charge kind of guy. That's one reason he rose so quickly through the ranks of soldiers he commanded. I studied him, like I would any opponent, looking for his strengths and weakness. He was strong, confident—maybe too confident—aggressive, and used to getting his way. I wondered if, under what he projected, he was actually insecure. Half of his armor was who he was and the fear anyone had to get past to face him, because after facing him, win or lose, you'd forever have to look over your shoulder. The criminal empire he represented would never allow you to live in peace. It didn't matter to me. He and I didn't have a problem. It was just a habit of mine to size everyone up who posed a threat, and Chapo fit the profile.

A few hours later, after he touched base with some others in the unit, he stopped by my cell.

I was drawing pictures from memory when he approached. I could tell he looked me over and compared what he'd heard about me with what he saw. His gaze traveled into my cell and took in the set up. He took note of how clean it was as well as how my jumpsuit was hung. Satisfied, he shook my hand again.

"You draw, ese?"

"Yeah, I do okay."

"Let me check out what you're doing."

I handed him the sketch of a cathedral I'd once seen.

"Damn, ese, you get down."

I could tell he was making small talk and knew where the conversation was headed. We talked for a bit and he finally came to the point.

"I bet Trigger was surprised when you popped out of your cell on his ass."

"It's never good to underestimate me."

"Simón, a lot of people have made that mistake with me too, and it's cost them their punk ass. So how did you do it?"

He looked directly at me and I didn't flinch.

I considered lying to him, but he'd know. I'm sure he learned exactly what happened that night and what I said just before I tore my door open. He knew I planned it all and he wanted to know how. A man in his position could make use of the knowledge. I stared back at him.

"It's not as simple as how I did it. I'm sure you understand. I'll get at you tomorrow in the dayroom."

"Órale, but I'll see you sooner. I'm going to the roof tomorrow with you."

We shook hands and he left. Later that night after Chapo had been locked in his cell, I called to Olaf.

"You up, Olaf? I got a kite over here for you."

"Yeah, let me get my line."

I slid a line under my door with a weight at its end so it would travel as far as I needed. Olaf slid his over mine and his weight had a small hook made from a staple on it so, when he pulled his line, it would hook my line.

"Did you get it?"

"Yeah, I got it."

"Okay, go ahead and pull."

In the kite, I explained what Chapo wanted to know and that I hadn't said anything because it wasn't my place. I also explained, since he showed me the trick, it would be up to him what I revealed.

"Sinbad, just tell him to come to me tomorrow night and I'll run it down to him. I figured once you came out on that idiot, the cat would be out of the bag, but it was worth it to see you work. I also respect that you came to me to ask what you should do about it. It says a lot about your style."

"It was the obvious thing to do."

"Well, most motherfuckers would have folded and ran their mouths. You did the right thing, old son."

The next morning I woke early, and when they called for roof I stuck my towel out of my bars so the unit cop would see it. As my door slid open I heard another door open as well and I knew it was Chapo's. I stepped out of my cell just as he came out. We shook hands.

"Buenos días," he said.

I nodded. "Buenos días."

I wasn't used to anyone going to the roof with me so I didn't say much, and when we arrived upstairs I immediately stretched and started my routine, which he watched as if I were the most interesting person in the world. When I finished, Chapo came close and said, "We have about ten minutes left up here and I want to get at you about a few things. I'd like to do it where no one else can hear."

"Yeah, I'm about done anyway. What's on your mind?"

"I'd like to know how you got out of your cell."

"Olaf taught me how to do it, and that's why I didn't tell you yesterday. It wasn't my place, and I had to check with him first. I got at him last night and he told me to tell you to stop by his pad tonight and he'll run the whole deal down to you."

"Órale, that's firmé. You know what, ese, I respect that. You know how to keep your mouth shut."

"You know the business."

He laughed. "Yeah, ain't that the fuckin' truth."

The truth was, I didn't want to tell him. If it were up to me, he would never know, but it wasn't up to me. I washed my hands of it by giving it back to Olaf. But I knew if it weren't for me, Chapo would never have found out about it and never would have been able to use it to his advantage.

It didn't take long for Chapo to put a plan in motion. A guy had come into the unit about a week before, named Medina, a.k.a. Magilla Gorilla. He had a number of robbery murders, and most of the murders were on kids who worked at AM/PM mini markets. That didn't sit well with a lot of people, including me. But when Chapo found out about it, it set him off, and every time he saw Magilla going to the shower or dayroom, he'd tell us that a piece of shit like that needed to be in a grave.

Magilla seemed unaware of how people felt about him. Either that or he didn't care, because he always laughed and boasted about his robberies. Of course, Chapo and the rest of the men talked to him and sent him drugs. I could see what they were doing. They wanted him to relax and feel comfortable, so when it came he'd have no defense. It wouldn't be easy. Magilla, even caught unaware, would be a handful. His nickname described him perfectly. He was big, and resembled a gorilla. In my opinion, there was something off about him, and he came across as a weird and creepy motherfucker.

I knew something would happen soon because Chapo, Nemo, Topo, and Apache would return to Folsom prison within the next two weeks. From what I observed of Chapo, he'd want to be there to see it happen. I didn't want to know any of the details, but since they were my dayroom partners it was obvious to me at least what they had in mind, and who had been recruited to move on Magilla. The order was simple: kill him.

The soldier sent after him was a gang member from La Jolla named Negro, who wanted more than anything to make a name for himself, and someday become a carnal. He had the mind-set for it. He didn't care he only had two months left on his sentence before he went home, and that served Chapo's plan perfectly. Negro was expendable, but he was also a loyal soldier who would do what was ordered and do it right. And at six two, 230 pounds, he was big enough—and aggressive enough—to inflict serious damage.

The weapon was a bone-crusher made of steel with an exposed blade about five inches long. Apache gave it to Negro while we were in the dayroom and he was out on the broom.

I wasn't told when or how it would happen.

After getting back to my cell from the dayroom, Chente called me to the bars and said, "They're going to punch that puto's ticket tonight."

"I figured it would be soon. All right now, gracias."

The next time the unit cop came to his control panel was for a shower change, and the next person to use the shower was Magilla. He passed by as usual in his boxers and shower shoes. I figured they'd get him then, but when I heard the shower door close and the water turn on, I sat back down and continued reading *The Annals of the Black Company*, a book I had just received from the library. If Negro hadn't made his move by then, he'd make it when Magilla came out. The only problem with the plan was the cop would see it all.

Negro came by and put the broom up against the wall, then took off his jumpsuit and shirt, leaving only his boxers and shoes. He pulled the bone-crusher out of his jumpsuit pocket and went to the shower. That's when I heard the shower door being ripped open.

It hadn't occurred to me that a domino could be placed in the shower door, where Magilla would not only be caught off guard but also without shoes.

"Hey, what the fuck, Negro."

That was the only thing I heard before it started. Somehow Magilla broke away from Negro. They were out of the shower area and fighting on the tier. Magilla punched and did everything in his power to keep Negro away from him, but it was useless. Blood poured from Magilla's chest, stomach, and neck. I heard the unit door open and the cop entered his control booth. When he saw what was happening, he ran toward my cell.

What could he do? He was behind Plexiglas, and all the yelling he did, telling them to stop, wouldn't make any difference. It would only stop when it was over.

Magilla slowed down and Negro moved in to finish him, but Magilla had played possum, and at the last moment swung his fist and connected with Negro's face, staggering him. As soon as that happened, Magilla tried to run for the unit door to escape the brutal stabbing. But he wasn't fast enough, and Negro caught him from behind and continued stabbing him viciously, stopping only when Magilla collapsed on the tier. Negro went to his cell and the door closed behind him. Medical staff rushed in to help Magilla and a gurney was brought in to take him to the hospital.

A few moments later, more than ten cops came into the unit and escorted Negro away. He would go to the hole for ten days and then return to the unit. The case would be referred to the DA's office, but they rarely prosecuted jail assault cases unless someone died.

A team of cops came and took pictures of the shower, the tier, and wherever they saw blood or evidence. They searched Negro's cell, but the knife had been passed along and then flushed. By the time they turned off the water so no one could flush anymore, the weapon was long gone.

Later we learned Magilla was stabbed a total of thirty-one times, had a collapsed lung and other serious damage, but would survive. I was surprised to hear the DA's office picked up the case and prosecuted Negro for attempted murder. He ended up taking a deal that would send him to prison for nine years. He'd sacrificed nine years of his life for the privilege to impress someone else.

Meanwhile, I went about my business as if nothing happened, and maybe part of that was true. I'd seen so much brutality over the years since my arrest, that one more stabbing didn't make any difference to me. But I was wrong. No matter how much you believe something so brutal doesn't affect you or change you, it does, unless you become a monster and lose your humanity completely. I could wear the mask of a monster, but at the end of the day I was only a scared twenty-one-year-old boy in way over my head.

Chapter 27

Adolescence, 1980–1981

Soon after my father left our house I was kicked out of Heights Lutheran. I really didn't care. I was sixteen and alone with nothing but resentment over my childhood beatings, abuse, bullies, and betrayals. Of course, I continued taking steroids and that only made things worse.

More and more often I was disqualified from fighting competitions for being too aggressive, and, although it frustrated me, I still received praise for my skill as a fighter. That year I won the Hapkido Middleweight Championship, and I was regularly invited to attend Black Belt seminars where techniques and the evolution of the art were discussed. I often demonstrated my technique and its effectiveness against traditional Hapkido styles at those events, but I never revealed that everything I did was fueled by anabolic steroids.

After being kicked out of Heights Lutheran, my mother went on and on about how it would look, and how she worked so hard to give me the type of home and opportunities most people only dreamed of. It was only school, and I didn't like being there anyway. Most days, I'd check in at school and then leave or go surfing early in the morning and not bother to go back. It all seemed like a waste of time to me. I couldn't sit still in class and nothing interested me. The final straw had been when a guy named Stuart told the principal I took a small stereo—which I hadn't. I punched him in the face and that earned me a ticket out of Heights Lutheran forever.

The following week my mother enrolled me in La Puente High School, and that marked the beginning of my criminal career. La

Puente High was full of gang members, and I knew a lot of them from the neighborhood as well as from my days at Sparks Elementary. The only difference was I wasn't a scared little boy anymore. Instead, if anyone attempted to pick on me or beat me up, I'd make them sorry the thought ever crossed their minds.

Of course, the reputation I'd so carefully groomed at Heights Lutheran hadn't reached La Puente, but it didn't take long.

For the most part I stayed to myself, but others usually were drawn to me because of my looks. As much as I tried to avoid people, nothing worked short of pushing someone away physically. I settled into school and, although I didn't particularly like being there, I went to class and tried to remain invisible.

During my third week at La Puente High I saw the basketball coach posting try-out posters, and as I read it he asked if I'd be going out for the team. I said I was seriously considering it.

"Good. I'm Coach Pilcher, the varsity team coach. You play?"

"I played shooting guard for Heights Lutheran's varsity team."

"Did you log time?"

"I was their starting guard."

"Well then, I'll see you at practice Monday. It's good meeting you."

"Same here, coach. I'm Bill."

He shook my hand and I walked away feeling better about the school, and I thought maybe I could make it work.

The following Monday I was in the gym before practice because I didn't have a class. I was shooting around when other members of the varsity team arrived, and soon a half-court three-on-three pickup game started. We played to thirty-six and during the game I noticed the coach watching. As soon as most of the guys who were trying out were there, Coach Pilcher put us through a series of ball-skill sequences, including dribbling, passing, and shooting. He then separated us by position and had us play each other one-on-one. I did well, but not great. I won four of five games, even though I hadn't practiced in a few months.

After a few practices, the coach cut a number of people who would not make the team. He sent others to the junior varsity team.

To that point, I had done well and logged time with the team. The previous year's starting guard had graduated and the position needed to be filled. I seemed to have the job locked in.

Another week passed and Coach Pilcher set his rotation for games.

I was the starting guard along with a fast point guard named Kenny. At the end of the week I came to practice with the rest of the team and was warming up when the coach called me into his office. I quickly ran to his office expecting to talk about game situations, but as soon as I walked into his office and looked at his face, I knew something was wrong.

"What's up, coach?"

"Sit down, Bill."

I sat, but I knew it wouldn't be good.

"Your counselor came to see me this morning. She pointed out that because you attended another high school and played ball for them, you're not eligible to play here until next season."

"Coach, that was a private school. It doesn't count. This is a public school."

"I'm sorry, son. I've argued with her, but there's nothing I or anyone can do."

I couldn't believe it.

"This is bullshit. There has to be a way around it. Just tell me. I'll do it."

"Believe me, I've tried. I've called the district offices and it's in black and white. You can't play."

A hole formed in the pit of my stomach. I didn't want anyone to see how it affected me, so I left and went to my counselor's office hoping something could be done to fix it. There had to be a way, but her answer was the same as the coach. I couldn't play.

I didn't go back to school that day. Instead I went to the beach and walked along the shore, not really doing anything except allowing my mind to wander. I didn't want to admit it, but I really wanted to be on the team. It would have given me a sense of belonging and a reason to make school a part of my life.

I blamed everything on my parents, specifically my mother. If it weren't for her self-serving reasons for making me attend a private school, I would have attended La Puente or Los Altos High and I would be able to play.

The thoughts fueled my anger as I drove to Go-Go's house, where we smoked pot and hung out the rest of the night.

I thought the anger would go away, but it didn't. On Monday when I entered the school parking lot, Kenny and another basketball player named Terry walked up as I parked my car. I realized how badly I wanted to be on the team. I was good enough, but because of some stupid red tape I wasn't allowed to play.

"Hey man, we heard what happened. Fuck, we needed you. Without you we're not going anywhere," said Kenny.

"You guys will do great. I don't even know what to say. I'm so pissed I could scream."

"Hey, why don't you practice with us before and after team practice so you're ready to go if things change, or next season," said Terry.

"Nah, that would only piss me off more and nothing's going to change. I'm fucked for the season."

We shook hands and I walked off. If I hadn't allowed my anger to rule my actions and thoughts, I would have taken up Terry and Kenny's offer, but I didn't. Instead, I never played again and my resentment grew.

I attended the rest of my classes that day, then went to the weight room to lift some weights and cool off. After lifting for a few minutes, I stopped. I couldn't focus. All I could think of was the team and how much I wanted to play, and it made me want to punch a wall. I showered and went to the parking lot to put my things in my car and go home when I noticed a beautiful black '56 oval window ragtop Volkswagen pulling into the parking lot a few spaces down from me. It was lowered to the ground with Porsche alloys and a high-performance engine.

The guy driving was Hispanic, tall, hair cut short and styled, and he was dressed to the nines. I had seen him and some of his friends around school but never really paid much attention to them. His car had my attention, but he somehow just fit in it and looked the part.

He got out and stood next to the car, with the stereo playing a type of Euro-disco. I continued to admire the car and took note of how much it looked like a show car. Everything was perfect. The paint, chrome, and wheels alone must have cost a fortune. It was a clean-ass California Volkswagen.

As he stood there, two Mexican gang members approached. They were Cholos, members of a street gang and the type of idiots I dealt with on a daily basis when I had attended Sparks Elementary. It was guys like that who always picked on me and bullied me when I was younger.

They heard the music the guy was playing and went to investigate. Seeing the car, and the guy who stood next to it, they saw an opportunity to mess with someone who looked like he wouldn't fight back. I sat in my car and watched. The two guys came up to the car and remarked about the stereo and how clean the ride was. Then one of the guys stuck his head in the car and turned up the stereo. Instead of the music becoming distorted, its rich bass pumped up to a heart-thumping sound, which meant his system was probably worth more than my entire car.

As soon as the stereo was turned up, the car's owner opened the driver's side door and turned it off, then put his keys in his pocket.

"Hey ese, turn it back on. What the fuck?" one of the Cholos yelled.

It was then I noticed who had yelled and why he seemed familiar. He took off his shades to approach the car's owner, and that's when I recognized him and his brother. It had been years since I'd seen Robert and Ernie Hernandez. The last time was the day they'd hit me in the head with a rock, taken my money, chain, and cross, and left me on the street bloodied and hurt.

My father fought their father that day, and I got my chain and cross back, but as I looked at them and remembered what they had done to me, my hand went to the same chain and cross I still wore. The hurt of that day came rushing back and a storm of rage overwhelmed me. I got out of my car and Ernie turned to me. He didn't recognize me. How could he? I looked nothing like the kid he and his brother had constantly bullied. He turned his attention back to what his brother was doing and forgot me. By then his brother had changed from just being curious about the car to being a thug. He pushed the driver up against his car and demanded the keys.

The guy was scared and Robert saw it, so he pressed him. He knew he'd get his way.

I went and stood next to Ernie. He seemed startled I'd appeared next to him, but he covered it well.

"What the fuck you looking at, ese?" he said.

"You and your punk brother still playing tough guys, huh?"

I was a good six or seven inches taller than him, and when it was obvious I was there as a threat he got pushy.

"Hey, fuck you, puto. Aquí para Puente."

"Man, you're still a bitch." I shoved him back. I had to admit, he didn't hesitate, and he knew what he was doing. His hands flashed and he punched at me in crisp combinations, which I sidestepped. I could tell he was a trained boxer who was used to taking people down quickly. He pressed me hard with more punches, but none connected. I easily blocked and avoided his hands, which were fast, but like most boxers, he used rehearsed combinations that he threw in any given situation. He knew what to do because he'd practiced the same punches over and over again—not because he knew how to apply it to a real fight with a real fighter. As soon as he dipped his right shoulder to throw a right hook, I struck fast with my right fist, beating him to the spot and connecting with his eye socket, stopping him in his tracks. I needed to end the fight fast and not get blindsided by his brother again. I picked Ernie up around the waist and body-slammed him into the concrete, knocking him out cold.

Robert watched what I'd done to his brother and came to help. I was no longer thinking. My vision had clouded red and the rage and pain those two had caused me as a child surfaced as if it had happened yesterday.

Robert never had a chance. I hit him as he opened his mouth to say something, and drove him to his knees with vicious punches to the face and elbows to the head.

The next thing I remember is waking up in bed at 2:13 a.m. I had lost more than twelve hours. A dangerous pattern had developed. Triggered by emotions like fear, hate, or pain, I'd lose control and black out. Of course, I continued to function, but I'd have no memory of what I'd done.

It never happened when I fought in competition because that was only business, but when emotions were involved, when the situation opened up emotional wounds that hurt me or brought back memories of when I was a victim, that old rage returned.

The following day I went to school, but I didn't want to see any of the guys on the team. I parked my car on the other side of the school next to the park. I just wanted to forget it and move on. I knew I'd see them eventually, but I hated hearing people tell me how sorry they were or how there was always next season.

By lunchtime I had reconciled myself to not being on the team by convincing myself I was already so busy that team practices and games would make my schedule impossible. A part of me knew I could have managed it, but allowing myself to believe, or at least pretend that the team would have been more trouble than it was worth, also helped me manage how upset I felt about it.

I sat next to my car listening to music and talking to a guy I'd met a few weeks previously, named Corban, when the guy who owned that '56 oval window ragtop came up. Again, I noticed how he was dressed.

"Hey, what's up, Bill? You got a moment?"

"Yeah, what's up? How do you know my name?"

"I asked around because I wanted to talk to you and say thanks for yesterday."

"Hey, don't sweat it. Those two idiots had it coming."

"Yeah, but what you did saved me from a major problem. He wanted my keys and who knows what would have happened then."

"It's cool man. Really."

He shook my hand. "My name's Adrian. Thanks for helping me out."

I watched him walk away.

"Who's that cat?" Corban asked.

"I don't really know, I just met him. But yesterday he had problems with a couple of them Mexican clowns who hang out by the handball courts. Anyway, I fucked their asses up. They weren't shit and had it coming."

"No doubt. Why'd you help him out?"

"Don't know. They just pissed me off."

Corban was cool, and we got along, but I didn't tell him the truth because that would be letting him get too close, and I didn't let anyone see behind the mask.

Like me, Corban got kicked out of his former school. He'd been caught smoking weed on the school campus, and since his mother couldn't deal with it he'd been sent to live with his father.

"Hey, I gotta get to class. I'll see you later. Take it easy," Corban said.

I sat there for a few minutes before I also went to class, but I couldn't stop thinking about Adrian's car.

About a week later, I walked home from school because my car had broken down. Although I put just about every dime I earned from working at the skating rink into the car, it was never enough and always needed repair. It would take at least a few weeks of saving to pay for the new fuel pump my car needed to get back on the road. Until then, I had no choice but to walk.

As I walked, I was wondering how much overtime I'd have to log before I could get the fuel pump, when I heard music. It was the same music Adrian played the day I fought Robert and Ernie. When I turned to look for his car, the black '56 pulled up next to me. Adrian turned down his stereo.

"Where you headed?"

"Home."

"Get in. I'll take you. We'll just stop at my pad real quick."

"Sounds good."

I got in his car and it was as if I'd stepped into another world—one I wanted to be a part of. He turned his stereo up and pulled away. I looked at the interior and it, too, was show condition. The entire car was a marvel. The thump of the stereo in my chest along with the roar of the engine sent my senses into overdrive. He knew what the experience would do to me. He knew I'd never be satisfied with anything less.

He turned toward the high school, and as we neared campus he opened the ragtop and hit his amps. His stereo jumped to another level and everyone within two hundred yards turned to look at us. I never felt anything like it, and Adrian smiled at me. It was his world, and as he drove slowly, allowing everyone to see, hear, and envy him, he kept his face straight as if nothing was out of the ordinary. He didn't stop or talk to anyone. It was as if he was telling everyone, look but don't touch.

I said nothing. I was too busy taking it all in, and I decided I wanted it. I didn't know it then, but Adrian made up his mind to give me exactly that.

When we arrived at his house I expected to find myself at the gates of a mansion. How else could he afford that kind of car? Instead, we arrived at a small home that was well taken care of, but there was nothing special about it except there were four other show-condition Volkswagens parked in the driveway and on the street just in front of his house.

All the cars had their original chrome, and nothing was cut, shaved, or altered. They were all 1965 and older convertibles or ragtops, lowered to the ground with Porsche alloy wheels and built chrome engines. Each one had a perfect paint job and was waxed and buffed to a shine.

Adrian saw how impressed I was.

"These are a few of our cars. The red convertible '62 Karmann Ghia is my brother, Julian's. He's our president. The blue-gray '57 oval ragtop is Luis's, our vice president. The black '59 ragtop is Francis's, and the red '65 convertible is Ruben's."

"Damn. These rides are clean. Where do you work? It must cost a fortune to afford and keep up these rides."

"I do a little here and a little there."

"Shit, got any openings? I work my ass off and I can't even afford a fuckin' fuel pump."

"Maybe, you never know."

He had me. I wanted to know more, but just then four guys came out of the garage behind the house. I noticed another car in the garage, but the door closed and it was blocked from my view. I didn't know any of the guys except one. Francis was in one of my classes at La Puente High, and he and Adrian were usually together.

"That's my brother, Julian."

"Who's this, Adrian?" asked Julian.

"This is Bill, the guy I told you about who beat down those two guys who were fucking with me."

Julian shook my hand. "Hey, thanks for looking out for my little brother."

I nodded. "They had it coming."

Francis smiled at me. "What's up, Bill? We have a couple classes together."

We shook hands and the other guys were introduced to me. Julian, Luis, and Ruben were all over twenty years old and said they had somewhere to be and left, followed by Francis.

"I gotta help them out. We're working on that grey vert." Adrian and I spent the next few hours together until I had to get to the studio to work out. He drove me home.

"How are you getting to school tomorrow?"

"Probably walking. My car's not running."

"I'll pick you up at around seven forty-five."

"Cool, thanks. See you tomorrow."

For the next two weeks Adrian picked me up for school and, after hanging out for a while after school, dropped me off.

When I saved enough to buy my fuel pump I put it in, but I didn't want to drive my car. I told Adrian I needed a new job so I could afford a car like his. I also asked him again what he did and if maybe there was a job opening where he worked. He smiled again and said, "Maybe. We'll check it out."

Another month of the same routine passed before Adrian showed up at my house driving his sister's BMW 320i and asked, "You want to work with me?"

"Of course," I said. "Yes."

"Get in. We need to talk."

I got in and we drove to a warehouse in Montebello. As soon as the car stopped I opened the door to get out, but he stopped me.

"Wait up. I need to talk to you. This isn't a regular job and I need to know you can keep your mouth shut. This isn't a game and the guys inside are serious as a heart attack."

He looked straight at me and I could tell he wasn't sure if this was a good idea.

"Listen, we've been hanging around with each other for a couple of months, and at first I thought you had some killer job that paid well, but since you never went to work I figured you probably were doing something like selling drugs. And since you always have good weed, it fit. Whatever you're doing is safe with me. You don't have to worry about that."

"Right on, but just so you know. I'm not a drug dealer. I do change-overs on cars."

"You do what?"

"You'll see. Let's go."

We went to the front of the warehouse and he knocked on the small door. A few seconds later Francis opened it and seemed surprised to see me, but then smiled and let us in. Working on a car inside were three guys I'd seen at Adrian's house, plus one more I'd never seen.

"Francis, Adrian, we need help lifting the shell. The new pan is ready," Julian said.

Everyone there grabbed a corner of the car by the bumpers. Francis got inside the car with a box cutter and Adrian walked over and stood next to what I assumed was the new pan, which was the underbelly of the car. Except it already had the front end, transmission, and Porsche alloy wheels. All at once, they lifted the body/shell off its original pan. As soon as they did, Francis cut the carpet, which was still attached and wouldn't allow the body to be lifted off its pan. Once that was done, they carried the body over and set it down on the new pan. Adrian lined it up as it was put in place and they started bolting it down. Adrian and Julian went off by the door to talk. I knew it was probably about me, so I waited.

"Hey Bill, grab me that torque wrench sitting next to my tool box," said Francis. "This baby doll is clean, huh?"

"Yeah, what is it, a '60?"

"'58 European convertible. It's Marco's, and when he pops out with it, everybody's going to eat cheese," he laughed. "Hey Marco, this is Bill. He's the one we were telling you about."

"What's the word, Bill? How do you like my new ride?"

"She's clean. What size motor are you going to run in it?"

He smiled at me. "It's a secret, but it's big and will blow the doors off anything around."

I imagined how the car would look when it was completely done, and I envied Marco. I wanted to be a part of that and have a car like his. I was still unsure exactly what was going on, but I wanted in.

Francis jumped into the '58 and sat on the floor where the driver's seat should be, his hands on the steering wheel and his head barely visible.

"Hey Marco, Darque Knights down. Everybody eats cheese," Francis yelled as he laughed.

Francis was always laughing or playing around, even in class. If I'd look at him, he'd smile so everyone knew he was up to something.

I watched Marco and Francis work until Adrian and Julian came back from their talk.

"Hey Bill, check it out. Adrian tells me you're cool and can keep your mouth shut. This is a serious deal and none of us want to get busted. If you want to back out, tell me now and there's no hard feelings. But if you decide to stay and we let you know what's up, we expect your loyalty and help," Julian said.

"I understand. I may not know exactly what's going on, but I have a good idea. Seriously, I thought you guys were dealing drugs and that's how you could afford your rides. Either way, I'm not going to say shit. I want in."

"Here's the deal. This '58 is stolen. We took it last night from San Diego and drove it back. Now it's Marco's because he bought a wrecked '58 for one hundred fifty dollars. We unbolted the wrecked body and prepared the pan for the '58 we stole. Once we got it, we unbolted it from its original pan where the serial numbers are and placed it on this one, which Marco owns and will register. The only other numbers on the body are in the form of a small plate under the front hood behind where the spare tire goes. Here, I'll show you."

We walked over and he lifted the hood.

"See that plate? Watch."

He got a screwdriver and broke the rivets holding it in place, then pulled another plate from his shirt pocket and Adrian handed him a rivet gun, which he used to rivet the new plate where the old one had been.

"Mission accomplished. This is now Marco's new ride. All we have to do now is finish bolting it down, connect all the wiring, put in the motor, and he'll pop out tomorrow night. We're all going to the boulevard."

"Let me get this straight. This bad-ass ride cost Marco a hundred fifty bucks? No shit."

Luis and Ruben came over to where we stood.

"Órale, Bill, it's all about the Darque Knights. We're now ten strong, and if you put one together, we'll be eleven," said Ruben.

We all shook hands. "Yeah, I'm in."

My thoughts were going a hundred miles an hour and I was smiling ear to ear. For the rest of the day, I helped them put the '58 together. By four that afternoon it was done, and I told Adrian I had to get to the studio to train and he drove me home.

The next morning after my run, Adrian picked me up and we went back to help put in the motor and get it ready for the boulevard that night. I barely slept, I was so excited. I kept thinking of the car I wanted for myself and how I could get the money I needed. The first thing I'd do was sell my car. I knew a guy who wanted to buy it but didn't have a lot of money. I would take what he had. The important thing would be to get started, and to do that I needed cash.

As we put the motor in and got everything put together, I realized that, although all of them knew a lot about Volkswagens, they didn't know much of anything about the motors and transmissions. They referred to a built motor as "big," but they didn't know the size of the crank, pistons, or cam it had. They could take a motor out and put it in with their eyes closed, but the inner workings of the engine and transmission were foreign to them.

By 11:30 a.m. it was done and Marco got inside and turned the key and the motor came to life with a roar. He was right. The motor was big. It had dual Weber 48 IDA carburetors and its response to the accelerator was immediate.

"Get in, Bill. Let's take a spin."

As soon as we hit the street, he opened it up and I could tell the work done to the engine was extreme and done right. I couldn't believe the car cost him under $200.

We drove around the block a couple of times and then came back to the warehouse, where we sat around drinking beer, smoking weed, and talking about stealing cars and how it was done the fastest. I learned the easiest way to get in was by popping out the back quarter window on the driver's side and then reaching in and opening the door by hand. One way to start it was to connect a wire with two roach clips on each end to the first and last fuse in the fuse box right under the dashboard on the driver's side. Luis pulled a pair from his pocket and handed them to me. We went to his car and he showed me how to do it. As soon as I placed the roach clips on the fuses, the lights on the dashboard came on.

"See those lights? All you have to do is push the car while it's in neutral, jump in, put it in second and pop the clutch, and it'll start. That's one way. Another is to open the front trunk. Here, I'll show you."

He opened the front trunk of his car and showed me the back of the ignition. There were three wires attached to it.

"Pull the wires out and touch them together and the car will start. Then let go of the bottom wire and roach-clip the remaining two together and the car will stay on. I can break into any car in less than fifteen seconds and start it in even less than that."

I listened to everything he said and drank it in. I wanted to know everything he knew and I was dying to try it all out.

That night, before we went to the boulevard, I called the guy I knew was interested in my car and made a deal to sell it to him. I needed quick cash, so I sold it for $1,000. The guy could hardly believe it and became suspicious something was wrong with it. But after driving and testing it out, the deal was made.

When the guys arrived at my house, they made a grand entrance. All ten of the club's members showed up and lined my street with their cars. You could hear them coming because their stereo systems were all playing the same song, and I swear I felt like royalty. I got in Adrian's car and we took off with Julian in the lead. It was a caravan of the baddest cars I had ever seen, and I was with them. I was a member of the Darque Knights.

From the start, I saw the type of reception we got from everyone at the boulevard where we cruised as well as in the parking lot where we stopped and many other car clubs were parked. Later, when we went to a dance club, the reception was the same. Everyone wanted to be around us. Guys wanted to be seen with us, and girls wanted to be with us. It was like we were some kind of celebrities. I watched it all with morbid fascination, and it was with this insight that I saw it. Most of the guys who seemed to be friendly at first glance, when observed closely, were actually envious and hated every one of us.

It wasn't just because of the cars, either. It was everything. From walking into the club without paying or waiting in line, to the way women responded to us. I say us because I had become one of them, but I could tell it was something that had been going on for a long time. The Darque Knights were all pretty boys. At least that's how I heard someone refer to us. We'd all been hand-picked, as Adrian later explained, to represent a certain idea, look, and concept.

Who were the Darque Knights? You had to be Hispanic, from the La Puente area, have a certain look, your car had to be a 1967 or older and stolen (change-over). Your car and you had to represent the club at all times, and above all else our business was ours and we stuck together. At least that's what the rules were. Later, I learned the rule above all others would be to watch your own back and trust no one.

For the next few days, Adrian and I planned everything about what my car would look like and where to look for it. The plan was to steal an original car, then steal a fixed up California-style one with the rims, engine, stereo, and everything I wanted, and then put those parts on my original car. If you planned it carefully, it would only take two cars.

I had found a wrecked '63 Volkswagen on a lot in Covina and bought it for $130. I had put it in a small warehouse in La Puente, about a mile from my house, that I'd rented for three days. That day, I unbolted the wrecked body and cleaned and prepared the pan for its new body. Once that was done, Adrian and I took his sister's car and went out looking for a clean '63, and another car that had all the parts I wanted. I was nervous. Not about stealing a car, but about making the deadline of three days to find the cars and put mine together. We drove to Pasadena because Adrian said he heard of a clean '63 sedan in an apartment complex, but assured me we'd find our mark even if the first one wasn't there. It was 9:45 p.m. when we got off the 210 Freeway in Pasadena.

"Let's stop at In-N-Out Burger and get something to eat. It's early and I'm fuckin' hungry," said Adrian.

"Yeah, me too. But I want to see if that '63 is there first, then go eat and come back and get it. I don't want to waste time if that ride's not there. I only have that place for three days and I want to make it count."

"Let's go check it out. It's only a few miles up the road."

Arriving at the apartment complex, we first checked the street for it in case it was parked outside, then we drove into the underground parking lot.

"Stop. Back up," I said. He put the car in reverse and eased back until I could see the red VW. We parked and got out, but even before we were fifteen yards away, I knew I wasn't interested. It was a '63 sedan. It was clean, but not to the level of perfection the rest of the club's cars were.

"Let's split. I don't want it. We'll have to keep looking. Know of any other ones?"

"Yeah, but they're in Orange County. Let's go eat and I'll call Francis and see if he'll give up some of his secrets. He has a list of cars and where they are."

As I got into the car, the sound of tires got my attention. I could hear the engine and the distinct sound of stock Tweety Bird mufflers of older Volkswagens. I saw the headlights first as it turned the corner of the parking lot and came toward us. It was a '63 and it was also red.

But the difference between it and the one we first saw was obvious even as it drove by and parked a few spaces away.

The '63 was perfect and fully restored. We waited a few minutes and then went to take a look at it. Even up close, the car looked as if it had just come off the showroom floor in 1963.

"Man, she's clean as fuck. What do you think?"

I nodded, but could barely hear Adrian. My mind was racing. My heart pounded in my chest and my eyes were locked on the '63. My focus was absolute. I reached out and touched the door handle and when I pressed it, it clicked open. I didn't bother to look around. I got in the driver's seat and pulled my roach clips and wire out and placed them on the first and last fuse. The dash lights came on.

"It's too early, Bill. We'll come back later."

"I got this. Later might be too late. I don't think it lives here."

Putting the '63 in neutral, I backed up. When he saw what I was doing, Adrian helped. As soon as we got it out of the parking space, we pushed it forward and, as it picked up speed, I jumped in, threw it into second, and popped the clutch. It started immediately. I didn't bother to look back at Adrian. I drove out of the apartment complex and in the direction of the warehouse. My heart pounded in my chest and ears. The adrenaline pumping through my veins was off the charts. To be perfectly candid, I loved it. I grew addicted to it and would later start to seek it out as if it were a drug.

Arriving at the warehouse, I drove it into the space next to the pan I had readied and got out. Even under the lights of the warehouse, it was perfect. Adrian arrived and walked in.

"Damn. You're crazy as fuck, but this baby doll is clean," laughed Adrian. "When I saw the dash lights come on and saw you were going to take it, I freaked. I couldn't believe you had the balls for it." He shook my hand. "You're down, ese."

"Let's call Francis. I want to know if he knows where any rides are with alloys and a big motor. I want to get it tonight so we can start by tomorrow."

We closed the warehouse and went to a phone booth and dialed Francis's number.

"What's up, Francis? I'm with Bill, we just got his '63. Yeah, it's clean. Hey, do you know where any big motors are?"

Adrian turned to me. "He knows where a few are, but wants to come with us."

"Tell him to get ready. Let's do this," I said.

We picked up Francis and he told us of at least four rides in Orange County that he described as "white boy fast with alloys."

Most of the guys in the club referred to fast rides as white boy fast, because, according to them, white guys always worried about the speed of their cars rather than how they looked. Therefore, their engines and transmissions were almost always built right and were fast.

We drove to Newport Beach and, just as Francis said, we found four rides within a mile of each other. We took a close look at all of them and all four of them had duel carbs and alloy wheels, but just one of them was complete. It had everything I wanted. It was a white '67 sun roof sedan with fully polished Porsche alloy wheels and Ricardo seats. It was close to show condition.

I decided I'd take it, but because Francis found it, a fee or tribute would have to be made to him. At first I thought he was joking, but Adrian explained it was always like that with us, and Francis usually went out twice a week just to scope for rides so he'd know where they were and get a finder's fee.

"What do you want?" I said.

"Not much." And in his best Godfather voice said, "I just want to wet my beak, that's all," then laughed. "Listen, Bill, I know you need the motor, trans, wheels, and stereo, so how about you give me them two Ricardo seats and we'll be even. Deal?"

"Let's do this."

It was close to midnight and raining lightly. The car was parked next to an Aston Martin, and I stuck my flat screwdriver under the corner of the back quarter window and popped the entire window out, then reached in and pulled the handle, opening the door. I got in and opened the passenger side door for Francis, putting the car in neutral. I released the emergency brake and backed it out of the driveway, pausing only to look around and listen. I pushed the car forward and down the street. I didn't want to start it there because the sound of the engine would wake its owner. Halfway down the block I got inside as Francis pushed and placed my clips in the fuse box and popped the clutch. The engine roared to life. Francis jumped in. "Let's go."

I put it in first and drove off. From the start I knew it was built right and to the gills. Its transmission had close-ratio gears and the roar of the engine sent chills up my spine. Under the dash was a huge monster tach that indicated the RPMs. Then suddenly, while I drove, the engine started to die. "What's wrong?"

"Fuck, I don't know," I said. I flipped the switches on the polished aluminum dashboard. The first one turned on the lights and the second one was for the inside lights. As panic set in, I flipped the third one and the sound of the electric fuel pump caught my ear as life flowed back into the engine. My panic wasn't because I thought I'd get caught, but because I thought I might not be able to make it to the warehouse, and I'd lose the ride.

I jumped on the freeway and opened it up. Damn, it was powerful, and Francis said, "This is the baddest motor around."

I knew he thought he should have kept it for himself, but it was mine now.

We arrived at the warehouse a little after 1:30 a.m., and as soon as I parked I turned on the lights and closed the door. Adrian came in and locked the door behind him. It was then Francis said, "You scored. Look at this motor." He opened up the deck lid and what I saw made me smile. The entire motor was chromed out with 48 IDA Webers and velocity stacks. It was beautiful, and it was mine.

I went through the entire car and found receipts for the engine and trans, built by Rimco and Small Car Specialties.

The receipts told me the motor was a 2180cc powerhouse that would blow the doors off of anything around. Francis was right. I had scored.

For the next two days and nights, Adrian, Francis and I worked on stripping the '67 of everything and placing its front end and trans on my new pan. Once that was done, we unbolted the '63 and called Julian, who brought Ruben and Renee—Francis's brother and another member of the club—to help us lift the body and place it on the pan.

As soon as they saw what I had, they all approved.

"Bill, this is one badass '63. When you pop out with it, you'll be holding down," Julian said.

"What are you going to do with the '67?" asked Ruben.

"Probably cut it up. I don't want it to be found around here because the cops may start looking around," I said.

"Let me have it. I'll bring a flatbed this afternoon and it'll save you the work of cutting it up." I knew Ruben had a connection with a car stereo place and could get some of the best stereo equipment.

"How about I give you the '67 and you hook up my stereo with amps and speakers?"

"Deal. I'll bring it by this afternoon."

By that afternoon, I finished putting my car together and Ruben took the '67. Everyone was gone except Adrian and Francis. I was tightening down my carbs while Francis and Adrian finished lowering the front end. The next day I'd change the door locks and take it to a place that specialized in interior and carpeting.

"Start this motherfucker up, ese," said Adrian.

I got inside and looked at my ride. Everything was perfect. I flipped the hidden switch for my electric fuel pump and turned the key. The engine came to life in its new body with a roar. I backed it out of the warehouse and Adrian and Francis got in. Revving the engine, I pulled onto the street, driving around the block to get a feel for the car. I don't know if I was happy, but for that day the void inside was satisfied. How could I have known that to stay satisfied I'd have to steal over and over again?

Chapter 28

San Quentin Death Row, 1993-1994

In these pages you may come to the conclusion that I am a contradiction. You would not be alone in thinking so. On a number of occasions I've even been referred to as "a perfect contradiction." I'm a man well-read who understands a progressive state of mind as well as the sensitivities of the soul. And yet the polar opposite exists side by side, in good standing. I'm a Neanderthal, a man ruled by primal instinct and an animalistic focus. I am both sides of the coin, and I make no excuses for who I am. I refer to it here in order for you to understand there is truth—and value—to both sides.

What may not be apparent is that I am afraid. Fear is at the center of this existence. Each day I live behind these brutal walls, I fear for my life and of disappearing as an individual. Fear triggers the inferno deep inside me that rebels and struggles against the opinion that I deserve to die, that I have nothing to contribute, and that I will be defined by my surroundings, thus becoming one with them.

Maybe I'm trying to prove it to myself as well. I made a horrible mistake—one I regret and think about daily since that night so many years ago when I lost control. Never far from my thoughts is the fact that I'm responsible for the loss of a life, and nothing I ever do will make up for it. So why try? Why continue with the struggle against this opinion? Because I am a human being. Because I regret it. Because I am responsible and wish to express my remorse and apologize for the pain I have caused.

This struggle, if you haven't guessed, is also against myself. I caused others to view me this way. It's solely up to me to attempt to change it.

In the months after the execution of Robert Alton Harris, I noticed certain developments taking place. My dreams and nightmares often had fields of color and music. Never before had that happened. My subconscious mind had always seen and interpreted everything in stark black-and-white images, where only numbers and equations quieted the chaos and storm. Now the fields of color, accompanied by music, moved in like the ocean tide, slowly and gently, but with an unstoppable force that threatened to drown me if I didn't drink in its influence and find its meaning.

I rarely spoke to any of the prisoners around me. Instead, I spent my days thinking of color—the intensity of its influence and its connection to emotions. I longed to speak to another artist about this, but none existed in my world. I was alone with my thoughts, dreams, and this new language made of color.

As all of these revelations were occurring to me, everything around me remained the same. Violence is something that never grows tired here, and when a particular person grows tired of performing it—when his thirst is quenched and he has been used and devoured—it jumps to the next willing person, like a disease.

One person who, for the span of less than fifteen seconds, would fall under the influence of violence was an African American man named Penmen.

I hardly knew Penmen beyond the casual nod while passing each other to and from the iron pile. I did not associate or have any type of relationship with him. However, as with all of the men on the yard, I was intimate with their habits, what made them tick, and their nature.

By that time, I no longer worked out with Sporty. He and the majority of the Mexicans on the yard ended up in the AC for an act of violence. Sporty had come out to the yard one day and stabbed another Mexican repeatedly until the gunner put four rounds into the wall just above his head. It had been over two years since the incident, and he wouldn't be back for another few years, if at all. After arriving in the AC, he'd stabbed yet another inmate. It seemed Sporty was well on his way to becoming what he considered a respected man.

After nearly five years on the iron pile, I also looked different from the twenty-three-year-old kid who struggled with 250 pounds on arrival. I weighed over two hundred pounds, adding thirty pounds of muscle to a six-foot-one frame. It made me look a lot like those gladiators I was once so impressed by.

I had eighteen-inch arms hanging, nearly twenty inches when flexed, a fifty-inch chest, a twenty-nine-inch waist, and less than six percent body fat. I looked like a machine, and I was a man whose body language, attitude, and appearance said one thing: "Don't fuck with me."

One overcast Friday, I considered not going out to the yard. I'd been out every day since Sunday, and I wanted to finish the portrait I was doing for a member of the San Francisco 49ers, but the call of the iron pile won out. I made my way to the yard after being searched thoroughly, which raised my attention. Being searched on the way to the yard was normal. Being searched so thoroughly meant the bulls expected something to happen. I wondered if maybe I was suspected of something, but that thought was quickly dismissed when I saw everyone being delayed because of how closely they were being searched. I looked to the gunners and there were more of them than usual. My stomach tightened as I continued on my way. Something was up and the bulls expected trouble. The only problem was, I had no idea what they expected. I had been out the previous day and nothing caught my attention. That's when it hit me. The bulls knew about it and I didn't because they were putting someone new on the yard, someone they anticipated would cause trouble. The classification committee in East Block meets on Thursdays and they had assigned someone to grade-A status.

I stepped onto the yard and made my way past the shower to a four-foot wall where I normally placed my things. It was also a perfect place to watch who was coming through the gate and how everyone responded to his presence.

Nearly the entire yard had been let out and no one seemed to be aware of the change in the bulls' attitude. But I trusted my instincts. I always paid attention to them and they were never wrong. I glanced at the gunner and he was also on alert, which meant someone would be coming soon. Just as my vision focused on the door where inmates continued to file out, I saw him. It was over a year since I'd seen Polo. That last time, he'd raised a sixty-pound dumbbell over his head and smashed it into the head of an unsuspecting prisoner who sat playing cards. He didn't kill him, but the man would never be the same.

The gate opened and he stepped into the yard. From the immediate response of most of the men, I knew things wouldn't end well. Personally, I had no problem with Polo. We normally nodded to each other whenever we crossed paths. As he made his way to the far end of the yard and surveyed the response to his arrival, our eyes locked on each other and we both nodded.

As soon as all prisoners were out on the yard, the bulls locked the gate and walked off.

Polo remained against the far wall. He put on his shorts and slingshot shirt, then seemed at a loss. No one spoke to him, and the tension on the yard was so thick you could cut it with a knife.

I noticed Polo had lost weight. The year he spent in the hole took fifteen to twenty pounds off him and he looked tired, as if maybe all of it was becoming too much for him.

Normally, he was five foot ten, about 210 pounds with piercing black eyes and tattoos covering his entire chest, arms, and back. He had long black hair and a dark complexion. Rumors said he'd been a hit man for the Hells Angels, but I rarely put much stock in rumors. True or not, it didn't matter. What mattered was what was about to happen.

I remained in my spot and watched. I didn't begin my normal routine because I knew we would be going in early. The minutes passed like the pulse behind a bruise, and I thought of a scene from Romeo and Juliet: *These violent delights have violent ends / And in their triumph die, like fire and powder, / Which, as they kiss, consume.*

I saw Penmen circle the yard. Every time he reached the iron pile, he stopped to do a set of bench presses, and while he did them another prisoner spoke to him, as if he were pumping him up. It's very common for a workout partner to talk to you while you work out, to focus your mind with words of encouragement. But I wasn't fooled.

I saw it for what it was. Penmen was being manipulated and it had nothing to do with lifting weights.

My stomach tightened, as if a fist took hold of it and squeezed. I knew something was about to happen, but something was off.

Penmen finished another set and began to circle the yard again. Polo crossed the yard in the direction of the drinking fountain and shower, which were less than ten feet from where I stood. As he neared, his path crossed Penmen's, and Penmen wasted no time. He exploded into a fury of punches that were aimed at Polo's face. Polo fought back, attempting to stop the attack. Whistles sounded and gunmen yelled, "Stop. Stop. Everyone down on the ground. Now."

Everything slowed down. I watched the two combatants still throwing punches. Then looked to the gunner, who brought his rifle up to his shoulder. Whistles continued to sound. My eyes returned to Polo and Penmen, who had separated, but were still in fighting stances, hands up, ready to resume their fight. Then a single gunshot sounded and Penmen staggered and fell to the ground less than a few feet from me. He looked straight at me, his eyes in shock as much as in pain, but very much focused on me. His right hand reached up to me and his mouth opened as if he wanted to tell me something. His eyes widened and I saw, before they glazed over and his mouth closed, that he was afraid, but it was much too late. He was one of them. The entire yard was ordered down to the ground. In the prone position, I looked up to see dozens of bulls at the gate, where Polo entered and was escorted inside. Then two African convicts carried Penmen to the gate, where he was placed on an orange gurney and taken away. Penmen died on the ground that day on Yard-1 of East Block's death row, looking at me and trying to tell me something. I knew all too well. It occurred to me then that the element I felt before, and recognized but couldn't place, was the approach of death.

Chapter 29

Orange County Jail, 1986–1987

The final months I spent in the high-power unit were relatively quiet. I continued my routine and wore the mask, which grew heavier by the day. I was tired, but determined not to show anyone even the slightest glimmer of weakness. To everyone, I was Sinbad or Mad Bill, a machine that never stopped or slowed down, and I'd do nothing to alter that perception. In truth, my life depended on it. Show weakness to a pack of wolves, no matter how strong or vicious you used to be, and they'll devour you. It's just how things are when you're locked up.

My release from high-power came in 1986. The classification committee found no true or factual evidence that tied me to the attempted escape from the roof, other than the word of an informant who was classified as "confidential." Nevertheless, I spent over a year in high-power with no write-ups and no confrontations with inmates or officers that they knew of. Therefore I was sent to unit-C, to another cell that held eight men. Each cell had a sleeping area and a dayroom attached that contained a shower, phone, TV, and large table.

As I waited for the unit cop to assign me a cell, I stood in the vestibule with my personal property rolled up inside my mattress. Nothing about the situation was new to me, but entering a new unit was always unsettling. I didn't know who would be there and who was running the unit. As I wondered about it, the vestibule door clicked open and Chente walked in.

"So the committee got tired of your ass too, huh?"

"Tú sabes, carnal. They sent me to keep an eye on your crazy ass so you won't get lonely," laughed Chente.

"Man, I'm glad to be out of that fuckin' box. I was tired of that program and the bullshit."

Chente nodded. "Who do you think's running things in there?"

"No idea, and I don't really give a fuck. Let's just get on with this."

The unit cop assigned us both to cell-4 in unit-C15. The two bunks were open because the former occupants had been severely beaten, and one had been stabbed.

"Maybe you'll fare better," the unit cop told us as he opened the unit door.

The cell was like any other eight-man cell I'd been in, but after being in a four-by-eight-foot cell for so long, it seemed huge. Four of the six men in the cell I knew from unit-A, and the other two I knew by reputation. All of them were Southern Mexican gang members, and since Chente and I had just come from the high-power unit, we were treated with a certain amount of respect. This was fine by me. The last thing I wanted to do was have to prove to anyone I shouldn't be fucked with. Luckily, it wouldn't come to that. My reputation preceded me. Word travels fast in prison, and everyone who heard of my reputation and how I took care of business seemed impressed enough not to want to see if it was all true.

I settled in and got into the flow of everyday life on the mainline. Going to the chow hall was something I enjoyed. Especially in the morning, when the rays of sunlight filtered through the windows and touched my face. I also enjoyed the familiar faces I saw there. Many said things like, "It's about time they let you out," or, "You look like someone I used to know." Others just nodded, but they all showed me the one thing I wanted: respect.

Within a month of being on the mainline I was in the dayroom having a cup of coffee just before breakfast when I heard all of the units being locked down. Within moments our unit cop came into the control area and locked us down, then came into the tier with three other cops. They had our pictures, and as they called out our names we stepped forward and were identified. My stomach tightened. It was too familiar. My mind went back to that night after we returned from the roof, the night of the attempted escape. It had been over a year since then, yet the memory was vivid. Once the count was done, the cops left and Chente looked at me.

"Hey ese, you been up to no good? Remember, we have our eyes on you." The last part he said with a Southern drawl imitating the classification committee lieutenant.

"Not me, but you know what, them placas didn't look happy. Something's up and it's serious as fuck."

Later, we sat watching TV and a large grin spread across my face. I'd been right. It all felt familiar because it was. I learned that earlier that morning an escape had been made from the roof. The inmates who escaped had used tools from the roof's equipment locker to break through the roof fence, then scaled down the building using the extension cords they found in the locker.

It turns out Olaf, the one and only Mountain Man who had lived next door to me for more than a year in high-power, had noticed the tools and extension cords, and they'd inspired him to come up with a plan.

What Olaf needed was the keys to the fenced area where the equipment locker was stored, so he befriended a cop, and over time he must have gained his trust.

On the day of his escape, Olaf took another prisoner with him up to the roof.

As soon as they were released from their chains, the prisoners separated. The new prisoner went to the lower level of the roof and Olaf made his way to the control bubble where he convinced his friend the cop to open the door and give him a cup of coffee to warm him up against the cold wind.

Because they were friends, and the cop trusted Olaf, he never paused. He opened the door to hand the cup to Olaf, but when he stepped out of the office Olaf made his move. He grabbed and hit the cop, knocking him out, then took his keys and threw them to the other prisoner, who unlocked the door to the fenced area where the equipment locker sat.

Olaf handcuffed the cop with his own cuffs and placed tape over his mouth so he couldn't call for help. Then he closed the office door, leaving the handcuffed cop outside on the roof with no way to get into his office and alert anyone, even if he managed to escape the cuffs he wore.

Olaf pulled out a steel bar and forced the fence open. Then he and the other prisoner tied together electrical extension cords and scaled down the building wall of the jail. As soon as they hit the street, they separated. After only a few days the other prisoner, who was facing twenty-seven years to life for murder, was caught a few blocks from the jail at a motel sitting by the pool in the company of a hooker.

Olaf, however, was nowhere to be found. When asked, the other prisoner said he knew nothing about his plans or where he could be found. A manhunt continued for Olaf with no results. Days passed, which led to weeks, then months. I often wondered where Olaf had gone and how he was doing. I guessed he left the state or country and would never be caught.

Then one afternoon, a man vaguely familiar looked at me through the TV screen. I turned up the volume and that's when I learned Olaf had been caught in Boston. Gone was the long hair and beard. The man on the TV screen looked nothing like the man I knew except for the flash of his ice-blue eyes.

In the months to come, he was put on trial for the forced escape and, acting as his own attorney, was able to convince a jury the reason he escaped and ran was because he feared for his life from the cops in the jail. He was able to demonstrate the abuse he suffered at their hands and that, if he hadn't escaped, they would have killed him. A jury of twelve found him not guilty. Later, he was sent to prison for the murder he was originally awaiting trial for and I've neither heard from nor seen Olaf since.

Chapter 30

Adolescence, 1981

There would be no turning back for me. I was addicted and I'd do anything to continue experiencing the high.

The ingredients were all the things that brought me the respect and reputation I was building. Not respect in the general sense, like the respect a doctor gets from society. The respect I'm talking about is street respect, based firmly on fear. I was so addicted to building my reputation, I thought of little else. My life became a circle, where everything revolved around getting more of the same.

By this time, I was involved in underground extreme fighting. I'd grown tired of being disqualified from tournaments for being too aggressive. I made it to the finals in an open tournament in San Diego only to be disqualified for knocking my opponent out in what was referred to as an "uncontrolled" hit—which couldn't have been further from the truth. I had complete control and struck my opponent with the precision of a surgeon. But in those competitions, "controlled" meant pulling one's hits—something I didn't believe in. So I quit.

As I went to my car in the company of my father, we were approached by a man who identified himself as a fight scout. He asked if he could talk with me about fighting in a league of fighters where I would never have to worry about being disqualified for being too aggressive, where knocking out my opponent was held in high regard.

I agreed to take a look at his league, and the following week my father and I stood in awe as two men circled each other in the center of a warehouse where hundreds of people placed bets and cheered their fighter. I watched with the eyes of a trained gladiator and an excitement grew inside me. I turned to my father and yelled over the roar of the crowd, "I can beat them." My father smiled and nodded.

Later, after watching three more matches, I spoke to the scout and agreed to a fight. It would take two to three weeks to set up, but he would call me within a couple of days to tell me all the details. For the scout, money was the reason to fight, and he explained I'd receive $2,000 if I won, $1,000 bonus if I knocked out my opponent, and $500 if I lost.

I smiled, leaving little doubt what I thought of losing, and he added that I could make even more if I bet on myself. I'd be the heavy underdog going in because I was unknown and people usually bet on a familiar face. Lastly, he explained the rules. There was only one: No weapons. Everything else was fair game, which basically meant there were no rules.

Over the next two weeks I trained with a renewed excitement and anticipation. I tweaked my style so I'd be more explosive, maintaining an attack for a longer period of time. Gone were the safety mechanisms in my mind. Never again would I pull a punch or kick. My beasts would be allowed free reign.

The night of my first fight, I sat in my father's car waiting. I fought second and wanted to be alone before the fight with my beasts and music, which always brought me an emotional edge and excited me. To Led Zeppelin's "Trampled Under Foot," I visualized what I'd do and how. My opponent had no face. He didn't matter. There was only my will and skill. Nothing would stop me.

There was a knock on the window. I opened my eyes. My father stood outside and nodded. It was time. We made our way to the side door of the warehouse, and as soon as the door opened the smell of cigarette smoke, sweat, blood, and women's cheap perfume assaulted my senses. I wore a hood that covered my head, my eyes were cast down, and with each step closer to my opponent I allowed myself to remember how I was once bullied and beat up.

When I entered the circle, without removing my hood, I knelt and closed off the world. Gone was the crowd, the smell, my opponent. I was alone in my cave and I called to my beasts. Rage and Pain leapt to my side as I reached for them. I opened my eyes and stood, removing my hood. For the first time I saw my opponent. He was Mexican, shorter than me by an inch or two, of dark complexion with gang tattoos, and he outweighed me by twenty pounds or more. But he looked out of shape. I took it all in at first glance, and also noticed he was at least twenty-eight or twenty-nine years old.

None of it mattered. I describe him here so you get an idea of who stood in front of me. To me, at that moment, he was just an opponent. It didn't matter if he was green. Within a few moments it would be over.

Taking off my shirt, I rotated my head, popping my neck joints and preparing myself. The signal to fight was simple. He stepped toward me.

His stance told me the type of fighter he was. Muay Thai. I knew the style and its fighters' habit of throwing long telegraphed roundhouse kicks to the legs and head, followed with short punches and elbows. The style was flawed and only effective against someone of the same style or an unskilled fighter. It wasn't useful, however, against a fighter who had combined the best of several fighting styles and honed them into an instrument of precision and power. He had only a puncher's chance to win, which was to say, he would have to get lucky and catch me with a wild swing.

I advanced on him and didn't give him a chance to study me. Striking out with a front kick aimed at his mid-section, connecting with his hip, I followed with punches to his face, ribs, and kidneys. Sidestepping me and shoving me away, he kicked my leg with a hard roundhouse and followed with a vicious spinning back fist, which grazed my temple. I backed away, giving him space, and he did exactly what he had been trained to do—close the distance with a kick to the head, which I blocked and backed away. I waited and baited him. Every time I backed away, his confidence grew.

The crowd's roar at what seemed like a victory for their fighter ended abruptly. Fighters with habits, when in trouble or on the verge of victory, revert to what they are first taught. Involuntary instincts override everything. Believing I was intimidated, he threw that tele-graphed roundhouse kick, which I'd been waiting for. As soon as he cocked his leg to whip it around, I moved in. In one motion I grabbed his leg in mid-air, and his torso, and using his own momentum I picked him up and slammed him into the concrete. I followed him down, pounding my fists into his face until my father's hands pulled me off him.

The fighter was unconscious. I glanced at him, then at the crowd, and roared my victory for the child I kept safe and protected inside me.

Fighting, stealing, and their by-products gave me a sense of my iden-tity, and I liked it. Even in the club, I soon distinguished myself and gave them a certain edge they'd never had. Before I came along, the club was a few good-looking guys with beautiful cars and a reputation built on the rumor that they stole cars. My very presence changed all that. Street gangs had no choice but to leave us alone. Other clubs respected us and no one dared mess with us because doing so would have earned them a one-on-one with me. Not that the other members of the club couldn't fight, because they could, I just brought a certain level of respect to us that was enough to give most people pause. Recognizing this, I became Sergeant of Arms, a title given to me as much for having the fastest car as being the club's most feared member. It was a title I took seriously. Every chance I got to boost my reputation, I took, at the same time making the club more and more notorious.

I loved stealing cars. Everything about it was a rush, and I wanted to be the best. In fact, everything I do that I like, I always try to be the best. I don't know the reason for this, but it's wired into me. This included being a car thief, and I worked hard at it. From the moment I stole my '63, I began perfecting my craft, everything from breaking into the car, to hot-wiring it. I noticed that whenever an alarm system was in place in a car, other members of the club would leave the car alone. I took that as a challenge and learned everything there was to know about car alarm systems. I'd purposely take a member or two from the club to a beautiful car I knew had an alarm system, and when they'd back down I'd disable the system and take the car.

I quit my job at the skating rink and thought only of cars, fighting, and surfing. School didn't enter into the equation, and although I still attended I had no interest in it at all.

During nutrition break at 10 a.m. on a Thursday, Adrian, Francis, and I sat next to his sister's BMW talking about a couple of cars I'd seen that I wanted to take a closer look at, when Ruben pulled into the parking lot and drove up to us.

"Hey, what's up? What are you doing?" Ruben asked.

"Nothing. Hanging out before our next class," said Francis.

"Want to go scoping? There's an area in Orange County I want to check out."

"Yeah, follow me to my house so I can drop off my sister's car and we'll go."

Scoping was a term we used to describe looking for cars to steal. We drove to Huntington Beach to scope for cars. Sometimes it proved to be extremely fruitful. Other times we looked all day or night and found nothing. This time, we drove by a street and Francis said, "Stop. Go down this street. There's a clean oval window behind that truck."

Ruben backed up and entered the street. A quarter of the way down we saw it, but it wasn't an oval window, it was two split-window rag-tops. One was on the street and the other was parked in the driveway. Split-windows were Volkswagens built only up to 1952, and in some countries until 1953. They were rare and priced above all other Cal Bugs. The problem was finding a pan and paperwork to use for a changeover. Nevertheless, we parked the car and checked out the one on the street. It was clean, mint condition, and fully restored. And so was the one in the driveway. I made a mental note of the address and, after looking at them for a few moments, we got back into Ruben's car and drove off.

At the end of the street Ruben turned right, but two police squad cars with flashing lights blocked us in—one in front and one behind us.

"Step out of the car with your hands up," the Huntington Beach cop yelled.

Once we were all out of the car, we were handcuffed, placed into the squad cars, and taken to the police station and interviewed separately. When a detective entered the interview room and asked me questions, I answered honestly.

"What are you doing in Huntington Beach?"

"My friends and I were looking at a pair of beautiful split-windows."

"Why?"

"Because I love VWs, and those are some of the cleanest I've ever seen."

"What were you going to do with them once you stole them?"

"We had no intention of stealing them. We were just admiring them."

It went on and on, but I told the truth. He didn't ask if I was a car thief or if we were out scoping cars. So I didn't give him that information. They didn't have anything on us, and the detective seemed upset once he realized we weren't the guys he was looking for. As we talked, he volunteered that vintage Volkswagens were being stolen in the area, and the two split-windows we were pulled in for were targeted the week before, but the thieves failed when the owner woke up and called the police. He explained that Volkswagens in the past year had become a hot item because of the California VW trend. Everyone wanted one. On that account, he was right.

We were released and I told my crew that scoping was no longer smart. Driving around looking at cars to steal later, especially in white neighborhoods, would get us arrested again. They heard what I said but didn't listen. Instead they joked about the cops and how we'd gotten away. This only upset me. There had to be a way to scope but not expose myself to the cops. The answer came a few days later when my girlfriend looked at an Auto Trader newspaper and complained she didn't have enough money to buy the car she wanted. She showed me the Auto Trader, and there on the front page was a picture and brief description of two VWs for sale. It was perfect and gave me a great idea. Instead of driving around, I'd simply scope out the cars in the Auto Trader and other newspapers and magazines. If the car interested me, I'd contact the seller and get more details. If the car passed that line of questions, I'd go to it, look closely, and, most of the time, take it. I told no one how I found the cars, only that I knew where they were located. I kept a log of their location, year, make, model, and goodies such as engine size and rims. When one of the club members needed something, I gave them the location, and of course I'd include a finder's fee. Most club members stole cars to fix up or to upgrade their own. I, on the other hand, saw the whole thing as a business. I made contacts at shops, other fences, and interested parties who needed car parts for vintage VWs and Cal-style VWs and to complete cars already changed over.

There was a huge demand for VW parts and complete changeovers. I was always busy with finding cars, stealing them, stripping them, and changing them over. I went about my business with Thursdays and Sundays as my days to steal, using the days in between to take care of what I'd stolen. Everything went well, except I found it difficult to find enough cars.

The cars in the magazines and newspapers were fine, but I needed more targets to keep up with demand. More and more shops and fences asked for parts and I had to say no. They also wanted the best parts. High-performance engines, transmissions, and wheels, and they weren't easy to find. I had to think of something. I hated not fulfilling orders. It bothered me and made me look unprofessional.

Again, luck was on my side. Go-Go and I were on our way back from the beach when I confided in him about my car, the club, and my small business. Soon he and I began stealing cars together. I still stole with the club, but Go-Go was fearless and he needed the cash. I also trusted him with my life. He was Pack. He was my brother, and that meant he'd never betray me.

I pulled up to a stop light and, across the street at a Carl's Jr., at least twenty Cal-style VWs sat in the parking lot. Every one of them was clean, and I decided to pull in.

"Let's see who these motherfuckers are and what they're doing," I said.

Pulling into the parking lot, I revved my engine. A short show of power and all eyes were on me. I parked, and we went inside to get something to eat. Most of the car owners were seated together having a meeting. After eating we got up and went outside, where some of the members were talking and some had their engine compartments open. Every engine was built to the gills, all with Weber 48 IDA carburetors. The engines were customized with chrome, brass, and anodized parts. Steel braided hoses were used instead of rubber ones. All of the cars were in show condition.

We stood by my car and one of their members came over.

"How's it going?" he asked.

"Not bad. I saw your cars and I decided to stop and take a look at them. They're clean."

"Is this your '64?"

"'63," I corrected him. "But yeah, she's mine."

"I heard you come in. What are you running?"

I smiled, but decided not to play coy. "2180." I opened my engine compartment and he whistled.

"Man, that's clean. Your whole car is. Are you with anyone?"

"Nah, I haven't found a club whose cars are clean enough."

As we spoke, other members of the club came over to look at my car.

"Listen, my name's Ron," the guy said. "I'm the president of our club. We're the Lightning Volks. We're going to caravan to Angelo's and cruise the place. We're also taking submissions for new memberships. Maybe you'd like to cruise with us and consider joining. Your car certainly makes the grade. Listen, just consider it. I know you've probably been approached by a lot of clubs, but believe me, we're the best and your car makes the grade."

I thought, *Makes the grade? My car makes all of these cars look bad.* But instead I smiled and said, "Yeah, I like your cars, but I want to think about it."

"Here, take a roll sheet so you remember what we're about. It has all of our members on it, our phone numbers, addresses, and our cars and engine size. All our members have these so we can communicate."

"Hey, thanks. Yeah, I think I will cruise with you. I like your club. Who's your Sergeant of Arms?"

"That would be Zach. He has the fastest car around and usually races V8s."

"No shit, huh."

"Yeah, he's that yellow '67."

We walked over to it and a guy of about twenty-three with blond hair and crooked teeth popped open the engine compartment with a shit-eating grin.

"What do you do in the quarter mile?" I asked.

"Fast," he replied. "Want to try me?"

"What, 14s?" He smiled. "13s?" He smiled more. "12s?" He just looked at me.

"That's fast, all right."

I didn't want to race him. What I wanted was to know who he was and which one was his car. When we pulled out of the parking lot, I stayed a little behind and watched.

"What's on your mind, brah?"

"I just solved our problem on where to find all the cars we need. Look at this roll sheet. There are over twenty-seven cars on it and every one of them is a mark. Do all these clubs have roll sheets and give them out? If they do, they're as stupid as fuck. Let's go to Angelo's and see what the deal is. The first car I'm taking is that smiling idiot Sergeant of Arms' '67."

"Man, if you could see the look in your eyes you'd fall out. You look like a mad criminal genius. Fuck, I gotta stop hanging with you. You're a bad influence and stealing is wrong. It's against the Ten Commandments. Why don't we stop and pray for a moment?"

"Man, shut the fuck up, you mumble mouth motherfucker. It's no wonder your girl can't stand you. Your breath stinks."

We both laughed and followed the Lightning Volks to Angelo's. When we arrived, I couldn't believe my eyes. There had to be over a hundred Cal VWs of every year, make, and model, and at least six or seven other clubs there. I never heard of the place. I always went to Whittier Boulevard in Los Angeles, where most of the Hispanics cruised, or Whittier Boulevard in Whittier and La Habra where the whites cruised. But this place seemed to be for a slightly older crowd that was from Orange County, and their cars were much more complete and polished.

That night three other clubs talked to me about membership. Of the three, only one gave me a membership form, which, like a roll sheet, had all of its members on it. I also learned of an upcoming event within six weeks called Bug-In, held once a year in Irvine, where VWs from around the country came together to race, show, sell, and hang out for two days.

I left that night with the location of over fifty marks and the possibility of hundreds more if Bug-In proved to be what everyone said it was.

Things were looking up and I got right to work. The next night, Go-Go and I got the yellow '67 from the Sergeant of Arms of the Lighting Volks, and a blue '61 ragtop from the other club who gave me their membership form. Both of the cars were placed in a small warehouse I rented in La Puente, and within three days I acquired a spare motor for myself—the one from the '67—and had $9,500 in my pocket from the shops and fences who bought everything I brought them. I gave Go-Go $3,000 and we prepared again for the next week and, of course, Bug-In. What I had in mind for that event would make me one of the most sought-after car thieves in Southern California and lift my reputation to the heights I'd always envisioned.

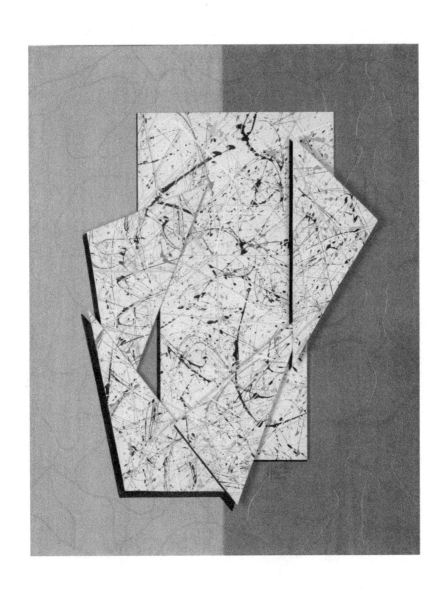

Chapter 31

San Quentin Death Row, 1994

The speaker to the right of my cell crackled and the desk officer announced, "The following inmate, prepare for escort. Noguera, 3-77, get up, get dressed, full blues."

I stood up from the five-gallon bucket I used as a seat when I worked. I'd known the moment would come, but still my muscles tensed over what was in store. Earlier in the week the Supreme Court of California ruled 4–3 confirming my conviction and against me receiving relief via habeas corpus.

I put on my blues, a pair of state-issued blue denim jeans, blue shirt, and boots. As I finished tying my boots, I heard the two bulls coming down the tier for me. Each step sounded like an approaching storm. I popped my neck joints, a habit I have when I'm nervous.

"Noguera, you ready?"

I nodded. What choice did I have? It's not like I could just say, "No, I'm actually not ready. Could you come back in, say, seventy years?"

I put my hands through the food port so the bull could place cuffs on my wrists, then I turned around so the chain attached to the cuffs could be wrapped around my waist and locked in place. Once secured, my door was keyed open and I stepped out on the tier. The bull to my right said, "Hold up, I have to double lock the cuffs."

I said nothing. I was still trying to take it all in.

"Let's go," said the second bull who stood behind me. I was escorted downstairs and into the captain's office where the new warden sat behind the desk. To his right, a captain and lieutenant stood.

"Please sit down, Mr. Noguera," said the warden.

Warden Calderon was appointed warden of San Quentin State Prison earlier that year, and this was the first time I'd spoken to him, although I'd seen him numerous times walking with one of his captains. I never saw a reason to talk to him.

Warden Calderon liked making an impression on people. He wore thousand-dollar suits, and his hair stylist probably charged more for a haircut than I spent in the store in a month. He came across as a guy who'd watched too many mob movies, and to me he looked like a peacock. He was the complete opposite of the former warden, Daniel Vasquez.

"Mr. Noguera, as warden of San Quentin I have the duty to carry out death warrants. I don't take this duty lightly, nor should you take it personally. I hope you understand. The California Supreme Court has confirmed your conviction and a date has been set for your execution. That date, set no more than sixty days from today, is December 16, 1994. Would you please sign here, indicating I have notified you of this, as well as choosing what method of execution will be administered?"

What? Was he kidding? I knew this was part of the process, but it takes on a whole new dimension when it comes down to signing the documents. It suddenly becomes real.

"Warden, I'm not signing anything."

"Mr. Noguera. You shouldn't take this personally. It's just a process."

Just a process? I shouldn't take it personally? Anger rose up my spine and my eyes came to life.

"Warden, nothing could be more personal than you trying to take my life. I don't care if you're just the messenger. The bottom line is, I'm not going to sign anything. Take that any way you like."

"You realize your refusal to sign will not delay anything?"

"Then you shouldn't take it so personally."

"We're done here then." He nodded to his bulls. "Take him back to his cell."

I was escorted back to my cell, and with each step my anger grew. It may only be a process to him, but to me, it was my life and it was personal. I had to think fast.

I had to get a stay and notify the Federal District Court that I sought relief, otherwise they'd move me to the first tier and place me on "death watch." That's when they place a cage in front of the cell with a bull in it 24-7. His job would be to watch the death watch prisoner to prevent him from killing himself. Can you imagine? They don't want me to kill myself, and will go as far as placing a bull in front of my cell around the clock, so at the end they can kill me. Not personal? All the smiling, reassuring faces they put on wouldn't change my mind. I too wore a mask.

The next morning at 10 a.m. I called a number of lawyers I knew and asked them for advice. I then called the California Appellate Project, and an attorney there agreed to secure my stay. She said it was a rather simple process and she'd file the required papers to notify the Federal District Court of my intention to seek habeas corpus relief and appointment of federal counsel. I agreed to call back by Friday, two days later, and see how things were progressing.

Meanwhile, after I hung up, I paced back and forth in my cell. I imagined the worst but forced myself to relax. Stressing myself out accomplished nothing. I would get a stay. I had a right to an appeal in the federal system, and all of those things would be granted.

I decided not to tell my family anything about it. What would it accomplish, aside from upsetting them? Imagine your only son—the son you held as an infant and watched take his first steps—calling you from death row to tell you he's been given an execution date. No, I'd keep it from them, and when I called them I'd lie.

Over the next couple of days I stayed inside. I didn't want to be around people. Instead I spent the days remembering and daydreaming about my childhood—the days before all the fighting started in my home—the only time I remember being truly happy. I thought about my parents walking hand-in-hand in a park near our home, often kissing, as my sister and I ran around and played. I remembered it as if it was yesterday, and I remembered my parents' laughter as they watched us. How could things have gone so wrong? How could I, at that very moment, find myself in a cell on death row with a pending execution date? How could all the wrong numbers have fallen into place so perfectly for me to be in that position?

I didn't know the answer. I took a deep breath and knelt down on the floor of my cell, closed my eyes, and shut out the world around me. Suddenly I was in my cave. The moisture from the spray of the waterfall touched my skin and I opened my eyes and stood. I took a deep breath and drew strength from my hallowed ground. I called and first Rage jumped through the mouth of the cave, followed by Pain. My beasts—my strengths and my weakness. I touched their damp fur and the fear subsided. Another presence appeared, and through the water came a small child, untouched by the water. Untouched by anything.

He smiled at me as the tears ran down my face. He was and is the only one I didn't wear a mask around. He knew me as I knew myself, because he is the part of me I protected from harm, the Radiant Child. He took my hand and smiled. He understood me, knew everything about me, and knew I was hurting. The gaping wounds from my past were still open and bleeding.

He led me to another part of the cave where I'd built a small gravestone so many years ago, when I was an eighteen-year-old grieving father. It read:

William Achilles Noguera
1982–83
Never Forgotten Son

Rage and Pain knelt beside us, and from deep inside me where that inferno burns, I drew strength from the two of them.

I opened my eyes and stood. Gone was the cave, my beasts, my Radiant Child. I was in a cell on death row at San Quentin State Prison and they were trying to kill me, but I wouldn't allow that to happen.

On Friday, I woke up earlier than usual, and after a morning cup of bitter black coffee, I washed and scrubbed my entire cell, then waxed the floor. I was killing time, waiting for 10 a.m. so I could call the attorney who agreed to file the required papers in the Federal District Court for a stay of execution and appointment of counsel. In the latter case, I had no choice. My funds were exhausted and I couldn't afford the cost of a defense team. The only funds I had were from the sale of my art, and I sent ninety percent of that home to my family.

I finished waxing my floor and washed my hands in my sink. I turned to grab my towel and found a friendly face standing at the door.

"Good morning, Bill."

"Good morning, Father O'Neil. How are you?"

"I'm fine, but it's you I'm concerned with."

"Not to worry, Father. I'm fine. I always am."

"That's what worries me, Bill. You're always fine, no matter what you're facing. You shake it off and continue. I need you to know that if you want someone to speak to, I'm here for you. It can be about anything."

"I know, Father, and I appreciate it. But really, I'm fine."

Father O'Neil came to see me every week since I'd arrived in East Block nearly seven years before. Being Roman Catholic, I took communion each week, confessed my sins, and took comfort in the fact that the church still considered me one of them despite everything.

"I have some good news," he said. "In the next few months a small chapel will be built here in East Block where we'll be able to hold services. We'll have to share it with the other faiths, but the fact that for the first time a Catholic service will be held on the row is a signal of progress."

"It is, Father." Although I said it, it wasn't heartfelt. I have little faith in buildings where people go to pray. I've never felt the presence of God in such buildings.

Since I was a small child my parents made me and my sister attend church every Sunday morning—Saint Joseph Catholic Church in La Puente. My parents never attended, but they would drop us off and then pick us up when the service was over. "Do as I say, not as I do," my father would say. This was a lesson I learned not to question early on, at least not where I could be heard.

As a grown man, I remained Roman Catholic. I followed the rituals out of habit, or maybe as a tribute to the idea of being Roman Catholic. But the fact was, the only church I believed in, the only faith I truly have even still, is between me and God. I will bow to no one—priest, saint, or common man—but each day I kneel before God. My faith and beliefs are simple because they involve only the two of us. Period.

After Father O'Neil left, I paced back and forth in my cage. Five steps to the door, turn, five steps to the back of the cage. On and on I paced until 10 a.m., when I finally dialed the number of the California Appellate Project.

"Operator, may I help you?"

"Collect call from William A. Noguera."

"Please hold."

"Hello, William?"

"Good morning, Ms. Schauer. I was wondering how things were going. As you can imagine, it's been on my mind."

"Yes, yes, I can only imagine. But you needn't worry. I filed the required papers for your stay of execution, as well as a motion for appointment of counsel, and the Federal District Court for the Southern District has accepted and granted you a stay."

Until that moment, I hadn't realized how nervous and worried I'd been, but her words took away the fist that gripped my insides.

"I can't tell you how relieved I am to hear that. Thank you for your help. I appreciate it greatly."

"You're welcome, William. As you know, the court will appoint an attorney for you, but there's no set time frame for this. An attorney will be appointed as one becomes available. I can come to visit you next week and discuss this further with you."

"That's okay, really. I have some ideas about this process and I'd like to take care of them on my own, but I appreciate the offer."

"Are you sure? It's no trouble at all."

"Thank you, but I'm fine. You've done a great deal for me already."

"Okay, if you're sure."

"I am. Good day, Ms. Schauer."

"Goodbye, William, and good luck."

I hung up the phone and took a deep breath. Since the Federal Court stayed my execution, I was under federal jurisdiction. I'd make contact with the federal attorney I knew of by reputation, one with a track record of getting reversals, and ask for his help.

I thought about Ms. Schauer's offer to come visit. Unlike the majority of the men here who would jump at the chance for someone to come see them, especially a woman, I had no interest in seeing anyone unless it was totally necessary. For me, every time I walk into the visiting area, I feel like a circus act. Most of the men here accept visits as part of being locked up.

Walk into any prison visiting area and you'll understand the circus act I refer to. Men accept visits from women they'd never be involved with if they were free. The women, deep down, know this but continue to return week after week because they finally have the guy they've always dreamed of—even if he's an illusion. The prisoner, for the illusion, is rewarded with a woman who will take care of him, give him money, food, quarterly packages, even drugs. There are some exceptions, but they're few and far between.

I don't have much in common with visitors. No matter if I enjoy their company and conversation, at the end of the visit they walk away and I stay here. It's more difficult for me to walk back to my cell after a visit than it would be to avoid visits altogether. It's like being in hell, and every once in a while looking up at a glass of ice water but not being allowed to drink from it. Just knowing it's there becomes an added torture.

Over the next few weeks, I wrote and received correspondence from that San Francisco attorney and his partner who I thought could help me. He agreed to petition the court for appointment. Until then, he'd research my case and get a feel for what was needed.

I also received a letter from a nonprofit website for artists called Intangible.org. They had seen my work and wanted me to become a part of their family of artists. As soon as I read the letter, I responded by requesting more information. I asked how they found me and inquired if they would be open to displaying my new body of work which no one had seen. This work was based on fragmenting an image into geometric abstract forms based on mathematical and rhythmic arrangements, as well as images based on my dreams. Those moving still-life, stark, black-and-white images I had always dreamed of were actualized in my work and I was finally ready for the world to see them.

Within a week I received a response, and after careful consideration I mailed Intangible.org a set of slides and pictures I hoped they would display. The response was immediate, not only from the people at Intangible, who were extremely impressed with what I sent them, but from a number of publications who saw my work on the Intangible website and were interested in interviewing me about my work.

I sat in my cage reading the words they wrote about my work and a sense of satisfaction overcame me. I'd taken another step in the right direction on the road to meeting my goals. It was just one step in a long journey, but it was significant.

Maybe the distraction made me momentarily forget where I was and who surrounded me, but the following day, as I made my way out to the yard, I still felt good. The minor success was on my mind and my elevated mood clouded my vision, blinding me to the tension and hatred leveled at me. I was so blind I didn't see or sense it until it was too late. Even then, I allowed my mood to alter my response. Entering the yard, I walked as I normally did to my spot where I placed my things, then warmed up before going through my martial arts routine. It was a beautiful day. The sun was warm and I decided to enjoy the sunshine for a few moments.

As I did, I felt it. My nostrils flared and I focused. I realized my mistake immediately, but I didn't have time to be upset at my stupidity—I had to act. A Peckerwood named Hellhound had approached me and stood a few feet away. Hellhound was a murderer, six feet, 225 pounds, and his face clearly betrayed his intent. He was angry and out of his mind. As soon as he got close I smelled the meth oozing from his pores, and I could tell he hadn't slept in days.

He accused me of putting a camera and microphone in his cell so his enemies could listen to his thoughts—hallucinations brought on by the meth. He was paranoid and unpredictable, but because I was still in a good mood I told him he should kick back because it was all in his head.

He continued to accuse me of everything from planting bugs in his mind to turning off the hot water in his cell, until I grew tired of his nonsense.

"Check this out, motherfucker. Take your punk ass off the yard. I don't want to hear this silly weak-ass shit," I said.

That's when I made my second mistake of the day. I turned to walk away, and before I took the first step he struck, hitting me hard on the side of the head. He partially connected with my left ear. The blow staggered me and I nearly fell. My vision narrowed and darkness threatened to swallow me. I hung between consciousness and unconsciousness, and for that millisecond everything slowed down. Then the inferno inside me—that place where everything ever done to me dwelled—erupted. I didn't think, only reacted to the danger I was in. I didn't know what he hit me with, or how much damage he'd inflicted, but my response was immediate and extreme. Darkness still threatened to swallow me, and my vision was clouded, but I struck out first with my left fist—a clumsy blow, but it was enough to center me and, most importantly, it located my target. I followed with my right fist, connected with his face, and smashed his nose. As he fell, I moved in and finished him with a kick to the side of his head. It was over. I stood, overwhelmed by anger, and saw blood draining from his face.

"Down. Everyone down."

I was so overcome with the moment, I didn't hear or see what was happening around me until the second I heard the distinct sound of the gunner chambering a round with my name on it.

"Noguera, turn around."

I turned and looked at him.

"Don't move or I'll put one in you."

I stared at him. He was threatening me and I didn't like it. I didn't care if he held a mini-14 pointed at me. At that moment, I was too angry to fear him or anyone.

Bulls poured out of the East Block doors and I was ordered to come to the gate, where I was cuffed and led to a holding cage, and then to the hospital for an examination.

Within the hour, I was in the AC cell. Anger still gripped me and I thought about everything that happened and what it meant. My biggest concern was my work, my commitments to commissions, and how long it would take to get back my grade-A status and get back to work. I second-guessed myself and wondered what I could have done to avoid the mess I was in, but, short of not going outside, I came to the conclusion there was nothing I could have done to avoid it.

The second day in the AC I received the 115 write-up and I got angry all over again. The gunner wrote it up as if I beat up Hellhound with no provocation. I had hoped the gunner had seen him hit me so he'd know my actions were a response to being attacked. It was obvious the gunner only noticed after the incident was well under way, and by that time I was doing the damage to Hellhound and he looked like the victim.

The way the 115 was written, I was facing at least a year in the hole. It was that simple. By the seventh day I accepted my fate. I would spend the next twelve months there.

The men around me in the hole told me about the damage I inflicted on Hellhound—a broken nose, fractured eye socket, and a couple of broken teeth. Part of me smiled, but another wanted to cry because of what I'd lose. I didn't care how much damage I inflicted on the idiot. The damage to my reputation as an artist mattered more to me. How would it look to the clients who trusted me with their orders? How would I appear to the people of Intangible? But most of all, I was angry about not being able to continue my journey toward that place where my vision, my imagination, and emotions became one in my quest for clarity.

As I worried about the consequences of the incident, I heard bulls coming, then the large outer steel door that closed me off from the world opened and two bulls stepped to the small area in front of my cage.

"Noguera, someone wants to see you."

The bulls looked familiar, but I didn't know their names. They cuffed me behind my back and escorted me to the second floor of the AC, where I was surprised to see Captain Hales sitting behind a desk. I hadn't seen him in a few years, not since I helped him win the bet with an associate warden at Folsom Prison who thought he had the best artist in the system. The pieces I created for Captain Hales proved that associate warden wrong.

"Good morning, Mr. Noguera. Please sit down. Imagine my surprise when I was told you had been placed in my AC for assault on an inmate. I looked over the 115 investigative report and it was pretty cut and dried. Except the medical report indicated your left ear was bleeding and bruised. The gun-rail officer's report states he only witnessed you assaulting the other inmate. So how did you sustain the injuries to your ear?"

I only stared at him.

"I'll tell you how. My gun-rail officer didn't see the whole picture, did he? I did some investigating of my own and, in speaking to Mr. Cutler (Hellhound), he admitted he assaulted you."

"I think the evidence speaks for itself, Associate Warden Hales," I said. "And congratulations on your promotion."

He laughed. "Normally this incident would be written up as Mr. Cutler being the victim and you the aggressor, but the evidence proves you were defending yourself even though he looks like he got hit by a truck. I'll write a memo for your file to document this finding, and I'm sending you back to East Block."

I hadn't expected that.

"You're serious? I really appreciate you taking the time to look into the situation, and finding the truth."

"Mr. Noguera, I'm doing this because it's not our policy to throw men in the hole for months or years for something they're not guilty of. I understand it has happened before, but not this time."

I thanked him, and that night I was back in my old cell in East Block. My job as phone coordinator and shower cleaner were restored. To my complete surprise, all of my property, including my art materials, were returned to me.

After setting up my cell that night, I sat on my bucket and looked out onto the bay, grateful someone remembered me and bothered to seek out the truth. I escaped a long term in the hole and realized it was because of my art. Never underestimate the power of art.

Chapter 32

Orange County Jail, 1987

Three years after my arrest, jury selection began for my trial, and still my lawyer wouldn't come visit me. In all that time, I still hadn't had the opportunity to sit down and really talk to my lawyer. I was frustrated and confused, but I didn't know how to change things. The truth was, I was intimidated by Martín Gonzalez. He had a certain presence about him that said, "I'm Martín Gonzalez, a lawyer, and I'm always right." Around him, I was inept and somehow like a child sitting at the grownup's table.

Maybe it was all of it; my frustration, the lack of any real participation in my own defense, and the visit with Maxine I had just left where the topic was mainly my thoughts about the defense my lawyer and mother were insisting we use—a defense based on my mother's twisted reality and her need to hide the truth and protect how she appeared to everyone.

As I left to return to my housing unit I was still so completely preoccupied I wasn't focused on my surroundings or the danger I faced.

I turned the corner into the holding cage area for inmates waiting for court, but since it was a weekend, it was empty. The sound of rubber shoes on cement made me look up in time to see a guy coming toward me. He was only a few feet away when he pulled a shank from his pocket. As I saw it, I realized the door ahead, which led to the main elevator, was closed. I was sealed off from anyone except him and the two other men behind me, also returning to housing. I took in all of it in the split second before the attack began. The men had one thing on their minds: killing me. The one with the shank stabbed at me

333

and moved closer, pressing me back into his crew, who came at me quickly from behind. I kicked as hard as I could into his groin and managed to give myself enough space to move. Taking advantage of that, I stepped to the side and punched him in the throat. Just as the others reached me, I grabbed his hand that held the shank and twisted it hard. The shank dropped to the ground and I kicked it away from us into one of the locked holding cages. My biggest concern was being stabbed to death, but the time I took to kick the shank away cost me. I turned to engage the two men behind me and took a blow to the face. Stars exploded my vision. I fell to one knee and tried to get up, but the damage was too much. While they beat me to the ground I covered up the best I could, but in a state of semi-consciousness I couldn't stop many blows. The next thing I remember was hearing an officer yelling for me to walk over to him and away from the three men who attacked me. I was on one knee and still my head swam. I was badly beaten. My head throbbed and blood flowed from my mouth, nose, and gashes on my face. My head began to clear, but I was sure I'd forgotten something, I just couldn't remember what. It seemed important, though, and as I rose on unsteady legs, I looked at the men who'd attacked me and I recognized them. The one who attacked me with the shank was one of Boxer's crew members, and Trigger and Shotgun's partner.

Then it all came together for me, like the snap of a rubber band. Boxer put a hit on me for what I did to Trigger in the high-power unit and for not respecting him.

My senses returned and anger set in. I was angry at myself for allowing those idiots to trap me the way they did. I walked right into it because I was distracted. I stepped toward the cop, who was a few feet away, then I looked at the guy who'd stabbed me. He smiled, but it was a wicked, twisted version of what a smile should look like. He thought it was over and he was taunting me. The cops were there and I was badly beaten, so he stood there smiling with his hands in his pockets, relaxed and confident. He was still relaxed and confident when I passed him on what seemed unsteady legs. Blood flowed from my nose, mouth, and the puncture wounds in my chest. Suddenly, I turned, moved in, kicked him in the face, and hammered him to the ground. I looked at him and his crew and returned my own twisted smile, made nastier with the blood that covered it.

"You're next," I said to the two other Mexicans. "Tell the puto that sent you to be a man and step up to the plate."

With that, I turned and went to the cops who led me to the hospital for treatment. I had a possible broken nose, cut lip, and contusions all over my body. I'd lost a lot of blood—most of it soaked into my jumpsuit, which hid the multiple stab wounds to my chest and ribs from the medical staff.

I didn't bring them to their attention. I knew the report would only show I was assaulted or involved in mutual combat. Boxer would want the report to confirm I was stabbed and dealt with. Mutual combat was not what he ordered. He didn't just want me stabbed, he wanted me killed. But instead what he got were my words to the two Mexicans. That would be a repeat of the slap in the face he got when I beat Trigger down after he gave him the green light to kill me.

As soon as I was alone in the hole, I took off my jumpsuit. I gently wiped the blood from the wounds with a wet towel. I found three small holes in my chest, but a scratch in my rib area hurt the most. None of the wounds threatened my life, but I washed them carefully so infection wouldn't set in. Then I took a bird bath.

I didn't realize how exhausted I was until I closed my eyes and fell asleep on the tiny mattress. I was safe and had cheated death once again. I wasn't ready to bow down to death. I'd fight it to the end, and possibly beyond.

Chapter 33

Adolescence, 1981

I became consumed by the stolen car business and by the admiration I received from people who knew. It gave me power and an identity I hadn't experienced before. When I walked into a club, all eyes turned to me as if I were an alpha wolf. Looking back, I understand the twisted appeal this image had for me, but as a young champion fighter, pumped up on steroids, I craved that respect and attention. It was a good identity to have, especially after so many years as a victim. After a year as a car thief, I drew admiration from some, and resentment and jealousy from others. Ultimately, it was some of those others who betrayed me. I attacked the Bug-In event in Irvine like it was a flock of sheep, and I included the rest of the Darque Knights to share in the spoils. It was all foreign to them. They couldn't see beyond the method they knew already—scoping, finding the car, stealing it, and changing it over or selling the parts. That's a painfully slow method, and they were lucky to get three cars a month.

When I exposed them to the thousand or more cars involved at the Bug-In event, they were overwhelmed. They never even imagined that world existed, and for them it wasn't a fit. But it was a world I not only fit into but thrived in. I interacted with the people at those events and spoke their language as if I were one of them. It was made easier because I worked at Precision VW and Porsche, a job I took in order to learn how to build high-performance engines. The owner, Mike, liked me and taught me everything he knew about VWs and Porsches.

Mike was a car thief and drug dealer before he opened his own shop, and I soon discovered he still had his hand in the cookie jar. I told him what I was doing, and Mike became one of my most trusted fences. I sold him most of the high-performance engines, transmissions, and parts I stole.

The Darque Knights saw how I worked with Go-Go to steal cars, secure contacts, and make more money from the Bug-In operation than they could ever imagine, but they weren't pumped up about doing the same thing.

Adrian was the single exception. Adrian had allowed me into his world and trusted me with his secret, so I did the same for him when he came to me. I explained my operation to him and let him know that, although I would remain the Darque Knights' Sergeant of Arms, my operation was between him, Go-Go, and me. I would gather the information, pick the targets, and deal with the fences. Adrian and Go-Go would steal the cars and strip, cut, or deliver them.

From the start, the three of us worked like a well-oiled machine. My business grew to heights only I had imagined, evolving into a high-end car theft operation that included Porches, BMWs, Mercedes, and whatever cars the clients wanted.

It's easy to say I was just a car thief, but to me it was much more than that. For me, stealing cars was an art form. Any idiot can pull a gun on someone and take what they want, but what I did was different. To carefully plan and study a mark, then skillfully take it and not get caught, was nothing less than pure poetry in motion. I took pride in being a car thief, like any professional takes pride in his unique talent and knowledge.

It's not that I advocate that lifestyle or try to justify stealing cars. It's just that at that period of my life it was my trade, and I experienced an intense elation at certain points in the process. Stealing a heavily guarded car gave me even more of that emotional rush. The harder the mark, the higher I got. Part of the excitement was from the risk and reward of the situation, but a huge bonus was knowing my reputation would grow with it.

With my new business in place, I had graduated to high-end marks and bigger possibilities. Of course, with more possibilities the risk of getting caught also grew.

Chapter 34

San Quentin Death Row, 1997–2000

Regardless of where you live—in prison or as a free man—state of mind plays a big role in the perception of the passage of time. When a student watches the clock waiting for the hour to end, time seems to stand still. For a man awaiting execution, time flies by. Weeks, months, and years pass in the blink of an eye. The very rules of time seem to change and conspire to taunt a condemned man and bring the impending doom to his doorstop in leaps and bounds.

By 1997, after nearly a decade in the same cell on death row, I noticed white hair at my temples and in the chin hairs of my Van Dyke. Time ignores none of us, but for me it seemed to take a particular interest.

I forged ahead, and near the end of the year it happened. My work as an artist received international recognition. The London *Guardian* ran a front-page article about my work entitled "Cellular Seurat," in reference to the French pointillist painter Georges Seurat. The article ended with the following paragraph:

> It is as an artist that Noguera wishes to be recognized. The progression that can be seen in his work in terms both of technique and emotional intensity, together with the increasing interest being shown by America's art establishment, testifies to his ability.

I sat back after reading the article and basked in a sense of accomplishment; but I was still nowhere near where I wanted to be. I had a goal and I'd reach it or die in the process. I pushed myself by recognizing it wasn't impossible. In fact, it had actually been done before. Granted, it was in a different time and circumstance, but Caravaggio himself, one of the world's most notorious and talented painters, was sentenced to death. Benvenuto Cellini, the famous sculptor, was also prosecuted for murder. Nevertheless, their work was accepted and revered. I found it interesting that their prosecutions for murder were only mentioned as a footnote, if mentioned at all. This encouraged me and fueled my desire to reach heights I previously never truly believed were obtainable.

By 1998, William Bonin, Keith Williams, and Thomas Thompson had all been executed by the state. Executions had gone from myth to a real possibility in California, and for many men the reality was too much. Some killed themselves. Others lost their minds. I could hear some of them from my cell screaming the entire night and sometimes into the day, finding peace only when sleep overtook them and numbed their senses. While the chaos went on and minds shattered, I found fertile ground to focus my mind and it blossomed into even more recognition.

In May 1998, Mark MacNamara, a writer for the *San Francisco Magazine*, came to see me about my work. He asked if I was represented by a gallery or dealer. I wasn't, and I really didn't know much about how that worked. He explained that most successful artists have an art dealer/gallery representing them. The representative gives the artist the freedom to work without the distraction of handling exhibits, exposure, and sales. With this freedom, the artist grows faster. Finding the right representative was the hard part. There are hundreds of them, but not all are honest. As an artist, and in my situation, finding honest and experienced representation would be the difference between swimming and drowning.

After our interview, Mark and I talked a while about the possibility of introducing me to a gallery owner he knew and believed would be interested in offering representation.

"I believe it's vital for you to be represented by a gallery that will not only exhibit your work but speak on your behalf. I know a German artist who is also a gallery owner and dealer. He'll understand how you feel about your work because he's also a very impressive artist. I've known him for a number of years and he has a reputation for being fair and honest. If you'd like, I could introduce you to him. He only speaks German, so when he comes to see you, his wife, who is his business partner, will accompany him to translate."

"Yes, I'd like that. The opportunity to exhibit where my work is understood is something I've thought about for some time."

"Call me at the end of the week. By then I'll have been in touch with Gerhard and Amanda Schumacher and shown them your work."

We said our goodbyes. He went his way to a normal life—a wife, family, friends, and freedom. I, on the other hand, went back into the belly of the beast—a world of hate, envy, torture, and death, where I live in a cage, awaiting my execution.

I waited until the following Saturday to call Mark MacNamara, and as soon as he began speaking I knew he had good news for me.

"I had the opportunity to show Gerhard your work and he was floored by it. He wants to represent you and wants to meet you as soon as possible."

"Wow. That was fast. Tell me, what pieces did you show him and what was his reaction?"

"I went by his gallery after speaking with him on the phone, and all I told him was I had something to show him. I brought a small portfolio of your work that included some of your earlier pieces as well as your new work that's on the Intangible site. He spent a long time just looking at it, and finally he looked at me and said, 'Magnificent. Who's the artist?'"

"When I told him about you and that you needed representation, he immediately asked to meet you and explore the possibility of exhibiting your work."

Within a month, I met with Gerhard and Amanda Schumacher, and we came to an agreement. They would represent me and handle my work. Instead of selling my originals and taking a percentage, which was usually forty to fifty percent, they agreed to buy all originals at double what they currently sold for.

My first exhibit was in Paris, France, at the Galerie Everarts in

September 1998. It was a group exhibit where I was the only prisoner whose work was being shown. As part of my agreement with Gerhard and Amanda, I insisted my work should never be shown with pieces by other prisoners. I didn't want the circus of being known as a death row artist. I wanted the respect and recognition for simply being a first-rate creator of fine art.

The next month the *San Francisco Chronicle* ran a front-page article about my work. This was followed by an exhibit at Winchester Contemporary in San Francisco entitled "New Visions."

Bay-area papers covered the exhibit and acknowledged my unique style and technique. In one article about my "New Visions" exhibit in the *Palo Alto Daily News*, an art critic wrote:

> Art is often more than just a pretty picture. It's about self-expression and evoking emotion. In the gallery, no artist makes a clearer statement than William Noguera. Noguera's pieces are unquestionably powerful. He uses a technique called pointillism, in which the picture is made up of millions of tiny black dots. Noguera's pictures are rich in detail and some of his works take up to three hundred hours to create. The subject matter expresses some of his concerns and emotion: regret, pain, violence, the desire for freedom, and the specter of death. While Noguera's nefarious past can easily overshadow the pictures, making them a curiosity, the quality of the craftsmanship allows them to stand on their own and Noguera's situation helps put them in context.

Having Gerhard's support, I concentrated solely on my work. My time was spent exploring the limitless possibilities that existed in my mind's eye, and the complexities of my work advanced quickly. A light switch was thrown, and my inner light allowed me to see with new eyes. I created *In God's Hands, The Encouragement of Sarah*, and a number of extremely complex hyper-realistic pieces that opened the floodgates of emotion and allowed me to express the heart-stopping scream I suppressed for so long. The scream was fully on display when

I created *Achilles Last Stand*, a piece that depicted in representational images the core of my pain—the very emotion that was both my strength and my weakness.

Yet, throughout that time, there was another part of my mind at work. My unconscious hours were spent in a world of abstraction, where geometric shapes and mathematical arrangements combined with color and rhythm to form a calm state. During my waking hours I thought of this and tried to make sense of it all. My conscious mind wasn't ready to accept and understand the progression and movement toward clarity that my subconscious mind firmly grasped.

Chapter 35

Orange County Jail, 1987

Before my ten days in the hole were up, a huge racial riot broke out in the chow hall and I was moved out to make room for a man who was involved. I went to a one-man cell right under a housing unit for men awaiting trial for murder. Those men were representing themselves, or at least they gave the impression they were.

They used a loophole in the law to obtain the legal title of pro per, or representing themselves, even though they also had attorneys. Because of their special status, they had extraordinary privileges compared to other prisoners. Their cell doors stayed open from 6 a.m. to 11 p.m., they had access to a phone the entire time, and their phone calls were free because they were made under the umbrella of "legal calls." They had court orders for supplies, pens, pencils, markers, paper, typewriters, computers, stereos, tapes, etc.

Normally visits were behind glass for prisoners in jail awaiting trial, but the men had court orders to have contact visits, not only with their lawyers but with the entire defense team. That included paralegals, witnesses, and agents of the defense.

I'd heard about the privileges they had, but never paid much attention to them until I stood at the bars of my one-man cell and looked upstairs at their reflection through the Plexiglas barrier. I watched them for some time, and they seemed unaware of my presence until the second day, when I went to the shower and on the way back I heard someone call me.

"Hey, Mad."

I looked up and saw a familiar face but couldn't put a name to it. I just nodded and said, "What's up."

I entered my cell and the door closed behind me. I tried to shave but the cuts and bruises were still visible on my face from the beating I'd taken, and made shaving difficult. Then the familiar face came to my cell.

"Hey, what's up, Mad? How you doing?"

"I'm all right, just finishing up my last couple of days in the hole—overflow."

"Yeah, I heard about what happened. You need anything?"

"Nah. I'm straight. Thanks all the same."

"Listen, where you going to go after you get out of the hole?"

"Don't know. It'll be up to the classification committee. It doesn't really matter."

"Why don't you come upstairs? Man, we got everything we need. You also know a few of the fellas."

I looked at him, not sure what to think. Was he setting me up? It was possible. I'm sure Boxer and his crew would continue with their politics against me in the hopes that someone would finish what they couldn't.

"Yeah. I'll check it out. It might be a good idea."

"All right. In the meantime, here's a few things to make your day cool."

He reached into his jumpsuit pocket and pulled out a small Walkman and earbuds, a few cassettes, a pack of Camel non-filters, and some candy bars.

"Man, right on. Where the fuck did you get a stereo?"

"All of us upstairs have them. Just some of the perks of being in the pro per unit. If you're serious, I'll go up to my cell and type out an order for you just like all of ours. Once your judge signs it, classification will have no choice but to house you with us. Write down your name and number for me and I'll have it done by this afternoon."

I wrote down the information he needed and handed it to him.

"I have court tomorrow. I just hand it to the judge and that's it?"

"Give it to your lawyer and tell him to ask the judge to sign it because you want to assist with your defense. You have a capital case, right? Well, the judge ain't going to deny it because, if you get convicted, you could argue on appeal you weren't allowed to assist in your defense, which is a reversible error. Besides, you got Judge Fitzgerald, right? He never looks at court orders. He just stamps them."

I knew my attorney wouldn't bother to do it since I couldn't even get him to talk to me. And my other attorney, a good guy but right out of law school, did everything Gonzalez told him to do. What could he do? Gonzalez was his boss. He hired him and brought him onto my case.

While I was thinking it over, I was handed a pack of cigarettes through the cell's food port. "Hey, I don't smoke, but thanks anyway," I said.

"Look inside. Just a little something to make the music sound better."

After we shook hands, he left. I sat on my bunk and opened the pack of smokes to find three joints and two hits of LSD.

The next day I entered court high as a kite, with the court order the familiar face had typed out for me. I gave the court order to my attorney's paralegal, Maribel Rodriguez. She was a good-looking busty brunette who flirted with me every chance she got. I smiled at her and she smiled back. My smile was more a product of the LSD I'd taken than anything else.

"Are you okay?" she asked.

"Yeah, could you have this signed for me so I can be housed in a different unit?"

"Why haven't you called? I've been worried."

"I can't use the phone while I'm in the hole."

"But are you okay? You look terrible."

For a moment I just looked at her, then realized she was referring to the cuts and bruises on my face.

"Oh, yeah. I'm fine. Could you get it signed for me? It's important."

That afternoon, as I was escorted out of the courtroom, Maribel handed me the court order.

"The judge signed it and a few other things." Her hand lingered on my arm. "Please be careful, Bill. I'll see you soon."

I smiled back, but it didn't reach my eyes. I was exhausted and I was coming down from the LSD. All I wanted to do was lay down and sleep.

Arriving back at the jail, I was escorted back to my cell right away. Being in the hole proved to be a nice perk. Otherwise, I would have been in a holding pen for over an hour then sent to chow. The only thing I truly wanted was sleep, and as soon as I lay down and closed my eyes it claimed me.

Suddenly, I was in my childhood backyard playing with an energetic four-year-old little boy. His laughter filled my ears as we chased each other around. I saw images of his eyes, my eyes, his smile, my smile. I knew I was dreaming because everything moved as stark black-and-white photographs. I didn't care. In those precious moments, I got the opportunity to be with him, feel his embrace, and hear his laughter and voice.

"Papa, I'm Superman. I'm going to save the world and you can help me." He laughed, then jumped into my arms and I hugged him.

"Sí, mijo. We'll save the world. I love you."

"Noguera. Hey, Noguera." I heard someone calling me but I didn't want to leave him. I fought to stay, but the voice persisted.

"Noguera." My eyes opened.

"Yeah, I'm awake."

"You have a legal visit."

"What time is it?"

"Nine p.m."

"Give me a few minutes to get ready. Are you sure I have a legal visit?"

"They just called from the visiting room."

I washed my face, the effects of the LSD still lingering, but I felt better than I had before I slept. I brushed my teeth and thought back to my dream. Emptiness filled my heart and tears ran down my face.

"I'll never forget you, son," I whispered.

My mask firmly in place, I stepped out of my cell and walked to the vestibule, where they put chains on me and then escorted me to the attorney visiting area.

"Booth C, Noguera," said the visiting room cop.

I couldn't imagine who was there, especially since my attorney never came to see me. I stepped through the security door and was surprised to see Maribel Rodriguez, my attorney's paralegal, inside the booth. She smiled and I smiled back as I entered the five-by-six-foot cubicle.

"Surprise," she said.

"Hey, how'd you get in here?"

"The court order. It allows for paralegals and agents of the defense to come visit you seven days a week, as frequently as needed and for as long as needed. Didn't you read the order?"

"Sort of. So you can visit me in these contact booths?"

She smiled and her eyes told me she had a lot more in mind than my case. I also noticed we were completely out of the view of the visiting cop.

"So what's up? What made you come all the way back to Santa Ana? I mean, it's nine o'clock, and it's a long way back."

"You did. I wanted to see how you were and to file the court order with the jail. I've already spoken to the watch commander and your ten days in the hole are up tomorrow. You'll meet the committee, then go to the pro per unit. Bill, are you all right?"

"I'm just tired and need a hot shower."

She smiled at me and I couldn't help but notice her low cut blouse and how hard she was coming on to me. I hadn't touched a woman in four years and here in front of me was a beautiful and sexy woman who acted as if she wanted nothing more than to have me for dessert. I decided to play it cool. The last thing I needed was more drama in my life. But I'm a man, and the visiting cop couldn't see us.

After another hour I went back to my cell and fell back to sleep, hoping to return to my dream. I never know when those dreams will come and give me moments to share with him. It doesn't happen as much as I would like.

The next day I returned to court to continue jury selection. I was placed in a large holding pen with about forty other men waiting for their date with a judge. As soon as I was inside the holding pen I pulled out the small piece of plastic I carried in my mouth at all times and slid it between the teeth of my leg shackles and opened them, freeing my legs. I did the same with the ones on my wrists. After what happened to me ten days before, I wasn't going to take any chances and give someone a chance to hurt me again.

The door slid open again and another small group of men came into the pen. My eyes locked on a particularly muscular Mexican who came right up to me.

"Órale, carnal. Where they move you to? I sent some things to you, but the trustee said they moved you out of the hole to make room for the vatos that stabbed up them niggers."

We shook hands.

"I'm in a one-man cell under the pro per unit. So what's the word?"

"It looks like Boxer and Trigger are behind that move on you. Are you okay?" Chente asked.

"Yeah. I knew it. I just got caught sleeping on the job."

"Well, your new look fits you better. A few scars and bruises will stop you from looking so damn pretty," he laughed.

"Hey, don't hate me because you're so fuckin' ugly. It's no wonder you turned to a life of crime. No one would hire your fuckin' ugly ass."

We both laughed.

"Hey, so how you going to handle this once you're out of the hole?"

"I'd like to put my foot in Boxer's and Trigger's asses, but I'll just keep doing what I normally do. I got a court order to be housed in the pro per unit, so we'll see how that goes."

"That's firmé. Those vatos have it made. Check it out. This whole pedo is political, so the only motherfuckers who will get involved are those in the same car with Boxer and his bunch of bitches. Everyone who I've talked to knows the business and sent their regards to you. They know you'll handle your business like you always do."

"You got that right," I said.

"Noguera, Whitman, Craft, and Santiago." The door to the pen slid open.

"All right, Mad, I'll see you soon." We shook hands.

"All right, Chente. Good looking out, man. I appreciate what you've done."

"I got your back, ese. Fuck Boxer and Trigger. They're just pissed off because of the ass kicking you dropped on their parade."

I was taken to Judge Fitzgerald's courtroom, where jury selection would continue for the next couple of months. It was an important process my lead attorney failed to participate in because he was in court on another case in Los Angeles.

That evening I was released from the hole and placed upstairs in the pro per unit, thanks to the court order Judge Fitzgerald signed for Maribel Rodriguez.

I knew some men in the pro per unit. The tier had a total of fourteen single-man cells. None of the men posed a threat to me, none of them had any affiliation to Boxer or Trigger, and none of them seemed to care about anything other than what was going on with them as individuals, which suited me perfectly.

To hear about all the privileges the men had was one thing, but to experience it was quite another. The stereos and electric typewriters, as well as all the things they were allowed to do, was a bit like going from being in jail to freedom, and we took advantage of it at every opportunity we had. Aside from the things we were allowed to have, there were plenty of opportunities to exploit the lax security on what we received and how we received it. Law books were a standard item used by the pro per prisoners. What the cops didn't know was that the Law Review (LR) Series was used to transport large quantities of heroin, cocaine, meth, pot, LSD, you name it, into the jail.

Most of the law books we received came from the jail law library. LR Series books, however, were different. They were kept across the street at the public library, which the public had access to. The LRs sat on a shelf where anyone could check one out. Instead of waiting for someone to turn themselves in to the jail with an ass full of drugs and risk him using them himself, or risking the drugs being contaminated from being inside of a human rectal cavity, they simply had a friend place flat packages of drugs they wanted inside the supplement sleeve.

The next day one of us would order the LR by filling out a law book request, and by that afternoon the particular LR was in the cell of the inmate who ordered it. It was that simple. The men then sold some of the drugs to keep the flow coming. The rest, they used. What I couldn't believe was the amount of drugs in the unit at all times. Searches were extremely rare, and when they were done we were given prior notice and a lieutenant had to be present because of the sensitive nature of the defense materials and other evidence we had in our cells. It was much more trouble than it was worth for the cops to do a real search.

My trial was fast approaching, which brought a great deal of stress to my life. I desperately wanted to escape and I did it with drugs. At first I used drugs from the men in the unit, then I got them from my attorney's paralegal. She visited me several times a week and proclaimed her love for me and her desire to be together. She was beautiful and sensual, but I knew her type—long term she was trouble, and I wasn't interested in a real relationship with her. There were times when I needed a distraction, and she offered that and more during her regular visits. She also showed up at my mother's home, and told her and my sister she loved me and that she would get me out because she was a major part of my defense. She claimed to be in charge of witnesses and had access to defense strategies.

It all seemed a little strange, but she was a nice distraction and I liked the drugs she brought me. Since attorneys, investigators, paralegals, and members of the defense were allowed to bring us supplies, Maribel filled highlight markers with cocaine, heroin, LSD, PCP, and any drug she wanted, then brought them to me. Since pro pers were hardly ever searched, I simply walked back to the unit carrying the drugs. It wasn't anything new. Most of the men in the unit had a paralegal, usually a girlfriend, bringing drugs or whatever they wanted. The girlfriends-paralegals were also being paid an hourly rate by the state for what was supposed to be legal work. Of course, the money was then kicked back to the prisoner they came to see. During my trial, I went to court high every time. It's the way I drowned out how depressed I was, and how I dealt with what was happening to me.

When my trial got under way, Maribel insisted I stop talking to Maxine or any other woman. When I didn't commit to her demands she went to my mother, who she already called "suegra" (mother-in-law), and told her she should convince me to be with her exclusively because she could get me out. My mother already lived in her own imaginary world, and when she came to see me she repeated what Maribel said to her. I explained that Maribel had no power to get me out because she was a paralegal. My mother was convinced what Maribel said was gospel and spoke to Maxine, who explained to her we were only friends but if it would somehow help, she would stop speaking to me.

The next time Maribel came to see me, I confronted her. A huge argument broke out. She had even gone to Maxine's roommate and talked to her, hoping to poison everything and make it impossible for us to remain friends. Maribel was out of control, and ruled by jealousy and hatred because I would not bend to her will. She made my already depressing existence worse.

Throughout that time, Maribel continued to visit and bring me drugs. But something was different. She only came during the shift of two particular officers who never searched her when she came into the jail. During our visits, I noticed exchanges between Maribel and the officers. I asked why the two cops went out of their way to mess with me as if they were jealous, and she just said she was being friendly so she wouldn't be searched.

Of course it was a lie. I learned from another paralegal, who visited another prisoner, that she'd seen Maribel in the parking lot on several occasions kissing the two cops. Everything came to a boiling point when a witness who was scheduled to testify in my defense told me during a telephone conversation that Maribel had come to her home and tried to convince her to go out on a date with one of the cops from the jail.

I refused her next visit, but she persisted until I finally agreed.

"What's wrong? Why didn't you want to see me?"

"Look, don't come to see me anymore. I know you're fucking around with the cops here. One of the other paralegals saw you making out in the parking lot. I see them tripping over themselves to escort you to your car when you leave."

"Yes, they escort me, but it's only to make sure I'm safe."

"Really? So I guess you didn't try and convince my friend Monica to go out with one of your cop friends last week?"

I had her. I knew she was lying. I knew everything I heard was true by the look on her face.

"It's not like that. Monica's lying. I'm in love with you, Bill."

"I don't want this in my life. I'm done. Don't come to see me anymore. If you try, I'll refuse the visit."

She started crying, but suddenly something much more sinister appeared on her face.

"You think you can just drop me?"

"I'm doing no such thing, because we were never together. It was all in your head."

"Fuck you. I'm not someone you can just push to the side. Who do you think you are?"

I just stared at her.

"I'll hurt you, Bill. I promise you'll be sorry. No one pushes me to the side."

I turned and left, never realizing I was underestimating her threat, which was a huge mistake. While it was true she didn't have any power to get me out of jail, she had the power to hurt my case. After leaving the jail she went to my mother's house and begged her to talk to me. When that didn't work, she threatened again to hurt me and make sure I never got out. She made the threat to several people, and as my trial proceeded we were blindsided by the district attorney's knowledge of confidential witness information that only Maribel had known about, thereby securing my conviction.

Chapter 36

Adolescence, 1981–1982

It was 2 p.m. and Mike was late. I had dropped him off earlier at his house after surfing the entire morning with Go-Go, Sandman, Brody, Silver, Matt, and the rest of The Pack. We agreed to meet at La Habra High School so he could introduce me to Cookie Monster, a local car mechanic who seemed to know most, if not all, of the people with the rarest parts for Porsches and VWs. I wanted to meet him because he knew a car thief with two sets of eight-spoke Empi wheels and I wanted them for the '59 ragtop I was building with the rarest parts and utmost care. It was my latest project and would be the baddest and fastest car I owned so far. Thinking I might be in the wrong spot, I walked over to the snack bar hoping I'd see Mike, but the place was empty. Growing impatient, I looked around, and that's when I saw her.

She walked from the opposite side of the snack bar with a girlfriend. I must have stared a bit too long because she looked at me and smiled. I smiled back. All I knew was that she was the most exotic creature I'd ever seen, and my heart pounded so hard in my chest I thought it would explode. She had a perfect complexion, tanned coco brown, straight black hair with sun streaked highlights, dark eyes that sparkled, dimples, and a body that showed clearly through her skin-tight clothes. But the most heart-stopping feature was her smile. It was perfect, and I found myself walking toward her without thinking. I stopped in front of her, but I was at a loss for words.

"Hey," she said. "How's it going?"

"Good. I'm Bill. What's your name?"

"I'm Vanessa, and this is my friend, Becky."

I nodded to Becky, but my eyes were focused on Vanessa. My senses took her in and I wondered what I'd say next. I never had a problem talking, so this was completely new to me.

"I like your hair, it's like a lion's mane," she said.

That seemed to bring me back to myself.

"What are you doing later? Can I give you a ride home?"

"I'm meeting my ride here in a few minutes. Oh, here he comes now."

"That your boyfriend?"

"No. He's just giving me a ride home. I don't have a boyfriend."

"If he's not your boyfriend, then don't worry about him. I'll convince him to let me take you home."

Just then the guy showed up. He seemed uneasy when I looked at him.

"Pick me up from school tomorrow. I get out at one-thirty," she said.

"I'll meet you here."

She smiled. "I don't go to school here. I go to Sonora. It's down Whittier until you hit Palm Street, turn right, and it's about half a block down."

"I'll be there at one-thirty. See you tomorrow."

As I walked to the parking lot, I looked back at her and she smiled. The guy taking her home seemed relieved. As I turned into the parking lot, Mike showed up.

"What's up, Hombre?"

"Nada, I was looking for you, so I went to the snack bar and man, I just met one of the most beautiful girls I've ever seen. I'm picking her up tomorrow after school."

"Oh yeah? What's she like?"

"Take a look for yourself," I said, just as she and her ride came into the parking lot.

"Who's the dick with her?"

"Who knows? Some ass-wipe giving her a ride home. Fuck him. Check her out."

"Yeah bro, she's clean, but trouble. My friend Ken went out with her a few times this year. Some dude didn't like it and pushed him around for it."

"Your friend should have put his foot in that cat's ass. Believe me, bro, the last thing I'm worried about is some punk getting in my face."

We got in my car and drove to Cookie Monster's house. He was a long-haired, wiry-thin Mexican who was jumpy as hell but had what I needed. After a few minutes he called the car thief, who came over. When he pulled up in his '58 ragtop we shook hands.

"Hey, Sinbad. How's it going?"

I knew this car thief—not well—but I'd seen him around and we'd talked a few times.

"I'm cool, Ron. You the cat who has the Empi wheels?"

"Yeah. I brought one so you can check it out."

Cookie Monster and Mike came up.

"I didn't know you two knew each other or I would have just told you who had the wheels."

"Don't sweat it. You did the right thing. Better safe than sorry." I shook Cookie Monster's hand.

"Thanks, man."

By that night I had all eight Empi wheels in my shop at home. They were in mint condition and four would soon be on my '59.

The next day at 1:20 p.m. I pulled into the Sonora High School parking lot. I got looks from a few guys standing next to a white '57 oval window with flames, but I wasn't interested in them. My focus was on Vanessa. I got out of my car and walked into the school, not sure where to wait since she hadn't told me.

For a second a thought crossed my mind: *What if she really didn't go to this school and was having a good laugh at my expense?*

The bell rang and a flood of students came into the halls. I stood by the front door hoping to see her, and just as I started thinking I'd been stood up she came walking my way. I smiled, all the doubt gone from my mind, and put a look of complete confidence on my face. I watched her, and as soon as she saw me she smiled.

"Hi. You look great," I said.

"So do you. I was afraid you wouldn't show up."

"Why? I said I'd pick you up. Couldn't you tell how much I wanted to give you a ride home yesterday?"

"I wasn't sure, but I'm glad you came. I couldn't stop thinking about you."

That surprised me.

"I've had you on my mind since I saw you yesterday and I couldn't wait to see you again," I said.

We walked to my car and a few of the guys who stood next to the '57 with flames were checking it out. One guy had his head stuck in the driver's side window, looking inside.

"You lose something?"

He pulled his head out.

"Nah, dude, I was just looking at your ride. She's gorgeous. What size motor are you running?"

"2180, 48's."

"That '57 with the flames is mine. Maybe you'd like to run them at four lanes on Friday night."

"I don't run for free—a hundred dollars a gear. I have five gears. Payment on the spot."

I was showing off, and as he thought it over I turned to Vanessa and gave her a long, intense kiss.

"Yeah, I'll run you. I'm Cory. What time do you want to line up?"

Still holding Vanessa, I said, "How about eleven p.m.? I'm Bill." We shook hands, but I could tell the guy didn't like me. He walked away with his friends and I opened Vanessa's door.

"Cory's right about one thing. Your car's hot."

I smiled. "Babe, you don't know how right you are. Let's go to my house and then I'll drive you home. Is that cool?"

"Yes. I don't have to be home until five."

We went to my house that afternoon and made love twice, then again at her house.

We couldn't get enough of each other and I thought maybe we could be a couple. As we made love, she made me promise to be only hers, and I readily promised. She was beautiful, exotic, and somehow vulnerable, all wrapped into one, and I wanted to protect her from the start. Best of all, she understood me—my moods, passions, and needs, as well as what made me tick. I immediately trusted her. That's something I'd never done with anyone.

I told her who I was. Not just Bill, or Sinbad the surfer, but a car thief, a fighter, and that I'd never trusted anyone before her. We spent the next hours, days, and weeks talking. I told her about my dreams and fears and she accepted me for who I was. Then a week after beating Cory at four lanes, she told me she was in love with me. I told her I'd fallen for her too and that she made me happy.

It became official. We were a couple and we went everywhere together. I introduced her to everyone: The Pack, the Darque Knights, and the fighters I trained with. It never escaped my attention how others looked at her, and how they seemed envious of me, which I enjoyed. I liked the way she looked on my arm, and when we went to clubs, people stared at her as much as they talked about me.

For the first time in my life I allowed someone to see behind the mask I wore. Instead of laughing at me or finding a reason to blame me for what happened to me, she embraced me harder and promised to protect me and my secrets.

I finally felt secure about myself and completely proud of who I was around her. But instead of taking the new positive element in my life and changing for the better, I did the opposite. I pushed forward, using the solid ground I stood on to be better at what I already did. I fed my need to be feared and respected, and continued to build up my reputation. The image I projected was like an aphrodisiac to Vanessa. She loved who I was and that my reputation extended to her. She wasn't just Vanessa anymore—she was my girlfriend, and with that she gained a new level of respect and admiration.

Within a few months of meeting Vanessa, I took her to watch me fight. My opponent was an African American who, to that point, like me, had never been defeated. I tried to explain the atmosphere at the fights. The people, the smells, the noise. But nothing I said prepared her for what she saw and experienced that night. My father, who normally was by my side at my fights in case I was injured or cut, sat with Vanessa prior to the fight and explained I was to be left alone before my fight—that I needed to go to a place to release my beasts, and that I did so only when I was alone.

As I entered the circle the crowd grew quiet. My hood covered my head and face. My opponent was already in the circle, and when he looked at me I slowly pushed back the hood to reveal my eyes and face. The crowd's response was immediate and their roar filled the warehouse.

Removing the hood, I allowed the weight of my eyes to fix on him. I popped the joints in my neck and put my hands up and squared into fighting position, yelling "Cho" from the deepest part of my gut, a martial arts form of centering.

From the start, I knew that my opponent was the best I had faced. He was confident, a martial artist, about six foot two, over two hundred pounds, muscular, and experienced. We were both cautious during the first few moments of the fight, connecting then backing out, not risking too much or doing much to the other. In one of our exchanges, he connected with my left eye and followed with strikes to my face and legs, sweeping me to the floor. I fell and he stood and watched me.

He didn't follow me to the ground because he wasn't comfortable there. I shook off the blows and flipped over onto my feet. I took his best shot and was still standing. I'd see if he could take what I could dish out.

I moved in. I didn't hear the crowd or feel their presence anymore. In the circle, only he and I existed. The fight lasted only a few minutes, but that's an eternity to a fighter. In my ten fights, I had knocked out all of my opponents, and I wasn't about to let that change.

He seemed to slow down, as if he was desperate to end the fight with one blow. He threw a combination of kicks, and as I backed away, blocking the blows, he jumped up with a flying knee aimed at my head. I caught him in mid-air, lifted him, and slammed him head first onto the floor. I backed away and watched him as he had done earlier with me. He was dazed and attempted to get up before he was ready. His fear of fighting on the ground made him get up—he thought I'd attack while he was down. I'm sure he studied me and knew, unlike him, my ground game wasn't a weakness. But that fear made him walk right into what happened next.

Still dazed as he got to his feet and squared off, I advanced, landing blows to his face, and finished off with a spinning back kick that connected with the back of his head. He crumbled to the ground in a heap. All of a sudden, the roar of the crowd engulfed me. Looking up, I caught Vanessa's eye and she smiled.

It was always like that with her. She never criticized me. She simply let me be me, and her responses during our most intimate moments encouraged me to push myself even harder.

Still, not everything in our lives was great. She confided in me she'd been abused as a child. Her father beat her, but since her parents were divorced and he'd remarried and lived elsewhere, she said she didn't suffer at his hands anymore. But I didn't believe her. I didn't press her either, because I knew how difficult and powerless a victim of abuse feels. All I wanted to do was protect her from harm, and if she wasn't ready to talk about it, I wouldn't make her. But deep down I sensed there was a lot more than she was telling me. I just never imagined the monstrosity or totality of the abuse, and how it would affect me and change my life forever.

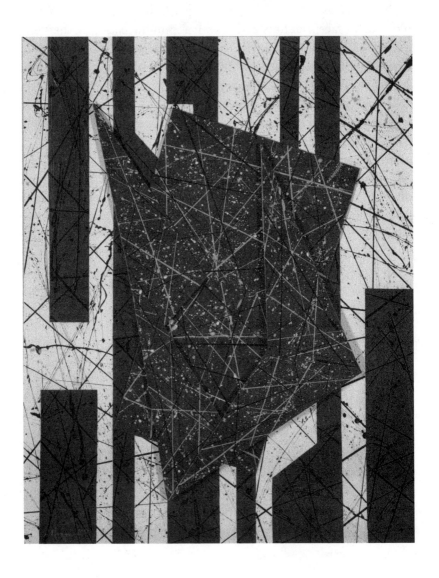

Chapter 37

San Quentin Death Row, 2000–2004

Jaturun Siripongs	February 9, 1999
Manuel Babbitt	May 5, 1999
Darrell "Young-Elk" Rich	March 15, 2000
Robert Lee Massie	March 27, 2001
Stephen Wayne Anderson	January 29, 2002

Like tolls from a ringing bell, the executions awakened the conscience of the men on death row and served as reminders of the sinister joke of our existence and the precarious path on which we walked.

I wasn't immune to the stress and depression, nor did I want to be. To do so would have blinded me to my emotions. I accepted my surroundings and everything that came with them. Indeed, these feelings are the very soil in which the subconscious mind and the creative imagination flower, opening the gates of future movement toward reintegration.

I used everything I experienced, both visually and emotionally, to create images, resulting in *Father's Rage, A Season in Conundrum, Little Boy Blue, Far from Heaven,* and *In My Time of Dying.* They were shown at Winchester Contemporary Art in San Francisco at an exhibit simply entitled "William Noguera," which received positive reviews and brought the attention of high-end collectors who wanted pieces created for them.

Unfortunately, and to my dismay, Gerhard refused to sell any of the originals that he bought. This frustrated me. I wanted my work to have more exposure and Gerhard wanted to show it only in his gallery, under his terms. But he had given me my first exhibit, and believed in me and my work enough to stand behind it. I believed I was indebted to him, so I kept my mouth shut and buried myself in my work. But no matter how much I tried to forget it, I couldn't. I was trapped by my commitment to Gerhard. I also had a responsibility to my family because I sent the majority of my earnings to them. The other portion I donated anonymously to various children's charities.

Over the next year I worked feverishly, pouring all of my frustrations into my work. I didn't know that feverish pace would turn out to be the very life raft that freed me from the imprisonment of my commitment to Gerhard. The escape came in the form of a letter from Amanda, Gerhard's wife. She wrote that they were extremely impressed with my newest body of work, and particularly with the speed in which I completed it. But because of the economic downturn, they couldn't purchase pieces as fast as I created them. They could only purchase one every quarter.

I read the letter twice. Whether she knew it or not, Amanda had broken their word to purchase all of my work in exchange for dealing exclusively with them. By changing the agreement to four pieces per year, I became free to sell and exhibit the rest of my work elsewhere. I called Amanda to confirm they'd only purchase four pieces per year. I expressed gratitude for everything they'd done for me, as well as my hope the economy would soon improve.

The following week I contacted Charles Linder, an art dealer and owner of the Linc Real Art gallery in San Francisco. I sent my résumé and photographs of my work, and expressed my interest in exhibiting my latest work at his gallery. To my surprise, he responded immediately and asked me to call him right away. He was very candid and said when he received a letter marked San Quentin Prison he wasn't going to open it until he noticed my name, which sounded familiar. Once he saw my work he recognized my style from the articles he'd read.

"William, your work is nothing like what anyone would expect to come from someone in your circumstance. The images you create are unique and powerful. They leave me wanting to gaze at them over and over again. I've never seen anything like it."

"Thank you. My images are unique because they're based on my dreams and imagination, then they're washed and fragmented with mathematical and lyrical rhythms. No image is the same because each image has its own number and emotional rhythm."

"Fascinating. I have an exhibit that opens in December and runs through January 2004. It's a group exhibit and I believe your work would be a spectacular addition. Would you be interested?"

"Absolutely," I said. "How many pieces do you need for the exhibit?"

"I believe three would be fine. There are four other artists exhibiting: Michele Manzoni, Rudi Molacek, Darrel Mortimer, and Jose Sarinana. They will all feature new work. It's unfortunate you won't be present for the opening reception. I'm sure the other artists would be interested in meeting the artist responsible for creating such wonderful work."

"I really appreciate this opportunity and I promise you won't be disappointed with the three pieces I create for the exhibit."

"I'm looking forward to it. By the way, William, the exhibit is titled 'Boxcar Wilhelmina: A Group Show.'"

"Interesting title. Again, thank you. I'll have the pieces arrive at your gallery a week prior to the exhibit. It's been a pleasure speaking with you."

I hung up and pumped my fist in the air. I called Paul Reinhertz, who I was introduced to the previous year. Paul had fast become—and still is—my most trusted and valued friend.

I told Paul about Amanda's letter and my upcoming exhibit at Linc Real Art in San Francisco. Finally I was free, back in control of how my work would be presented and where. After I hung up the phone, I sat back on my bucket to take everything in. This was good. I had about three months to create these pieces. My work would be allowed to stand on its merit and my voice would once again be heard.

All of this happened at a time when the world around me was in a state of chaos. Two more men on death row were killed. Smokey, from San Gabriel, was stabbed on the yard for his part in the senseless murder of a child and infant as he carried out a hit, which he bragged about. The other man was Chico Gonzales, who probably never thought as he went to the yard that it would be his last walk. An argument with another prisoner escalated to a fight. He took a punch so hard it lifted him off the ground and broke his neck from the impact. Unconscious, he fell and struck his head against the cement, crushing his skull.

Several others took their own lives instead of facing the depression and chaos that exists inside these walls. To avoid a similar fate, I escaped into the world I created.

Over the next two months I created the pieces for the exhibit. The first two, *Slave to Love* and *Sunrise*, were of ballerinas in motion poses. Their bodies were a testament to the rigors of their profession. The geometric fragmentation of the images was based on a mathematical arrangement and rhythms, which quieted the storm of chaos inside me.

The final piece, *Drops of Jupiter*, was a hyper-realistic montage arranged in a mathematical order. It represented the images of my subconscious mind at work during sleep, brought to life for everyone to see and experience.

Satisfied with the work, I signed each one, then signed, dated, and placed my fingerprint in blood on the back.

I smiled and packaged the work. The next day I'd ship them, and by the end of the week Charles Linder would have them. When I send my work out into the world, there's a part of me that goes with it, allowing me to escape and leave this place. My work isn't just a portrait of who I am as an artist—it's also both a figurative and literal vehicle of escape.

Since I was still doing four pieces a year for Gerhard, I busied myself with creating another piece for him, but something had changed. Where I used to look forward to it, I now dreaded it. I didn't want to send him any more of my pieces knowing they'd sit in a storage locker until he allowed people to see them. For me that meant my work was being subjected to imprisonment, a fate I abhorred.

I send my work out into the world incomplete, like orphans reaching for a first handhold in a stony world, searching out the sensitive observer. Like mirrors, the pieces reflect the viewer's passions, fears, secrets, and memories, no matter how well hidden. It's only in the eyes of the observer that the final ingredient falls into place, at last becoming concrete, breathing life and emotion into the piece. When the observer leaves, the piece once again enters a state of waiting. The works I sent to Gerhard would only come to life when he allowed them to be seen.

The exhibit at Linc Real Art came and went. My work was well received, and I sold all three pieces to a collector who'd attended the show. My true goal has never been to sell my work. I need to sell to meet my responsibilities, but my true artistic goal has always been freedom and clarity.

Less than two weeks after the exhibit at Linc Real Art, I spoke to Paul, and he asked me how I felt about the Vallejo Artists' Guild, which was considering me for a solo exhibit.

"I'd love to have a solo exhibit with them, but what made them consider me?"

He laughed. "I submitted a proposal for you. I'm now a member of the board, and next Thursday the entire board will meet to vote. If your work receives the majority vote, you get the exhibit."

"Paul, even if I get the exhibit and I start working right away, I won't have enough finished work for a solo exhibit."

"I've thought of that. I'll speak with Gerhard and Amanda about the exhibit and ask to borrow the work they have. I'll explain the exhibit will give them and the work they own exposure."

"I hope they say yes. Otherwise I won't be able to do the exhibit."

"You should consider putting together your own private collection of your best work. That way you'll always have enough to exhibit and won't be at someone else's mercy."

"You're right, especially now that I've decided to leave Winchester Contemporary Art."

"Why did you decide that?"

I explained my reasons. I don't know if he fully understood, but he accepted and respected them.

After that, I began working on what would become my private collection. Since I no longer worked for anyone, I didn't have to meet someone else's aesthetic standard. I slowly allowed myself to wade into the waters of color and abstraction. It was a new beginning—one that would take many years for me to become fully comfortable with. But since freedom and clarity had always been at the heart of my expression, I moved toward freeing myself from the old pictorial formula. I would allow my work to reflect changes that took place within. These changes represented a new language based on my surroundings, geometry, emotion, and color.

The following Sunday morning, I was called for a visit. I thought it was a mistake, and asked the tier bull to double check.

"Hey, Noguera, the front desk said you're scheduled for an eight a.m. visit. It's no mistake."

"Thank you, boss. I'll get ready."

"You have about fifteen minutes. I'll be back."

I nodded and got ready. I wasn't sure who it was and wondered if it was Paul. Maybe he had an answer about the Vallejo exhibit. Suddenly, I got nervous. I really wanted the show and the recognition it would bring. It represented so many things—recognition, respect, acceptance, and movement toward the goals I was driven to accomplish.

A few moments later the bull returned.

"You ready, Noguera?"

"Yeah, boss."

"Didn't think you had a visit today. It's nice someone remembered you."

He was right.

I went through the strip out. As I put my clothes back on, I thought about what the bull had just said. *It's nice someone remembered you.* My thoughts went to my work. I wouldn't give them a choice. I would be remembered because my work wouldn't let anyone forget I was once here. My mark would be undeniable.

I stopped just inside the visiting area and gave the floor bull my name and number. He escorted me to the five-by-eight-foot steel mesh cage where I would have my visit.

"C-5," the bull announced, and the other bull let my visitor into the cage. After the outer door was locked, the inner door was opened for me to enter. I turned around, placing my hands through the door slot so the cuffs could be removed.

I smiled at Paul and we shook hands.

"Hey, brother. How you doing?" I said.

"Okay, Bill. I'm here. I'm alive," he said with a smile.

Paul and I get along so well because we're both comfortable with who we are and neither has any desire to change the other. We agree on some things and disagree on others, but that's fine. I respect him as a man, and at nearly seventy-five years old, he's earned it. He's a retired teacher, an active Sufi, a practicing martial artist with over fifty years of experience, and he's a good guy to boot.

"Okay, so you look like you found a gold brick," I said. "What's got you smiling ear to ear?"

He laughed. "Nothing gets past you. It's nothing. I'm just happy to be here enjoying a cup of coffee with you."

As much as I wanted to ask him about the Vallejo Artists' Guild's board meeting, I didn't. The way he was smiling, I figured I'd gotten the exhibit, but he wanted to milk it for all it was worth. Finally, he asked, "How does the title 'Redemption' grab you?"

"It's powerful and has a great deal of significance for me. Why do you ask?"

"It's the title of your solo exhibit with the Vallejo Artists' Guild. A vote was taken Thursday and every member voted in favor, except one. That member was outraged. Hey, some people have such closed minds, they can't be reached. The rest of the members are extremely moved by your work and happy about the exhibit."

He still smiled.

"There's more, isn't there?"

"Oh yeah. I spoke to Gerhard and Amanda. They've agreed to loan a few pieces for the exhibit."

I shook Paul's hand and expressed my thanks for what he'd done.

"Don't thank me yet. The exhibit's in December. You have ten months to prepare. It's you and your work that'll be under the microscope. I did the easy part. The ball's in your court."

He was right. Over the following months, I created a new body of work, including a number of oil and acrylic paintings that I would allow people to see for the first time.

I knew I needed to find new representation—someone who would push my work to the next level of the art world. From the years of reading about other artists and their successes and failures, I knew success was as much about who you knew as it was about talent. For many artists in history, that was the difference between being well known and never being heard of.

I wrote a number of letters to art dealers, galleries, and art organizations that I thought could help me meet my goals over the coming months.

Finally I received a response from Clayton Tate and his organization, the Modern Art Foundation. I sent them a letter with pictures of my work, but somehow his response had been lost in the prison mail system and I received it two months later.

I read his words carefully, which were encouraging and full of promise. Most importantly, he was interested in representing me. In his letter, he said my work was visually striking and emotionally driven, which caused him to react physically to the images. He asked me to call him as soon as possible.

When I spoke to him, I apologized for the delay in calling him, and explained I'd just received his letter.

"Don't worry about it, my friend. I understand you're not at the Ritz-Carlton. I'm just glad to hear from you. Tell me, are you working on anything now?"

"I am. I'm preparing for a solo exhibit with the Vallejo Artists' Guild, which will feature a number of new works. I'm in the process of finding new representation to allow me to evolve and not control my artistic direction."

"I totally understand where you're coming from. I've worked with Barry 'Twist' McGee, Andy Warhol, Jean-Michel Basquiat, and I've produced concerts for Iggy Pop. I know all artists need freedom to grow and express themselves. Here at MAF, that's exactly what we stand for."

I noticed he liked to name-drop, but didn't think it was necessarily a bad thing—especially if it was all true.

"Mr. Tate, I'm encouraged with what you've said, but let me explain exactly what I'm interested in. I've spent the past eighteen years evolving as an artist, and I'm sure that in ten more years I'll be a different artist than the one you're speaking with today. I'd like to not only exhibit work but to record this process as a portrait of my own development as an artist. I want the seriousness of my voice in this medium to be heard, and to earn the respect and acceptance of my contemporaries. I want my work to transform the sensitive observer, at first glance, to the emotional state I experience when I created the work."

"You speak powerfully about your work, and frankly I'm a little shaken. I never would have expected what I'm hearing to come from a voice calling collect from death row. It gives me chills and brings into perspective the images you create, which moved me from the first time I saw them."

From that first phone call, Clayton Tate, his assistant art director, Jennifer West, and I began a union that provided me with the types of exhibits I wanted. It also brought attention and respect to my work. Of course, there were always those people around who, no matter what I did, always condemned me, my work, and anyone who stood behind me.

As the exhibit with the Vallejo Artists' Guild drew near, I finished the work I would include, thinking long and hard about the placement of a number of new color paintings. Working in color was a new and difficult language—one I had yet to feel comfortable with. Nevertheless, I told myself not to worry and pushed ahead.

The day of the "Redemption" reception, my work hung on the gallery walls. Paul walked through it as we spoke on his cell phone.

"Everything is framed, hung, and looks great. I'm sure you'd be very pleased with how your work looks. People are still arriving and it looks like a large turnout. They're here for you. Speaking of being here for you, there's someone here who wants to speak with you. I'll let you two talk."

"Hello, William. How are you?"

I recognized her voice immediately.

"I'm fine, Jennifer, and you?"

"Fantastic, and completely thrilled to be in the presence of your work. I love your new pieces. From the conversations I've heard, everyone is shocked at not only the photo-realistic images and abstract paintings, but their ability to draw the viewer in and pull at their heart strings. I'm so happy for you, William. Your work deserves the attention it's getting."

"Thank you. This is all bittersweet to me because, once we hang up, I'm cut off from the world. But knowing my work continues to breathe life and emotion into those who truly see and experience it gives me hope. It's as if a piece of me has escaped into a world, and in the fertile minds of viewers, true transcendence occurs."

"You have a way of describing your work that's truly poetic. I look forward to working together."

As I hung up the phone, a certain finality overcame me, as is always the case. Once that connection from the outside world is cut, loneliness is even more pronounced. I busied myself trying to think of other things, trying to escape the overwhelming weight of the world I lived in, and longing for the one I wanted to be a part of again.

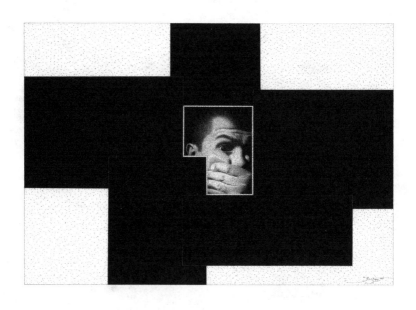

Chapter 38

Orange County Jail, 1987

I was accused, tried, and convicted. My so-called lawyer, Martín Gonzalez, who actually worked for my mother, protected her interests and secrets during her divorce, and he protected them again during my trial. I objected but it didn't matter. He was instructed to stage my life as one of privilege, happiness with loving parents, and, of course, of innocence. He did exactly that, sacrificing and silencing me in the process.

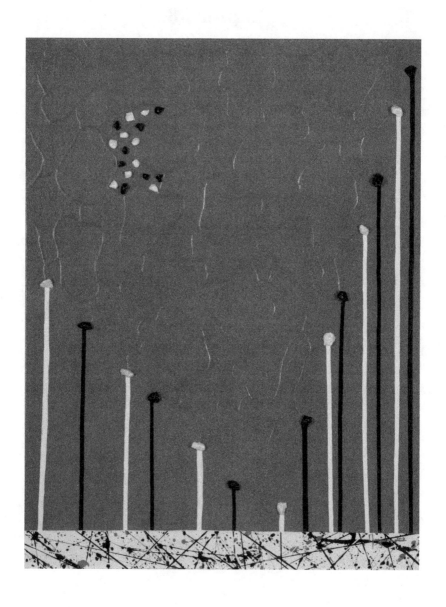

Chapter 39

Adolescence, 1982

My father started dating Vanessa's mother, Loretta. They really didn't go out. They were simply having sex. They met when I asked my father to pick me up from Vanessa's for a fight I had that night. I was there putting together a 1960 convertible VW I had started a few days earlier. What no one knew was that it was going to be a gift for Vanessa. Loretta was well aware of my criminal activities and was fine with me bringing a stolen car to her home.

My father pulled up to the house in his van while Loretta was outside, and they talked. The next night I came by to resume work on the convertible and noticed my father's van in the driveway. I walked into the garage and found Vanessa sitting in a chair, staring at the ground.

"Hey, Vanessa, what's my dad's van doing here?"

"He's inside with my mother."

I could tell from her tone that something wasn't right.

"What's wrong? Are you okay?"

She didn't respond, so I knelt down to her.

"She always does this, you know. It's like the only thing she cares about."

I could see she was upset, but I didn't understand what she was talking about.

"What do you mean? What does she do?"

"She's inside fucking your dad."

Not many things catch me off guard, but I would never have guessed she'd say that. She seemed disgusted by it.

"I don't want to be here. Would you take me somewhere? Anywhere but here."

"Yeah, come on. Let's get out of here. Is there anything else wrong? You know you can tell me anything."

"I know. I just need to be away from here."

I sensed there was something else, but I didn't press her. If she just wanted to be somewhere else, I could give her that.

A couple of nights later I stopped by my father's house and asked him what was up with Loretta.

"Nothing really. She's really forward and wanted me to come by. The next thing I know, we're in bed."

"Listen, what you do is your business, but it upset Vanessa, and from what I hear, you aren't the first by any stretch of the imagination."

"Yeah, I gathered as much. She's into some way out shit."

"I don't care, and I don't want to know. Just think about what I said, okay?"

It was the first time my father took what I said to heart, and he stopped seeing Loretta. Although we never talked about it again, I believe the "way out shit" she was into was what scared my father off rather than what I said.

The next week, Loretta asked me to stay over for the weekend because she and her boyfriend, Don, were going to Las Vegas to gamble. That wasn't anything new. I spent the night so often it felt like a second home. Of course, it still seemed a little strange to me, but what seventeen-year-old would complain? Besides, I'd experienced the same type of behavior from my parents my entire life. My mother often bent and twisted the rules to fit what was important to her. Granted, my mother wouldn't allow my sister's boyfriend to sleep over, but in other regards my mother's behavior and parenting skills were just as bad, or worse. Since my parents' divorce, my father refused to pay child support, so to continue with a lifestyle she was accustomed to, my mother moved to insurance fraud.

If my mother wanted new furniture, kitchen appliances, or a car, she'd burn her house or vandalize it so the insurance would pay her. She did it a number of times over the years and on a number of occasions asked for my help. One of those times was because she wanted a new car. I offered to steal whatever car she wanted, change the VIN numbers, and do all the paperwork. But she didn't trust VIN numbers and stolen cars, and feared the consequences of getting caught. What she wanted was for me to wreck her Monte Carlo. She'd report it stolen to collect the insurance money. I did what she asked and soon she had her new car.

Since I operated a successful high-end car theft ring, my mother expected me to pay for living at her home. I didn't mind. It was worth it to me. With my mother I had an ally and alibi. If the cops asked whether I was home on a particular date and time, she covered for me.

This, in my mother's mind, made her an accomplice to my crimes, and that was a secret she wanted to keep hidden. Since she was involved, I had to pay. It was that simple. If I was arrested, she bailed me out. In her mind she was being a good mother. She took care of her son and did what she had to do. To a seventeen-year-old, it seemed like a great deal. But that's why seventeen-year-olds need responsible parents. A true parent would have been horrified. Even today, my mother wouldn't see any fault in what she did and would argue vigorously that she was a great mother.

I finished the VW and gave it to Vanessa, which she did not expect. She was wide-eyed and thrilled to have her own car. At the same time, I finished my ragtop. I painted it black and put on the eight-spoke Empi wheels that I'd bought from Ron.

Everything seemed to be on track. I worked with Mike to supply high-end cars—Porsches, Mercedes, Corvettes, Cobras, and even Ferraris. I got anything the list required and delivered them to different warehouses near El Centro, California, where they were readied and taken across the border into Mexico.

Stealing cars never got old. Each list I received was a challenge. From finding the cars to delivering them and collecting my fee, every part excited me. I attended parties in some of the most exclusive homes in Los Angeles and Orange County to meet the owners of the cars I needed. I learned their habits, their alarm systems, and anything that could give me an advantage. I studied marks with an obsessive eye for detail. Nothing escaped my observation. To me, all of it was business, and I prepared myself for it just as I did for the ring. I wanted to be the best. I loved it.

I built a reputation as a car thief and it wasn't long before law enforcement heard of me. They frequently pulled me over to check the VIN numbers of my cars, or they'd impound my car so they could look for evidence to prove I'd stolen the car and changed its numbers.

I knew the cops didn't just decide to mess with me. Someone had to have given them information, and that someone had an agenda. It became clear that the informant was in the club because no one outside knew the kinds of details the cops had. I knew it wasn't Adrian or Go-Go. If either of them talked to the cops I'd already be in a prison cell because they knew everything—where I'd stolen the cars, who my connections were, and what warehouses I used.

I was confident neither Adrian nor Go-Go would ever betray me. I made them more money than either had ever seen, so they needed me. That alone was enough to keep them quiet. No, the informant was one of the club members. Though I continued to be Sergeant of Arms, I didn't steal with them or include them in my new enterprise. That made some members angry and jealous.

I didn't have anything concrete about the identity of the informant, only suspicions. It was possible one of our members simply told a girl what we were doing and expressed hatred for me, and that she was the informant.

I spoke to Adrian and we came up with a plan to catch the rat. He would tell other club members about what we were supposedly doing, and we'd wait and see which story surfaced with the cops. It didn't take long. Within a week the head of a specialized unit covering car thefts in Southern California pulled me over and took me in for questioning. I denied everything from the start, making the cop angrier by the minute. Finally he said he knew I'd taken a pair of Porsches from Balboa Island, which I gave to a member of a New York crime family as a token toward future business deals.

I kept quiet and he let me go, but I had the information I needed. There was no New York crime family and I certainly hadn't given a pair of Porsches from Balboa Island to anyone. It was a made-up story

Adrian floated to one specific club member we suspected of being the informant.

I drove to Adrian's house and picked him up so we could meet with Go-Go and talk.

"What's up? You've been quiet as fuck. What's on your mind?" said Adrian.

"I got pulled into the cop house today and the head of the highway patrol task force questioned me about some shit."

Adrian sat still for a few seconds. "One of our stories surfaced, didn't it?"

He knew what that meant. One of the club members was the informant and something had to be done about it. We didn't say a word until we picked up Go-Go in Huntington Beach, then I ran the whole deal to them.

"Okay, who's the fuckin' rat?" said Go-Go.

"Adrian, who did you tell the story to about the New York connection?"

Adrian just stared at me. "I told Javier."

Javier was one of the newest members of the club and seemed fearless when it came to stealing. But he and I never got along. He thought I should include him in my private business because he had earned the respect. But I simply told him, "No one's stopping you. Get yourself a fence and set up your own shop. It's that simple. But my business is mine. My game, my rules, and my people—no one else."

The subject never came up again, but he resented it and wanted me to fall. His mistake was going to the cops.

"So let's deal with this quickly and quietly. Adrian, you tell Julian what we've discovered. Tell him I'll deal with it, but I want Javier gone from the club. No ifs, ands, or buts about it."

"What are you going to do?"

"I'll think of something creative, but he won't forget it."

Adrian seemed nervous about it, but he knew I was right. He liked Javier, but he'd have to tell his brother that Javier, a guy he raised his hand for, was an informant.

Go-Go and I drove Adrian home that night after midnight. I did it on purpose so he wouldn't be able to talk to Julian about it until after I carried out my revenge. Adrian didn't pick up on anything, but Go-Go did, and as soon as Adrian was out of the car, I allowed my anger to seep out and the rage to boil over.

"Okay, Adrian's out. What's the plan? I know you got one, so let's have it. I'm in, no matter what. You know I'll back you up 'til the wheels fall off."

"No doubt, brah. I see you. I always have. Here's what I got. Before this bitch knows what's up, let's take his ride and burn it to the ground in front of his pad."

"Damn, that's a clean ride. Sure you want to handle it like that?"

"Yeah, I'm sure. If we just take it, he won't know anything other than someone took his ride. I want this motherfucker to know why and that we know he's an informant."

Javier lived in a residential area of La Puente and kept his ride in his garage. I knew his car had a good alarm, but it was connected to his battery and that was plain stupid.

After entering his garage, I slipped under the rear of his '63 convertible and cut the battery cable. No battery—no alarm. We pushed it out of the garage and into the street, and right in front of his house, we lit it on fire.

The next morning, I got a call from Julian and he asked that I come by his house. Go-Go spent the night, so he came with me. As we pulled up, I noticed most of the members of the club had their cars parked outside of his house. Adrian met us outside.

"I told Julian what we discovered and that Javier's an informant, but he wants to talk to you."

I nodded and walked into his garage.

"What's up, Julian? You need to talk to me?"

"Yeah, Adrian told me about Javier, but what other proof do you have? And why is he here?" Julian asked, looking at Go-Go.

All the other members seemed confused. Julian hadn't told them why the meeting had been called and they looked at me for an explanation. I didn't bother explaining Go-Go's presence.

"Proof? I'll give you proof."

Julian liked Javier and hung out with him a lot. They were stealing partners. He was hoping I'd mess up and the crew would turn on me for accusing a club member of being an informant.

"Check this out. My proof is that someone has been talking to the cops. I've been pulled into the cop house and my cars were impounded because someone in our crew is a rat. I know it wasn't Adrian or Go-Go, because they could sink me easily. The informant was someone who knew about my operation but didn't have the details to have me busted. So how do you set a trap?" I looked at all the members.

"I'll tell you how. You bait with cheese. I didn't know who the rat was but suspected Javier."

"Wait up." Renee spoke up. "You're accusing Javier of being a rat?" It's what Julian hoped for. It was the reason Javier wasn't there, even though he called Julian as soon as he discovered his car was torched.

"I'm not accusing him of being a rat. He is one. All of you know that Javier and I don't get along, and he's pissed I won't include his punk ass in my business. For that reason, and because he's a bitch, he went to the cops."

I had their attention, so I pressed on.

"When I suspected one of us was telling, I spoke to Adrian and he told Javier I had given a couple of Porsches to a New York crime family member toward future business deals and that I'd taken them from Balboa Island. Within a week, I was pulled into the cop house and questioned about the New York deal. That's my fuckin' proof. We made the story up, fed it to the rat, and he ate it up. Only Adrian and I knew this. Case closed."

Everyone was silent. Then Julian said, "Is that why you took his car out of his garage and burned it last night?"

"Damn straight. How else do you treat an informant? As far as I'm concerned, once he became a rat, he stopped being one of us and deserves no protection."

"Did Go-Go help you?" asked Julian. But he knew he'd lost. Go-Go stepped up to him.

"Yeah, it was my idea. Fuck Javier. And if you don't like it, fuck you too." Julian looked at me.

I told him, "You're on your own against Go-Go. I won't save your ass." Renee got between the two of them and Go-Go smiled.

"Yeah, that's what I thought."

"Listen, Javier is out. There's no doubt he told on Bill, and I won't be caught dead around a rat. I may have handled it differently, but Bill did what he had to. I got no problem with that," said Renee.

Everyone nodded, but I could tell some of them didn't like it. The tension was thick and it wasn't over by a long shot. Javier had his friends among us, and since I spent more and more time away from the crew to develop my operation, Javier got close to some of them and they liked him. Julian, Marco, Ruben, and a few others were on Javier's team, and that didn't escape my attention. But instead of confronting them, I left it at that. I did what I set out to do and that was catching the rat, and everyone knew I was right.

Of course, being right doesn't always make you popular, or liked. But I didn't care. I thought I was invincible and powerful. I didn't need friends. I wanted respect. What I didn't realize was that someone may respect and fear you while you're standing in front of them, but when your back is turned the knife is suddenly plunged in and twisted.

Over the next few months, business returned to normal, but I changed my habits. Everything, including the warehouse I used, was switched. I spent even less time around the club. I sold my black '59 ragtop and drove a white-on-white '62 ragtop I took from San Diego. I poured thousands of dollars into building, from the ground up, a '56 356 (A) convertible Porsche. I had taken it from the Beverly Hills Hilton as soon as I saw it sitting in the parking lot of the hotel. I didn't hesitate. As soon as I changed the VIN numbers, I took it to Crazy Ben, the best body and paint man in Los Angeles. He'd worked on it over the next few months to make it perfect. Not that it needed it. When I first took it, it was in mint condition. But like all of my rides, I improved it. I wanted to put my personal touch on it and to change the appearance so it couldn't be identified.

Meanwhile, I spent as much time at Vanessa's house as I did at mine. I moved my gym equipment to her house as well as my martial arts gear. But the more time I spent with her I noticed things seemed out of place. I couldn't put my finger on what was wrong. When I'd ask her, she'd say it was nothing. But I knew better. Still, I let it go. I didn't want to upset her and ruin what we had. All I wanted was to see her smile and hear her laugh.

That laughter would stop, or at least change, a few months later. Her father, who usually took her out twice a month, was scheduled to come by to pick her up on Saturday. Since she was usually gone the entire day, I went to the studio to put in some extra work in preparation for an upcoming fight I had in Mexico. I spent the better part of the day in the studio and it was already dark when I finished. I drove home, took a shower, and, just as I finished shaving, my mother knocked on my bathroom door.

"Billy, Vanessa's on the phone. She's crying."

I opened the door and went to the phone.

"What's wrong?"

"Please come get me. My father hurt me. He's coming now. Please come get me."

"Vanessa, who are you talking to? Get off the phone."

I could hear her father's voice clearly as he ripped the phone from her and slapped her. She screamed and cried out.

"Who is this?" her father screamed into the phone. "Bill, is that you?"

I heard his words as I dropped the phone and ran out the door.

Rage filled my every fiber. Her father was a bully, and as I drove to her, memories filled my mind of when I was beaten and abused by everyone around me. A red haze clouded my vision, but the nearly twenty-minute drive kept it at bay. When I arrived I thought clearly, holding back the rage that threatened to consume me.

I didn't bother knocking, just walked into the house, straight into Vanessa's room, which for the first time struck me for what it truly was. A cage. She was on the corner of her bed, as far as she could get from the door, holding her legs as close to her chest as possible, where she rocked back and forth.

"Vanessa, are you okay?"

As soon as she heard my voice she looked up and ran into my arms.

"It's okay. He won't hurt you anymore. Shhh . . . it's okay."

Her body shook and trembled as she cried. My eyes searched her room. A mattress on the floor. Absolutely no furniture, pictures, posters, or dolls. Nothing. I don't know why I never noticed it before.

She shook violently and her high-pitched wail filled my ears, reminding me of a tortured animal. I sensed his presence before I heard him, but I turned to find Manny Sanchez standing in the doorway. I put myself between him and Vanessa. As I did, I noticed the bruises on her face and body and I responded by shoving Manny back. He wasn't a small man. Six feet, over two hundred pounds, and confident with his macho act.

"Touch her again and I'll break off the hand you used and beat you with it," I said. I shoved him again. "Not so tough now, are you? Let's see some of that tough guy act you love to use on Vanessa."

He realized why Vanessa called me.

"C'mon, Manny, hit me."

I shoved him back again. Rage poured into me and I opened myself up to it. But Vanessa touched me and I stilled.

"Bill, please take me somewhere else."

I turned, picked her up, and carried her to my car and drove away. The rage drained away and concern filled me. We arrived at my house and my mother saw what her father had done. Bruises ran down her back and legs, and she had cuts on her face and lip.

I didn't know what to do. What could I do? I couldn't go to the cops. I'd never dealt with anything like that before. I knew I couldn't just hide her at my house. Later, while Vanessa showered, I called my ex-girlfriend's father to ask for his advice. I worked for him at his painting company when I was younger, and besides being a good man and father, he was a cop. The next day I drove Vanessa to his home, and as soon as Bud saw her he became angry.

"Did your father do this to you?" he asked.

Vanessa started crying. "He gets angry and hits me."

Bud asked us to come in and brought out his camera. He took pictures of the abuse she'd suffered.

"Bud, I don't know what to do. I can't just keep her at my house, and if Manny comes to get her, I can't stop him unless I beat him up, which I almost did last night when I saw what he did."

"You don't want to do that because you'll end up in jail. No, Vanessa can stay here for a few days, and if her father shows up I'll deal with him."

I was relieved but knew it wasn't over. At some point she'd have to go home and would be exposed to the abuse again. Since she left without saying where she was, Loretta called around until she found her. By the next afternoon, Manny showed up at Bud's house. I wasn't there, but Manny had no idea Bud was a cop. When he made demands and threatened to call the police Bud showed him the pictures he took of Vanessa, then showed him his badge.

"Go ahead and call the police," Bud said. "I'm sure they'll be very interested in seeing the abuse you inflicted. It'll be a pleasure to book you myself. Please make the call."

Manny left without much else to say. Within two weeks, Vanessa returned home. She had to. She had school and she couldn't just stay at Bud's forever. Everything seemed to return to normal, but Loretta started giving me the cold shoulder. Nothing obvious, but I noticed the difference. I continued doing what I'd always done and didn't let it bother me. I worked to expand my car delivery business and competed in fights every time I had the opportunity.

As my senior year came to its final weeks, I received a call one morning when I returned from my run. It was Vanessa. She was in the hospital. She'd been in a car accident while driving to my house. I rushed to the hospital and found her sitting on a bed. Loretta was there, too. As soon as she saw me, Vanessa got up and we hugged. But Loretta wasn't as affectionate to me. I was told what happened, and Loretta blamed me.

"She had this accident because she was going to see you, and because you gave her that car."

I couldn't believe it. What could I say? Technically, you could say I was to blame. I did give her the car that was now totaled. She rear-ended an El Camino because her foot slipped off the brake pedal, and she was on her way to see me. Minus a few bruises, Vanessa wasn't seriously injured, but someone had to be blamed and I was the scapegoat.

A few weeks later, my luck ran out. I was celebrating my eighteenth birthday on Wednesday, June 17, 1982. Vanessa and I spent the night at the beach. We made plans to go dancing that Saturday at a club where the Darque Knights were VIP guests. I was also enforcing club security and had to be there early. I told Vanessa to get a ride to the club and meet me later that night after I finished bouncing. As bouncer, I screened who was allowed in, enforced dress code, and stopped any trouble or fighting inside the club. That night I failed to detect trouble and paid for it dearly.

Vanessa arrived with a few of her friends just as the club reached its maximum capacity. She looked great. I couldn't believe how much she'd changed since we first met. Gone was the straight sun-streaked hair. In its place was a styled loose perm that gave her already womanly features an attractive sophistication. She dressed differently too, in order to fit into the world I lived in.

I'd also changed. I'd cut the lion's mane of hair I'd worn as a symbol of the beasts I controlled, and instead had a short and styled cut. I did it to fit into the world of high-end car owners, and to acknowledge my confidence in who I was.

Vanessa and I made our way to the dance floor. We loved to dance, spending hours at it. Nothing seemed to matter when our bodies moved to the rhythms pumping through the mega speakers. The club was crowded, and as Lime's "Your Love" started to play, a DJ known as Darque Star, a member of our crew, dedicated the song. "This jam goes out to Bill and Vanessa, Darque Knights down."

I was bumped from behind. I turned to see who hit me and I noticed a little boy who couldn't have been more than eleven years old hurry past me.

"What the hell is that kid doing in here?" I said to no one in particular. I stopped dancing, and took hold of Vanessa's hand as we followed the little boy, who tried to make his way through the crowded dance floor. He reached the stage and I knew he'd have to turn around and come back because there was no exit through the stage. I stood waiting for him, holding Vanessa in front of me. He saw me and I smiled at him. The kid smiled back, and as he approached me he bumped into a guy who was dancing. The guy, not expecting to get bumped, tripped and nearly fell. As he recovered, he spun around, pulling a knife and flicking it open. He moved as if he was going to stab the kid. Music played and lights pulsed, but people continued to dance, unaware.

I didn't have time to reach the boy, so I yelled from the deepest part of my center, "Hey, over here."

The guy focused on me and I could tell he was high and mad as hell. Anger controlled him as he pulled his arm back to stab me. It would have plunged into Vanessa, who I still held in front of me. I pushed her out of harm's way and heard him say, "Taste this." Seconds later the knife plunged deep into my stomach.

I had a split second to ready myself for the vicious attack, and although it was difficult to see because of the atmosphere in the disco, I caught the knife with my hands, cutting them open in the process, but avoiding a much worse stab wound. I struggled to hold the blade away from me, but someone on the dance floor bumped me hard from behind, loosening my grip on the knife. As soon as I lost my grip, the guy stabbed deep into the area next to my groin. Once the blade went in, he pulled up, opening me and cutting my femoral artery.

Vanessa screamed and I heard the echo of it course through me as my body turned to rubber. Blood poured out of my upper thigh as the blood pressure in my entire body drained away. I staggered to the ground, panic gripping my senses. I had to get away from the danger or the guy would finish me. I drew on all my strength and stumbled out of the club onto the sidewalk, where I fell. I hoped someone would call my mom and dad. I was dying.

I went into shock. My hands curled up uncontrollably. Vanessa cried, "Bill, please don't leave me. I love you. We're supposed to be together forever. Please, someone call an ambulance."

I was cold, covered in my own blood, and terrified. I tried to tell the crowd to tell my mom and dad I'd be home late for dinner. My thoughts were foggy as my life flashed before my eyes. Suddenly, Go-Go sat beside me. He took off his belt and tied a tourniquet tightly on the wound.

"I'm here, brah. Damn, I leave you alone for a minute and you go get yourself stabbed. It's just a scratch. Stop being such a pussy."

I was too far gone to respond, but if I was going to die I wanted Go-Go with me. I looked at Vanessa one last time before I lost consciousness. As I did, I smiled and looked past her into the crowd. A few feet away, Javier stood laughing at me. Then darkness swallowed me.

Chapter 40

San Quentin Death Row, 2004–2007

In the weeks after my "Redemption" solo exhibit with the Vallejo Artists' Guild, I busied myself with new work and answered questions from reporters and critics. It overwhelmed me to realize so many people had seen and interacted with my work. But along with the positive interest my work created came skepticism, shock, and even hatred from a few.

"Why should he be allowed to work?"

"Shouldn't we lock him up and throw away the key?"

"Why should he have a voice when his victim can't speak?"

There will always be people who only see the bad no matter what I do. I couldn't please everyone. But even as I told myself this and tried not to be affected, in truth, it bothered me. I wouldn't have been affected as much if critics simply proclaimed my work to be horrible— but the criticisms were deeply personal and affected me as a human being more than just as an artist. Some of them actually wanted me to be killed.

A week later I received a letter from Gerhard through his gallery manager. In the letter I was accused of dishonesty for creating new work and never offering it to him. It said I failed to honor our agreement, which made it obvious that his wife, Amanda, had never told him of the letter she wrote to me that ended the agreement. Nevertheless, I immediately wrote a letter back to Gerhard and enclosed a copy of Amanda's letter to assure him that it was she who broke her word, and not me. I concluded by expressing that I appreciated everything they had done for me and would be forever grateful.

The end of the relationship with Gerhard concerned me even though I'd done nothing wrong. My reputation in the art world was of utmost importance to me, so I didn't want anyone to think I'd broken a contract. I had followed the terms of our agreement to the letter, but once Amanda voided the agreement, I sought other options.

I never heard back from Gerhard and still don't know if he ever received my letter. Maybe it was intercepted and kept from him. Maybe he still believes I didn't keep my word. Regardless of what he thought, my conscience was clear.

In May of 2005 I got an exhibit at the San Francisco Design Center Galleria. With the help of Clayton Tate and his Modern Art Foundation, my work got more attention. I believed I'd found a home—a place I could explore and express my emotions freely.

Clayton sent me pictures of the neo-expressionist works of Jean-Michel Basquiat, a famous artist he claimed to have been close to. Somehow his work spoke to my Radiant Child and brought my subconscious and conscious states together as one. Never before had color spoken to me in a language I could understand so clearly. I had studied and allowed the works of Rothko, Still, Motherwell, Pollock, Miró, Matisse, Gorky, Mondrian, and countless others to move me. But when I saw the primitivistic style of this artist, all the pieces fell into place. Color, shape, rhythm, and my beloved numbers came to life and filled me with such emotion I could hardly contain the tears. I kept all this to myself, but I was changed, and would never be the same again.

As the year came to a close, the State of California's death machine came to life again, taking the lives of Donald Jay Beardslee, Stanley "Tookie" Williams, and Clarence Ray Allen. Surprisingly, the executions had little effect on me. I don't mean to give the impression those men's lives didn't mean anything, but compared to how I reacted to the first execution, where I nearly had a nervous breakdown, my reaction was minimal. I believe my subconscious mind had constructed a wall to protect itself and ensure its survival.

Still, the State of California couldn't execute death row prisoners as quickly as they killed each other. The sheer brutality behind these walls would shock even the most bloodthirsty men. I wondered what all the people who marched against the death penalty would say if they knew the very people they supported were often planning to take another prisoner's life.

It shouldn't shock anyone to know the men here pursue murder as a solution to their problems, while the State of California seeks the same solution with its legal death machine. Whether a robed official or a death row prisoner orchestrates the act, the result is the same. Both have political agendas, and both are flawed.

Rather than focus on any single issue and be consumed by it, I allowed myself to experience it all. In doing so, I developed a new body of work, "Structured Chaos," that incorporated my surroundings—its impulses, energies, and struggles for space. The first piece of the series, *Birth*, followed by *Gothica*, marked the start of freeing myself from my pictorial formula and speaking in a new vocabulary of abstraction.

In March 2006, with the help of the Modern Art Foundation, I received my first solo exhibit in San Francisco at the Space Gallery. The exhibit was titled "The Escape Artist: Shadowed Views from the Private World of William Noguera."

As the opening reception approached, I became painfully aware that I would be under the microscope more than ever. But wasn't that what I wanted? If it wasn't, I would've been happy to keep my work to myself. No, I wanted my artistic voice to be heard. A child's voice deep in my subconscious reminded me: *I am here. I am somebody. I made this. Won't you stop, look, and feel?*

The exhibit was a success. More than four hundred people attended the opening reception. I was amazed at the response and the magnitude of the exhibit. A few weeks before the reception I created some drawings of my cell, and from those drawings an architect and artist, Francisco Recabarren, created a detailed replica that was placed in the gallery. During the reception, which my father attended along with my half-sister, Tatiana, I called the gallery and spoke to the audience through a speaker inside the replicated cell, making it poignantly clear that I was speaking to them from my cell on death row. Critics called me a "visionary" and my work "chillingly beautiful" and "technically impeccable." Affirming what the critics thought of my work, collectors paid between six and twelve thousand dollars for each of my pieces.

To say I was pleased was an understatement. I was overwhelmed by a sense of satisfaction and accomplishment. During an interview with a reporter, my father said, "I'm proud of my son. Look what he's created. All of these people are here to see his vision. A lesser man would never carry the burdens he does with such dignity." My father's words completed the circle for me. I had the attention of the only man I ever loved or needed approval from. Sadly, it had come at such a high price.

A week after the Space Gallery reception, someone from Stanford University's film department contacted me. They were interested in producing a short film about my work that I would narrate. I agreed to do it, and production started right away.

Soon after I had exhibits of my work at the Four Galleries in San Francisco and at the Centre Pompidou in Paris, France. By the end of that year, the *San Francisco Weekly* gave me the front page of their publication, "In Pen and Ink," and ran a detailed five-page article about me, my work, and my journey as an artist.

In just a little over a year I went from the shadows to the spotlight. My work was in demand. Collectors from San Francisco, Los Angeles, Chicago, and New York sought my pieces. Magazines and publications featured my work in their pages. With the new celebrity I experienced the high of success and the low of losing my most prized possessions.

I returned from the yard late in the day. I was tired, and as I placed my yard roll on my bunk, I glanced at the metal shelf and locker that sits just above my sink. Something was wrong, but it didn't fully register. I went to the sink to wash my hands and that's when I realized what was wrong. My heart pounded in my chest and my stomach clenched tight. I stepped back and looked on top of my metal shelf and locker. I stood on the toilet so I could search the entire top of the locker, but I already knew my sketchbook was gone.

The sketchbook contained drawings, thoughts, emotions, and ideas from the past twenty years. I had last worked in it the night before.

Every picture I'd ever drawn, painted, or created had first been purified there. In the more than five hundred pages was the purest portrait
of me that existed, and someone had stolen it. I searched my entire
cell, just in case I was wrong. A true part of my soul existed in those
pages, and I could feel that it was no longer in the cell with me.

Only a bull could have taken it. When the bull on duty passed by I
stopped him.

"Excuse me, boss. Did you search my cell?"

"Nah, Noguera. I just got back from a hospital escort. What's
wrong?"

"My Book of Thoughts is gone."

"I'll check the logs and see who searched it."

He left to check, but I knew it was useless. The bull who took it
wouldn't have left a trail. It had to be a regular in East Block. A new
bull wouldn't know about it. Just about all the regulars knew me and
my work, especially about my Book of Thoughts. During searches it
was always a major attraction.

The bull came back. "Noguera, according to the log, I was the last
one who searched your cell and I'll admit, I looked at your Book of
Thoughts, but that was three days ago. I'll go downstairs and inform
the lieutenant."

A few moments later a unit meeting was called, but I knew no one
would admit taking it. What I couldn't figure out was how they carried it out. The book was big: twenty by twenty inches, leather bound,
and nearly three inches thick. It was priceless to me and obviously
some bull thought it was worth the risk to take.

Every time I look into the eyes of one of the bulls I wonder if he
was the one who took it. I never created another book, nor will I
ever. Every few months I have someone search for it online, hoping
someday someone decides to sell it. I'd like nothing better than to
open its pages and reunite with the pieces of me I lost.

Sadly, it would happen again, but from those I trusted to protect me
and my work. In April 2007, I had another exhibit at the Space Gallery in San Francisco, followed by a screening at the Mendocino Film
Festival of the short film created by the student at Stanford. The film

was named after my hyper-realistic montage, *Ghost in the Material.* Everything was moving along well, and I was grateful.

But I knew something was wrong, though I refused to believe what my instincts told me. A few months later, I entered and won the *San Francisco Weekly* Best of San Francisco Masterminds Grant Competition. When I asked Clayton what the prize was, he told me there wasn't one. He said the award was in the form of a future exhibit, which I knew was untrue. I knew that the Masterminds Grant Competition awarded five thousand dollars to the winner. Nevertheless, I didn't challenge him. I began to realize that Clayton wasn't the artists' savior he portrayed in the media.

Later, when I asked him when my family would receive a check for the sale of my work, he became angry. He said he would send it as soon as he could, but added that he'd spent over fourteen thousand dollars on my promotion and exhibition costs, and that those costs would be paid for with my work. It's a simple swindle—an old trick that he would be familiar with from his days as the owner of a record label. Find an artist, pay to give him exposure, and, once he's in debt, demand that the rights to the work be transferred to the label for payment.

Clayton Tate's Modern Art Foundation claimed to be a nonprofit that received donations in order to offset the costs of organizing artist exhibitions. During a conversation with him and his art director, Jennifer, I made it clear that his dealings with me were suspicious.

"Clayton, art dealers and galleries normally take forty to fifty percent of sales. I understand this arrangement and it's fair because the gallery dealer only gets paid if they make a sale. However, you claim to not take any money from artists, yet here you're charging me for every cost you incur in reference to my work, whether you make a sale or not. That's not what you advertise. I'd rather we come to terms on a set percentage for you to take only when you sell my work."

"We're a nonprofit and that arrangement violates the rules of a nonprofit. We couldn't possibly do that."

"That's bullshit and you know it, because what you're doing is exactly that. The only difference is that we're not agreeing on a set percentage, which benefits you. You're simply taking most of the profits, if not all of them, and calling it payment for costs, whether you sell or not. What happens if nothing is sold? My debt to you continues to rise, and at the end, how do I pay you?"

"Well, the debt must be paid."

"Funny that you never mentioned that before, or to all of the magazines and publications that have interviewed you. I suppose you'd take some of my work as payment for my debt?"

"I'm sure we can work something out, my friend."

"Listen, forget the exhibit you're trying to set up. I'm not going to pay for anything else until we agree on a set percentage for sales. Right now, I'm the one taking on all of the responsibilities and costs. The way I see it, your organization has never received the attention it's getting now. Correct me if I'm wrong, but it's because of me. When was the last time you were given a front page or a feature article prior to me signing with you? Years? This has to be settled before we go on or we won't be doing anything else together."

Later that night, I called Jennifer. I believed we'd become friends and I thought I could trust her. During our conversation I told her of my plans to leave the Foundation, and she told me she had decided that she could no longer work with Clayton either. She knew he was lying to me, and to other artists too.

I asked point blank, "Is Clayton attempting to take all of my work?"

"Clayton is a snake and has stolen from other artists. He plans to do the same to you unless you stop him." She said she planned to establish her own organization, and she asked if I'd consider being her first client.

"What will your standard artist agreement be? What percentage will you take from sales?"

"My gallery will be a for-profit enterprise and I will only take forty percent of sales. Nothing else. Everything you consign to my gallery will be on this scale. I give you my word. You'll never have to worry about your work with me as your dealer."

"This sounds good. Tell me, is Clayton ever going to give my family the proceeds from the sale of my work? Because as of yet, they haven't received a dime."

"After speaking with you earlier today, Clayton said he sent your family roughly thirty percent of what he sold. But the thirty percent is only what you know he sold. What you don't know is that he's been selling prints of your work. Since it's impossible for you to prove how many he's sold, he's keeping one hundred percent of the profits from the prints. I'm so sorry, William."

I was speechless and couldn't believe how stupid I'd been.

"I know you don't have any reason to believe what I've said, especially since I never told you what Clayton was doing, but it's easy to prove if I'm being truthful or not. In July, we have your solo exhibit at the Yerba Buena Center for the Arts, as well as the film screening of *Ghost in the Material*. This is a great venue for you. But if you choose to cancel it because of what I've told you, I'd understand. However, if I were you, I'd take the exhibit, and right after, tell Clayton you have placed all of your work in your family's name. If his response is positive, then I'm wrong. But if he gets angry, then you'll have your answer, and proof I'm telling the truth. You see, you have no defense against Clayton because you're in prison. But your family is a different story."

Jennifer also told me that Clayton had been sued by many other artists for exactly the same thing: stealing and copyright infringement of intellectual property rights. I hung up the phone still reeling from the sucker punch. Luckily, all of my pieces were at Jennifer's apartment, and she assured me that Clayton would not be allowed to take them, and she was the one who was in charge of setting up the upcoming exhibit. I decided to be patient and follow her advice to take the exhibit and film screening since a venue like that would benefit my portfolio. But as soon as it was finished, I would confront Clayton.

In the weeks leading to the exhibit, I didn't call Clayton and only spoke to Jennifer. I communicated everything through her. I couldn't stomach talking to him.

After the exhibit, once I confirmed with Jennifer that my work was back at her apartment, I dialed Clayton's number. He answered on the second ring, accepted the call, and as usual went into his dog-and-pony show.

"William, my friend, I'm so happy you called. How are you?"

I could play his game too, so I followed suit. I didn't want him to suspect anything. I wanted his responses to be spontaneous.

"I'm doing well. I just read the article in the *San Francisco Chronicle* about the exhibit. I'm pleased with it."

"This is only the beginning. I'm going to make you a star. I believe truly that you're the next big thing. I hope you're also pleased the exhibit didn't cost hardly anything since the Center did us a favor."

"I am happy about that and also about the money you gave my family. Thank you."

"Of course. I'm happy to handle your career. I also spoke to my lawyer about setting up a trust for your family which I'll be happy to handle too since I know about these things and have handled other artist's affairs in the past."

"That sounds good, but how would that work? Would my work belong to my family?"

"Yes, of course. They'll solely benefit from your work. But so no one can steal from you, we'll place all of your work and rights in the Modern Art Foundation's name. That way you and your family will be protected."

"It's always been my intention that ownership and rights to my work be held by my family in case something happens to me. That's why, a little over a month ago, I signed ownership and all rights of my work over to my family and had all of the documents notarized. They now own it all."

"What? Who the fuck do you think you are?"

"It's my work and my intention has always been for it to benefit my family when I'm gone, so I just made it official."

"You son of a bitch, pissant motherfucker. I made you what you are. You owe me."

I let him put the noose around his neck. He kept yelling and screaming and I just listened. When he slowed down, he realized he'd lost his temper and made a mistake. That's when I cut into the conversation.

"You're taking this pretty personally. It seems you never intended for my family to benefit from my work—you were counting on benefiting. Thank you for being so honest about it and also about all the prints you've sold and never told me about."

"I have costs and you owe me."

"Clayton, from this moment on, you no longer represent me, my work, my family, or anything to do with me. I'll send you a letter today to this effect, terminating everything."

I hung up the phone and never called Clayton Tate again, nor had anything to do with him or his organization. In the coming weeks, Jennifer also left the Foundation to form her own organization, Phoenix Art Agency. I became the first artist she represented. To settle the debt Clayton claimed I owed him, Jennifer arranged for me to give him *Samo*, an original portrait of Jean-Michel Basquiat. At first I was against giving him anything since he had already stolen from me, but eventually I agreed. What I didn't know then, and wouldn't know until it was too late, was that I'd be bitten again by an even bigger snake.

Chapter 41

Adolescence, 1982

I was pulled down into the fog. The darkness surrounded and threatened to drown me. The more I struggled to get free, the deeper I sank. I heard laughter and knew they were laughing at me. In an instant I was no longer a powerful young man, but a small, helpless child.

The next instant I stood at a distance watching the child struggle. At my side stood my beasts, Rage and Pain. I knew if the child didn't win the fight he'd be dead. I couldn't let that happen. The longer I watched, the more the familiar red haze clouded my vision, and I needed to help him.

I closed my eyes and willed myself into his place. Suddenly, it was me who fought the darkness, the moving black-and-white images tinted red with rage. It grabbed at me, wrapping me in greedy arms to pull me down and consume me.

I screamed and fought to free myself, and, when I finally woke, I tore at the tubes in my arms that my unconscious mind mistook as a threat. I screamed my frustration, and then realized Vanessa held me down, and she was the one screaming.

"He's awake. Someone help me. He's going to hurt himself."

I stopped. The fragrance of her perfume brought me around to understand that I was safe. But I was still in the grip of fear.

"Vanessa? Where am I? What happened?"

"Oh Bill, you're awake. You've come back."

I tried to sit up, but the pain stopped me. I realized I was in a hospital. Still confused, I tried to understand what I was doing there and what had happened. Vanessa was still crying and calling for someone to help, which added to my confusion.

Finally a nurse arrived. I tried sitting up, but my right leg felt as if it had been ripped off and sewn back on.

"Mr. Noguera, you're in the hospital. You've been in a coma for the past few days and you must calm down or you'll tear the stitches in your leg and possibly open up your artery. You nearly died. You've suffered a great trauma and need to heal."

I was tired, the exhaustion overwhelming. I pushed back the sheets to look at my leg. What I saw nearly made my heart stop. The inside of my upper right thigh looked like it'd been slashed with a piece of glass and sewn back together with a thick cord. The wound was eleven inches long. I gasped at the sight of it.

Then it all came back to me. The club, the kid, the knife, Vanessa crying as I faded away, and Javier's laughter.

I was still so tired I couldn't think straight. Exhaustion dragged me back down, and I closed my eyes and slept.

When I woke again, my throat was on fire with thirst. I attempted to sit, but then remembered my wound. Vanessa was asleep in a chair next to the bed. I didn't want to wake her, so I tried to reach for the pitcher of water and cup. I must have made too much noise because she opened her eyes and smiled at me.

"Vanessa," I tried to talk. "My throat is dry." God, I felt like hell. She poured me a cup of water and I drank slowly.

"How long have I been here?" I asked.

"It's Thursday. You came in Saturday, so five days."

Just then the doctor came in.

"Mr. Noguera, welcome back. How are you feeling?"

"Sore, but I'll live. Who used the can opener on me? My leg looks like Dr. Frankenstein worked on it."

"That would be me. I'm Dr. Benson. You had a lot of damage to your artery. The wound was large and you lost a lot of blood. We lost you a couple of times during the surgery. I'd say you're very fortunate to be among the living."

"So what's next? When can I get out of here?"

"We'll have to see how your progress comes along. Please understand this is no small matter. It's going to take months, maybe longer, for you to walk again. A lot of muscles were damaged and cut in the attack. You'll have to go through therapy and learn to walk again. For now, be grateful you're alive."

"Wait a minute. What do you mean months? Give me a week or so and I'll be fine."

"If you're not patient, you could do more harm to yourself. Let me be candid. The damage you sustained is substantial. I've been told you're a martial artist and fighter. Quite frankly, being in the shape you're in is what saved you. It'll take you a few months to walk again, and even then you'll have a noticeable limp. Too many muscles have been damaged for you to compete at the level you once did. You also sustained cuts to your right hand, which severed some tendons. I'm sorry, Mr. Noguera. You need to be patient. Although, who knows, you may prove me wrong."

Another week passed before I was discharged from the hospital. I was eighteen, depressed, and extremely vulnerable.

Another shock waited for me when I arrived home. My '62 ragtop wasn't there. It had been parked at home the night I was stabbed, and someone tried to steal it. As the thieves backed it out of the driveway, the exhaust system scraped the pavement and the noise woke my sister. She scared them away by yelling at them. To prevent another attempt, my car was stored at a friend's garage.

Then my sister told me something no one else knew.

"Billy, I didn't recognize the guys who tried to take your car, but the driver of the car they jumped in to get away looked like Javier."

That was good enough for me. I knew it was him, and the image of him laughing at me while I lay dying on the sidewalk fueled my recovery. I stayed away from everyone during the weeks I spent gaining strength and attempting to walk. Within three months I was running and training again, and the depression soon lifted. I took my daily dosage of steroids again and it became clear that those who counted me out had made a huge mistake.

Finally I was ready to make an appearance. My confidence returned, along with my strength and anger. More than anything, I wanted to see the look on the faces of those who'd wanted me dead. I guess that's a big part of who I am. Count me out, bet against me, tell me I can't possibly succeed, and I promise, I'll prove you wrong.

During that time Vanessa and I became much closer. I learned she refused to leave me while I was on the sidewalk that night. In the ambulance, she held my hand and talked to me. It was only when I went into the emergency room and to surgery that she was forced to leave me. Even then, she never left the hospital. When I came out from surgery she sat at my side, refusing to leave until I finally opened my eyes.

During my recovery, she opened up like never before. It was then she told me the secret she was most ashamed of and, worst of all, blamed herself for.

I learned that her mother had been sexually abusing her. It started soon after her parents divorced, when she was nine years old. At first it had been during baths, then while she showered. Her mother would touch her in inappropriate ways. As she grew older the abuse escalated to oral sex. Later she was forced to take nude photos with strangers, and to watch her mother have sex with multiple men.

I listened as she told me but didn't know how to respond. She made me promise never to tell anyone, and I kept that promise, but it tore at me. Each time I saw her, I wondered if she had been abused again. She thought it was her fault and was afraid to share her secret because of what people would think of her. I'm ashamed to admit that her fear was justified. I saw the blemish and scar on her every time I looked at her. I didn't blame her, but I couldn't forget it or pretend it didn't exist.

Since my brush with death, the only thing I concentrated on was recovery. Once I regained my strength, I called Mike to set up a meeting. I was back and ready to open my operation again. I heard all the rumors and knew the void I'd left remained, and that everyone involved suffered for it. I also knew Javier had set up his own operation and it was time to pay him a visit.

I went to Mike's shop to tell him that nothing had changed and I'd resume business as usual beginning the following week. He gave me a list of cars and told me, "All bullshit aside, you need to be careful. Javier and a few others from the club have been operating a crew since you've been out of commission. I've heard that Javier has bragged about being the one who tried taking your ride. I know he's an informant. He's dangerous, and still running around with Julian and the other club members. It looks bad."

I knew all of this, but thanked Mike anyway and left. It was time to handle some loose ends. First, I went to Crazy Ben, who had worked on my '56 the past few months. It was finished and I was anxious to see it. As he lifted the car cover to reveal his work, a huge grin appeared on my face. It was perfect. Black with a white top, and the paint shone like a mirror. Ben was a genius. I paid the balance I owed him and drove to Go-Go's place in Huntington Beach, where I spent the night. Early the next morning we met with the rest of The Pack to surf. It had been a long time since we'd all surfed together—ever since I nearly died. It was good to be with them, like being home.

"What's on your mind, Sinbad? You look a thousand miles away and a storm seems to be brewing," said Sandman.

"A lot's happened, brah. I'll be fine. I just need time for my soul to heal."

"Your soul? I knew a poet lived under all that bravado, but remember this: If ever you need someone to talk to, I'm here. No matter the cause. I'll always be your brother and help. We're Pack and we stand together."

As Go-Go and I drove back to La Puente, I told him about the talk with Mike and that we'd be getting back to business. But first, we were going to pay a visit to Julian. He continued to run with Javier and formed a new crew. And much worse, my word was not being respected, and that pissed me off.

As I turned into the street where Julian lived I saw cars in his driveway. Marco, Ruben, and Luis were all there, and a red '57 convertible Ghia I'd never seen before. I knew it was Javier's. I drove by and kept going.

"Where are you going? I thought you wanted to jam these motherfuckers."

"I do, but I'm going to do it right."

I drove to Renee and Francis's house and told them Julian was still doing business with Javier, Marco, Ruben, and Luis. I told them I was going over there to settle it. Then I told them Javier was involved in the attempt on my car the night I was stabbed. They asked how I knew and I told them my sister had seen him. I wanted them there as witnesses only.

We all drove to Julian's house together. Adrian pulled up. We shook hands and all he said was, "I've tried talking to Julian, but he won't listen."

"Don't worry about it. I'll handle this. Stay out of it."

I walked into the garage where they were all talking and acting as if they hadn't heard us pull up. As I entered, flanked by Go-Go, Renee, and Francis, I saw the fear in Julian's eyes.

"What's up, Julian? What's this rat doing here? I thought I told you I didn't want to see him anywhere near us." I looked at Javier. "You're a rat and it's time we see if you can back up that mouth you can't keep shut."

Renee spoke next. "Hey Julian, what the fuck? You're all doing jobs with him when we know he's no good?"

"Why isn't he any good? Because Bill said so?"

"Yeah, I said so. His actions speak for themselves. He knows I torched his car. If he wasn't a rat he would've confronted me. Wouldn't you? Tell me, Julian, if I called you a rat and burned your car, would you let it go? That's what I thought. But check this out. You are who you run with. Javier's a rat, so that makes you a rat, too. Fuck you, Julian. I know you and Javier were behind trying to take my ride. None of you are worth two shakes of a dick, and I'm here to collect on the debt this bitch owes me."

I walked up to Javier and shoved him into the wall.

"Come on, tough guy. Here I am. Let's see you back up all the talk. You thought it was funny when I got stabbed. Yeah, I saw you. Fuckin' rat."

I slapped him and allowed rage to pour through me. He grabbed a wrench and took a swing at me. I didn't hesitate to punch him in the face and slam him to the floor. I turned and saw Go-Go and Julian engaged in a fight, but it was over before it had a chance to get started. Go-Go smashed his fist into Julian's jaw, and he crumbled to the ground. I looked at Ruben, Marco, and Luis.

"I can't believe you'd side with a rat. I'm done. I won't associate with motherfuckers like you. If I ever see any of you again, I'll do to you what I did to this rat."

I walked away that day, no longer the Sergeant of Arms of the club, and no longer a member. They were on their own as far as I was concerned.

In the weeks that followed, I got back into the swing of my operation as if I was never away. Members of the club came by to talk, assuring me they weren't involved, nor would they ever have any dealings with Javier and his crew. I told them all I was out for good. The Darque Knights were tainted. Some members dropped out the night I confronted Julian and his inner crew, including Adrian, who continued to work with me. But I really didn't care. When I said I was done, I meant it.

Since telling me about the sexual abuse her mother inflicted on her, Vanessa found the strength to stop the attacks. It didn't sit well with Loretta, and she figured, correctly, that I somehow gave Vanessa the courage to take a stand against her. I kept my mouth shut and didn't break my word by confronting Loretta. However, because life with Loretta was so stressful for Vanessa, I arranged for Vanessa to move in with a friend of mine. She enrolled in the nearby school, but after a month Loretta convinced her to return home. Loretta also wanted me out of the picture in order to regain control over Vanessa and resume her abuse.

Five months after I was nearly killed, I appeared to be completely healed, but I knew I wasn't the same. The damage I suffered, physically and psychologically, handicapped me. My leg still hurt and was weakened by all the muscle and tissue damage. I often woke up with migraines so intense I couldn't see, believing I still lay bleeding to death on that sidewalk. I was damaged and took it hard. For so long I'd seen myself as invincible, but that was gone. Uncertainty and doubt dogged me. It drove me to push even harder. I needed to be whole again. If I couldn't, I was sure I'd end up on that sidewalk again, dead.

Sometimes life smiles on us. God, in His ultimate grace, allows goodness to touch our lives, and it's in these times we feel in His presence an overwhelming sense of love.

That October, as I was driving Vanessa home from school, she suddenly asked, "Bill, do you like kids?"

Of course she knew the answer to the question. I often told her how much I loved kids, and that when I became a father I'd make sure my child never had to go through what we had. I'd always protect and love my child more than anything, more than life itself.

She'd seen me play with children, and how, for a brief moment, I'd allow myself to be a child again too.

She smiled, but tears welled in her eyes.

"Bill, I think you're going to be a father."

I pulled over. "Are you sure? I mean, how long have you known?"

"I'm not sure, but I think I am. Are you happy?"

I kissed her. "Of course I am. I'm going to be a father."

I placed my hand on her stomach. "It's a boy. In my family, it's always a boy first."

I smiled again. For the first time in my life I felt whole, and not just a false sensation achieved through fighting competitions or stealing cars. It was pure and good. In fact, I had become a father the very moment our child was conceived, marking a climactic moment in my life.

We confirmed we were pregnant, and, although we were happy, we kept it to ourselves until the time was right. The first to know was my family. I invited them to dinner to make the announcement. Everyone was happy. My grandparents, Victor and Flor, told me how proud and happy they were, saying I needed to first think about my new family and always protect and honor them. I hugged and kissed them and swore I wouldn't fail.

Next, I told the entire Pack and asked them all to be my child's godfathers, which they readily accepted.

"Have you named our godson yet?" asked Brody.

I smiled. "William Achilles Noguera. He's going to be a great man some day and inspire many people."

Vanessa started showing by her twelfth week, and it marked a time to change and ensure my son would have everything he needed. I got a job as an apprentice with a friend's company, California Plumbing. I wanted to change, but it wouldn't be easy. I continued operating my business, thinking I could gradually turn it over to Go-Go and Adrian. In truth, a part of me wanted to change, but another part of me knew I wouldn't. My operation and fighting were part of who I was. Life without it would be like life without my skin.

Nevertheless, I worked hard at the plumbing job and held onto it. In my spare time I built and carved a cradle for my son. When he arrived, he'd sleep in a bed made by his father's hands. I took great pride in it. I already loved my son more than words could explain, often having complete conversations with him while Vanessa looked on.

"You know he doesn't understand what you're saying, right?"

"He doesn't have to. He hears my voice and knows it's his father, and that's good enough for me."

Soon, Loretta learned about our child and didn't take it well. She placed more restrictions on Vanessa, hoping it would make things between us a living hell and break us apart. Her behavior made no sense to me at all.

At the beginning, Loretta had encouraged our relationship to grow by never placing any restrictions on us whatsoever. But as she felt herself losing hold of Vanessa, she changed her approach. In Loretta's mind the answer was simple. Get rid of me and she'd regain control.

Her opportunity came four and a half months into my son's life. If I had understood the danger, I'd never have left. But how could I have known? Preparing for a fight was a major undertaking that required me to give my full attention or risk major damage or death. But maybe I'm still making excuses for failing to protect my family.

My fight was in Mexico, and before leaving I took Vanessa out to lunch.

"Bill, do you have to go? I mean, I'm going to miss you."

"I'll miss you too. But I'll be back in a few days. I'm going early to prepare, but I'll be back as soon as I can."

She nodded. "Please be careful. I love you."

"I love you too. Don't worry so much. I can't be beat."

I touched her stomach. "I love you, son. Don't forget to practice your kicks and punches."

I laughed and Vanessa smiled, shaking her head. "Easy for you to say, since he's not punching and kicking inside of you."

After we ate, I took Vanessa and my son to her house and drove off. I never thought it would be the last time I would see my son alive. The last time I would touch her stomach and feel him kick and move. The last time I would be the same.

My grandparents had tasked me with protecting my new family, and I failed. I was so focused on my fight, so confident and ego-driven, that I failed to sense Loretta's plan to murder my son, then murder me. I was only gone four days, but it was plenty of time to carry out the first execution.

I returned to a quiet house. Nothing seemed out of place.

"Hola, mom. Cómo estás?"

"Oh, mijo. I didn't hear you come in. Cómo te fue?" my mom said as she looked up and saw me. "Oh mijo. What happened? Dios, your face."

I kissed my mom's cheek.

"No es nada, mom. A lucky hit. But I won. The swelling will be gone in a few days."

"Let me put some ice on it. Can you see?"

"I'm fine. Has Vanessa called?"

"No, not yet."

That was strange. Usually when I was gone she called my house every day to see if I had called or returned. I went to the living room phone and dialed her number. It rang seven times. I hung up and dialed again. No answer. I looked at the phone. A sense of dread crept up on me. Something was wrong.

Instinct took over. I ran to my car and sped to Vanessa's house. I drove in a state of panic. Something was terribly wrong. The house was dark as I pulled into the driveway and I relaxed for a moment, thinking I was wrong. She'd just gone out. I got back in my car, but something stopped me. Looking at the house again, I got out of my car and knocked on the front door. No one answered. By this time I was tied in knots, gripped by fear.

At the side of the house I jumped the wall, landing in the backyard, where I was met by the dogs.

"How you doing, girls? Where's Vanessa?"

I walked to the back of the house and looked through the sliding glass door. The house seemed empty, but I couldn't shake the feeling in my gut. I circled to the side of the house to Vanessa's bedroom window. Reaching up, I tried the window and it slid open. I grabbed onto the window frame and jumped up to look inside. The room was dark but I could see Vanessa curled up on her mattress. I lifted myself through the window and knelt next to her, kissing her head.

"Vanessa, I'm back. I was worried. Is everything okay?" As I said this I reached for her stomach. Her hand caught mine and pushed it away. She sobbed and trembled as she fell forward into my arms.

"Oh, Bill. I'm sorry. God, I'm so sorry. Please forgive me. I was trapped. I was scared. She pushed and pushed and I didn't know what to do. I needed you, but you were gone. God, why did you have to leave?" she cried.

"I'm here. I won't leave again. It's okay."

"No, no, no. It's not okay. It'll never be okay. Our baby's gone."

I froze, pulling back to look at her. "What do you mean, our baby's gone? What happened?"

My voice started to rise as anger crept to the surface.

"Vanessa, what happened?" I repeated.

"Please forgive me," she cried. I could tell she was in physical pain, but her emotional distress was manic.

I lowered my voice. "Vanessa, it's not your fault. Just tell me what happened." Unable to stop, I cried, "What happened to my son?"

"It is my fault. I let her kill our son. She had it all set up with the doctor."

"Wait, what doctor?"

"Oh God, Bill. The doctor. He aborted our son. My mom told me she made a doctor's appointment for a check-up. When we got there they examined me, then said something was wrong and that a small procedure had to be done to help protect me. I was scared and alone, but my mom told me not to worry, everything was going to be okay. I felt pressured. When I woke, I found out she lied. Nothing was wrong. She planned it all and set it up to take away our baby. Please forgive me, it's my fault I let our baby be killed."

She held me as I cried from the deepest part of my soul. And from that place I looked up to heaven and screamed my grief, my rage, my pain. A part of me died that day, along with my son. He was murdered for no reason. And I blamed myself.

Chapter 42

San Quentin Death Row, 2008–2010

There is no greater personal expression than the creation of art. It allows me to render my truest, deepest emotions, to share myself and all that I hold dear with friend and foe alike.

I've always distanced myself from other artists in prison, so when Jennifer placed my pieces in an exhibit entitled "The Prison Project," I was very unhappy with her. I was focused on new work for an upcoming exhibit in May at the Braunstein/Quay Gallery in San Francisco. A news reporter sent a letter requesting an interview and asked about my views and involvement with the Prison Project exhibition. I read the letter, and as each word registered, my jaw clenched tight. I'd just gotten out of a situation like this, and here she was, doing exactly what I made clear I never wanted—for my work to hang next to the work of other prisoners. I had worked hard to gain respect for my work from the art world, and she risked ruining all of my efforts.

I called Jennifer to confront her. "Hi, William," she said in an excited voice.

"Hello, Jennifer." I didn't hide how upset I was, and she picked up on it right away.

"What's wrong? You sound angry."

"I am. Imagine my surprise when I learned my work is in an exhibit hanging next to pieces by other prisoners—rapists, child molesters, child killers, and God knows who else. Imagine how I felt when I learned it was you who placed me in the exhibition after I told you my work is never to be shown with work by other prisoners. I've worked very hard over the past twenty years to distance myself from prison artists. How dare you ruin that?"

"I'm sorry. When the exhibition curator called me, he said you were the only incarcerated artist in the show. The other artists would be from all walks of life and live in their own prisons through their state of mind: economic, environmental, and forms of mental illness. Please believe me. I had no idea the exhibit would place your work next to other prisoners."

She started to cry. "I just wanted to get you into an exhibit so you'd believe in me, but I've ruined everything." When I heard her cry, my anger died down. I was still very upset because she'd lied to me.

"Don't cry. You were obviously lied to. I don't blame you for that. But please, in the future, if something doesn't go as planned, just tell me. I don't want to find out through a third party. Okay?"

"I was afraid of losing you as an artist."

"Don't worry about it. Let's move on. It's already forgotten."

"You're truly a great friend and I thank you for trusting me with your career. I promise never to let you down. Now are you ready for some great news?"

"Of course. I could use some right about now." I wanted to trust her. I needed to. For too many years I trusted no one and I was starved for normality. The luxury of friendship was only a concept because of the fear that it could go wrong and cost me my life. I'd have to approach my association with Jennifer differently than my association with criminals and murderers.

"I've made all the arrangements for Jesse Hamlin to come interview you. He's a writer for the *San Francisco Chronicle*, and he's very interested in your story and work. And they're giving you the front page. Isn't that great? I'm so excited."

"That is great news."

"There's more. Ruth Braunstein picked out all the pieces for your exhibit at the Braunstein/Quay Gallery. She said she's never seen work that evokes the drama and emotion that yours does. When I brought all of your works to the gallery, she asked to be left alone with them and she closed the doors, locking everyone out for the next hour so she could experience your work intimately. When she emerged, she asked that I tell you, 'Thank you,' and said you'd understand."

I hung up the phone satisfied and complete. I knew Jennifer didn't understand what Ruth Braunstein meant when she said thank you, but I did. Ruth Braunstein was the rare "sensitive observer." My work came to life for her, breathing emotion, freeing my voice and ideas to affect her with no obstacles in between. She heard and understood me through my work. I couldn't ask for anything more.

As promised, after the interview with Jesse Hamlin, I was given the front page of the *Chronicle*'s Datebook Section for the Arts. One of my black-and-white hyper-realistic neo-cubist images covered most of the page. The headline read, "Letting His Creativity Run Free Behind Bars." At the same time, an article also appeared in *Style Century Magazine* entitled "A Studio on Death Row," and, in *Arts and Opinion Magazine*, "Art as Lifeline: William Noguera."

With the success I experienced, I should have been happy and content, but something wasn't right. Every time I spoke to Jennifer, I was left thinking I'd been lied to or that something was hidden. She said all the right things, always telling me how much she respected and appreciated our friendship. But more and more it felt like a smoke screen. I wanted so desperately to believe she truly saw me as a human being and that we shared a friendship based on mutual respect. But my gut told me otherwise. I began to investigate things Jennifer said, but nothing really jumped out to confirm she was lying. It wasn't until Jennifer went to Miami months later for the annual Art Basel fair that I heard back from some of my sources.

One source told me flat out, "William, I hate to burst your bubble, but she's playing you. You remember the gift you created for the artist Stanley Pierce for his wedding? He never got it. Jennifer kept it and it's hanging in her apartment. She's also been selling prints of your work through her website and numerous other sites. And I hear she's sold some of your originals that you don't even know about."

I waited for her return from Miami to confront her. I didn't expect things to be so bad, and I still didn't want to believe it. Could I be so naive? I respected her, trusted in her, and most of all I believed we were friends. I had even given her small gifts of my work as a token of my appreciation. I was angry and hurt by everything I'd learned. I didn't know what to do. If I fired her, I stood the likelihood of losing more of my work. I also didn't know if what I heard was even true. My sources could be wrong. Or maybe I just didn't want it to be true.

A few months before, a high school friend, Melissa, contacted me. We started talking on a regular basis. Melissa and I had gone to La Habra High School together. Back then, she dated a guy I knew, and we always got along well. For some reason, after nearly twenty-seven years, she wondered whatever happened to me, then found me and reached out.

Since I was unsure how to handle the situation with Jennifer, I asked Melissa for advice. It's one thing to deal with convicts and killers, but I was at a loss as to how to address this kind of situation. Melissa suggested I not jump to any conclusions, and to ask about the wedding gift I made for Stanley Pierce to see what her answer was. In the meantime, she would investigate the online sales of my work to try and clear up whether or not the rumors were true.

From the very start of the conversation with Jennifer, I knew she was guilty of everything. She admitted to never giving the wedding gift, *Adam's Eden II*, to Stanley. She said, "I fell in love with it and couldn't stand parting with it." I asked why she hadn't told me and once again she cried, saying she was afraid I'd think badly of her and leave. I understood it was all an act, the tears, the crying. It was how Jennifer got away with lying and stealing. She had led me to believe she'd accomplish so much for my career, but I had to act fast and find a way to get my work out of Jennifer's possession before she sold or stole any more of it.

Shortly after our last conversation, Jennifer said she'd come visit but never showed up. I was going to use the opportunity to terminate her as my representative in person, and to give her detailed instructions to hand my work over to Melissa and Tatiana. But she became extremely evasive, disconnecting her phone and moving to another location.

After months of not being able to meet, Melissa, my sister Tatiana, and I met to decide a plan of action. They'd retrieve all of my work and other intellectual property. The plan was sound, but its execution wasn't so easy. Jennifer refused to return calls, canceled meeting appointments, and made a myriad of excuses not to meet with Melissa and my sister. I sent a registered letter that terminated our professional relationship. Still, no response.

Finally, in fall 2009, Melissa and Tatiana arranged to meet Jennifer at her apartment in San Francisco. Armed with power of attorney and executorship to my trust, they informed Jennifer she no longer represented me or my work. Her response was simple: "There it is, take it."

While preparing the pieces for transport into Melissa's car, it became evident that many pieces were missing. They questioned her about the missing pieces, as well as the digital scans used to make prints—which I paid for with my gift of *Samo* to Clayton Tate. She refused to give any answers, or to sign a receipt acknowledging the transfer of the work in her possession.

Altogether, I lost nearly two dozen original pieces, digital scans of over twenty-five pieces, fifty-three certificates of authenticity, fifteen artist proofs, and all sales records for the work Jennifer had sold. In the two years Jennifer and Phoenix Art Agency represented my art, neither my family nor designated charities received a single dime. Everything Jennifer sold, she kept.

After returning to Los Angeles, Melissa conducted an inventory, professionally photographed the pieces, and ensured that proper copyright was in place. Most importantly, she began investigating the whereabouts of the missing pieces. She uncovered more facts too. Jennifer was selling original pieces and prints all over the Internet and through various third-party art dealers. Jennifer consigned the work without my permission or knowledge, advertising original works and prints for sale.

Melissa made a list of the missing originals and some of the facts. She reported the missing pieces to the police department and sent certified letters and e-mails to Jennifer demanding answers and the return of the missing pieces. Jennifer's responses were condescending— she didn't think she owed anyone an explanation. According to her, she had expenses for representing me that entitled her to keep one hundred percent of the proceeds. When Melissa relayed this to me, I couldn't believe it had happened again. Never in my worst nightmare did I expect Jennifer to steal from me. But her self-proclaimed mentor was Clayton Tate, and that was his self-made reputation. In Jennifer's case, the bad apple didn't fall far from the tree.

Weeks passed, and Melissa uncovered more of Jennifer's dishonest dealings. She consigned a dozen original paintings and drawings to a Bay Area art dealer several years earlier but had basically abandoned the work. Melissa contacted the dealer to retrieve the pieces and discovered that Jennifer owed the gallery over two thousand dollars. We reached an agreement to trade a framed drawing in exchange for the release of the consigned pieces. Melissa retrieved twelve originals and fifteen artist proofs.

Melissa contacted Jennifer again, telling her she'd retrieved the pieces and at what cost. She requested the return of the disks Jennifer was using to make and sell prints, that she remove all reference to me and my work from her website, and that she stop selling prints of my work. She refused, and was extremely combative and hostile.

Melissa also insisted on the return of the final five missing pieces— major pieces featured in numerous publications. They were never returned; all of the pieces are considered stolen and unaccounted for to this day. They include *Echo, Moved to Tears, The Divine Proportion, Adam's Eden,* and *Ghost in the Material.*

Melissa, who proved to be a true friend and assistant, helped me connect with California Lawyers for the Arts. After writing a letter about my situation, I was placed on a list of artists seeking legal representation. In the meantime, I busied myself with searching for new gallery representation. I was aware of my need to be extremely selective in who I submitted my portfolio to, but now Melissa would be able to help safeguard against predatory art dealers.

By the end of that year, I received two letters that gave me hope. The first was from California Lawyers for the Arts. I opened the letter and read it over and over: "We found a lawyer who will represent you." The news was actually better than I'd first realized. A very large firm with offices around the globe read the summary about what happened and offered their services to protect my rights against Jennifer and anyone else prior to her representation who had infringed on my intellectual property rights. Manatt, Phelps, & Phillips, LLP, would act on my behalf to recover what was stolen from me, and fight to enforce and protect my legal rights as an artist. The other letter I received was from a group called the Organization of Independent Artists, in New York, another group Melissa recommended I contact. I was invited to join and show my work in a group exhibition at the New York Law School.

I took a deep breath, and exhaled. It was the first time in over a year I was able to relax. I was relieved to be able to pick myself up again, dust myself off, and move forward.

Every time I experience trauma and pain it's a shock to my perspective, but my ability to translate the experiences into and through my work is elevated and enhanced. Never before had it been so laser sharp as when I truly accepted my surroundings.

That's not to say I didn't acknowledge it before. However, I consciously kept any reference to my surroundings out of my work, afraid it would somehow place me in the same catchall category of prison art. I convinced myself the viewer didn't need those images to grasp the emotion I experienced, even if my emotional state was a result of my surroundings. But there's some truth gained in knowing where an emotion was born in order to give it perspective.

I touched on something important when I started the "Structured Chaos" series. I used cut pieces of mathematically arranged canvases that were painted based on rhythms and emotions, and then bonded to Masonite panel. I washed the panels in paint dozens of times, creating the impression that the geometric canvas shapes floated in a sea of paint held in place by three-dimensional biomorphic roots.

As each idea gave way to the next, I used Masonite instead of canvas to build a three-dimensional structure that rose from the base panel. This illustrated the landscape of my confinement with weaving rhythmic spirals, zips, and drips of color that characterized the complexity and nakedness of my mind. I encased these glimpses into the philosophical and psychological undercurrents of my mind in hard-edged geometric shapes to communicate the boundaries and struggle for space I experienced every day.

The first of these neo-constructivist wall sculptures was *Touch*. From there, a door opened in my mind, driving me to create more of these unique sculptures. I developed this idea even further when I incorporated the San Quentin Prison newspaper into my work, which resulted in the series *Take No Prisoners*.

About the same time I wrote an artist statement to give the world an opportunity to understand my theories and purpose in creating art. It read as follows:

My evolution as an artist has been long, lonely and sometimes frustrating—with long periods when nothing was satisfactory.

My early beginnings were in a realistic visual repertoire that evolved into my present abstract style rooted in geometry, Constructivism, Color and Set Theory. Only when I accepted my surroundings using the purity of my senses, did I break through to a place where the intensity of mind and vision were given full play.

The results: I created a language to convey what I see happening around me, and within me. This language brings the multifaceted dimensionality of my mind together through an alphabet of shapes, numbers, color, and images that portray the energies, feelings, thoughts, and emotions I experience. This enables me to communicate, and make real to the viewer the very emotions that possess me when I create the work.

With each work, I walk and sometimes stumble, searching with driven sincerity for that road which eludes even the most focused of us—the road toward clarity and freedom.

Not long after I wrote the artist statement, I started hearing a new artistic voice demanding to be heard. July 12, 2010 marked the opening of the group exhibition with the Organization of Independent Artists at the New York Law School, entitled "Summer Salon Show." That's when I took my retreat and sat down to write the story of my life. There is much I didn't write about because it wasn't paramount to how I find myself in this cage on death row. One more part remains, which will bring everything full circle.

I do not look forward to sharing this part of my life story. It's difficult to call forth these memories because they are so painful. Even after thirty years, these wounds are easily opened and the primal soul-wrenching agony consumes me. A father never stops being a father.

Chapter 43

Adolescence, 1982–1983

My world was destroyed and all I could ask was, *Why?* I asked myself over and over again, but the magnitude of the murder of my son still never fully registered. I was in shock, and with each heartbeat the rage and pain overwhelmed me. I couldn't bear the grief, and I blamed myself for not keeping my promise to protect Vanessa and William.

In my mind, I imagined holding and loving William, and doing everything a father and son do together. I watched his first steps, heard his first words, cheered him on the first time he rode his bicycle and caught his first wave surfing, and beamed at his prom and graduation. I pictured his beautiful smile. As I explored each of the would-be memories, I lost more of myself to the crushing sorrow of having lost him. I couldn't eat, sleep, or function. I just laid in bed and cried. The fragments of my soul would never come together again.

To escape, I drank, used drugs, and allowed the pain to rule me. I was a mess. Each time I thought of my son, I was destroyed all over again.

A week later, I went to Vanessa's house. There were questions I needed answered, and only she could answer them. No sooner had I knocked on the door than I was confronted by Loretta.

"What the hell do you want?" she asked.

"I need to talk to Vanessa," I said.

"No you don't. Get the fuck off my property," she said through tightly clenched teeth.

Ignoring her words, I asked why she'd murdered my son. I threatened to go to the police to expose the sexual abuse she'd inflicted on her own daughter since she was nine years old. I called her a child molester. That stopped her cold in her tracks.

"I know everything," I said. "The photo sessions, the sex, the abuse, everything."

"You can't prove anything," she yelled.

But I could see it in her eyes. Everything Vanessa said was true.

She slammed the door in my face, and as I walked to my car the door opened again. This time Vanessa came outside to talk.

"I heard what you told her. She's afraid you'll go to the police."

"Let her think that. I don't care," I said, pacing back and forth. I was crying and shaking. Vanessa stopped me and we hugged.

"We need to talk. There's things I don't understand."

"I know. I'm sorry, Bill."

We drove to a park a few blocks away from her house and walked in silence. Not really knowing how to start the conversation, I stopped and faced her.

"I'm dying inside. I don't know if I can go on like this. Please, help me understand how you let this happen. How? Damn it. How the fuck did you let them murder our son? He was just an innocent baby."

She tried to hold on and bring me close again, but I stayed stiff.

"No. Tell me. I need to know."

She cried. Her body trembled and I felt worse for yelling at her. I drew her in close and held her until she stopped crying, and she quietly said, "I don't know. I've asked myself the same question and just don't know. I was scared and alone and she pressured me. Bill, please forgive me. It's my fault. I killed our son."

"No. No you didn't. I should have been here. I should've protected him. I'm the one to blame. No one else."

Victims of abuse often blame themselves for what's happened to them. The abuser gains power over their decisions and completely dominates them. Vanessa was just such a case. I didn't know it at the time. How could I? I took blame because it's the father's responsibility to protect his family, his child, and I failed.

I went home that day with a bomb ticking inside me. Every passing moment destroyed me. What do they say? "Time heals all wounds." I'm proof that's not always true.

Each passing day was worse than the last. My mind fractured and I lost touch with reality. Grief, pain, and death stalked and pushed me into a realm of intense psychosis. I heard and saw things that weren't really there, things urging me on and feeding the inferno of rage growing inside me.

During one of the episodes, I sat in my workshop looking at the cradle I crafted for my son, when suddenly I heard a knock at the door. I turned and there was a little boy of about four. He stood there crying and looked up at me. "Why didn't you protect me, Daddy?" Wounds appeared slowly on his body, then opened and bled. He screamed. I closed my eyes, and when I opened them again I was alone.

Anger gripped me as I grabbed the cradle and smashed it with my fists, ripping it apart. Sobbing uncontrollably, I picked up the pieces, carried them to my car, and drove to my hallowed ground. I knew something was broken inside me and I was trying to fix it. I went to the only place I felt safe—where I found peace.

I hiked hours to reach my cave. Ducking behind the waterfall, I was met with emptiness, but it mingled with the solitude I always found there. I was safe, and no one would find or hurt me there except the demons inside me. I knelt to meditate, calling my beasts and the child I once was, but nothing happened. Over the next two days I tried over and over, but still nothing came. Finally, I understood a part of me was lost—dying or already dead. I gathered the pieces of my son's cradle and buried them inside my cave, constructing a small grave that held the only pieces of him I ever held.

On my return home I continued on a downward spiral, becoming obsessed with knowing what they'd done to my son and how his life had ended.

I went to the library with my sister. In the pages of the book, *A Child is Born*, I saw pictures of what my son looked like before he was murdered, and learned the atrocities he'd endured. He wasn't just a fetus, like many would argue. He was my son, a baby, my child. He was alive. At four and a half months in-utero he was a tiny version of a fully developed infant—with fingers, toes, a tiny nose, everything human. I learned the methods used to abort babies thirteen weeks and older, and found myself sobbing into my hands. My God, he had suffered. He felt everything as he was dismembered piece by piece. The graphic realization only added to my already fragile state of mind and fed my psychosis.

Everything suffered because of this—my martial arts training, my business, everything. The only thing increasing was my hair-trigger temper. I'd always been quick to anger, but now anything set me off, as if I wanted an excuse to be consumed with a rage so intense it had a mind of its own.

It was also during that time I learned from a well-connected street source that Loretta hired someone to implement the second part of her plan—to murder me. Honestly, I welcomed it. I wouldn't be as easy to murder as my son. I'd be ready for it, and I maintained a heightened sense of awareness. I constantly checked and rechecked everywhere I went. I doubled back to see if I was followed by Loretta's hit man. Late at night, I walked the perimeter of my house to see if it was being watched. Some would say I was paranoid and psychotic. But it wasn't paranoia, it was anticipation. I wanted Loretta's contract killer to show himself and come for me because I wouldn't be her next victim.

Though the contract killer never came, I later received confirmation from several sources that a hit man had, in fact, been hired. The sources were Loretta herself, and later, during my trial, from the mouth of one of her friends.

The discipline and control I'd possessed my entire life faded as each day passed. I didn't care anymore. I existed in my own world, surrounded by pain and rage.

Chapter 44

Adolescence, 1983

April 24, 1983 started off no different than any other day. On the outside, I probably looked and acted much like I normally did. However, inside, the grief was unbearable, and I couldn't make it stop. A part of me thought I deserved to suffer—ultimately I blamed myself for everything. I could only understand that I failed. I had no one to talk to about the mounting and overwhelming sense of loss and grief.

The only person I believed would understand and help me through my anguish was my father. But he was in Colombia and didn't know his grandson was dead, and it wasn't a conversation I wanted to have over the phone. I had no one to talk to or cry with. I was alone in my sorrow. As time went by it was more difficult to speak with Vanessa about what was destroying me inside because she believed I blamed her, so I kept my heartache bottled inside, trying to hang on and get through it all.

That evening, I picked up Vanessa on my motorcycle, a 1983 Kawasaki GPz750. It wasn't cold and I wanted to ride. I drove up her block, but she was waiting at the corner. She smiled, and as soon as I stopped she sat on the back seat and said, "Let's go," and kissed me.

We rode off, and at the first light we came to I asked, "Why were you waiting at the corner? Did Loretta do something?"

"No, she has one of her new boyfriends coming over and I didn't want to be there." I nodded. She smiled and kissed me again.

We went to a house party in Covina. A guy I'd met during a business deal invited us, and when we arrived he was out front waiting but appeared disappointed I hadn't brought my car.

"What's up, Bill? Where's your ride?"

"At the house. I felt like riding tonight. This is my girlfriend, Vanessa."

"Hey, Vanessa, what's up?"

She nodded her greeting.

"You guys go on inside," he said. "Make yourselves at home. Grab a beer, whatever you want. Mi casa es su casa."

"Right on, man. Thanks." I needed this. I smiled for the first time in a long time.

I took a deep breath and went inside holding Vanessa's hand. For the next few hours we listened to the live band and relaxed—just a couple of kids at a house party. Anyone who saw us saw a nice couple having a good time. No one could have guessed how things would end that night, not even us. If I had, I never would have taken Vanessa home.

We left the house party before midnight and went to a local burger joint on Arrow and Grand Avenue. We stayed around a while longer to eat and talk, then drove to a spot in the hills near La Habra where the lights of the distant city are a beautiful panoramic view. It was a quiet place where we could be alone and enjoy each other's company.

I noticed Vanessa seemed happier than usual. We stood leaning against my motorcycle. She was in my arms while we kissed gently. She pulled away from our kiss to smile.

"Bill, I love you. I don't want to lose you."

"Why do you think you'll lose me?"

"I've almost lost you twice now. Once when you were almost stabbed to death, and since we lost our son you've been different—distant and angry."

"We didn't lose our son. He was murdered." My muscles tensed and anger bubbled to the surface.

"I know, and I'm sorry. But maybe you could be happy again." She looked at me. "I think I'm pregnant."

I felt as if I'd been struck by lightning, and I couldn't breathe. I didn't move. I was in shock. Her words took me by complete surprise. Finally, I spoke.

"Are you sure? I mean, how long?"

"A little while. Are you happy?"

"Yes, of course I'm happy, but I'm afraid. I won't let anyone hurt our baby like they hurt William. He suffered. He felt what was done to him. I saw pictures of how he would have looked before, and he was fully formed and alive—a beautiful child."

I got upset. My stomach tightened, my mouth went dry, and panic set in. My mind and emotions were in overdrive, and I vowed to protect our second child. We left our spot and I drove her home. A few blocks from her house, at the light, she told me to drop her off at the corner where I picked her up. I turned my head to look at her.

"I'm driving to your house and walking you to your door just as I always have. I'm not hiding from anyone and I'm not going to let you walk home alone."

"Please. I just don't want to argue tonight, and I want to go to sleep."

The last thing I wanted was to upset her.

"What if I pull over a block from your house and I walk you the rest of the way. No one will know I'm there."

She nodded, and we headed to her house. I parked a block away in a parking lot beside a baseball field, and we walked the rest of the way.

We arrived at the house and it was dark. I walked Vanessa to the porch, and as we kissed goodnight the door suddenly burst open. I instinctively put Vanessa behind me and faced Loretta.

"What are you doing here, you son of a bitch?"

"Making sure Vanessa gets home safely."

"She doesn't need you for anything. Get the fuck out of my house."

Loretta got angrier, but at that moment I didn't really care how angry she got anymore. Vanessa touched me and I turned to her. The look on her face said it all. She didn't want to stay there. I turned to walk away with Vanessa, and that's when Loretta hit me on the side of the head so hard it made my ears ring. I spun around to face her and she swung at my head again, barely missing another blow. Because it was so dark, I couldn't see that Loretta held a wooden tonfa, a type of wooden baton-like weapon used in some martial arts. As she swung at my head a third time, I caught and ripped it from her grasp.

"Big man, you think you're something, don't you? You weren't so big when I killed that monster growing inside of my daughter. Do you know why I killed it?"

Loretta laughed, then spat, and I started to tick like a time bomb. Everything—all of it rushed to the surface. I was losing control, so I tried to turn and escape. But she poked me hard in the middle of the chest with her finger.

"Because it would have been just like you. Yeah, big man. One down, one to go."

She poked me even harder again, and while she spoke my vision turned red.

"You're next," she said as she spat in my face.

Images flashed before my eyes. In a split second I saw the cradle I'd labored to make, I saw myself burying the fragmented pieces, touching Vanessa's stomach and feeling our baby move, missing his first words, and all the things I imagined we'd have done together. Then all the thoughts and images of what I'd learned about how he'd suffered surged through my mind. A father never stops being a father. I started to shake, but I moved to walk away. I had to escape. Loretta slapped me hard across my face again. I heard a pop in my head and my vision went completely red. Agony, pain, rage, grief, and heartbreak engulfed me, and that's the last thing I remember.

Over the next eight months, I was worse than ever. Not only did I fail to protect my son, I lost control and was responsible for the loss of a human life.

What happened haunted me. I couldn't get past any of it and felt I should be punished. Those thoughts manifested during every waking moment. I started to self-destruct. My anger faced inward onto myself, and I became an even more distant loner. I couldn't shake the guilt or shame. I searched for the person I once was, the guy who competed in disciplined martial arts competitions and reveled in stealing cars, but I only found emptiness. I was a mere shadow of my former self, and worst of all, I knew it.

In a desperate attempt to find my way back, I drove to Huntington

Beach at 2 a.m. I walked to the water, taking off my shirt and shoes, and dove in. The cold water took my breath away, but a calmness set in. Honestly, I wasn't sure what I'd do. I considered swimming until exhaustion overwhelmed me and allowing the ocean to claim me. I swam on, passing the end of the pier. I remembered the first time I swam that far. It seemed like a lifetime ago. Where was he? That guy I used to be? I pressed on. My shoulder muscles burned, but I needed to keep going. I needed to find my way back. Suddenly it was there. That burning anger I always relied on. My only true constant. I stopped swimming, took a deep breath, and looked back to the shore—easily half a mile. As I swam back to shore I thought of William and allowed the tragedy of it all to burn inside of me. As I reached the shore, exhausted and in agony, I accepted that I would bear the burden.

Vanessa was mistaken. She wasn't pregnant. I think she hoped for it, and a part of her wanted to replace what was taken from us. I took it like a man who'd been chained and whipped. It was another deep gash in an already bloodied soul. Or maybe the opposite was true. Perhaps it was preparation for what was to come, hardening me, like the folds of a Katana sword as they're bent and hammered to produce "shadows," a process that increases its strength. Maybe it's why I wear a ring that reads, "Soul of a thousand shadows."

Nevertheless, I forged on. I competed in fights I should never have taken. I found a certain justice in pain, and routinely allowed myself to be hit before letting my rage surface and brutally beating my opponents.

I also resumed stealing cars at an even more alarming rate. I was undisciplined and was arrested on multiple occasions. I made mistakes but didn't care. I'd make bail and continue on my path of self-destruction.

Late one night I was driving home from the city of La Habra when a black-and-white cruiser behind me started flashing its lights. I pulled over and two cops walked up on either side of my car. One stood on the driver's side, the other behind the passenger side bumper with his gun drawn. I placed both hands on the steering wheel.

"Step out of the car, Mr. Noguera."

I was relieved. For a moment I thought I was finally being arrested. It had been months since that fateful night. But that night it was about cars, specifically the beautiful '62 convertible I drove. It was a car I'd only finished recently.

"Step out of the car, Mr. Noguera, and put your hands on top of your head."

I did as I was told. The cop stepped behind me and patted me down, then cuffed my wrists. I was turned around as the head of the car theft squad pulled up behind us. "Mr. Noguera," he nodded. "Good evening. This is one beautiful car." He looked inside. "Amazing. This may be the best one you've put together for yourself. How many has it been? I've seen you with ten? Twelve?" He answered his own question. "Yes, at least. Well, I told you I'd someday catch you. And this is that day."

I didn't respond and didn't care what he said. I'd beat him every time we met. Why should this time be any different?

"Take him to the station and book him. Grand theft auto. Though I'm sure it won't hold him very long, will it, Mr. Noguera? No matter. This time the charge will stick."

As I was placed into the back of the cruiser, a large flatbed pulled up behind my car.

"Hey, Lieutenant. Scratch my car and you'll pay for the paint."

"I wouldn't dream of scratching it. Besides, I'm sure the rightful owner will love what you've done to it. You're an artist, Mr. Noguera, and this is quite the masterpiece."

I was booked and within a couple of hours released on bail. But something about the Lieutenant's demeanor bothered me. He knew something I didn't. I'd never seen him that confident in all the years we'd faced each other. It was as if he'd already won.

On the third day after my car was impounded, I called the Lieutenant. By law, he had five days to prove the car was stolen. If the original owner couldn't be found, then the car would be returned to me. It was a game we'd played for years and I always won because of how difficult it was to check every reported stolen car throughout the state. I could have taken the car from anywhere, which made it that much more difficult for him.

I dialed his number, using the card he'd given me. He always told me if I ever needed to "talk," meaning to rat someone out and save my own skin, he'd always lend an ear. That would never happen. After the second ring, he answered.

"Hello?"

"How you doing, Lieutenant?"

He recognized my voice and said, "Mr. Noguera. I was just talking about you to the district attorney."

"Really? Is he going to help wash and wax my car before I pick it up?"

"Actually, no. We were talking about the '62 and how tomorrow at ten a.m. the legal owner will be driving from Santa Barbara to identify it. Ms. Christine was on vacation, which is why it wasn't done days ago."

As he spoke, my stomach tightened and my mouth went dry. Someone had talked, and the list of people who knew where I'd taken the '62 from was extremely short.

"Lieutenant, you're swinging in the dark again. I'll be by the day after tomorrow to pick up my car."

"Not this time, Mr. Noguera. You have a nice day." He hung up.

I tried to recall the entire conversation. First, he knew where I'd got the car because someone told him. Second, and most importantly, its original owner would be there the next day to identify it, meaning it hadn't been ID'd yet. The owner had to see it in person, but even then it would be difficult to ID since I'd changed it so much. Maybe the owner wouldn't be able to. For a moment, I allowed that idea to give me hope. Nah, if my car was stolen and the cops had a car they said was mine, I'd ID it quickly, especially if it looked as good as that car.

I made up my mind—the owner would never see the car. The Lieutenant made a big mistake telling me the owner would identify it the next day. I'd take it back that night. It wouldn't be easy. The '62 was held at the police station impound yard. But it was either that or sit back and let fate take its course.

At 1 a.m. I approached the impound yard and climbed to the top of the twenty-foot wall. About one hundred feet away I saw the white top of my car. At first glance I knew I was faced with a bad situation. If I jumped into the yard it would be difficult to get out, so I needed an escape route.

I retreated back to my motorcycle and rode home to pick up a small pair of bolt cutters and the tool bag I always carried to hit a mark. I rode to the corner of Colima and Hacienda Boulevard to make the first of a series of phone calls. Each call I made got me closer to the impound yard.

I knew the yard had two tow trucks working the night shift, and I made calls to draw them out. I disguised my voice to request an emergency tow. I told the dispatch operator I was at the corner of Colima and Hacienda. I jumped on my motorcycle and rode to the next street corner, Gale Avenue and Turnbull Canyon Road. I made another call to request service, but this time I said I was in the opposite direction, near Puente and East Temple Avenue. Finally, I rode to a telephone booth a block from the impound yard and made the last call to request a tow in yet another direction.

I parked my motorcycle and ran to the yard to watch the action from across the street. First one, then the other tow truck left the impound yard from out of the main entrance. The impound yard had two entrances—one gate for civilian business and the second gate for the police. As soon as the second truck was gone, I ran across the railroad tracks and heard a train horn bellowing in the distance as it approached. It was then or never. In seconds, I climbed over the twenty-foot wall, landing on the impound yard pavement, and ran to my car and got inside. I shut the door and took a deep breath, inhaling the scent of my car. It would be the last time I'd drive her.

I hit the electric fuel pump, and its sound filled my ears. I turned the key, which had been left dangling in the ignition, and the engine roared to life. With the lights shut off, I drove toward the police gate, which was far from the main office and out of earshot. I got out, cut the lock off the gate, and slid it open. Then I drove quickly to the house of a guy I knew, but who had no connection to my car stealing business. I parked my car in his locked garage and gave him instructions to let no one see the car or know about it. I explained it was my car, but the cops were looking for it, and that I'd be back in a few days to strip and cut it up. I asked him for a ride and he dropped me off a few blocks over from my house. I jumped several of my neighbor's backyard fences to get to my house through the back door. As soon as the cops discovered the '62 was gone, they'd come for me. I crept into bed, and within ten minutes the cops surrounded my house and the Lieutenant was banging on my door.

I opened the sliding glass window next to the front door.

"What the fuck? What are you doing here at two in the morning?" I wiped my eyes as if he'd awoken me from sleep.

"Where were you tonight?" asked the Lieutenant.

"Right here, Lieutenant. Why?"

He looked at his partner. I could see he was unsure.

"What's the problem? Why are you here?" I asked.

"Would you step outside for a moment, Mr. Noguera?"

"I'm not stepping outside from nowhere. What's this about?"

As I said that, my mother had woken and stepped to the window to see what was happening.

"What's going on? Why are you bothering my son? You have nothing better to do?"

"Mrs. Noguera, has your son been home all night?"

"Yes. Can't you see you woke us up?"

The Lieutenant asked to speak with my mother alone, so I left but hid in the dark hallway to listen in.

"Mrs. Noguera, this is a serious matter. I need your help."

"First of all, it's Ms. Salinas. I'm divorced. Now, what do you want? I'm tired and want to go back to sleep."

"Has your son left the house tonight?"

"No."

"I noticed he has fresh scrapes to his arms. How did he get them if he hasn't gone out?"

"He was pulling weeds and gardening right over there next to the chain-link fence. The wires cut him."

I heard the Lieutenant instruct his partner to check if it looked like someone had, in fact, been working in the garden.

"Yeah, Lieutenant. Looks like quite a bit of work has been done, and there's a sharp wire that keeps the roses protected."

There was a long pause.

"Both car engines are cold and haven't been driven tonight."

I had them now, so I walked back into my room with my mother.

"Well, Lieutenant, are you going to tell us why you came here to wake us up? Please tell me there's more to it than being worried enough to make sure I'm asleep and safely in bed."

"I don't know how you did it, but you'll go down for this. You're involved. I know it. Someone got into the police impound yard and took the '62. I know it just happened because the gate was found open and it wasn't like that less than half an hour ago."

"I haven't left my house tonight. My car was left in police custody and you allowed someone else to take it?"

"It's not your car. You stole it, you son of a bitch," he yelled.

"I own the car, the pink slip is in my name. Correct me if I'm wrong, Lieutenant, but you have no proof I stole anything since the supposed original owner never identified it."

He glared at me and it all set in. He realized his mistake. He was so happy thinking he'd finally caught me that he'd boasted, giving me a piece of information that I used against him to eliminate the case. No one came to identify the '62, making it the last time he and I played our cat-and-mouse game. I was tired of it, anyway. Sooner or later, my luck would have run out.

On the morning of December 20, 1983, I woke with a start. I sensed something was wrong. I got out of bed to get ready for my daily run, leaving through the back door of my house. I ran the usual five miles as I'd done countless times before, but a part of me knew it was the last time. I memorized every scene, every scent, promising myself I'd someday return.

The week before, I did the same thing when visiting my son's grave in my secret cave.

"I'll never forget you, son," I said, as I placed my hands on the rocks covering the buried pieces of his cradle. "I'll hold you inside my heart forever."

I returned from my run and woke my mother. I planned to take her and my grandmother to the Los Angeles Jewelry Market later that morning. It was a few days before Christmas and I wanted them to pick out jewelry they liked for their Christmas presents. As they readied, I showered and took my dog for a quick walk. While I walked him I felt I was being watched. I stopped, then looked around and continued back to my house. Moments later, with my mother and grandmother in the car, I pulled out of our driveway heading to the 605 Freeway. As we reached the end of the street, an unmarked police car pulled in front of us and cut us off. At the same time, another unmarked police car pulled up behind us. With weapons drawn, they ordered me out of the car.

"Put your hands where we can see them," yelled a cop.

I opened the driver side door and stepped out with my hands on my head.

"He's on bail," my mother cried. I turned to look at her, but instead caught the weight of my grandmother's eyes. She gave me the sign of the cross and whispered, "Qué Dios te bendiga, papito."

I read her lips—those words were familiar. She'd said them to me since I was a small child. Closing my eyes, I took a moment of comfort in her words, and turned to face the chaos.

Guns were pointed at me as I was forced to kneel and lay face-first on the asphalt. I was rushed from all sides. Knees pushed into my back and the cold steel of handcuffs bit down on my wrists. My ankles were cuffed.

"Just in case you get any ideas of using your feet," one of the detectives said.

They threw me down face-first into the back of the unmarked police car, and before the door closed I turned my head to look outside. There, on her knees, my grandmother cried. Immediately rage boiled to the surface and I struggled to comfort her.

"Easy, you're not going anywhere. Relax."

"What's the charge?" I asked through clenched teeth.

"Oh, it's a doozy. How's murder grab you?" said the detective. I looked at him and he smiled.

"Yeah, I thought that'd get your attention. Welcome to hell."

I closed my eyes. It was finally over.

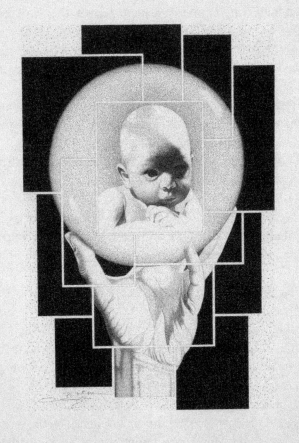

Epilogue

My father came to see me today, June 4, 2014. He usually comes every few years, which I understand. He's seventy-six and it hurts him to see his only son a prisoner, like this. Our moments together are usually spent far away from anything emotional. We understand words aren't necessary, but deep down we both suffer. My father is a strong, hard man, who will never allow me to see him weak. He knows I blame myself just as he blames himself for my circumstances, so we pretend to be okay and life goes on.

I love my father and know I let him down. I failed everyone, including myself. No matter what I do, I can't change what I've done. For that I'm truly sorry. I have many regrets. My actions caused a great deal of pain, and I accept responsibility for that. I hope by writing my story, some good will come of it. Perhaps a life can be saved, spared, or changed, before it's too late.

I don't know why I'm so driven—why art and its creation calls to me with such passion. I just know I must answer its call with a sense of urgency. How long I have left here is not up to me. However, with each piece I create, I'm at the verge of a breakthrough and will finally find what I've searched for my entire life. This allows a sense of satisfaction to heal me. Knowing all the pieces of me, through my art, have escaped these barbaric and brutal surroundings, to live long after I'm gone, gives me the greatest satisfaction of all. Art is not a luxury. For me, it's a necessity.

I sometimes sit and look out the dirty window directly in front of my cell and wonder if I'll ever see the end of this. Over thirty years have passed since I was placed behind these walls. Everyone has gone on with their lives.

I wonder about my son, William, and what he thinks as he looks down to see his father struggle as I do. Does he wonder if I'll fall? Or does he know, as I do, that no matter what, I will pick myself up and rise again? A father never stops being a father.

The face that stares back at me in the mirror is different now. My Van Dyke is nearly all white. Where there was once smooth skin, lines mark the many years I've spent in this concrete and iron cage. But in an instant, my eyes come to life. He's still there—that child. Suddenly, he smiles at me. All is not lost.

Addendum

In 1998, when my art began receiving international attention, I anonymously donated portions of the earnings to children's charities. I recognized that I owed a debt to society because my past actions caused pain and suffering, and I wanted to repay part of that debt by giving to others. However, at the time, I remained anonymous, and avoided truly giving the most important thing I could. Myself.

I only briefly mentioned donating to charities in *Escape Artist* because my intentions were never to receive praise for giving to those in need, a good deed that we as humans should do selflessly. Yet, since finishing my memoir, I realize it is my responsibility to lead by demonstrating to others, including prisoners, the true meaning of rehabilitation. The William A. Noguera is a private trust that was founded to continue giving to charities—in my name—setting an example of how to live in a selfless manner.

Further, in my effort to give back and provide a service to the general public through the experiences I have lived, I accepted the invitation to become a collegiate guest-speaker. I now lecture to MBA students on professional ethics and corporate responsibilities, providing an insider's view of ethical erosion and the consequences that arise from grandiosity, greed, and corruption.

It is my hope that others can learn from what I've experienced, and that I can serve a higher purpose and change other people's lives for the better. I possess the potential to grow further and vow to do so in the months and years that follow, no matter where I find myself, for the true measure of a man is his capacity for generosity and compassion.

Glossary

WORD OR SLANG PHRASE	DEFINITION
AB	Aryan Brotherhood, a white prison gang
AC	Adjustment Center
BGF	Black Guerrilla Family, an African American prison gang
Bone-crusher	Deadly handmade prison knife
Bottle Stopper	A cop; police; prison guard
Bull	Prison guard
CDC	California Department of Corrections
Camarada	Friend; partner; comrade
Carga	Heroin
Carnal	Brother; or Mexican Mafia member
Carnalito	Little brother
Cellie	Prisoner you live with
Changos	Monkeys; derogatory term for African Americans
Chicanos	Mexicans
Chicans	short for Chicanos, slang for Mexicans
Cholos	Mexican street gang members
Clavo	Package; usually drugs
Clecha	Schooling
CO	Correctional Officer

Cómo estás?	How are you?
Cómo te fue?	How did it go?; How was it?
Dispensa	Sorry
Eme	Spanish for the letter M; used to indicate the Mexican Mafia (La Eme)
Emero	Mexican Mafia member
Es un placer	Used as a greeting; "It's a pleasure (to meet you)"
Ese	Guy; dude; man
Firmé	Good; "solid"
Gang and Plank	Shank; knife
Gavacho	White guy
Gesca	Pot; marijuana
Guerrilla	Black Guerrilla Family (BGF) members
Grandes	Dollars
Kite	Note
La Raza	Our race; our people; Mexicans/Latinos
Leaning Tower	Shower
Me dicen	They call me; I'm called
Mi casa es su casa	My home is your home
Mijo	Son
Moan and Groan	Phone
Mucho gusto	Nice to meet you
Muertes	Deaths; murders
NF	Nuestra Familia, a Northern Mexican prison gang
No es nada	It's nothing
Nombre	Name
Norteños	Northerners; Northern Californian Mexican gang members
Órale	All right; Yes; a form of greeting

Órale pues	All right now; Yes; a form of greeting
Palabra	Word
P/C	Protective Custody
Peckerwood	A white convict
Pedo	Problem; trouble; stuff; thing
Perros	Dogs; partners; friends; road dogs
Placa	Cop; police
Ponte trucha	Stay alert
Ponte verga	Be alert; Stay on your toes
Puedo	I can; Can I?
Puto	Fag; derogatory term for homosexual
Qué Dios te bendiga, papito	God bless you, son
Qué pasa?	What's happening?; What happened?
R&R	Receiving and Release
Road dog	Partner; friend
Simón	Yes
Soda	Coke, cocaine
Soy	I am
Suegra	Mother-in-law
Sureños	Southerners; Southern Californian Mexican gang members
Tiempo	Time
Tú sabes	You know
Twist and Twirl	Girl
Varrio Nuevo Estrada (VNE)	Los Angeles street gang
Vatos	Guys; dudes
Watcha	Check it out; Listen
Woods	Short for Peckerwoods
Ya estuvo	Enough; stop

ABOUT THE AUTHOR

William A. Noguera is an author, lecturer, and award-winning artist.
He resides at San Quentin State Prison.
His official website is www.williamnoguera.com.
Visual art created by William is available for exhibition bookings and for collectors and private purchase.
Financial proceeds are privately donated to charity organizations and are used to sustain the operations of the William A. Noguera Trust.